Anne Bourne
707 East Palace Avenue #16
Santa Fe, New Mexico 87501

SANTA FE

BIRD'S EYE VIEW OF THE CITY OF

SANTA FÉ, N.M.

1882.

1. Palace.
2. H'd Qrs. Dist. N.M.
3. Post of Fort Marcy.
4. Government Corral.
5. First National Bank of Santa-Fe.
6. Second National Bank of New Mexico.
7. Cathedral.
8. St. Vincent Hospital.
9. Academy, } Sisters of Loretto.
10. Chapel, } Sisters of Loretto.
11. Convent, } Sisters of Loretto.
12. St. Michaels College.
13. San Miguel Church. Erected in 1582, distroyed by Indians 1680, rebuilt1710 by the Marquis de la Penucla.
14. Congregational Church.
15. Guadalupe Church.
16. M. E. Church.
17. Presbyterian Church.
18. Episcopal Church.
19. Oldest Building in Santa-Fe.
20. Palace Hotel, P. Rumsey & Son.
21. Exchange Hotel, Reed & Bishop.
22. Capitol Hotel, Gray & Bailey.
23. Herlow's Hotel, P. F. Herlow.
24. Santa-Fe Planing Mill, P. Hesch.
25. Cracker Factory, D. L. Miller & Co.
26. Post Office.
27. Depot.
28. Gas Works.
29. Fisher Brewing Co.'s Brewery.

Santa Fe

A MODERN HISTORY, 1880–1990

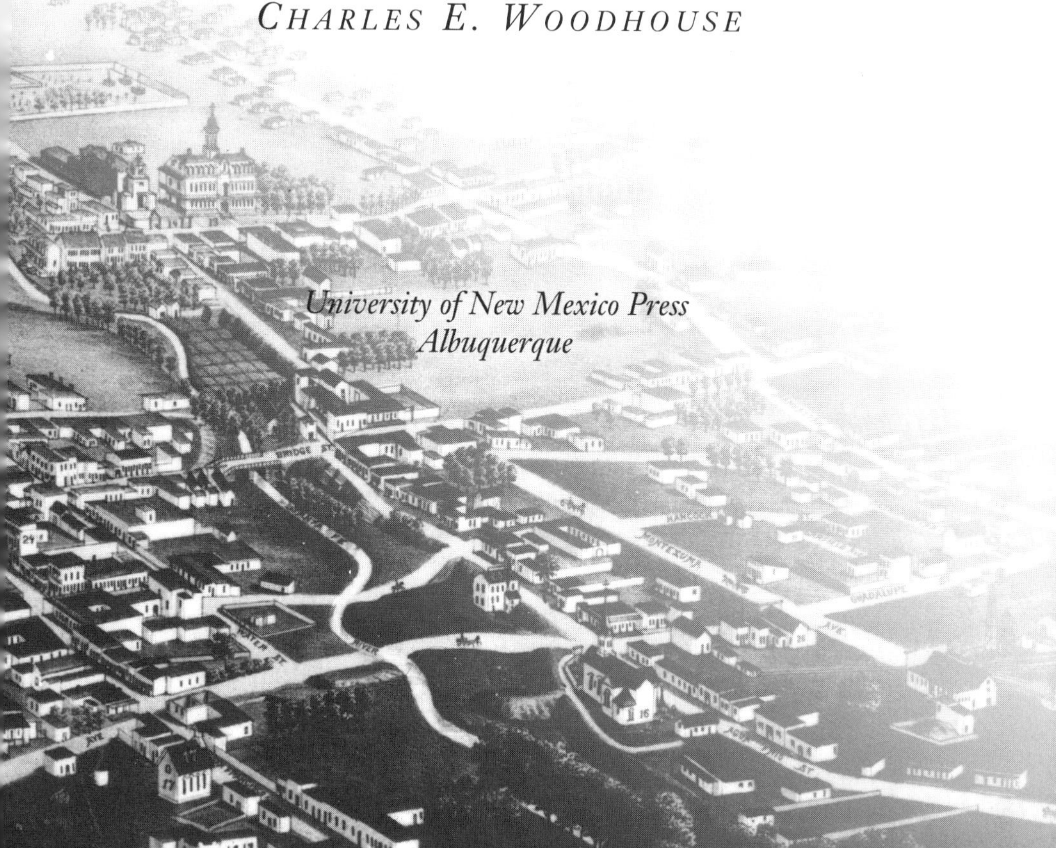

Henry J. Tobias

and

Charles E. Woodhouse

University of New Mexico Press
Albuquerque

FIRST EDITION

Library of Congress Cataloging-in-Publication Data

Tobias, Henry Jack.
Santa Fe : a modern history, 1880–1990 / Henry J. Tobias and Charles E. Woodhouse.—1st ed.
p. cm.
Includes bibliographical references and index.
ISBN 0-8263-2331-6 (alk. paper)
1. Santa Fe (N.M.)—History—20th century.
2. Santa Fe (N.M.)—Social conditions—20th century.
3. Santa Fe (N.M.)—Politics and government—20th century.
I. Woodhouse, Charles E.
II. Title.
F804.S257 T63 2001
978.9'5605—dc21
2001001829

Frontispiece
1. Illustration of Santa Fe, 1882.
Courtesy Museum of New Mexico, neg. #23306.

Contents

List of Illustrations

Acknowledgments

IN THE PROCESS of creating this manuscript we have relied on the knowledge, goodwill, and patience of a host of agencies and individuals without whose help the attainment of our goal would have been much more difficult. It is our obligation and pleasure to offer them the recognition that is rightfully theirs although they bear no responsibility for the product.

The major resource at our disposal was the library of the University of New Mexico. Its varied collections and branches, The Center for Southwest Research, The William J. Parish Memorial Library, the data bank of the Bureau of Business and Economic Research, the Fine Arts Library, the Engineering and Science Library, and the Medical School Archives, and their good-humored and efficient personnel have all been essential to the completion of our task. In Santa Fe, the resources of the State Records Center and Archives and the Museum of New Mexico's history and photograph collection, with its unique materials, have been equally valuable and indispensable. The Special Collections Library of the City of Albuquerque provided materials that were invaluable as did the Sangre de Cristo Water Co. of Santa Fe.

Special sources brought us to city, county, and state agencies as well as private institutions. Michael Burkhart, Walter Burke, and Gloria Taylor, all of the College of Santa Fe, provided much needed information about their institution as did Richard C. Rindone of Santa Fe Community College, and Ed Nagel and Marie Kimmey of the Santa Fe Community School, Esther Hamerdinger of the Office of the Registrar at New Mexico Highlands University, Amy Holt at Eastern New Mexico University, Miriam Meyer and Judy Bosland of New Mexico State University, and Tom Field of the

Office of Institutional Research at the University of New Mexico, did likewise. Dr. Bill Simpson of the New Mexico Commission of Higher Education and Henry F. Borgrink of the State Department of Education provided their expertise at every request. Mariano Lucero of the Department of City Planning did likewise. We owe our gratitude to these institutions and persons.

Individuals who contributed their efforts to our work are legion. The standout is Dr. Suzanne Simons, who read the manuscript, listened, and offered her own wisdom. Others, who contributed to narrower themes, are Robert Meiering (golf), Harry Moul (planning), James P. Miller (education), Allen Stamm (building), Bernard McEntee (horse racing), M. Eugene Sundt (Los Alamos), and Wilson Hurley (art). They gave of their special areas of knowledge and materials. Others, such as Maurice Rosenthal, Chris Kelly, and Lucinda Sachs gave of their knowledge and wisdom, while A. Samuel Adelo informed us of Spanish language usage. We may have inadvertently omitted some persons in our effort to recall the entire list of those who aided us, and we apologize for any shortcomings.

Each of us recognizes the role of a special person in our lives who listened to our problems in creating the manuscript. The encouragement of Paulette Bailey and Carol Higgins, who listened patiently and offered advice, requires our special attention and gratitude.

Preface

TO DESCRIBE THE history of Santa Fe since 1880, we must first consider the previous experience of the city. By that date it was nearly two and three-quarter centuries old and still reflected strongly its earlier existence, first as a Spanish colonial and then as a Mexican provincial outpost. The American political presence after 1846 provided a new chapter to that history, but it did not erase the old. Rather, it overlaid it, adding a new dimension to the city's internal life and external appearance. How much of the older periods remained and what the latest period added were vital and interacting elements in the lives of Santa Feans after 1880.

The introduction of new elements in a history, however, cannot be treated as mere overlay. Each new element affected the older living realities, creating new combinations. Just as the Spaniards changed the lives of the original native inhabitants so too were these later arrivals affected by their new surroundings. And as the Hispano population changed even as it retained much of its old character, so too did the Anglos bring much that was new to the already existing society even as they were modified by the old. Each was affected by the presence of the other. Such is the nature of the human experience over time as people respond to the exigencies and opportunities of environment, both physical and human.

The focus of this work, as we have chosen to define it, is Santa Fe itself. This endeavor involves a problem of delimitation—to separate the city of Santa Fe from its existence as a regional center to a focus on its internal condition. This does not mean that the researcher can ignore completely the role that the city played as a provincial and state capital, but to concentrate on what the city meant to its own inhabitants rather than to the outside world.

The initiative for the thrust of our history derives partially from the sparsity of a certain kind of historical work about Santa Fe. Writings about the city in English are certainly not lacking. Descriptions of the city at the end of the Trail that bore its name before 1880 were not only numerous but depicted its life and physical attributes in both favorable and unfavorable terms. Occasional travelers wrote a good bit about it.

In the second and third decades of the twentieth century, when Santa Fe began to acquire a different identity, another wave of American writing about the city appeared. By then New Mexico had become a state and a considerably larger number of Anglos had put in their appearance as residents, drawn by reasons of health as well as the attraction of new cultural and physical vistas. Anglos had been there long enough to sink roots into the community and to gain a perspective of themselves as the latest residents in what was a long and complex history. The writing of the city's history at that time leaned heavily toward the description of political and artistic events, but economic and social factors received relatively little attention from scholars. Thus, many questions about the condition and evolution of the population remained scarcely examined.

In recent decades Santa Fe has been the subject of many studies, but these have often concentrated on specific groups or topics. The artistic climate of the city in the twenties and thirties, for instance, has received an inordinate amount of attention. But such works are more often than not about individuals or small circles of persons who lived there and what the local environment did for them and to a lesser extent what their presence did for Santa Fe. Interest in the mundane existence of the mass of Santa Feans who did not paint or write and did not concern themselves with such matters is far less common. Our interests lie more heavily in that direction.

The place of ethnicity in Santa Fe requires comment. Interest and concern for Native Americans may have been admirable from the anthropological, humanitarian, and aesthetic points of view, but few of them lived in Santa Fe. The Hispano who worked for the highway department and the Anglo owner of a drugstore, however, attracted little attention. The mostly Anglo writers, who often held romantic views of both the physical environment and the people about whom they wrote, formed by class and education a group unto themselves and often interpreted what was important about Santa Fe from the perspective of their ideals and the persons who exemplified them. The result was a skewed and partial view of the city. Its function as a state capital, the very large employment in government occupations, and the social and economic welfare of the local population received little attention.

An organism as old and complex as Santa Fe has an endless number of facets that bear examination. Unfortunately, human endurance and publisher's concerns limit what may be included in any finite work. Such considerations compel authors to weigh, sift, and select what they consider vital to their presentation. Thus the general relationship between Anglos and Hispanos in the city's modern history assumes precedence over all other ethnic relationships.

Ethnic terminology, that is, names assigned to particular groups of persons in the city, can be a complicating and confusing issue. Often, the various designations involve differences of viewpoint within the groups themselves. Generally, we have chosen to treat the subject as simply as possible. Native Americans, Hispanos, and Anglos define the major groups. Who they are is clear even if such terminology was not always used by the inhabitants themselves.

Our history is divided into two main parts. The first nine chapters carry the narrative from the coming of the railroad to New Mexico to the end of World War II—roughly from 1880 to 1945. Within that period one major emphasis rests on the political and socioeconomic life of the city. The other major subject matter is the appearance and development of the archaeological and artistic threads that slowly began to shape the town's character and offer new goals.

The last four chapters deal with the half-century that has passed since World War II. They examine thematically the material for the entire postwar period: political and cultural expansion, social and economic development, and ethnic interaction and change. Unlike the first nine chapters, the period since World War II is one of less dramatic, but nevertheless, serious evolution that makes this approach, to our mind, a better way to describe the life of the changing city than a purely chronological arrangement.

History may be written in many ways and no one way will satisfy all historians or lay readers. We hope that our method will offer enlightenment, while recognizing that other methods and subjects might also help provide explanations of the city's multi-faceted and ever-changing history.

ONE

Some Historical Background

AMERICAN POLITICAL DOMINANCE in New Mexico began with the arrival of General Kearny's army in Santa Fe in 1846. When his forces entered the city, New Mexico and its capital were nearly two and one-half centuries old as Spanish colony, Mexican province, and town. Santa Fe's existence and basic character had been shaped by the Spaniards' law and practice as well as their language and the Catholic faith they brought with them. Some of these characteristics remain visible and strong in the modern state and city to this day.

New Mexico's colonial development progressed under limits imposed by its physical environment and its location relative to other populated centers. Its great distance from Mexico City, the political center of colonial New Spain and, later, independent Mexico, proved to be a crucial determinant of how New Mexicans could respond both to the wishes of the central government and to their own local problems. Given the myriad issues faced by late colonial Spain in the early nineteenth century and the young Mexican republic between 1821 and 1846, New Mexicans often had to decide for themselves how to deal with their problems—they could expect little support from the outside.

The disappearance of the old Spanish political order and its replacement by an independent Mexico affected the political life of New Mexico deeply. Representative institutions appeared on a provincial level and experienced revitalization on the municipal level.[1] Greater autonomy now existed than under the old Spanish state. Yet, there was disappointment that the altered governing system under the Mexican republic remained incomplete and, at times, ineffective and confusing.

New Mexico's economic order also changed dramatically under Mexican sovereignty. While Spanish mercantilism had restricted commerce with foreigners, the Mexican republic favored trade with outsiders. This change of policy, which fostered the establishment of contacts with the Americans, led to the formation of the trade route known as the Santa Fe Trail.

In the early days of the Spanish conquest in what became New Mexico, Santa Fe had quickly become an administrative, military, and religious center and never relinquished that position under Spanish or Mexican rule. The longevity and status of that tradition remain no small element in the sense of importance and uniqueness that pervades the history of the city to this day. The tasks assigned to officials by higher authority of state and church, as well as its isolation within the vast territory in which it stood, gave it an unusually high degree of visibility. Its unique political and economic position drew to it successful and active persons from throughout the province, a process that in some respects and in broader contexts continues to the present.

The work of Ralph E. Twitchell, the best known of the Anglo historians of Santa Fe, offers an example of this perception. Writing in the early twentieth century, he saw the town's historic sphere of influence as extending "on the East to the Mississippi, to the unknown regions of the North, to the Pacific on the West . . . and to New Biscay on the South." Recognition of their responsibilities by local authorities and the place of the Native American in the scheme of settlement and colonization, Twitchell continued, made Santa Fe "a center of the greatest civil and military importance."[2] He offered his readers the picture of a city of imperial scope in its outlook and operations.

The history of Santa Fe, however, must also be measured in the context of its own immediate environment—as a place in its own right. Given these parameters, it presented a more humble image than the grandeur-filled one invoked by its broader provincial functions. In this context, Twitchell himself noted that the poverty of Santa Fe's people had contributed to its failure "to achieve that degree of importance or distinctive character as a municipality attained by the capitals of others of the northern provinces of New Spain." Along with its poverty, he suggested that the almost constant warfare with the Native Americans had sapped its vitality.[3]

The evaluations of contemporary travelers confirm Twitchell's view. Never legally a *ciudad*, the most independent urban civil entity defined by Spanish rules, Santa Fe attained the status of *villa*, the next lower rank. In 1776 Fray Francisco Dominguez, on a visit there, noted that

> when one hears or reads "Villa of Santa Fe," . . . the seat of political and military government . . . such a vivid and forceful notion . . . must be suggested to the imagination that the reason will seize upon it to form

> judgments . . . that it must at least be fairly presentable. . . . [B]ut its appearance, design, arrangement, and plan do not correspond to its status as a villa . . .[4]

As a villa compared to others in New Spain, he concluded, it "lacked everything."

If the Catholic cleric downgraded its urban character to that of a marginal villa in 1776, the American soldier, Lt. Zebulon Pike, writing in 1807, described Santa Fe as a village, looking like a fleet of flat-bottomed boats.[5] On the other hand, when one contemplates the level of urban development in the Southwest in 1850, just after the establishment of American authority, Santa Fe's population of 4,846 was large compared to Dallas's 2,743 and Los Angeles's 1,610, while Tucson, Phoenix, and Denver did not appear in the census at all.[6]

The realities of Santa Fe's existence reflected conditions on New Spain's and Mexico's northern frontier. Scholars have pointed to the sense of community that pervaded Spanish colonization and settlement. Writing of the northern frontier, Oakah Jones informs us that "the large majority of the people on the Spanish frontier in the colonial period consisted of real settlers established in formal communities, and absolutely dependent upon tilling the soil and raising livestock for their livelihood." The early Spanish town, he concluded, "was a self-contained rural-urban unit."[7] The municipality was an urban area that included rural environs with agricultural lots assigned to each resident.[8] With limited trade opportunities a fact of economic life, self-subsistence was a necessity.

Santa Fe also largely fits this description. However much scholars have concentrated their attention on soldiers, politicians, and priests, the city displayed important features of its agrarian character. Although Spanish plans insisted on the concentration of settlers to attain security, Santa Feans chose to scatter along the Santa Fe River to achieve convenient access to farm plots and to control them. For them, agricultural considerations took precedence over the needs of defense.[9]

Studies of colonial Santa Fe attest to its strong rural economy in the late eighteenth century. Even at that relatively prosperous time the products most profitable for export—furs, hides, and weavings—were not directly products of local production; a majority of the city's population engaged in farming and stock raising.[10] Twitchell, writing of that period, noted that residents of Santa Fe, outside of officeholders of the Crown and the presidial garrison, "cultivated small parcels of land by irrigation" and that "[m]ore than three-fourths of the area comprising the settlement was devoted to agriculture and small gardens."[11] Marc Simmons's conclusion that Santa Fe, the most urban of New Mexican towns, was hardly an example of true urbanism appears well taken.[12]

How much of the population of Santa Fe engaged in agriculture is difficult to determine. However, the demands of subsistence and the limited amount of suitable land available restricted agricultural production to family use and a bit more. Members of the immediate and extended families performed the required labor. Farming was the business of the family but not necessarily the only family business. Farmers were of all social categories and all segments of society bought, sold, and traded agriculture's fruits. The pervasive nature of the occupation bespeaks it as a fundamental activity in a population of relatively few specialists.[13]

Municipal government in New Mexico under Spanish and Mexican rule reflected traditional forms modified by local exigency. *Ayuntamientos* or *cabildos*, town or municipal councils, governed towns of any size. *Alcaldes*, local officials with judicial, civil, and legislative duties, generally carried out the functions of administration.[14] Whichever agency ruled at any given time, the major areas of official activity appear to have been judicial and police functions. How effective they were depended on the quality of the individuals, the means available to them, and the character of the community itself.

However new the American political presence was in 1846, it was preceded by American economic influence. The trail that bore Santa Fe's name had been established between New Mexico and Missouri after Mexican independence a quarter-century earlier. By the time the American flag was raised in Santa Fe, as historian David Weber put it, New Mexico "had grown as dependent upon the United States for markets and merchandise as it had once been on central New Spain."[15]

The effects of American trade, however powerful, did not overwhelm New Mexico or Santa Fe. Americans were not the only merchants. New Mexicans had produced their own merchant class, which engaged in commerce across the great plains to the east and even more in the transshipment of goods from Santa Fe to Chihuahua and to California. That commerce opened new opportunities for muleteers, translators, and others with skills valuable in the exchange of goods.[16] Thus, trade had already affected the socioeconomic character of New Mexican society. The driving force of that intercourse, however, was due less to the central provinces of Mexico and increasingly to contact with the Americans.

Santa Fe had been changing under Mexican administration. In the last years of Mexican rule there were efforts to deal with its growing complexity. A proposal in the legislature to lay out municipal ordinances contained paragraphs relating to sutler tents in which liquor was sold, public beneficence, weights and measures, police, jails, education, and sanitation. Historian Lansing Bloom noted that General Kearny's code of law, issued in 1846, relied heavily on these preexisting measures for guidance.[17]

The American military occupation of Santa Fe initially interrupted the course of municipal legislation by limiting civil government. Only with the creation of American territorial status in 1850 did efforts resume to delineate the powers of the city. The first territorial legislature of 1851 formally reestablished the political prominence of Santa Fe as the seat of government. That same body incorporated the city on 4 July 1851, designating an elected mayor and board of common council as governing agencies. The legislation accorded the city considerable powers to license commerce and to regulate public behavior, including the authority "to prevent furious and unnecessary riding of any horse or animal within such city," as well as to levy and collect taxes.[18]

The American military occupation also introduced new elements and dynamics of economic, political, and social activity. The entry of over 1,600 troops under Kearny alone altered the pace of economic change, placing a severe strain on housing space and the availability of certain foodstuffs for men and even more for animals.[19] Although this original large force did not long remain, smaller numbers did. Their presence and Santa Fe's position as a military headquarters became an important factor in the life of the early territorial city.

Nevertheless, the older strains of even a modified semiagrarian town did not disappear. A few months after the city's incorporation, in January 1852, the second session of the first legislature repealed the act and Santa Fe was not incorporated again until 1891.[20] County officials and the probate court assumed the duties of governing the community.

What motivated the reversal of incorporation is uncertain. Twitchell attributed it to lack of approval by local politicians and "on the ground of economy."[21] Another expanded explanation noted that "the inhabitants of Santa Fe, who were unaccustomed to be taxed for the maintenance of a municipal government, found the city's charter to be distasteful. . . ."[22] Santa Feans appeared unwilling to assume the obligations of urban residence.

One might consider that New Mexicans had also resisted new taxation when instituted by the Mexican government in 1837. They had viewed fees for vehicle or animal entry into the city and for entertainment as nothing more than support for "luxury and waste of a few in Santa Fe. . . ." The platform of the rebels of 1837 included clauses that rejected plans of reorganization or taxation.[23] Hard times and bad management provided sufficient cause for the uprising when added to the Mexican government's new imposts.

Such attitudes toward direct federal taxes, which New Mexicans had never paid, may well have carried over into the new period of American territorial history. Despite appeals by early territorial governors, the legislature would not pass laws levying taxes on land, but did levy them on merchants. The tradition of no tax on land continued. In part, the attitude of the Hispanos seemed to imply, as one scholar put it, that the Anglos had seized the country and should pay for its upkeep.[24] It also reflected a strongly agrarian tradition.

Between 1846 and 1880 Santa Fe experienced close to two generations of an American presence. That reality affected Santa Feans, a heavily Hispano community, in a variety of ways, altering older modes of life by the necessity to adjust to new reference points of politics, economics, and culture. The new "Anglo" population, a designation that arose later for non-Hispanos and non-Native Americans, was numerically small. However, it was strongly anchored in politics through ties with Washington, close interaction with the military, and in its knowledge of the new legal order brought to the region with the American assumption of political power.

The Anglos, a small but powerful minority, differed from the long-resident Hispano population in major respects. The Catholic Church, for example, so important both politically and culturally in the Spanish and Mexican periods, now faced new challenges of permissible diversity and secularization. In addition, with the arrival of French Catholic clergy who came during the fifties, New Mexican Hispano Catholics encountered a different authority and energy within the Church itself.

While the appearance of religious diversity was one dimension of change, that within the Anglo community itself brought much that was new to Santa Fe. Protestantism was a powerful force among the Anglos. Masonry, too, was strong. German-Jewish merchants formed a tiny but influential new contingent in commercial circles even if they did not express themselves in a formal religious presence. But such elements were small numerically and did not impinge heavily on the existing Hispano majority.

Ethnic social interaction also became a new fact of life. Because the Santa Fe Trail and the Southwest were judged too dangerous a place for Eastern women to travel, Anglos arrived mostly as single males. Given the circumstances, many married local Hispano women. A student of the subject found that in 1870, 63 percent of Anglo family men in Santa Fe had done so.[25] By 1880, one of every three Anglo married men had wedded a Hispano woman.[26] However, while ethnic boundaries were pierced without great difficulty, the early results of such unions tended to assimilate the Anglos who married into Hispano families and their children were raised as Hispano Catholics. Anglo names of Hispano families provide clear evidence of that process to this day.

Education, a potentially powerful instrument for cultural change, progressed only slowly under the auspices of the new political forces. Without formal obli-

2. *End of the Trail at the Plaza, ca. 1869.*
Courtesy Museum of New Mexico, neg. #11329.

gation to assert itself as schoolmaster, the American national government did little to alter existing conditions of widespread illiteracy. Local government and religious organizations in particular, however, saw both obligation and opportunity in New Mexico's scholastic wasteland and asserted themselves despite limited means, cultural differences, and difficulties posed by isolated frontier conditions. Santa Fe had become an early beneficiary of these efforts as Catholic schools, primarily, opened and established themselves as important new fixtures in the community. Their foothold would prove a powerful instrument of both cultural change and continuity.

Differences of usage and custom began to alter the appearance and functioning of the venerable town. For example, American architecture and building materials became prevalent in the town's center. Perhaps the greatest changes, however, resulted from the powerful presence of American goods and commerce geared to the needs and desires of a consumer population and the broader territorial requirements of the new American political presence.

The city's population grew between 1850—when New Mexico first appeared in an American census—and 1880, from 4,539 to 6,635, an increase of about 39 percent. However, in the same period the population of the entire Territory of New Mexico expanded from 61,547 to 119,565 or about 49 percent.[27] In light of the broader comparison, Santa Fe's growth appears vigorous but not spectacular.

The qualitative character of that growth is more revealing as a measure of change than its quantity. As its population grew, the town's economy diversified. It became not only a retail but also a wholesale center of commerce. New forts and the creation of reservations for Native Americans contributed to that process. Large commercial enterprises, such as those of the Staab, Seligman, and Spiegelberg families, came into existence and flourished between 1846 and 1880 with business that related both to Santa Fe itself as well as to the entire Territory of New Mexico.[28] William Parish, an eminent regional business historian, described the integrative effects of their operations that linked growers, merchants, and users as a "commercial revolution."[29]

Although the effects of the merchants' enterprising ways upon the old city were strong, they were less than tidal. Increasing availability of consumer goods and opportunities to create services brought the Anglo arrivals and the older Hispano population into new relationships with each other and modified the internal ways of each group. Essentially, the Anglos brought with them the skills they practiced in the East. The political and economic power of the newcomers made it incumbent on the Hispanos to adjust, and the Hispanos' response can be shown in the changes of their labor force from 1850 on.

In that year, traditional Hispano ways of earning a livelihood were still dominant and farming remained the underlying reality. Anglos did not come to farm; of the 278 persons listed as "farmers" in the 1850 census, only ten were Anglos. As late as 1870 farmers and farm laborers formed 51 percent of the Hispano labor force in Santa Fe.[30] And in 1880 Hispanos, with 45 farmers and 185 farm laborers, retained the same agricultural preponderance over Anglos in agriculture as they had in 1850. However, the reduction of farming practitioners to 15.5 percent of the total labor force by 1880 reflected the increasing entry of Hispanos into other occupations as well as the growth of a nonagricultural Anglo population.

Already in 1850 about one-fifth of the employed Hispanos plied skilled crafts (predominantly as shoemakers, tailors, and blacksmiths), while another third worked as unskilled laborers. By 1880 about 20 percent of Hispanos were in occupations new to them. Some became lawyers, nurses, Catholic teaching sisters; others now operated food stores and kept saloons, and in government they had become policemen and jailers. Still others served as clerks in a variety of institutions as well as in stores and engaged in new skilled crafts as millers, bricklayers, and painters, and in semi-skilled occupations such as housekeepers,

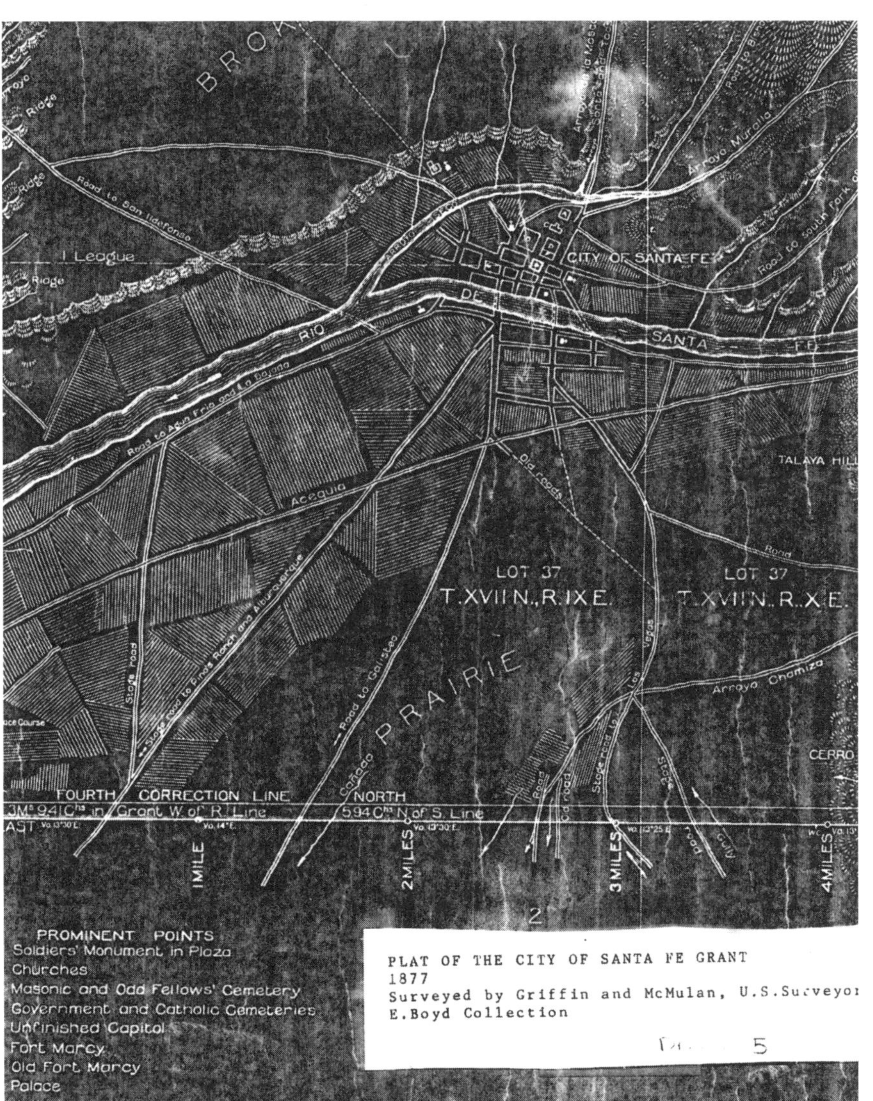

3. Plat of Santa Fe Grant, 1877.
Courtesy New Mexico State Records Center and Archives.

seamstresses, and laundresses. In addition, there were those who served as service personnel in hotels, as errand runners, and waiters.

Thus, the Hispano population had begun to exhibit the occupational diversification that existed among Anglos in this early period of urbanization. As the total of Anglos employed doubled in size between 1850 and 1880 (from 405 to 858), the number of different occupations they practiced increased almost threefold (from 55 to 154). Similarly, the total of Hispanos employed increased by almost half (42 percent) and the number of different occupations they pursued more than doubled (from 31 to 74).

For the Hispano population, these changes that paralleled the Anglo experience meant an increasing shift to a cash economy and away from traditional subsistence farming, barter, and unpaid domestic labor. The shrinkage of agriculture led to an increase in the sale of foodstuffs and a growing number of grocery stores appeared in the hands of Hispanos situated in local neighborhoods.

The economic roles of women began to change. Access to manufactured cloth brought forth seamstresses and dressmakers from within the Hispano community.[31] The presence of prospering Anglos created opportunities for a large number of Hispano laundresses, the women so engaged comprising nearly a third of the Hispanos working in new occupations. In these ways Hispano women began to earn money for work formerly limited to the family household, while formerly unpaid family farm workers could now earn cash in nonfarming occupations.

The increasing variety of occupations and conversion to a cash economy brought Hispano residents of Santa Fe into relationships with the Anglo newcomers based on interdependence and common interests. Hispanos were becoming dependent on Anglos for employment, at first in occupations serving household needs; Anglos, in turn, relied on Hispanos for such services. Anglo merchants, in addition, counted on Hispano customers.

While Anglos introduced occupations that provided opportunities for Hispanos, they also entered occupations that Hispanos had held before the territorial period. This was particularly true in the skilled crafts. In 1850, 89 of the 116 Anglos in the skilled craft category held occupations similar to those of Hispanos, as did 85 of the 122 skilled Anglos in 1880. The potential existed for common economic interests to develop on the part of the two groups as well as for competition.

The growth of Anglo and Hispano interrelationships remained limited. The large majority of the Hispanos still spoke Spanish and lived lives firmly rooted in their own family, residential, and customary mold. Early Anglo settlers often had to learn at least a modicum of Spanish to get along. The schools of Archbishop Lamy, the famous prelate whose presence dominated the church in Santa Fe, while not dedicated to preserving Spanish, taught in a manner that served as a transition from Spanish to English. Protestant schools did the same.[32] Nevertheless, formal education remained beyond the means or opportunity available to most Hispanos, and their cultural traits continued intact, interrupted only by their increasing contact with the growing Anglo presence.

The coexistence of the two groups making their living primarily in different ways gave rise to conflicts of interest when the needs of one group impinged on the other. It is in this context that modern local government developed in Santa Fe. Santa Fe retained its position as the territorial capital, but its local government remained minimal. While Anglos almost totally dominated the small number of federal positions (including the territorial governorship), Hispanos were beginning to appear in local positions and they dominated the territorial legislature. With the repeal of Santa Fe's incorporation in 1852, the county was left as the source of money and personnel. The probate court became the seat of executive authority in the county and the probate judge the principal agent of government charged with the administration and enforcement of law. Not until 1876 did the creation of an elected county commission introduce a deliberative body between the territorial legislature and the community with power to regulate local activities.

Early efforts to develop public services revealed the need for municipal government in Santa Fe and reflected the diverse and competing interests. Two principal areas of concern drove the early efforts to develop services: protection and support for the residents who farmed for their livelihood and the maintenance of safety and order, sanitation, and convenience deemed necessary for life in a growing urban environment.

The sharp decline in the portion of the Hispano labor force engaged in farming shown in the census from 1870 to 1880 should not obscure the extent or political strength of farming interests in the city or the impact of farming operations on the city's policies and practices. A surveyor's map of 1877 (See page 9) depicted farmlands on both sides of the Santa Fe River to just southeast of the cathedral and then again west of Galisteo Street south of the river. Agriculture north of the river began west of Burro Alley.[33]

Given the uncertainty of water resources in the entire community, concern for its supply in the city received attention as early as 1861. In that year, the legislature passed an act to examine the possibilities of increasing the flow from the Santa Fe River that coursed through the city. Voluntary subscriptions and labor required of white males between the ages of 18 and 45 (except ministers and federal employees) who resided on or near the river "from its source to the last house of the settlements of Agua Fria" would finance and build any project adopted.[34]

This plan produced no action, nor did a second one authorized in 1864 to construct a dam to create a reservoir. Even a year later, when a diminishing water supply was judged to be causing "great hardship in the entire community, which they cannot longer endure," and the legislature ordered the probate judge to "at once proceed to the work of constructing a dam," the residents took no more action than before.[35] A new law in 1865 added provisos for protection of the proposed dam, calling for guards and requiring stiff fines and jail terms for actions that would harm the structure.[36] After 1866 a minimal reservoir was completed but no further action was taken until 1879.

Other efforts by the government to provide services illustrate the division of interests between residents devoted to farming and those concerned with the needs of commerce and urban amenities. There was a marked tendency for the legislature to impose the costs of protecting agricultural operations on the farmers and landowners directly and those of urban safety, sanitation, and convenience on the county.

In 1859 the legislature authorized the construction of "a market house for the city of Santa Fe for the free use of all persons wishing to sell foodstuffs, but for no other purpose." Food sold at any other corner market house incurred fines. The county sheriff was charged with overseeing its cleanliness and given permission to use prisoners under his supervision to fulfill that purpose. In what was obviously a project to promote sanitation, the legislature authorized the county to pay for land and building, to put prisoners to work on construction, and to fund personnel in charge of the house operation.[37]

As Anglo residents dependent on commerce developed needs that threatened the resources of Hispano farmers, as in the case of the water supply, and as governmental funding tended to favor the urban services over agricultural needs, both groups acquired interest in the exercise of authority and the development of public policy. When the city was eventually incorporated, the ethnic division of political power that prevailed would be replaced by a pattern of equal participation in local government to accommodate the distinctive concerns of both groups.

By 1880 Santa Fe had developed a social and institutional infrastructure that was distinct from its traditional status as political capital and Catholic bishopric. Its growth as a commercial center, the terminus of the Santa Fe Trail, nurtured an awareness of the city's relationship to the broader American economy. While conscious of its traditional preeminence in New Mexico, questions arise as to the city's sensitivity to the changes that were occurring beyond its boundaries.

Las Vegas prospered in the seventies and, along with Albuquerque, both towns were thriving as centers of agrarian production and markets. They presented potential challenges to the proud capital. Yet, as long as business continued in the accustomed pattern, Santa Fe felt secure enough.

Nor was that sense of assurance shaken by early news of the approach of the railroad into their area. Having adapted so well to the Santa Fe Trail, Santa Feans viewed this prospect as an extension of the past—an improvement of the existing system. Because the oldest and most prestigious commercial firms and the most important federal offices were located in their town, it did not occur to them that the new mode of transportation could bypass the largest and most important town in the territory. Moreover, in the absence of a formal local government, Santa Fe business leaders and lawyers saw themselves as continuing their leadership role. This set of circumstances may well have bolstered the certainty of their expectations.

A community as small as Santa Fe, however, had neither the internal resources nor the external controls to dictate the direction the railroad would take. The geography of railroad building had a logic of its own that the small town could not alter. Therefore, when confronted by the incipient economic revolution caused by the railroad, which largely ignored the town's existence, the Santa Feans had to reconsider their fortunes. Recognition that one era had closed and a new one was opening, however, would not come immediately. Thus, it is with the main line of the railroad bypassing the city in 1880 that the history of the Santa Fe Trail ends and that of modern Santa Fe begins.

TWO

The Railroad and Santa Fe

BY EVERY MEASURE, the arrival of the railroad in New Mexico may be likened to other seminal events that dramatically changed the Southwest's course of development. Just as Oñate's expedition had introduced a new culture to New Mexico and as the Mexican-American conflict changed the political relationship of the region to the United States, the railroad altered its economic orientation to the eastern states. As a result, the area experienced economic and social change at an unprecedented rate.

The innovations introduced by railroads did not impinge on all places alike. Albuquerque and Las Vegas, located on one new main line, would flourish as a result of their placement. By contrast, that the main line bypassed Santa Fe and closed the Santa Fe Trail deeply threatened the economic prominence it had long enjoyed. It would force upon the city a new consideration of its future.

The railroad builders had their own perspectives and motives as they moved westward. Historian James Marshall elucidated their strategy for construction and development in the West. He noted:

> It is a singular fact that the Atchison, Topeka and Santa Fe, in common with our Western railroads, prospered and became powerful by building straight into undeveloped or thinly settled country. . . . They prospered by developing the country through which they passed, thus creating their own business, and by establishing through transportation routes to the Pacific Coast over which much traffic necessarily had to pass.[1]

Moving primarily to fulfill their objectives, not those of local communities, the railroads followed their own dictates when interests between them clashed.

The "fatherhood" of the "Santa Fe railroad," as it was known in the West (in the East it was called "the Atchison"), is attributed to Cyrus K. Holliday, an Easterner who moved to Kansas in 1854.[2] Holliday claimed authorship of the road's charter, introducing it to the Kansas legislature in 1859. Originally named the Atchison and Topeka Railroad Company, the charter indicated that the company would construct and operate a railroad between Atchison and Topeka, Kansas and "in the direction of Santa Fe."[3]

In 1863 a stockholders meeting added "Santa Fe" to its title. Probably more than anything else, the path and business of the Santa Fe Trail drew the keen attention of the Kansans. When "the first spade of dirt" was thrown in 1868, Holliday forecast the extension of the line to Santa Fe, a dream he had long cherished.[4] The name addition may also have been made to attract state and federal support for land grants.[5] Railroad historian L. L. Waters mused that it must have been a great feeling for Holliday when the first train reached Santa Fe; no other achievement "would symbolize quite so much."[6]

The arrival of that train in Santa Fe on 9 February 1880 generated a celebration and much excitement. Nevertheless, there was also disappointment. Rather than having a position on the main railroad, the city found itself on a branch line from Lamy, some eighteen miles to the east.

How did it happen that Santa Fe became a side issue rather than occupying a major position on a line bearing its name? Historians point out that more than one survey indicated that the terrain made it difficult to build into the town.[7] Other factors also contributed to the route selection. Timber in the mountains and coal at Cerrillos to the east, for example, served to divert the road to the southeast of Santa Fe, toward the rapidly developing Rio Grande valley.[8]

The railroad behaved in accord with its reason for being—to haul freight and people. The costs of building in one direction or another were measured by the ultimate profit to be gained. Railroad historians point out that the entire trade of the Santa Fe Trail "meant only a few hundred box cars of freight each year" and that Santa Fe itself in the late seventies "was no longer a good business center—a few boxcars a month could handle its freight business."[9] Santa Fe's lack of commercial promise, then, must also be included among the reasons for the railroad's reluctance to build its main line through the city.

Santa Fe's ultimate fate as a subsidiary railroad center began to emerge in the late 1870s. Viewing the prospects early in 1878, the *Weekly New Mexican* expressed confidence in New Mexico's future. The railroads, it judged, "must come, for there is no other place for them to run. They all want to carry our merchandise, minerals and cattle. . . ." That forecast was already changing New Mexico. "Commerce, enterprise and progress," the paper continued, "are commencing to wake the echoes among the ancient fossils of mediaevalism that have been slumbering in these valleys and hills ever since the European found his way to the country."[10]

The bright hopes of the townsmen, however, flew in the face of the economic realities of the seventies. The problem was not that Santa Fe County ceased to grow, but that other areas were growing far more rapidly. Ranked third among the counties in population in 1870, by 1880 it had fallen to sixth place. In the seventies the value of farms in Santa Fe County actually fell while they nearly doubled in Bernalillo and tripled in San Miguel Counties. Wool production, one of New Mexico's most important trade commodities, demonstrates the trend clearly. Despite the fact that Santa Fe County produced 28,918 pounds in 1870 and 48,628 in 1880, Bernalillo County produced 166,960 in 1870 and 1,169,925 in 1880, while San Miguel County produced 186,626 in 1870 and 640,893 in 1880.[11] As a production center Santa Fe County was falling far behind its neighbors, a fact quite evident to the railroad builders.

At the same time there was uneasiness in Santa Fe about its relationship to this drama of imminent change. Slowly, awareness of the possibility was emerging that the city might be bypassed by the railroads. With commerce uppermost in mind, but considering other factors as well, the *Weekly New Mexican* let its readers know that

> the time seems to have arrived when Santa Fe must decide upon a course to adopt which shall affect the future of this particular locality with respect to railroads. The assurance of permanence in values . . . , the securing and enlarging its trade and importance; the profits resultant from the influx of invalids . . . , and of tourists . . . these hardly need demonstration. There needs no assertion of the fact that with railroads passing Santa Fe, leaving it one side, its commerce and importance will depart, and its many attractions will not be sufficient to outweigh the inconvenience and delay of reaching it. . . . We deem it useless . . . to assert the certainty of the decay of the city should it [the railroad] pass some distance from us.[12]

The perspective of the railroad was forcing Santa Feans to consider their specific fate as a town as distinct from its position as a capital speaking for its territory.

As direct negotiations began between the roads and the city, Santa Fe's difficulties became increasingly evident. Meeting first with representatives of the expanding Denver and Rio Grande Western (D & RG), "the principal men and landowners" of the city and county were told that the line would build into town "if sufficient aid should be given . . . to justify the Company in so doing."[13] The D & RG sought $200,000 in cash and bonds, twenty acres of land for a depot, and a free right-of-way through the county. The city and county representatives countered with an offer of $94,000, the legal limit to which the county could encumber itself, and a suitable depot site.[14] No agreement was reached.

The *Weekly New Mexican* defended the rejection of the road's proposal. It viewed the road's policy of building up small terminal towns at the possible expense of Santa Fe as a mistake. With the bulk of business and banking capital in the city, the presence of two railroads would allow Santa Fe to compete for commercial ascendancy, but a disproportionate debt would be a handicap. Taxation on behalf of railroads for temporary advantage had left a trail of bankrupt towns along western railroad trunk lines. Even the rise of real estate values would not, the paper counseled, be adequate compensation.[15]

With the D & RG out of the picture, Santa Feans awaited the approaching Santa Fe line (AT & SF). By March 1879, however, indications were strong that the road would not come directly to the city. "From the limited knowledge which I have of the country," wrote W. B. Strong, the Santa Fe railroad's general manager, "I should suppose that we could only reach Santa Fe by a branch."[16] The *Weekly New Mexican,* which published the letter, expressed discouragement, but noted, "we have faith that our city will yet come out all right."[17]

Just past mid-year of 1879 the tension grew. The AT & SF had already secured a right-of-way through Bernalillo and along the Rio Grande to the southwest. "It is almost a certainty," the *Weekly New Mexican* noted, "that the road will pass down the valley of the Galisteo by Los Cerrillos."[18] The paper reiterated its fears for Santa Fe if no railroad reached it. Decay would be inevitable.[19]

Meetings with AT & SF representatives in mid-July revealed the line's terms and the choices available to the city. First, the road asked for a donation of $175,000 and depot grounds in return for which it would "build the road and operate it in connection with our main line." Alternatively, the city could build a road "to the satisfaction of our chief engineer," the line furnishing the rolling stock and operating the road. In that case, earnings would be applied to the upkeep of the line. A third choice would be for Santa Fe to build, equip, and operate a road on its own account, with the company agreeing to do business with it.[20]

The newspaper clearly took sides. Admitting the existence of some opposition to the coming of the railroad, it defined the naysayers as people who had more in the past than they could hope for in the future. Whatever the local effects, the paper forecast that the railroad's coming would bring "wonderful and novel changes which will promote their [the people's] welfare incalculably."[21] The reduction of freight costs, the unlimited promise of the livestock industry and agriculture, the exploitation of coal and iron resources and precious metals were all presented in the best light. For Santa Fe, even the loss of a direct line was not a fearful fact. The paper stressed, rather, that "The assertion that 'Santa Fe is the pleasantest place in New Mexico to live,' has become an axiom." As a residence and health resort it would grow. Coal at Cerrillos would bring new residents to the city. It would remain a civil and military headquarters. "Its historic romance," it prophesied, "will cause many visitors to come to it, and it needs only to be known to be appreciated." Gloomy predictions for the city's future by ambitious neighbors, it concluded, were "as ill-founded as premature."[22]

To decide the issue of a branch, a special election was called of those who owned taxable property (the property of a family head not exceeding $300 was exempt from taxation) in Santa Fe County. The propositions placed before the voters called for the issuance of county bonds in the sum of $150,000, requested in two separate propositions to be donated to the railroad to assist it in the construction of a railroad branch to the city of Santa Fe. The election was set for 4 October 1879.

The paper put forth its best effort on behalf of the propositions offered. W. H. Manderfield, a county commissioner and an editor of the paper stood behind them. The September 27 issue carried numerous separate editorial items each entitled "Vote the Bonds." The message was clear: "to vote against them will be suicide."[23]

Yet, the arguments revealed contradictory views that had been evolving over a period of time. Where earlier fear of debt had led to support of those who refused to accept the D & RG offer, now fear of isolation justified debt in the name of great prosperity. Where doubt had existed about marked increase in property values, now editorials stressed the direct personal benefit to property holders. The paper had moved from a position of caution and anger at the railroads' seemingly excessive demands to one of desperation should the results of the vote be negative. Images of great commercial and banking wealth and competitive position had changed to stressing the beauty of the city and its importance as an administrative center. No railroad meant hotels and stores without patronage, the loss of position as a capital, and a town in which the very streets would be deserted. The presence of a railroad would assure Santa Fe its position as New Mexico's leading town, a chance to be "what Denver is to Colorado." Santa Fe's fate, it appears, was to have a railroad and prosper or not have one and die.

The results of the bond election proved that the large majority of holders of taxable property in Santa Fe County wanted the railroad. The proposition calling for $79,000 dollars of bonds passed by a vote of 191 to 72; the second proposition for $71,000 dollars passed with a vote of 192 to 67. The large majority of voters lived in the city of Santa Fe and the two city precincts voted overwhelmingly in favor—191 to 19 and 192 to 13, respectively. The rest of the county precincts together voted 10 in favor and 54 against both propositions.[24] Clearly, the city property holders and those in the county did not see eye to eye on the value of the railroad.

The *Weekly New Mexican* rebuked the opposition, dismissing their arguments as weak. Moreover, the city, which would pay almost the entire amount of the taxes to implement the program, was seen as the proper place to decide the question. However, the paper took strong exception to an article printed in the *Denver Tribune* that described the election as largely an American victory over the Mexicans. "Had the leading Mexicans worked against voting the aid to railroads," the *New Mexican* stated, "it would not have been voted . . ."[25]

The paper's analysis appears essentially correct. Of nine precincts in the county, the seven outside the city of Santa Fe itself contained no Anglo-surnamed voters and the results were overwhelmingly opposed to passing the bonds. In the two city precincts, where slightly over half the voters were Anglo surnamed, the vote was overwhelmingly for the bonds. The issue of opposition, therefore, would appear to have been more along the lines of city against county, or urban area against rural area, rather than Hispano against Anglo.

With a place on the main line of the AT & SF gone, Santa Fe lost an opportunity to retain its commercial power in the new order created by railroads. Santa Feans did not, however, end their efforts to gain connections with other lines. In March 1880 the D & RG signed an agreement with the AT & SF not to build south from Española for ten years.[26] That left the former's terminus some 34 miles north of Santa Fe. To overcome that obstacle, some of the same Santa Feans who had fought the earlier battles for rail connections, Lehman Spiegelberg, Bernard Seligman, Antonio Ortiz y Salazar, Zadoc Staab, and Charles H. Gildersleeve among them, incorporated a new narrow gauge road under the name of the Texas, Santa Fe and Northern Railroad.[27]

The point of the new line was to link Santa Fe with Española, thus overcoming the force of the agreement between the AT & SF and the D & RG. After a promising start, money problems beset the new railroad entrepreneurs and the work languished. It was only in 1886 that an Ohio syndicate took over the project of completion, to the apparent relief of its originators and subsequent board members. Early in 1887 the line was completed, giving Santa Fe a connection with Denver. However, the AT & SF, unhappy about the amount of freight traffic heading north, tripled its rates on freight moving south, actually worsening conditions in Santa Fe.[28] In any case, by that time, other completed rail connections left the Santa Fe extension to the D & RG, in the opinion of the latter's historian, "an unimportant branch line."[29] Santa Fe's new attempt to retain commercial power proved too little, too late.

The decision to build a branch line from Lamy to Santa Fe affected the city immediately. The creation of a depot and railyard followed directly from it. As early as November 1879, the New Mexican reported attempts to buy land for the depot and noted problems raised by owners asking exorbitant prices.[30] However, by the time the first train arrived in February 1880, the depot had already been built.[31] Throughout 1880 and 1881, a water tank and windmill, a coal house, an engine house, and a number of other structures went up.

The expected development of the land adjacent to the new railyard soon led to the creation of a subdivision of lots east of the depot by local businessmen. Thomas Catron, Antonio Ortiz y Salazar, Luciano Baca, Abraham Staab, and Robert Longwill, among others, platted an area known as the "Valuable Building Lots Adjoining AT & SF Depot" for projected commercial and residential purposes.[32] Laid out in rectangular fashion with 224 lots, the subdivision may have been the first in Santa Fe to reflect American land development patterns, if one sets the military apart.

4. Santa Fe Railroad Depot, ca. 1908.
Courtesy Museum of New Mexico, neg. #66658. Photo by Jesse Nusbaum.

However, the hopes for the rapid development of the new subdivision ran into problems. High prices followed high expectations. When the lots went on sale in September 1880, the *New Mexican* judged them expensive "but not more than the situation warranted."[33] Nevertheless, over the space of several years the results of speculation and use proved less than brilliant. In the fall of 1881 about eight to ten houses were under construction. Commercial building in the area was somewhat more successful, but a recent study of 120 structures in the area showed that only seventeen, mostly residences, had been built before 1900.[34] Another study of land use that described how the area looked in the mid-1880s defined 129 lots in the Valuable Lots subdivision as speculative and without structures upon them.[35]

All in all, the picture of development in the area indicated no boom of the kind experienced near the railyards of Albuquerque and Las Vegas. The new district, calculated to be a new town, did not displace the traditional plaza as the leading commercial and residential sector of Santa Fe. In that sense, whatever immediate ado the railroad's arrival created, it disappointed the long-term expectations of those who had counted on the creation of a newer, more modern, and larger Santa Fe.

Whether it was anxiety induced by the threat to its traditional supremacy or urgency produced by the appearance of rail traffic, the early eighties fired up new energy in the city. Within the space of a few months major projects of modernization were launched. Most conspicuous was the creation of a gasworks and the beginnings of a waterworks.

The first project completed was the gasworks. Incorporated in April 1880, its backers were some of the established business figures of the city, such as Willi Spiegelberg, Abraham Staab, and James L. Johnson. They were joined by such publicly important persons as William H. Manderfield, the editor of the *New Mexican*, Eugene A. Fiske, William Breedon, and Antonio Ortiz y Salazar. Located behind the Masonic temple and using coal to produce the gas, the new enterprise, which went into operation in December 1880, provided power to illuminate the city and to end, as the *New Mexican* put it, "those dangerous and greasy lamps and candles which through three centuries have dimly shone upon the labors of past generations. . . ."[36] It was estimated that some 1,200 burners would be necessary to accommodate the demand.

The issue of water was more delicate. Given the importance of water rights in the arid West generally, the problem of urban and rural water use could not be so easily settled as the gasworks. Earlier attempts to procure water had not resulted in victory for urban sectors of the city. Despite a legislative order in the mid-sixties to build a dam, no definitive action had resulted. In 1879 the

New Mexican was still calling for a widening of the passages in the Santa Fe River to improve the flow and for a prohibition of sheep and goat herding in the streambed.[37] Wells were an important source of water in the residential areas of the city.

Whether the coming of the railroad contributed to action taken to improve the water supply at that time is moot, although the *New Mexican* frequently linked the two events. Incorporation of the Santa Fe Water Works came in December 1879 and of the Santa Fe Water and Improvement Co. in October 1880. At that time the company proposed to build a system of three reservoirs and received a franchise from the county commission enabling it to act on the proposal. A disastrous fire in Las Vegas's New Town in September provided evidence of the urgent need for a water system lest Santa Fe suffer the same fate.[38]

Despite considerable financial difficulty and opposition from residents along the Santa Fe River, the effort to procure a modern water supply for the city achieved at least a partial success. The "Stone Dam," Santa Fe's first storage reservoir, was built in 1880–1881.[39] Water mains were laid throughout the principal streets and to the dam and the water began to flow on 31 March 1882. Discussion of the issue of the conflict generated by the new waterworks belongs elsewhere, but like the gasworks, the timing of the water system accompanied the railroad's appearance in Santa Fe, giving a new sense of impetus and progress to those who sought to create a modern future for the city.

The creation of such facilities was presented optimistically in a leading historical work that appeared in 1888. H. H. Bancroft's *History of Arizona and New Mexico* noted that "During the past decade its [Santa Fe's] quaint old, Mexican, one-story adobes have given way to a considerable extent to brick blocks and residences of modern style."[40] Bancroft's congratulatory conclusion on behalf of modernization, however applicable in the time he wrote, would prove to be quite at odds with the cultural driving forces of the city a quarter-century later.

The presence of the railroad had an immediate effect on the pace of life in the center of town. Visitors of all sorts arrived in large numbers—miners, capitalists, workers, and tourists.[41] Their appearance confirmed local expectations that interest in the city and growth would follow the arrival of the new transportation system.

The increased human traffic, however, also had its less desirable aspects and revealed the town's lack of preparedness to deal with the unaccustomed influx. Vagrants contributed to an unsettled feeling in the community. Even before the railroad arrived, its approach had brought such nomads in sufficient numbers to warrant the creation of their own rating system for Santa Fe homes: S. U. for stand up and eat, C. V. for cold victuals, O. O. H., ordered out of house, and so on.[42] Crowding and insufficient services added unpleasantness. Filth and garbage in the streets, not entirely absent before the railroad arrived, proved an embarrassment. Action by the county commission established a system of garbage collecting carts in 1881, which brought a sigh of relief from the *New Mexican*.[43] Inadequate hotel accommodations also attracted much attention from the press, which was following the building of the new Palace Hotel with much interest.

While the immediate shock of visiting crowds could be adjusted to and rectified in a relatively short time, the commercial future of the city and the problem of space in the center of town presented longer-term problems. The failure to create a new town in the depot area proved crucial in this matter. While the arrival of the railroad in Albuquerque had led to the building of an entirely new city, the relatively slow and weak development of Santa Fe as a rail center placed new burdens on the traditional commercial district around the Plaza.

Given the failure of Santa Fe to gain a place on the main line, no large-scale influx of new capital followed. That left immediate new investment in city development or enlargement of the old commercial district in the hands of the already established business leaders and property holders. They were willing, as noted above, to invest in a comparatively modest real estate development in the depot area, but the opportunity to produce a new commercial center was a more complex matter.

The very idea of a new town raised difficulties. The *New Mexican* opposed the concept, seeing in it a recipe for the kind of conflict that had arisen in Las Vegas and Albuquerque with the separation of new and old towns.[44] One could ask, too, why Plaza merchants should want to create a potentially competitive situation for themselves.

Yet, the Plaza district was crowded. Leading the charge for enlargement of this old commercial area, the *New Mexican* called on property holders there to make room for new businesses. Its larger scheme involved connecting the Plaza and the depot. To accomplish this the paper urged the widening of San Francisco Street and the next street to the south, which in the spring of 1881 became known as Water Street, and for widening the bridge across the Santa Fe River to provide access to every kind of traffic.[45]

Discussion in the late winter and early spring of 1881 revealed the problems of the city in responding to the railroad's presence. Any progress on Water Street required the agreement of all the property holders of the area. The county lacked authority to confiscate property and the funds to overcome all resistance. Power to act thus remained with the property holders themselves.

The county commission, under the chairmanship of Sol Spiegelberg, an old-line merchant, organized a public meeting on 15 March 1881 to discuss the issue. The assemblage chose a committee composed of Gov. W. F. M. Arny, William M. Berger, and Adolph Seligman, supplemented by Sol Spiegelberg, Gaspar Ortiz, and Felipe Delgado, to call on Water Street property owners to persuade them to allow the straightening of the street. That meeting also resolved itself into an association on improvements. Despite the subcommittee's efforts, however, it could not gain the unanimity needed to proceed.[46] By late April, the effort had fizzled.

This process displayed an impasse in Santa Fe's development. Without the economic energy to create a new town or to enlarge the old commercial district, growth, if not modernization, stalled. One historian attributed the failure of the Water Street project to the lukewarm efforts of the old-line business leaders to back a movement that may have been contrary to their closest interests.[47] Certainly, such large-scale merchants as Staab, Spiegelberg, and Ilfeld expended considerable effort on upgrading their existing local businesses during this same period, even as they publicly supported the Water Street project.[48] Whether it was shock at the change in Santa Fe's fortunes, conservative shortsightedness, lack of a boom mentality, or fatigue, Santa Fe's old leadership reacted too weakly to overcome the city's new circumstances. They did not open the doors of Santa Fe wide to whatever opportunity the railroad's coming presented and thus contributed to the city's decline as a center of commerce. Left moot is the question of whether anything could have prevented the altered course of history introduced by the Santa Fe railroad's decision to bypass the city with its main line.

How Santa Fe fared as a result of the new era of transportation involves looking at immediate and longer-term considerations. The modest development of a new business area in the city around the depot was a direct and immediate result of the railroad's coming. Other signs are less direct but nevertheless persuasive. Thus, the most general data indicate a decline in population. In 1880, Santa Fe had a population of 6,635, but by 1890 it had fallen to 6,185.[49] Between 1890 and 1900 the city's population again fell, to 5,603.[50] Such absolute declines had not occurred before. By comparison, the growth of Albuquerque made it larger than Santa Fe by the turn of the century. A mixed picture emerges of immediate new development and a longer-term population decline.

Perhaps the greatest change incurred by the introduction of rail transport lay in the city's place in the territory as a business center. Without question, the closing of the Santa Fe Trail as an artery of trade with Santa Fe as its terminus aborted a process that was underway for well over a half-century. Wagon trains gave way to railroad boxcars and the loading of agricultural goods took place at Las Vegas and Albuquerque, close to where that kind of production took place. In an economic sense, Santa Fe slowly ceased to be the business center of New Mexico's import and export economy.

In the generation that passed between 1880 and 1900 Santa Fe was also outdistanced as a manufacturing and industrial center, insofar as such imagery could be applied to late nineteenth-century, urban New Mexico. In 1880 Santa Fe County contained 21 enterprises classified as such; in 1900, the city of Santa Fe itself housed 39 such establishments. By way of contrast, Bernalillo County in 1880 had only three enterprises, but by 1900 Albuquerque alone had 102 of them, nearly a fourth of the total number in the territory. Capital investment for these enterprises reached $61,459 in Santa Fe County in 1880 and $82,055 in the city in 1900. By contrast, Bernalillo County had $32,500 of capital in such enterprises in 1880 and Albuquerque alone reached $793,644 by 1900.[51] Economic development, while not dead in Santa Fe, clearly fell far behind Albuquerque and there could be little doubt that the railroad stood firmly at the center of these changes.

Santa Fe's place as a financial center declined as well. Until the latter years of the seventies it alone contained nationally chartered banks that catered to a territory-wide clientele. The First National Bank since 1870 had loaned money to mining interests, merchants, ranchers, and the Territory of New Mexico itself.[52] The Second National Bank, also in the city, was a good bit smaller but nevertheless quite active. By the late seventies, the commercial growth of other towns had led to the creation of new banks throughout the territory. Las Vegas in 1876 had a private bank in the name of the Raynolds brothers who reestablished it as the First National Bank of Las Vegas in 1880. In 1879 the San Miguel National Bank of Las Vegas opened its doors. In 1878 Albuquerque, too, experienced the opening of the Central Bank, which became the First National in 1881. Over the next decade new banks appeared in Socorro, Deming, Silver City, and Roswell.[53]

Under the pressure of such new competition, the financial resources available in Santa Fe shrank. Reporting resources of $919,655 in July 1882, the First National of Santa Fe showed $679,777 in July 1890. Similarly, the Second National Bank (the Spiegelberg bank), with reported resources of $366,412 in July 1882, showed $294,548 in July 1890.[54] In 1892 it closed its doors, its directors choosing not to renew their charter. While these declines were not disastrous, they nevertheless displayed a significant shrinkage in the business of both banks as other banks in the territory established themselves in their own local areas.

Commerce, the lifeblood of the Santa Fe Trail and the base on which territorial Santa Fe had grown and prospered, showed signs of decline after

1880. The causes lay in the new competition of rapidly growing towns on the main line of the AT & SF and changes in the methods of business that accompanied the railroad. The ability to replace inventories much more quickly than in the past and the increase of liquid capital as seen in the growth of banking affected the ways in which business was done.[55] The results were frequently unhappy for the old established firms in the city.

After an initial flurry of activity, a number of businesses experienced difficulty. J. L. Johnson and Co., one of the largest houses in town, was the first to falter and then fail. Caught between the practice of providing long-term credit that was characteristic of prerailroad days and the suppliers' newfound means for demanding quick payment for their goods, the firm failed in March 1881.[56] Lehman Spiegelberg, senior member of his family's enterprise, wrote plaintively in 1884 that despite the long-term advantages it would bring, "times are not as good as before the railroad."[57] As noted, by 1892, the Spiegelbergs, the principal shareholders in the Second National Bank, had closed both the bank and their large store and returned to the east after a stay of forty-six years. In January 1882, L. Hersch and Co., a smaller firm with a long history in Santa Fe also went under, a victim of "dull times and poor trade."[58]

Other firms chose to move elsewhere. In the eighties, Albuquerque became the new home of D. J. Abel & Co., a wholesale tobacconist, and of (Noa) Ilfeld & Co., a dry goods and clothing store. J. G. Albright, publisher of the Santa Fe *Democrat*, also moved to the growing new town and opened the Albuquerque *Morning Democrat*.

Less conclusive, but nevertheless instructive evidence, lies in the listings of McKenney's business directories. The 1882–1883 volume carried 236 listings for Santa Fe, but the 1888–1889 edition contained only 191.[59] While such losses did not constitute grounds for panic or mass desertion, they indicated a downhill trend that boded ill for the old commercial center.

The new transportation system, which, as noted earlier, brought a new order of credit, also led to the appearance of new credit-reporting agencies. The firms of Bradstreet and R. G. Dun and Co., then separate, had moved rapidly westward after the Civil War.[60] In 1872 Santa Fe had 24 listings in Bradstreet while Albuquerque had 20.[61] In 1897, almost a generation after the railroad's arrival, Bradstreet's carried 93 listings in Santa Fe and 217 in Albuquerque—at a time when the cities were roughly the same size. Thirty-eight of Santa Fe's businesses and 114 of Albuquerque's were actually rated for their capital and trustworthiness.[62] Santa Fe had fallen far behind Albuquerque in numbers of firms using the Bradstreet and Dun's credit rating systems.

Changes in Santa Fe's workforce in the years 1880–1900 also tend to confirm the declining state of commerce. The town's population fell about 16 percent in those years and the labor force about 23 percent.[63] The loss of working persons and of total population reflects the heavy loss of adult workers and reduced commercial and development opportunity.

Within the labor force itself the changes induced by the railroad reflected the continuing economic distinctions between Hispanos and Anglos. The Anglo labor force fell about 36 percent and the Hispano about 18 percent. The number of Anglo merchants dropped by nearly half, while Hispano merchants fell marginally. Nongovernmental clerks declined among both Anglos and Hispanos. Anglo-owned businesses and their Anglo employees were far more heavily involved in commerce than Hispanos generally and the losses reflected their greater decline.

The numbers of servants and workers, both Anglo and Hispano, also declined. A significant reduction of disposable income could account for a lesser ability to employ servants. Hispano workers, in this instance, were more affected than Anglos. Anglos and Hispanos shared equally in the 50 percent decline of skilled workers and foremen. Carpenters in particular exemplified losses here and reflected the reduction in construction activity.

Conversely, the number of Hispano farmers rose sharply during the period. Some 161 additional Hispanos reported farming as their occupation in 1900 as compared with 1880. This suggests that in the face of declining urban forms of employment Hispanos from farming families fell back on their traditional use of landed property and farmed to live. Perhaps Santa Fe's Hispanos, with agriculture still available to them, were less vulnerable than Anglos to the reversal of economic fortune caused by commercial decline. As a result, Hispanos could remain in Santa Fe, while Anglos were more likely to leave. Overall, the whole population suffered the effects of the city's changed economic situation.

Despite the efforts of the leading citizens of Santa Fe, they could not overcome many of the economic consequences introduced by the external forces of the railroad. The city, which was already exhibiting loss of economic leadership to other locations before the rail lines arrived, found itself losing population, capital investment, and commercial enterprise as never before; even the branch line to Lamy did not offset the disadvantage created by the absence of the main line. The era of growth fostered by the Santa Fe Trail was over.

Nevertheless, the behavior of the civic leaders in the face of new problems confronting the community displayed a determination to work together. At first this solidarity focused on maintaining commercial survival. The nearly unanimous approval of the railroad bond issues transcended diversity otherwise apparent between urban and rural precincts. The creation of new public services arose out of awareness that the city needed improvements—even if it involved private profit. That the establishment of a waterworks would produce tensions by threatening the interests of users dependent on irrigation merely reflected the continuing existence of diverse economic forces within the town.

The critical limit of solidarity was that the responsibility for civic welfare under conditions of a revolution in transportation now had to be shouldered by businessmen in the absence of an established municipal government. When such narrowly local tasks as straightening streets, expanding the area available for business activity, and linking newly created areas with older ones arose, the absence of institutions representing broader public interest over private interests was an obstacle to rapid change. The coming of the railroad laid bare the city's vulnerability as a community, not only due to economic competition from other towns and the endangerment of its territorial political position as capital, but also to loss of pride as a traditional leader in the region. The issue that came to the fore was whether Santa Fe could achieve the civic coherence necessary to rebuild its economic welfare and protect that political legacy prized by all.

THREE

The Political Development of Santa Fe

AS NOTED EARLIER, Santa Fe has been the political center of whatever administrative form New Mexico has taken—province, department, territory, and state. That distinguishing fact at times cloaked it with an exalted image that exceeded its presence as a city. As a community with a life of its own, it found itself compelled to consider its internal condition under the new pressures of the modern world.

Under American rule the city retained its political prominence. The introduction of other institutions that used it as their headquarters—the American army and the Catholic Church as bishopric—even enhanced its status, but it remained undefined by their purposes. Lacking a sufficient legal identity of its own, Santa Fe was nevertheless more than an extension of these institutions. When issues of a local public nature arose, solutions had to await the action of the territorial legislature or follow the energies of private citizens. Early in the territorial period the majority of Santa Feans probably preferred such informality, the heavily rural character of the place providing its own traditional answers to recurring problems.

By the time the railroad arrived the city had become a far more complex social and economic organism than it had been when the Americans first appeared. It required greater control over its internal affairs to solve the new problems and conflicting demands of its changing population. To some extent, the creation of the county commission system in 1876 brought Santa Fe a step closer to availing itself of an independent voice. Yet, even if county commissions by their makeup proved sympathetic to its increasingly urban needs, they did not have a mandate to use the resources of the county unequivocally on behalf of the city, although they did respond to aggressive city leadership when the occasion arose.[1]

The railroad's appearance soon changed conditions in the territory sufficiently to threaten Santa Fe's traditional place of political leadership. The rapid growth of Albuquerque and Las Vegas, possessing advantages derived from their main rail-line positions, led them to seek incorporation quickly to control their own fates. Albuquerque in particular moved apace, first incorporating in 1885.

Santa Fe, however, took no action in this direction. Even the discovery in 1886 by Census Commissioner William B. Sloan that the city had been incorporated in 1851 and his assertion of the continuing legality of that act did not change matters.[2] Attorney William Breedon disagreed with Sloan's view, while C. H. Gildersleeve, another important personage, responded to Sloan's interpretation that "we do not yet desire a city government."[3] Those opinions disturbed Sloan, who believed that incorporation meant progress, which required the municipal exercise of authority.[4] Nevertheless, Santa Fe continued to exist without incorporation for a few years more.

Meanwhile, enjoying rapid population and financial growth, Albuquerque exuded confidence in the future and, as a concomitant of that mood, political ambition in the present. As the town sought a larger place in New Mexico's sunshine—to become its capital—it encountered the entrenched positions of Santa Fe merchants, lawyer-politicians, and traditional interests, all determined not to relinquish their political status. And even if the commercial dominance held by Santa Feans had begun to slip, their hold on political power did not follow suit and was, in the early 1880s, still expanding.

Resistance to the widespread political and economic power of capital politicians had emerged even before the railroad arrived. The interests of such Santa Feans as Thomas B. Catron and Stephen B. Elkins, who came to the territory as young lawyers after the Civil War and became politically and economically influential, drew them into enterprises that affected the lives of persons very far from Santa Fe. Their involvement in the Maxwell Land Grant in Colfax County proved a source of considerable conflict in the mid-seventies arousing the resentment of many local persons and interests there.[5] Some Santa Feans were sufficiently attuned to such hostility as to blame William R. Morley, Sr., the location engineer for the AT & SF and an enemy of Catron's from Colfax County, for the report that recommended bypassing Santa Fe on its main line.[6] Although the Santa Feans' suspicion proved unfounded, they were apparently becoming sensitive to the idea that other areas of the territory might inflict pain on them.

As early as 1873, New Mexican Democrats had stamped those who grouped around Catron and Elkins as a "ring," a kind of mysterious and unholy cabal.[7] By the early 1880s some southern New Mexicans, Democrat and Republican alike, associated with this putative Santa Fe Ring, began to resent its growing power. They believed that the Santa Fe leadership by itself was accumulating a disproportionate share of patronage and territorial assembly representation, to mention only the Ring's assumed political greed.[8]

Albuquerqueans, with a strong sense of confidence, were discussing their future in the early mid-eighties as the territorial capital. With a view towards their city's incorporation, they propounded that its grant ought to include "some five miles square," predicting that "the time is not far distant . . . when it will all be laid out in streets and squares and all occupied by the city."[9] This space was necessary, the local paper, the *Morning Journal*, asserted, because "As the political capital and commercial, railroad and manufacturing centre of such a community, . . . Albuquerque is destined soon to become a very considerable city. . . ." The paper reasoned that "As Albuquerque is to be the capital of the coming state . . . it is important . . . that it should be made as attractive as possible. . . ."[10] While such thoughts occupied Albuquerqueans, they saw no need for haste, believing the issue would "settle itself in its own good time."[11] Evolution and the survival of the fittest would decide.

Santa Feans noted the attitude of their burgeoning neighbor to the south. The *New Mexican*, as cited by the *Morning Journal*, promised to aid Albuquerque in many respects "except as to getting the capital to Albuquerque."[12] While claiming impartiality on issues related to New Mexico's advantage, the *New Mexican* noted pointedly, "We are prepared to be impartial since it may be easily gathered . . . that we consider this the permanent capital of a future great state. On that point we stand firmly prepared to advocate Santa Fe's claims against every other place."[13]

Powerful Santa Feans did more than talk. Quietly they prepared to strengthen the position of their city against any challenge with stone and mortar while Albuquerque bided its time. In the fall of 1883 and the winter of 1884, according to historian Twitchell, then in his early legal career, such legal and political figures as Catron, William W. Griffin, and Antonio Ortiz y Salazar, merchants Abraham Staab and the Spiegelberg brothers, and even Archbishop John B. Lamy devised policies to secure the capital at Santa Fe.[14]

When the territorial assembly session began in February 1884, Governor Lionel A. Sheldon's message calling for a penitentiary provided the Santa Fe contingent and its allies with their opportunity to act. The need for such an institution had general support and the measure passed without difficulty. The location of the facility, however, was not decided upon immediately. A number of towns hoped to acquire it, including Las Vegas, Cerrillos, Socorro, and Bernalillo, among others.

Before the location of the prison was decided, a surprise bill to erect a capitol building at Santa Fe was introduced. That aroused a political storm. To the

Albuquerqueans the idea was outrageous. The *Morning Journal*, frustrated in its ambitions for its own town, saw in the undecided site of the penitentiary a lure by which the Santa Feans sought to gain support for their capitol bill.[15]

The major issue was the capitol bill itself. The Albuquerque paper depicted the penitentiary bill as a false pretense. Its purpose, it claimed, was to aid an economically ailing town. "The real object," the *Morning Journal* railed, "is to help Santa Fe out of her present hard times. . . ." If Santa Fe needed charity it should be voted an appropriation.[16]

The Albuquerque press questioned the need for the new capitol structure. There was enough space for public business in the Old Palace, the existing facility. If there was a shortage, the *Morning Journal* charged, it was "because a large portion of the room that should be occupied by public offices, is appropriated by private users. Citizens of Santa Fe are occupying for their private purposes almost one-half the room that belongs to the public." Attorneys and others in Santa Fe, the paper charged, were seeking space free of charge.[17] The accusation was not without merit.

The Santa Fe press supported the capitol bill. Although it defended the legislation, the *New Mexican Review* did not offer reasons for constructing the new building. Instead, it counterattacked, charging Albuquerqueans with delaying tactics so that they could become stronger and remove the capital to their town later. In addition, it advanced arguments that Santa Fe should retain the capital because "geographically, climatically, and financially, Santa Fe is the best place in New Mexico for the seat of state government."[18]

Beyond that, Santa Feans argued on the basis of political will. The majority of New Mexicans were for it. Depicting the Albuquerque opposition as that of selfish newcomers, the paper cited Governor Sheldon's support on the grounds of tradition and a general Hispano desire to keep the capital where it was. "I have discovered," the governor said, "that the native population of the territory, with great unanimity, is favorable to Santa Fe as the capital. . . . Santa Fe has been for generations a sort of governmental and religious shrine . . ." and "the feeling of the native citizens in this matter is not only natural but commendable."[19] However correct and sensitive these arguments may have been, they did not address directly the need to construct a capitol building in 1884.

The stand taken to defend the location of the capital involved a shift of position from the early eighties among Santa Feans. Arguing for tradition as opposed to strong modernization, which they associated with the "American" town of New Albuquerque, they may have been tacitly admitting that their town, by the mid-eighties, was beginning to feel its slippage as a commercial center. To emphasize tradition, wittingly or not, may have been an early step in a process of rethinking the basis of Santa Fe's future development.

When the dust of the legislative session settled, the city had become the home of the new penitentiary. In May 1884 the territorial legislature's board of managers, composed of Governor Sheldon, William Breedon, and Antonio Ortiz y Salazar, voted two to one in favor of the capital as location for the prison. Governor Sheldon cast the nay vote, citing free land in Las Vegas and the willingness of local financial capital there to encourage prison manufacture, the availability of raw materials, and the limited rail resources in Santa Fe as the reasons for his opposition. But he did not persevere. The *New Mexican Review*, in reporting the meeting, noted that the proponents gave no reasons in favor of the Santa Fe location.[20]

The penitentiary must be viewed as more than an improvement in New Mexico's law enforcement condition. To be designed in the Norman style with walls of stone twenty-five feet high, its 108 cells were envisioned also as an economic enterprise. It was to contain workshops, and trunks, brooms, and hosiery were among the early products listed as possibilities for manufacture there.[21] The inmates themselves, in addition, were viewed as a source of labor for various projects outside the prison. Finally, these inmates were regarded as consumers whose needs had to be attended.[22] With these perspectives in mind, the value of the facility to the community could be considerable and Santa Fe interests would not let it slip through their fingers.

The erection of the penitentiary coincided with the national victory of the Democratic Party in 1884. That opened the path to appointment of a Democratic territorial governor in New Mexico. President Grover Cleveland's choice was Edmund G. Ross, who, as a Republican senator a generation earlier had cast a crucial vote against the impeachment of Andrew Johnson. He had suffered political demise for his action, became a Democrat, and in 1882 moved to Albuquerque. There Ross threw himself into public life as a journalist and a critic of the territorial legislature.[23]

To Ross, the curse of New Mexico was its "Rings." All the rapacious combinations were, in his eyes, concentrated at Santa Fe as the capital and commercial center of the territory "regardless of political divisions."[24] As an anti-Ring advocate, Ross and the Santa Fe political leadership clashed repeatedly. Ross felt in March 1887 that "the people of Santa Fe, under the influence of the Ring, were almost a unit against it (his appointment) and bitterly hostile."[25]

Ross's stance undoubtedly limited the full benefit that Santa Fe sought to derive from the penitentiary. In February 1887 he pocket vetoed bills permitting the use of convict labor, which he felt competed with free labor. And again in February 1889 he vetoed portions of a bill permitting the use of convict labor at the capitol building, but also on the streets and bridges in or near Santa Fe and repairing the banks of the Santa Fe River. "I submit," Ross queried, "whether this is fair to the other cities of the territory. All our towns . . . are taxed for the support of these convicts. . . . No one community should be permitted to monopolize that labor. . . ." If it were to be done, he suggested, then there should be a proportionate defrayal of the public expense.[26]

Nevertheless, the presence of the penitentiary did bring benefit to some Santa Feans. Local merchants sold supplies to the institution, although not without producing friction among themselves. The Spiegelberg firm complained in 1886 to Governor Ross that the penitentiary purchasing authority bought "without advertising for bids" almost exclusively from one firm. The company demanded changes "as will enable us, as well as other merchants, to compete honorably with the one favored firm."[27] The successful seller was apparently merchant Bernard Seligman, whose services Governor Ross sought as territorial treasurer.[28] By 1890, however, Abraham Staab held a near monopoly on sales to the penitentiary.[29] Apparently, whichever party held office favored influential merchants of that party for the supplying of that institution.

Similarly, the one effective industry created in the penitentiary, brickmaking, also served the powerful. Thomas Catron ordered 400,000 bricks from the facility without a written contract in 1890 in exchange for which he was to give equivalent value in machinery to the institution. Shortly thereafter, equivalence was abandoned. Only the reorganization of the penitentiary administration by the legislature, and a desire to avoid outside criticism when an opportunity to gain statehood was under consideration, led to a suit against Catron. In 1894 he was forced to pay for the bricks.[30]

Santa Fe's political influence in the territory thwarted Albuquerque's effort to become the capital. Allied with representatives from Bernalillo, who may have been fearful of Albuquerque's growth, and representatives from northern counties, the Santa Feans squelched the capital removal bill while passing the act to build a capitol building.[31] The *New Mexican* depicted an easy victory when it observed that the decision reflected the will of "a hundred thousand Mexicans and fifteen thousand Americans" against "six to eight thousand Americans mostly living in new towns along the railroads . . ."[32]

For a few years, the success of the Santa Feans ended Albuquerque's efforts to become the territorial capital, but the issue reemerged in the early nineties. Albuquerque's continued commercial and population growth encouraged its renewed campaign. In 1891 the Santa Feans blocked another capital removal effort, but a new sense of uncertainty revealed itself both within the city and in commentary around the territory. The Socorro *Chieftain* noted that the issue was closed for two years until the next legislative session, but added that Santa Fe should take warning and put its house in order.[33] Indeed, the charge of lack of progressiveness against the capital took on an urgency against the background of the removal issue. The *New Mexican* itself suggested that the best way to end the conflict was to build a modern, attractive city including some sidewalks and lighted streets, and prodded Santa Feans to "wake up and bestir yourselves."[34]

Throughout the legislative sessions of the early 1890s Albuquerque continued its attempts to become the capital. A disastrous fire on 12 May 1892 destroyed the capitol building. The report of the Capitol Committee of the House of Representatives alleged arson, but condemned the "lax, careless, insufficient oversight" of the capitol commission and its custodian and expressed doubts as to the immediate rebuilding of the facility.[35] The loss endangered one of Santa Fe's arguments for retaining the existing location of the territorial government.

The town, however, hung on. When Miguel A. Otero became governor in 1897, he convinced Congress to designate the capital permanently at its existing site.[36] The territorial legislature had reaffirmed the city's position even earlier when it authorized the construction of a new capitol building in 1895 with Congress approving the sale of bonds for that purpose in 1897.[37]

Nevertheless, the city remained nervous. When the bonds did not sell well, prominent local citizens and organizations stepped forth to ensure progress on the project. Archbishop Placidus L. Chapelle, Solomon Spiegelberg, Abraham Staab, Marcelino Garcia, and L. Bradford Prince, among others, produced a preliminary fund of $2,550 for that purpose.[38] The new capitol building was completed in 1900 and, for the remainder of the territorial period, Santa Fe's position remained secure.

What Governor Otero confirmed for Santa Fe in the late nineties received reconfirmation when New Mexico achieved statehood. The state constitution adopted in 1910 named the city as its capital until changed by an election called for that purpose. The document provided, however, that "no election shall be called . . . prior to the thirty-first day of December, nineteen hundred and twenty-five."[39] Santa Fe, as capital, was safe for nearly another generation. By that time the issue of capital relocation was moot.

The challenge to Santa Fe's political status as New Mexico's capital, although unsuccessful through 1891, nevertheless forced Santa Feans to confront some of their problems. The city was increasingly perceived by other towns and by elements within Santa Fe itself as backward. One means of alleviating that condition was for the city to assume greater control over its own destiny. The political solution to accomplish that end was to incorporate—an action that was not well received, as earlier noted, as late as 1886.

In 1891, incorporation again became an option for Santa Fe. Among the new considerations were changes in the territory's statutes on the subject. The numbers necessary to petition for corporate status were lowered while amendments to the 1884 laws took account of growing urban populations and the physical areas necessary to accommodate them. Santa Feans, who watched closely the course of legislation and were wary of excessive costs of government, found satisfaction in the small number of officials authorized to govern cities as well as the limits on permissible taxation.[40] However minor the recent statutory changes were, they provided a reassuring starting point for adoption of a new legal status for the city.

More visible to many as incentive for change was the deplorable condition of services and of the streets. Complaints were constant. In June 1886 the *New Mexican* felt called upon by popular clamor to protest sanitary conditions in which animal carcasses dragged off by the county garbage cart from the plaza were dumped onto a common a few blocks away, soon returning as a sickening stench. Dissatisfaction with county authorities resulted from such poor performance. And, despite the fame of Santa Fe's summer climate, often dubbed "salubrious," the state of the streets in late winter offered a source of frequent complaint. "While the snow lasts," the *New Mexican* groaned, "the disgraceful condition of the streets of Santa Fe is not apparent, but when the snow melts, well, don't talk."[41] A few weeks later the paper commented, "Santa Fe will be incorporated in a few weeks, the mud and lack of pavements have settled this question."[42]

Economic issues also provided a powerful impetus for change. Underlying such concerns was the condition of the county, which in the early 1890s lay embroiled in conflicts over elections and financial difficulties. As the incorporation bill passed through the legislative process, Santa Feans expressed their approval for the measure by pointing up the benefits for property, how the city would be viewed inside and outside the territory, and the unemployed, as well as for the attraction of new financial capital.[43]

Conversely, as the movement for change gained momentum, the adverse effects of failure to incorporate also received recognition. New building and city improvements, it was predicted, would cease and stagnation would engulf the city. Without incorporation, property values would fall around the Plaza and the eastern section of town. In light of that, the south side would establish itself as a new city.[44] One outside capitalist, E. T. Webber of Denver, shut down building operations on the block he was constructing and was cited in the *New Mexican* as saying that "he doesn't have to spend money in a non-progressive town" and would wait to see how Santa Feans behaved before he spent another dollar there.[45] The whole issue assumed a tone of crisis in the press reminiscent of the efforts to lure the railroads a decade earlier.

As in the case of the railroad, prominent citizens took the lead in organizing a campaign to push incorporation to a successful outcome. A letter to the

New Mexican on 13 February 1891 asked plaintively, "Will the business men of Santa Fe take hold and push this matter to a conclusion? Can not a public meeting be held . . . where every citizen . . . may have an opportunity to discuss freely the merits of incorporation . . . ?" On March 9 a meeting of some 600 citizens took that step at the courthouse. Lehman Spiegelberg presided, Candelario Martinez acted as secretary, and B. M. Read and Henry Becker acted as interpreters. A prefatory meeting of leading businessmen had already decided on the need "to enlighten the masses" and impress upon all the need for action. S. Wedeles was part of a committee chosen at that meeting to give a report and it was he who addressed the crowd on March 9.[46]

Most of the organizers of the public meeting favored incorporation. Wedeles dwelt on its benefits for the poor and middle classes and noted that $1,000 had been subscribed to defray the preliminary costs of taking a census as prescribed by law. Aniceto Abeytia spoke more cautiously of the need for a frank discussion and careful explanation of the benefits. In the end, a committee of fifteen was chosen to carry out the necessary steps for incorporation. Its members were Sol. Spiegelberg, Celestino Ortiz, Frank Chavez, Frederick Grace, Candelario Martinez, Geo. W. Knaebel, Benj. M. Read, Marcelino Garcia, Aniceto Abeytia, E. L. Bartlett, Meliton Castillo, J. G. Schumann, G. D. Koch, A. L. Morrison, and C. F. A. Fischer.[47]

The question of what to include in the incorporated area received considerable attention. Discussion centered on the issues of size and population as they related to taxation and consequent attitudes toward incorporation. Since the relationship between taxation and benefits to be derived from incorporation could be the crux of any dispute, early attempts to define the city's boundaries brought suggestions to include as large an area as possible. This, it was argued, would dilute the tax burden as well as allowing Santa Fe to become a worthy capital and first-class city.[48] Another viewpoint, expressed by E. L. Bartlett, argued for a smaller area that could serve as an example to areas where opposition existed. The benefits, he believed, would convince them to join later.[49] The issue of potential opposition appeared crucial in the last analysis—it was more important to incorporate a smaller area than to risk failure.

The area finally defined for incorporation after a series of revisions was a modest one and five-eighths miles from east to west and one and six-tenths miles from north to south. Fischer's brewery was the best-known landmark on the eastern boundary, while a point some 200 feet west of Dunlop and Irvine Streets served as the western boundary. The southeast corner of the penitentiary marked the southwest corner of the square and the northern boundary's most important landmark was the military cemetery.[50] The required census included 3,880 inhabitants.[51]

The election to decide incorporation took place on 2 June 1891. The outcome was decisive: 709 in favor, 102 against. Upper Santa Fe voters (those living north of the river) registered 311 for and 72 against; lower Santa Fe (south of the river) voted 392 for and 30 against.[52] If, indeed, a powerful opposition ever existed, it was overcome either through persuasion or careful boundary delineation designed to leave serious opponents outside the incorporated area. As was so often the case in Santa Fe, an exuberant celebration followed the announced election results with every source of steam whistle and anvils called into active cacophony while a large crowd partied on the Plaza. Legally, Santa Fe had become a city.

The act of incorporation set in motion a new phase in Santa Fe's political history. Now the city faced the prospect of solving its problems through the instrumentality of its own elected officials and the use of its own funds. Immediately ahead lay the need to create a political structure, such as a government and wards; form the infrastructure for a modern city; and deal with the quality of life therein.

On 17 June 1891 the board of county commissioners announced ward boundaries for the election of city officials. The Santa Fe River became the northern boundary of the First and Second Wards and Don Gaspar the east-west boundary between them. The First Ward lay to the east of the line and the Second to the west. The river also served as the southern boundary of the Third and Fourth Wards, while Shelby Street and Washington Avenue became the east-west boundary between them. The Third Ward lay to the west of that line and the Fourth to the east. The city-limit line became the outer boundary of each ward.[53]

The same meeting of the county commissioners named July 2 as election day for the newly incorporated city. The board's notice provided for the choice of a mayor, city clerk, treasurer, and two aldermen from each ward. By mid-June, political and election talk were in full swing.

Seen through the pages of the *New Mexican*, the discussion of city government took on a modest cast. Letters to the editor expressed the desire for a minimal expenditure for governance with a heavy emphasis on the welfare of business and real estate interests. Published opinions also stressed the view that improvements heretofore paid for by subscription should be equitably defrayed by all who benefited through moderate taxes.[54] Such opinions sought to avoid any politically partisan tone by emphasizing the good of the city above all.

And, in fact, a so-called "businessmen's nonpartisan ticket" received support from the newspaper and public meetings organized to select such a government.[55] The *New Mexican* castigated and ridiculed the opposition for being antiprogress and venal.[56] The July 2 election fulfilled the *New Mexican*'s hopes when the nonpartisan slate received the approval of the voters. Only one member of the opposition, Richard Gorman, attained an alderman's place, in the First Ward. William T. Thornton became the first mayor of Santa Fe. Indeed, only the First Ward, the southeast quadrant of the city, displayed considerable opposition to the *New Mexican*'s list of candidates. There the vote went against J. D. Hughes (for city clerk) and Marcus Eldodt (treasurer), although they both succeeded in the city as a whole.[57]

The "businessman's nonpartisan ticket" did not survive that initial election. A Republican attempt to repeat the format in 1892 did not gain Democratic support and the "nonpartisan" slogan passed out of existence for a time. In the mid-nineties the Democratic characterization of the Republicans indicates the broad reasons for lack of agreement. In 1894 its party resolution defined the role of government to administer "in the interests of the whole people, and against the classes created and fostered by the special care of the Republican party."[58]

Democrats reiterated this theme in April 1896.[59] It may be that a "nonpartisan" designation for a businessman's ticket at a time when business was not thriving and Santa Feans were returning to agriculture did not suit those who questioned that what was good for business was necessarily good for them. In both 1894 and 1896 Democratic slates prevailed.

The inability of political forces to rise above parties meant that the party would become the major instrument to organize political activity. Many of those who served in office between 1892 and 1910 had held office or position in county or territorial government prior to city service. Their experience ensured that the place of political parties would extend into the new city politics. Moreover, the parties were quite capable of dealing with the constituencies and problems that existed in the new political entity.

Territorial party politics could also affect the city newspaper. Influential Santa Feans, such as Republican editor Max Frost of the *New Mexican*, found it necessary to adjust to changes of party control. In the mid-nineties, when Democrats held sway in the territory for a few years, Frost leased the Santa Fe newspaper to Democrats, fearing bankruptcy if it did not receive contracts for public printing. The Democrats relinquished control to Frost when the Republicans regained power in 1897.[60]

Generally, both parties shared political power in the generation between 1892 and 1910. The Democrats held an edge in citywide races for mayor and city clerk with the treasurer's place equally divided. City council races also found Democrats slightly ahead in numbers elected. Neither party dominated any ward, although the Third leaned slightly toward Republicans and the Fourth toward Democrats.

Political parties in New Mexico had long functioned to overcome ethnic distinctions.[61] Concentrating on the needs of the city and the flaws of the other party reduced ethnicity to a present but also negotiable factor of city politics. The 1892 election demonstrated that partisan divisions would not be dispensed with—they were providing a basis for ethnic cooperation. The *New Mexican*, in that year, floated a series of trial balloons. While generally committed to the Republicans, the paper promoted nonpartisan government. On March 7 it published a letter suggesting the virtues of "a union ticket made up of good men regardless of their political tendencies." All of its suggested candidates, except for city clerk and one member of the board of education, were Anglos. Two days later on March 9, an article entitled, "A Sensible Ticket for City Election," provided a new slate with Hispanos named for treasurer, city attorney, two councilmen, and three members of the board of education. The next day, on March 10, the paper added "Another Good Ticket," with Hispanos listed for mayor, one councilman slot, and three slots on the board of education. The newspaper's broadening concept of good men capable of holding any position seemed to bow to the presence of ethnic consciousness.

Nevertheless, Anglos did well in the heavily Hispano town. In citywide offices between 1892 and 1910, Anglos served seven times as mayor and Hispanos three. The city treasurer post showed a similar disparity. The office of city clerk favored Anglo candidates six times to four for Hispanos.

In the more locally centered ward elections for city council and board of education, the choices reflected the existing ethnic balance more strongly. City council posts in particular displayed a marked tendency to pit candidates against their ethnic fellows. In the First Ward Hispano ran against Hispano seven of ten times, in the Second Ward eight of ten times, and in the Third Ward nine of ten times. Only in the Fourth Ward did ethnically matched candidates occur as little as half the time.

The board of education races showed a less consistent pattern. The beginnings of a public school system where only parochial schools had previously existed may have sharpened religious distinctions. Only in the First Ward, where about 82 percent of the population was Hispano, did matched ethnics run against each other eight out of ten times. In Wards Two, Three, and Four, candidates matched each other ethnically in no more than half of the races.[62]

Overall, Hispano candidates for city council outnumbered Anglo candidates by a fair margin—about 57 percent of all contenders. The First and Second Ward candidates of both parties were heavily Hispano; Third Ward candidates were heavily Anglo. The Fourth Ward candidates split evenly for both parties. Board of education candidates, however, showed a majority of Anglo candidates with a marked preference for the Republican slates. Still, the ethnic balance of the ward races clearly distinguished itself from the experience of the citywide races.

In the generation between incorporation and statehood the city displayed its mixed ethnic and political character. Only Democrat Dr. J. H. Sloan served more than one term as mayor and Anglos dominated the holding of that office. The council offices reflected more of the ethnic concentration in the city with the First and Second Wards south of the river returning a heavy concentration of Hispano officeholders, while Anglos tended to win in the Third and Fourth Wards north of the river.

Unlike the mayoralty races, one finds a few persons returned to the council a number of times. Marcelino Garcia in the Second Ward served five times and R. L. Baca served six terms for the Fourth Ward, but the large majority of councilmen served only one or two terms. City government in these early years apparently did not offer a career in itself although many persons who gained it often attained political prominence later, including Ralph E. Twitchell, Thomas B. Catron, and Arthur Seligman, who served as mayors or councilmen or both before statehood.

The first years of city government were busy ones. The city ordinances published in 1893 attest to that. A volume of over one hundred pages, it revealed a heavy concern with basic infrastructure and quality of life issues.[63] The many ordinances dealing with the presence and disposition of animals indicated how rural Santa Fe still remained. Cattle, horses, mules, burros, goats, sheep, and swine received specific enumeration as species that could not run at large within the city limits. The disposal of dead animals as well as offensive odors occupied the new city fathers as both nuisances and health hazards.

The behavior of citizens themselves received detailed attention. Creators of public disturbances, the use of firecrackers and the discharge of weapons, drunkenness and indecent exposure, sports likely to frighten horses or injure persons, disturbance of religious worship, and horse racing in the streets had to be defined as unlawful. Prostitution and the smoking of opium gained attention in a chapter on nuisances. The great concern with such matters was typical of a small, unsophisticated Western town.

As for the long-term development of Santa Fe, city officials at least undertook the first steps toward making it livable. The construction, operation, and maintenance of a water supply system to fulfill domestic and public purposes received considerable attention. Ordinances dealt with both the Santa Fe Irrigation Co. and the Water and Improvement Co. for the laying of pipes, the placing of hydrants, and the creation of a reservoir. They also sought to align the needs and rights of the users of irrigated water with city requirements that could conflict with them. The introduction of electric lights and the creation

5. Roman L. Baca, six-term city councilman. Courtesy New Mexico State Records Center and Archive, photograph collection, photo #52055.

of a sewer system also received due attention. It would have been too much to expect a complete solution to all those new and complex problems. Under that forgiving maxim, these first years of city government may be described as a busy, fruitful time in the creation of a modern American city.

The relatively small number of changes included in the revised ordinances compiled in 1911 tend to uphold that judgment. The most noticeable changes reflected the presence of new technology, such as the licensing of automobiles and motorcycles and their operators. The speed of such vehicles was generally set at twelve miles per hour, with an eight mile per hour limit on streets surrounding the Plaza.[64]

The appearance of the city also began to take on a new importance. By 1911 the historical virtues of the Old Palace had already been recognized and a whole new concept of saving and building a city that would recognize the old Spanish-Pueblo architecture and heritage had begun to be formulated.[65] New ordinances reflected concern with care of the Plaza and the beginnings of parks to beautify the town.[66] Beyond these changes, much remained the same as in 1893.

Nevertheless, the formal legal cadences of the town's ordinances should not hide the rancorous panorama of daily life there. The diversity of needs, fed by economic and cultural differences, led to a range of behaviors that had to be sorted out to accord with the new legal arrangements and institutions created by incorporation and legislation. Grievance and advantage jostled each other continuously as the various sections of town sought to gain their share of attention and political parties asserted themselves as instruments to achieve desired goals.

Some of the complaints reflected the newness of the ordinances. The police received criticism for behaving either too weakly or too oppressively. Objections were raised concerning the prohibition against killing fowl in one's own backyard and taxing wood haulers and poor laundry women, while other protests dealt with the nonperformance of duties by city agencies, such as the failure to clean the streets or collect garbage.[67]

Differences within the city received airing as new services came into operation. As street lights appeared, the north side received highly favorable treatment while the south side registered its dissatisfaction.[68] Complaints about garbage collection from the south side were frequent.[69] With time, some of these complaints were assuaged, but the competitive clamor for such services remained.

Commentary based on ethnic distinctions was rare in these early years after incorporation. One could hear an occasional remonstrance against "sixteenth-century portals" in favor of "nineteenth-century awnings."[70] Attacks aimed at individuals, however, received sharp rebuff. A report that Republican mayoral candidate Manuel Valdez had been called a "Mexican" in a disrespectful manner called forth a rebuke that he was a native of Santa Fe and an American citizen—and not even a professional politician.[71] Such exchanges, however, appear relatively rare. New Mexico's wide experience in intergroup relations did not require retranslation from the days of county government to the new structure of the city and remained muted in the press.

The issue of the city's water supply touched a deeper chord. It was cast in terms of water rights, but the problem lay in the growing urban character of the city as compared with its agrarian past. That past, in part, posited the Hispano as the property holder and agriculturist. As soon as pipes began to be laid in the river in 1881, challenges arose from property owners along its banks, including irrigators and entrepreneurs, to what they considered encroachment upon their rights.[72] The *New Mexican*, in turn, denied the loss of any vested rights and stressed the value of the new pipes for all.[73] Speakers at public meetings held in June 1881 had displayed great suspicion of the water company's motives in seeking to control the flow of the precious liquid and defended the ancient and hallowed rights of the irrigators and their families to have it.[74] Meetings between property owners and the water company at that time produced no agreement. In late June 1881, the paper reported that "a party of Mexicans" had stopped pipe-laying work and that Sheriff Romulo Martinez had disarmed them.[75] In time the sides achieved a modicum of understanding, but in 1883 there was still an instance of smashed pipes and the diversion of water back into the riverbed.[76]

After the city's incorporation, extensions of the waterworks continued. The city granted a twenty-five-year franchise to the Santa Fe Water and Improvement Company for the services required: fire protection, domestic use, irrigation, and street sprinkling.[77] Mains were extended into the south side in the following years and a new dam opened two miles above the city in 1894. Santa Feans found amusement in the use of several hundred goats to tamp down the earth for the evolving structure.[78]

Given the uncertain nature of rainfall in New Mexico, water problems resurfaced during periods of drought. In 1893, irrigation flow was occasionally cut off. Downstream problems followed upstream solutions. In 1895, the *mayordomos* of the Santa Fe *acequias*, seeking relief for better irrigation, addressed the legislative assembly with a petition of 550 signatures.[79] In 1904 another drought again raised the issue of the use of water for irrigation. The *New Mexican* sought to uphold the preservation of the water supply for the city's 7,500 persons, maintaining that they "were primarily and first legally entitled to the use" and had been for centuries. The city, the paper held, was "the natural and legal successor to those who first appropriated the water. . . ."[80] It accused the mayordomos of acting as though the entire supply was theirs on behalf of "a few corn patches" and at the expense of the entire community.[81] As if to demonstrate the episodic nature of such problems, a few weeks later a deluge left Water and DeVargas Streets under water and the paper reported the reservoir higher than it had been in three years.[82]

Beyond the disputes over water use rights lay the deeper question of adequate supply. The estimated cost of a proposed new dam at Granite Point in Santa Fe Canyon in 1911 led to abandonment of the project.[83] Only in 1918 and 1919 did the matter arise again, when the water company informed the city council of the urgent need to develop the supply further.

Partly by chance, the city's incorporation in 1891 occurred in the same year that a public school system in New Mexico achieved legal affirmation. Public education had developed very slowly after the American assumption of political power. Unaided by the national government, the territorial legislature sought at various times to deal with the issue, but faced formidable obstacles. Lack of wealth, opposition to property-based taxation, and tensions centering around culture and religion all played their part in hindering the creation of an effective educational system.[84] In 1870 illiteracy stood at 78.5 percent.[85] Yet, a more detailed look reveals actions after 1850 that were moving New Mexico from the virtual absence of means to provide formal education toward the beginnings of an institutional structure. In 1872 the legislature had legalized a poll tax for school purposes and a county system of supervision.[86]

Religious institutions had never awaited government action. Archbishop Lamy labored to build schools from the time of his arrival in 1851. By the end of the fifties his efforts had resulted in the formation of the Loretto Academy for girls and St. Michael's for boys—both in Santa Fe. Early Protestant efforts to establish schools did not fare as well, but were also making headway before the railroad arrived.

The flow of immigration from the East and the desire for statehood gradually increased pressures for further action to strengthen education.[87] After 1875 philosophical differences between Catholics and Protestants over the purposes of education and the place of religion in the schools led to considerable controversy over the issue of public funds going to sectarian schools. Such battles had long been fought in the East. Out of them, Catholic leaders had adopted the position of a need for parallel systems, each supported by portions of public funds. Protestants saw the answer in a single nonsectarian system.

New Mexico, with its strongly Spanish and Catholic background, presented unique conditions. While county systems became public bodies, the composition of school boards often remained dominated by Catholics and even included clergymen.[88] Regulations and practice, therefore, did not necessarily go hand in hand.

During the late mid-seventies, Governor Samuel Axtell, backed by Secretary of State Ritch, opposed by New Mexico-based Jesuits and, later, Bishop Jean Baptiste Salpointe, waged battle over the issue.[89] Finally, under the leadership of Governor L. Bradford Prince, a new school law passed in 1891, which established common schools and created a territorial board of education (it included the president of St. Michael's). The law stated that no sectarian doctrine would be taught in public schools but went no further. Under the new structure, county boards remained virtually autonomous.[90]

In the mind of the new superintendent of public instruction, Amado Chaves, the 1891 law offered a real common school system. Expected serious sectarian and cultural problems arising out of the requirement that English be taught in all common schools did not develop.[91] Schools of any kind appeared welcome enough to New Mexicans to blunt the force of philosophical and cultural purity.[92]

With strongly established Catholic and newer Protestant schools already present, public schools began modestly in Santa Fe with the passage of the new law. At the end of 1892 the city schools had an attendance of eighty pupils while that of the religious schools approached five hundred.[93] Limited data make comparisons between attendance at public and church-supported schools difficult up to 1910. However, the parochial schools appear to have upheld their numbers. Occasional figures indicating the total numbers of school-age children compared to those attending public schools show 587 in school out of 1,168 in 1896 (about half) and 606 out of 1,930 in 1905.[94] In 1910, of 1,914 school-age children, 469 were enrolled in public schools, while an estimated 850 were enrolled in private or sectarian schools.[95] While the public schools appear to have made some headway, they did not dominate the city's educational scene.

The physical plant of the city schools also advanced slowly at first. In 1896 its property value stood at only $2,000 and classroom space was largely rented. By comparison, the property value of the Catholic institutions alone stood at $84,000.[96] In 1902 the city schools' property value was still only $5,000.[97] A great change came early in the century, however, when city officials led by Thomas Catron, then president of the city board of education, sought to persuade the federal government to turn over the abandoned Fort Marcy property to the city for educational purposes. These efforts succeeded and in 1904 seventeen acres with many buildings, valued at $65,000, passed into the board's hands.[98] Accompanied by a school bond issue for the construction of a high school and ward school building, Santa Fe's public educational facilities began to catch up with the sectarian school plant.

As Santa Feans moved toward incorporation, Congress was taking steps to end a troublesome and unsettled issue in New Mexico—the issue of land grants. After decades of unsatisfactory solutions that left (and leaves) many Hispanos embittered, Congress created the Court of Private Land Claims in March 1891. It sat mainly in Santa Fe during the years of its existence.

Santa Fe's own claims to land title had never been confirmed. In 1874, Gaspar Ortiz y Alarid, probate judge for the county, had petitioned the surveyor general, an office set up in 1854 to investigate land claims, to confirm a four-square-league tract on behalf of the inhabitants of the city.[99] The claim was still pending in 1891 when the new court was established. Given the importance of the claim, it was one of the first cases presented to the court when it moved to Santa Fe.

An original suit by the Santa Fe Board of County Commissioners as trustee on behalf of the inhabitants of the city in 1892 was found lacking in authority. The city, now incorporated, filed a suit on its own behalf in 1893. The defendant, the United States, demurred, finding no cause of action in the petition and failure to disclose that adverse claimants existed under Spanish grants.[100] The United States contested Santa Fe's claim as successor to the Spanish villa or to four-square Spanish leagues by operation of law. The Court of Private Land Claims upheld the city in 1894 but the government appealed the decision and the U.S. Supreme Court reversed the finding. Since the Court of Private Land Claims had rejected the claims of conflicting grants, the Supreme Court held that without valid grants, all title was vested in the U.S. government.[101]

To end the uncertainty and provide relief, Congress passed an act in 1900 that quitclaimed to the city all the lands within a Spanish league (2.63 miles) for parks, streets, unoccupied lands, and public places, and to the city in trust for all persons claiming title to individual holdings by actual possession or under title for a period of ten years. It reserved for the United States all land and buildings held there and excepted lands covered by private land grants previously confirmed by the Court of Private Land Claims. It was, in effect, a grant de novo to the city, and attorneys, in passing upon land title covered by a city deed, did not need to go back beyond 1889.[102] The city breathed a sigh of relief. The *New Mexican* touted its benefits, confessing that the question of titles had somewhat retarded the city's growth and had kept real estate values down.[103] Compared to other parts of New Mexico, Santa Fe had gotten off with a minimum of difficulty.

By 1912, the date of New Mexico's entry into statehood, the basic outlines of modern Santa Fe's urban legal condition were settled. New Mexicans had reaffirmed its position as the capital, its legal status as a city had been carried through by the town's citizens themselves, and the basic issue of land proprietorship had been settled by the courts. Where the city would go from its beleaguered condition as a place off the railroad's main line was only beginning to emerge and requires an examination on its own terms.

In addition to the above-noted legal issues, the beginnings of modern bonding as city and capital began. Both town and state jurisdictions had to operate harmoniously in the interests of all. State properties needed to be integrated into the surrounding city for reasons of health, convenience, safety, and appearance. Individual city dwellers had to face the requirements laid down by a new city government establishing its own physical identity.

The first state legislature introduced measures and principles to unite city and state structures. It appropriated funds for street paving around the capitol and in front of the Old Palace. At the same time it laid down the principle that private property owners, whose holdings abutted those streets would have to contribute one-half of the cost of paving.[104] State and city residents were cemented together physically to create the new state capital.

The location and functioning of the penitentiary also came into play. Its brick-making capacity became a factor in the street paving around state buildings. Moreover, labor for such projects would be supplied when practicable from available convicts.[105] Sewers also had to be improved in the state facilities so as not to pollute the Santa Fe River and had to be connected with the city system where possible.[106] Santa Fe was gaining considerable financial advantage from its position as capital out of these arrangements. Such changes also contributed to the impetus toward modernization.

Even as city and state capital were linking themselves through pipes and bridges into a modern entity, persons of imagination and determination were in the process of rethinking the entire future direction of the city. Three years before statehood, in 1909, the territorial legislature had been persuaded to establish a museum for the territory to be housed in the Old Palace. No act or building would achieve greater importance as a new starting point for a city that had struggled for thirty years to find itself after the demise of the Santa Fe Trail. The results of the territory's action and the use made of it by the city require separate and detailed attention.

FOUR

The Search for a New Direction: Archaeology, Health, and Civic Organization

OVER TIME, Anglo residents of Santa Fe became increasingly aware of its cultural complexity. The city's proximity to the Native American pueblos had been important in the life of the community from the time of its creation. While Anglo contact with the pueblos was somewhat limited, interaction with the overwhelmingly Hispano population was an omnipresent fact of life. Although even some early Anglo newcomers had displayed a modicum of appreciation of their ethnically mixed surroundings, as generations passed, sensitivity toward New Mexico's past and its persistence heightened and produced a sense of obligation to preserve what they saw before them.

The earliest institutional sign of this interest was the formation of the Historical Society of New Mexico in 1859. Well-educated persons, mostly Anglo, but including some Hispanos, took the initiative in its creation. They defined their purpose as "the collection and preservation . . . of all historical facts, manuscripts, documents, records and memoirs, relating to this Territory; Indian antiquities and curiosities, geological and mineralogical specimens, geographical maps and information; and objects of natural history."[1] Active in its work of collection and full of promise, the society did not actively survive the Civil War, which diverted the attentions of its members and drew Southern members to the Confederate cause.

It was not until late 1880 that the society reconstituted itself. Several of its original members, Major David J. Miller and Captain Louis Felsenthal among them, issued a call to renew the work of collection and preservation begun a generation earlier.[2] Even before formal reorganization took place, influential citizens of Santa Fe secured permission from the Department of the Interior and the territorial governor to utilize several rooms in the Old Palace for the purposes of the society.[3]

W. G. Ritch, secretary of the territory and new president of the society, in delivering the inaugural address on 21 February 1881, recognized 1880 as an auspicious date for renewal, marking the second centennial of the Pueblo uprising against the Spaniards as well as the year in which the railroad arrived, both landmarks of New Mexico's history. He reaffirmed the need to collect historical materials of all kinds as the society's basic purpose but raised an additional responsibility and a sense of urgency. Because the railroad brought new interests and people to the region, Ritch noted that "Antiquarians and curiosity hunters are with us in large force, and collecting and carrying away by wagon loads that which legitimately belongs to the local historical society." He also expressed fear of the corrosive effects of American "energy" on archaeology and ethnology. The society's duty, he concluded, was "to snatch from oblivion the wonderful evidences of the prehistoric people of the Southwest."[4]

But Ritch was neither modest nor defensive in his delineation of the organization's tasks. He envisioned a center of scientific knowledge in the Southwest akin to the Smithsonian Institution. It would fulfill a unique niche in relation to education, society, commerce, and politics. Nothing could do it better than a local organization and no better location could exist than Santa Fe. The city was the capital of the territory and the center of its political, military, ecclesiastical, and commercial history, "the most ancient and voluminous specimen" of all.[5]

To link the fate of the society with Santa Fe and its status as a "specimen," Ritch called for the Old Palace to be the permanent seat of the organization. He went further, asking, "why not engage in a National Museum . . . a National Historical Society in the Southwest; where there is an historical field of magnitude, having an historical edifice . . . situate[d] in the most ancient historical center of the Nation."[6] Influential Santa Feans and New Mexicans in general flocked to its banner. In addition to Ritch these included leading political figures such as L. Bradford Prince, a chief justice and future governor; the most prominent merchants, the Ilfelds and Spiegelbergs; the most prestigious Hispano families, the Oteros, Ortiz y Salazars, and Senas; and the leading attorneys, Louis Sulzberger, Frank Springer, and Thomas B. Catron, to name a few.[7] Few cultural enterprises could have matched the wholehearted support accorded the revival of the society.

The field of interest defined by the society's charter was broad and inclusive. It was historical, encompassing the Spanish and Anglo experiences; archaeological and ethnological, involving old pueblo ruins as well as the crafts of the contemporary Indian villages; and scientific, embracing the natural history of the region. No area of scientific or historic interest was omitted.

Ritch connected the renewed society with the future of New Mexico and Santa Fe. Noting the role of such organizations in other states, he cited the resources granted them in the form of quarters and financial grants. In his eyes, New Mexico's historical society deserved no less, given its important mission. Ritch's address contained many ideas that would affect the future of Santa Fe. The city as historical specimen in itself, the territory as an archaeological repository, and Santa Fe as a center of activity devoted to historical and archaeological concerns all resonated in his words. The images, however premature they were in terms of immediate action, nevertheless carried the dim outlines of an agenda that lingered among those who shared Ritch's vision.

While the society's interests were promising for a growing sense of communal identity and purpose, they did not progress without problems. The society found itself beleaguered, having to assert itself time and again to retain its Palace space. Its supporters were forced to write impassioned pleas to senators, to New Mexico's congressional delegate Antonio Joseph, and to the U.S. Secretary of the Interior to prevent disruption.[8] For a time, calm prevailed. In 1888, Antonio Joseph informed Judge L. Bradford Prince, a leading advocate for the society, that the secretary of the interior had advised New Mexico's secretary of the territory "not to disturb the Historical Society of New Mexico in possession of the Legislative chambers in said palace building."[9] Nevertheless, in 1905, the need for revenue to keep the building in repair led A. A. Keen, the New Mexico commissioner of public lands, to inform Prince that the rooms would have to be rented, in this case, to the Republican Central Committee of the territory.[10]

The most successful activity of the Historical Society of New Mexico—collecting materials—produced problems of its own. Its report of 1909 described expansion into new rooms of the Palace and noted that by 1906 acquisitions had so outstripped space that the collections could not be arranged for display "because it was impossible to do so properly."[11] By the time this report appeared, however, changes were occurring that ended the society's unique position as an institution devoted to preserving New Mexico's past.

The society under Prince's leadership performed labors for a quarter-century that benefited Santa Fe. Accumulating varied historical and anthropological materials, it pushed the city into the forefront of the territory in such matters. Edgar L. Hewett, on the threshold of becoming a cultural leader in the city in 1909, wrote to Prince praising the quality of the Pueblo collections of the society, judging them almost sufficient as they stood to adequately represent some of the region's pueblos.[12] Visitors flocked to the Palace to view its holdings, some 8,000 in 1907 and over 10,000 in 1908.[13] The society published brief reports of an historical nature occasionally but with increasing frequency after 1903 and held public lectures to enlighten the local populace. It did all that the energies of such devoted leaders as Prince could accomplish within the framework of a local cultural organization receiving limited funds from the territorial legislature.

In 1909 the territorial legislature opened a new era for New Mexico and Santa Fe's heritage by creating the Museum of New Mexico. The success of the museum's backers lay in broad-based changes in the fields of archaeology and anthropology at the national level. These developments set the stage for action among persons in New Mexico who represented institutions in those fields of study.

During the last decades of the nineteenth century, science in America was undergoing rapid change. Starting with the Civil War, Washington had begun to centralize its activities, a process that continued after the conflict. Exploration and surveying in the West boomed under the aegis of the Geological Survey, the Weather Bureau, the Coast and Geodetic Survey, and numerous other agencies, many growing out of the Smithsonian Institution.[14] In 1879 Congress created the Bureau of American Ethnology as an adjunct of the Smithsonian. The latter institution, formed in 1846, devoted no small part of its resources both to the study of linguistics, archaeology, and ethnology, as well as to diffusion of that knowledge. In so doing, it dominated American anthropology until university departments emerged at about the turn of the century.[15] Museums, too, became a major instrument in the diffusion of information. By the late nineteenth century they no longer contained mere miscellaneous collections of objects, "cabinets des curiosites," but materials grouped according to theoretical orientation.[16] The major museums served as focal points for anthropological research, teaching, and the development of theory.

For American anthropology, the Native Americans inevitably constituted a major subject of study. Their presence forced a constant stream of questions and comparisons that preoccupied White Americans, such as: Were the Native Americans in any sense brothers of White Americans? Was there any justification for taking their land from them? The study of linguistics and archaeology, in light of a growing status for the sciences in the nineteenth century, placed these questions within the framework of scientific investigation in which the Smithsonian and other major museums played a powerful role.[17] As the lens of scrutiny moved westward, New Mexico could not escape the consequences of such examination.

When Congress created the Bureau of American Ethnology in 1879, it provided "that all the archives, records, and material relating to the Indians of North America, collected by the geographical and geological survey of the Rocky

Mountains, shall be turned over to the [Smithsonian] Institution. . . ."[18] In that year, a collecting party led by Colonel James Stevenson, following the lead of John Wesley Powell, the director of the new agency, who had been impressed by the Pueblo communities and ruins a decade earlier, and including Frank Hamilton Cushing in its makeup, arrived in New Mexico. Cushing went to Zuni in western New Mexico and had three months, originally, to study that society. He stayed much longer, becoming the first American actually to live among the people he was studying and to become an "anthropologist as hero."[19]

If Cushing's labors marked the beginning of the modern anthropological enterprise in New Mexico, then Adolph Bandelier brought the study of the Native American and the historic past closer to Santa Fe itself. Operating under the auspices of the newly created Archaeological Institute of America (AIA) and with the support of Lewis Henry Morgan, a leader in the comparative study of human societies, Bandelier arrived in New Mexico's capital in August 1880.[20] In his correspondence with Morgan, Bandelier had shown concern about the collecting of artifacts and about the attitudes of the Europeans toward American records.[21] Beyond these concerns, however, the new activity signaled the arrival of anthropology and archaeology in New Mexico.

In the last years of the nineteenth century, the AIA, after an initial start and subsequent hesitation, recognized the need to accord American archaeology an expanded place in its research and publication plans.[22] Its deliberations led it to foster the creation of local affiliated societies in the West. One consequence was the creation in 1903 of the Southwest Society with an office in Los Angeles. Its secretary, Charles F. Lummis, was an old New Mexico hand, author of the popular volume, *The Land of Poco Tiempo*, and a friend of Bandelier. In 1904 Colorado, too, organized a local affiliate of the Institute.

By 1907 the AIA took a second step to upgrade its work in American archaeology. It created the office of director of American archaeology "to direct and coordinate all work undertaken by the affiliated societies of the Institute." This was to be followed (and was) by the establishment of a School of American Archaeology to receive students and carry out research.[23] In so doing the Institute was following a path it had previously established in Athens, Rome, and Jerusalem. The study of American archaeology now achieved an organizational status equal to its older classical brethren.

The Museum of New Mexico grew out of the AIA's actions to create a school of archaeology. Viewed as a valuable prize, the location of the new school sparked a lively competition for its possession. Charles Lummis proclaimed it "the most important scientific establishment ever made in an American city."[24] Mexico City, the University of New Mexico at Albuquerque, Colorado, Los Angeles, and Santa Fe all sought to give it a home.

6. Frank Springer (L) and Edgar L. Hewett (R), early archaeological study leaders. Courtesy Museum of New Mexico, neg. #7362.

The School of American Archaeology was actually founded in 1907. The condition of archaeology in New Mexico had been greatly strengthened since Bandelier's departure in 1892 when financial support for his research dried up. Such persons as John R. McFie and Frank Springer, both influential figures in the territory with considerable interest in the subject, had established themselves in New Mexico in the eighties and nineties. McFie played a key role in the creation of the Archaeological Society of New Mexico in 1898, under the influence of the young archaeologist Edgar Hewett.[25] National legislation for the preservation of antiquities and the cliff dwellings at Mesa Verde brought new attention both to archaeology and the Southwest. Certainly the time was propitious for the AIA's action.

The conjuncture of strengthened interest in archaeology in New Mexico and the activity of the AIA generated the forces that made the Museum of New Mexico possible. In 1902, Prince tried to persuade the Smithsonian to establish a national museum branch in Santa Fe, using the Palace as attractive bait, but his efforts came to naught.[26] The Palace, which through inadvertence on the part of the federal government had become territorial property in 1898, became an instrument to attract the interest of the AIA.

It was also through the efforts of Frank Springer and John McFie that the person destined to lead New Mexico's archaeological establishment, Edgar L. Hewett, appeared on the scene. Hewett, a Midwesterner and a teacher, moved to Colorado, discovered archaeology there and in New Mexico, and came to Frank Springer's attention. Springer invited Hewett to Las Vegas to lecture on the Native American ruins and persuaded the board of regents of New Mexico Normal (now Highlands University) to name him head of the new college.[27]

By 1900 Hewett's archaeological interests led him to Washington, where he met leading figures in the field, several of whom were highly placed in the AIA. In 1903 Hewett lost his position at New Mexico Normal and committed himself to archaeology by pursuing a doctorate in Europe. In 1906, working in Colorado, he was appointed a fellow in American archaeology by the AIA. A year later, when the AIA created the directorship of American archaeology, Hewett received the position.[28] Hewett, as link with the AIA, and McFie, who worked in New Mexico, launched a campaign to lure the proposed school of archaeology to Santa Fe.

As early as 1907 the New Mexico legislature reacted favorably to news of the planned School of American Archaeology. By joint resolution it requested that the U.S. president designate the Palace as a national monument with use and custodianship granted to the AIA, which would locate the school there. It also offered an annual appropriation to encourage the new institution.[29]

In 1909, after the school's creation, some negotiation, and resistance in the legislature, that body passed an act establishing the Museum of New Mexico.[30] The new law located the School of American Archaeology in Santa Fe and placed the Palace under a board of regents, which, in turn, granted the AIA free

7. Judge John R. McFie, archaeological society leader. Courtesy Museum of New Mexico, neg. #10258.

use of the property for the school and museum. The director of the school was also to be director of the museum.

The museum became a new cultural center in Santa Fe. Its board of regents included the president of the Archaeological Society of New Mexico, McFie, who also became president of the board. Hewett became the school's director. The success of McFie, Hewett, and their supporters opened the path to new cultural standards and interests for the city. It would also allow the revitalization of the town as a cultural leader in the territory, replacing its lost commercial primacy of thirty years earlier.

The leaders of the new archaeological establishment and their political allies envisioned the school in grand terms. Governor George Curry, in his message to the legislative assembly in 1909, recommended approval of the AIA's terms to locate the school in Santa Fe as "the only institution of its kind on the continent." He cited historic interest in the city and its Palace as well as "unrivalled opportunities for archaeological investigation near Santa Fe and in all parts of New Mexico" as reasons for acceptance.[31] Charles Lummis depicted the new American School on a par with the AIA's operations in Rome, Athens, and Jerusalem.[32] Political and cultural forces had combined to acquire what seemed a most worthy and logical institution in the very heart of Santa Fe. The lofty terms in which the new institution was couched reiterated Santa Feans' earlier image of their city as an imperial outpost and center of trade. If some of the earlier characterizations had faded after the railroad bypassed the city, they now received the beginnings of a new cultural equivalent.

In institutional terms, the Historical Society of New Mexico now suffered the presence of a powerful competitor. While retaining space in the Palace, it was nevertheless forced into a subordinate position vis-à-vis the museum's board and fought a rear-guard action to maintain itself between the years 1909 and 1913. Isolated and local as compared with the national connections of the newly created museum, and relatively amateur in its operations as compared with the museum's full-time director and his strong support in the legislature, the society, led by Prince, lost its battles for primacy on political and professional grounds to the archaeologically oriented personnel of the museum.

How much Prince's enemies, after his long political career, contributed to his disadvantage is difficult to measure. One of his major supporters, Ralph E. Twitchell, an attorney of note, and later, the best-known local historian of Santa Fe and New Mexico, bitterly opposed the school at first, seeing in the AIA's child a loss of credit for New Mexico and "little less than bare-faced effrontery" on the part of those "who would take the benefit of others' work by wiping out a going institution. . . ."[33] Twitchell originally preferred alliance with the University of New Mexico and for New Mexico getting all the credit.

The major focus of the society had been New Mexican history; that of the archaeologist was Native Americans. The shift of emphasis may have fostered a concern among Hispano intellectuals that their heritage was being slighted. In 1913 they had already created the Society for the Preservation of Spanish Antiquities. Led by Benjamin Read, an historian in his own right, and supported by Hispanos and Anglos such as Ralph Twitchell, its objective appeared to be to foster exactly such research and preserve such knowledge that had been relegated to a secondary position by the defeat of the historical society.[34]

The antiquities society sought statewide support. Still in existence in 1918, its leadership included the former driving force of the historical society, L. Bradford Prince, and such well-known figures as Archbishop J. B. Pitival, Bronson Cutting, Antonio Lucero, and Felix Martinez. Hispano surnames dominated county vice presidencies and a mix of Anglos and Hispanos (including Twitchell) graced its board of governors.[35] How well it functioned is unclear, but it indicated clearly that Hispanos and sympathetic Anglos believed that a gap existed in the vision and work that was emerging from the museum's establishment.

Another persistent theme in New Mexico's and Santa Fe's history focused on climate. The glories of New Mexico's moderate temperature, low humidity, and copious sunshine had long been noted favorably by travelers. It was a permanent asset that could, under proper conditions, serve as a magnet for settlement or tourists. It was more than mere pleasantness, however, that made New Mexico a special place in terms of climate. The extra ingredient came from the perceived relationship between climate and health.

Sixteenth-century Spaniards had described the physical well-being of the native population, and Americans in the nineteenth century continued in their favorable evaluation of the climate and its meaning for health.[36] Josiah Gregg, a doctor and sickly himself, whose classic volume, *Commerce of the Prairies*, fired the imagination of Easterners for several generations, made much of it. Easterners regarded the West in general as a more healthful environment than the older, more heavily settled and polluted seaboard.

New Mexico and the entire high plateau of the eastern Rocky Mountains gained added luster by virtue of their altitude. Medical theories popular in the latter decades of the nineteenth century laid great weight on the curative value of thin air for relief from respiratory diseases. Mineral springs, present in many locations of the region, supplemented the reputation of the area as a natural health resort.[37]

However, until the railroads were built, the remoteness of the Rockies and the difficulty of travel prevented any large-scale utilization of the region to restore the ailing population of the East. Once created, the new transportation system became an important artery for those who sought cures for many ills. Local agencies, eager to attract new settlers, advertised the virtues of their towns for health seekers with an enthusiasm that recognized few bounds.

New Mexicans created the Bureau of Immigration in 1880 to attract business and investment of all kinds.[38] Laudatory descriptions of the climate and health occupied no small place in the literature produced by the Bureau for wide distribution, and the railroads aided in this endeavor. William Ritch, an early president of the Bureau, who had come to New Mexico for his own health, led the early campaign to attract Easterners for physical renewal.[39]

The lengths to which Bureau literature went to extol the virtues and curative powers of New Mexico's climate appear today to approach the fantastic. In 1883, the *Illustrated New Mexico*, its chief publication, noted that in the presence of that environment "pulmonary complaints generally experience relief if the disease is not too far advanced. Frequent instances of aggravated cases in consumption (tuberculosis) . . . have received relief and life prolonged to ripe old age. . . ." Continuing the list, it stated that "Rheumatism, cutaneous and venereal diseases experience speedy relief," and "Heart diseases and nervous complaints would be out of place in this rarified and electric atmosphere." Medical statistics demonstrated, the *Illustrated New Mexico* went on, "that 'New Mexico is by far the most favorable residence in the United States for those predisposed to or affected by phthisis.'" And like the climate, the mineral springs were credited with "almost invariably" curing, among other ailments, "gout, scrofula, stiff joints, skin diseases as a class, ulcerations and enlargements of the glands . . . mental exhaustion, spinal disease, sciatica, lumbago, paralysis, St. Vitus dance, and all nueralgic [sic], or nervous afflictions . . . diabetes . . . and all blood poisons and female diseases." Like the Spanish explorers before them, the *Illustrated* found "extreme healthfulness" among the local populace.[40]

Beyond the general claims of a healthful environment lay one specific attraction that surpassed all others—the hope of arresting or curing tuberculosis. Toward the end of the nineteenth century that dreaded killer claimed the lives of 150,000 persons annually in the United States and the number of those infected was tenfold higher.[41] Fear of the disease was monumental and therapies of that time held high hopes for fresh air, sunshine, low humidity, and high altitude, qualities New Mexico possessed in abundance.

Given these circumstances, New Mexico became heavily involved in the effort to attract those "chasing the cure." Research published in 1915 indicated that by then between 20 to 60 percent of all households in most New Mexican towns had at least one stricken member and perhaps 50 percent of Albuquerque's population consisted of tuberculars and their relatives.[42] Such numbers affected the development of the territory, contributing to the creation of hospitals and boarding houses, service industries, funeral homes, moving and storage firms, real estate agencies, and, not least of all, to the development of the medical profession itself. Moreover, no small segment of the "lungers" were well-educated persons with sufficient resources to afford the long period of enforced idleness required by treatment and who contributed greatly to the development of New Mexico.[43]

Santa Feans, accustomed to a role of leadership, sought at first to establish a claim to lead the territory in health as it had in most other matters. Even before the railroad arrived, in 1878, the *Rocky Mountain Sentinel* announced that when it did come, Santa Fe would become "the sanitarium of the United States."[44] Indeed, the city did have a good start. St. Vincent's Hospital, founded in 1865, was already caring for tuberculars, although that was not its primary function. Santa Fe based its claim for leadership on the presumption that it had the best conditions to offer consumptives and health seekers in general. If these were properly advertised, the *New Mexican* stated, "thousands of health-seeking tourists would come, instead of hundreds."[45] In fact, in the early eighties St. Vincent's undertook a building program to enlarge its facilities, partially, at least, to accommodate health seekers. It was completed in 1886.

Behind the open call for health seekers, however, a more restricted invitation appeared at times. Even as the *New Mexican* called for a sanatorium, it suggested that it be "for a wealthier class of invalids."[46] In late 1886 attempts were made to establish a world-class or national sanatorium with financing by wealthy Eastern philanthropists, but it came to naught. In July 1891, the paper was still calling for a sanatorium and hotel combined, where the afflicted would be assured "all modern conveniences and comfort."[47] A few days later, the *New Mexican* again called for an effort "to attract here a well-to-do class of health seekers and tourists who annually expend vast sums of money in patronizing health resorts. . . ."[48] One cannot resist paraphrasing: "Give us your rich, your coddled masses, yearning to breathe free." As late as 1896, however, Santa Fe still had no sanatorium of the type the *New Mexican* sought. All the ingredients were there, but even by 1920 it had not appeared.

In 1901, a health resort, according to a Santa Fe Railroad brochure, was "any place where one's physical condition may be bettered by baths and medical treatment or by merely being out in the open air, engaged in hunting, fishing, riding, walking, etc."[49] Colorado, and Colorado Springs in particular, had a strong head start in actually developing such institutions.[50]

All this did not mean that serious health care did not come to Santa Fe. St. Vincent's sanatorium burned in 1896, was rebuilt, and reopened in 1910 as a seventy-five-bed structure on Palace Avenue. It was the largest facility in the city. In 1901 Sun Mount Tent City came into existence as the first private sanatorium and later reconstituted as the more permanent Sunmount Sanatorium.[51] Diaz Sanatorium followed in 1906. These institutions formed the corpus of traceable sanatoria in Santa Fe.

A variety of factors acted to bring untold numbers of tuberculars to New Mexico who did not inhabit sanatoria. The financial burden of not working for a year while paying for care, the difficulty of maintaining a strict regimen of therapy, and the degree of disability relative to the stage of the disease, contributed to the numbers of afflicted persons who lived in boarding and rooming houses. Some of them worked and mingled with the local population and affected the atmosphere of the cities in which they resided.

All in all, Albuquerque and other towns, such as Silver City, attracted more tuberculars than Santa Fe. In 1908 New Mexico ranked fifth in the nation in hospitals, sanatoria, and day camps. Just past the middle of the second decade of the century, Santa Fe ranked behind Albuquerque and Silver City in beds for the same category of institutions.[52]

One may speculate as to why Santa Fe did not establish leadership. It was the best known town in the territory. Yet, the greater ease of rail connection to Albuquerque, its more Anglo character, open space, and its milder winters, may have made it a more suitable location than Santa Fe. Then, too, the fact that the medical profession itself organized earlier in Albuquerque than in Santa Fe, where there was no medical society until 1909, may have contributed to choice of location. To that must be added the slowness of the town in rebuilding St. Vincent's sanatorium after the fire of 1896 and its desire to cater to wealthier sufferers.

One must also consider the negative side of the presence of the disease bearers. Fear of the infected grew as knowledge of its contagious character spread. In 1894, the Bureau of Immigration noted that "No contagious or infectious disease is allowed to enter the precincts of the [St. Vincent's] sanitarium, but it is conducted solely for the benefit of the weakly and invalid."[53] By 1901, territorial legislation forbade the hiring of tuberculars as teachers and in 1907 a law prohibiting spitting was enacted.[54] These new immigrants clearly carried an element of danger that made their presence a mixed blessing.

Health, or at least tuberculosis, remained a source of immigration for New Mexico and Santa Fe up to World War II. Whether lodged in health-related institutions or not, many sufferers brought their talents to Santa Fe in this early period. The city would be the beneficiary of their skills as would other New Mexico towns, but Santa Fe did not dominate as the destination of this immigration.

Although Santa Fe's commercial primacy declined in the first decade after the railroad's appearance, no adequate replacement for that lost economic activity became apparent. The decline itself, as noted earlier, was not precipitous, a condition that may have contributed to the slowness of adaptation. Hopes that a railroad might still come to reinfuse traditional avenues of commerce, especially in the eighties, remained alive. The determined efforts that surrounded city incorporation in 1891 still stressed that urban improvement of Santa Fe would result in attracting commerce and growth.

The business community did not institutionalize itself in any convincing fashion after 1880. Although Santa Fe created a board of trade in 1882, that agency reflected the heavy presence of the older merchants such as Spiegelberg and Seligman along with political-legal, banking, and press interests—W. W. Griffin, Max Frost, and L. Bradford Prince.[55] They did not change their habits quickly. In Albuquerque, by comparison, the years prior to incorporation in 1885 had witnessed the creation of a board of trade that acted in effect as a town government.[56] Outside of its concerted efforts to draw railroads into the city, campaigns to retain it as the capital, and the efforts for incorporation, the board in Santa Fe did little. The emphasis of these efforts was to hold or regain what the city was losing rather than to create something new.

In 1891 a second business organization, the Commercial Club of Santa Fe County, took preliminary steps toward formation. Beyond the stated general desire to advance the best interests of Santa Fe, a goal held in common with the board of trade, the new club sought only to establish "a place where business men can entertain visitors to our city in a suitable manner."[57] Only in October 1895 did the organization take on a formal existence. The two organizations retained separate identities and managed to behave antagonistically toward one another. Neither organization, despite memberships that included the most influential businessmen, entrepreneurs, and lawyers in town, became a driving force in advancing new directions for the city.

Nevertheless, changes in attitude did occur among the business groups between the early nineties and the later years of the next decade. Replies to letters of inquiry addressed or referred to the board of trade about business prospects in the city illustrate these. By 1907, Santa Fe was no longer touted as an agricultural bonanza. "It [Santa Fe] is a fine place for residence, but not much of a place for farming," one reply to an inquiry stated.[58] The prospects for commerce, too, were played down as was the notion that immediate prosperity would follow immigration. "It takes some time," the board's respondent noted, "before newcomers can become well enough established to make a living. . . ."[59] And again, Santa Fe "is not a commercial center, but men who are competent can always find something to do if they can wait round a little for an opening."[60] Other letters related to business opportunities even suggested going elsewhere: "[B]eing the capital of the Territory and residential rather than a commercial city, doubt if you could make a go of it here. Write the commercial club of Albuquerque."[61] The board suggested trying Moriarty or Estancia to a prospective drugstore opener on the grounds that "we already have three Drug

Stores and that is all the town can carry. . . ."[62] Such sober and modest views were far removed from the open-ended commercial boosterism of the eighties and early nineties.

In place of the common fare of economic growth usually fostered by local business organizations, the board of trade now offered a different Santa Fe. The fine climate and scenery, as always, received due notice. More important, however, was the depiction of the city as a residential, rather than a commercial or agricultural center. How deeply a new concept of Santa Fe had penetrated into the board of trade's repertoire of comments appeared in a letter to the New York office of the *London Times*. "It is our idea," it read, "and with the fact that it is the capital of the Territory to help us, to make it [Santa Fe] rather a residential place and place of resort, than to give it a commercial aspect, which it can never have."[63]

The other themes of the new directions sought by Santa Fe—health, historic interest, and archaeology among them—also received attention in board of trade letters. Nevertheless, it was the decided shift from commerce to these new interests and the persistent references to the city as a residential town and capital that defined the change of attitude. Moreover, by 1909 this change was viewed as how it ought to be. "Up to perhaps two years ago," one response declared, "no real effort was made to systematically beautify this the Capital City . . . , and because of the natural aridity of our soil and the poverty of resource this entails, no scheme can be taken up except the general one of developing this city along its natural lines." The letter concluded with the possibilities inherent if Santa Fe attracted the School of American Archaeology.[64] The business community was joining hands with the adherents of the new cultural interests.

The growing federal interest in conservation and the creation of national parks also created new attitudes in Santa Fe. In the early nineties considerable hostility existed toward such government efforts, and particularly the work of John Wesley Powell, who sought to withdraw land from the public domain as government reservoir sites and, therefore, from entry to settlers.[65] Such goals clashed with existing views of a community still seeking new population and agricultural development. In 1894 the *New Mexican* sneered at Powell's report and the U. S. Geological Survey, which suggested that little government land could be irrigated.[66] Hewett himself, seeking national parks and the consequent withdrawal of acreage from private use in the first years of the twentieth century, may well have lost the renewal of his presidency of the Normal University at Las Vegas in 1903 as a result of his views.[67]

By 1906 Powell had passed away and the torch of conservation had passed to Gifford Pinchot under the aegis of President Theodore Roosevelt. By that time national parks and forests were of great positive interest to those who were beginning to conceptualize a new Santa Fe. In 1904, objections to them on the territorial level still existed when they concerned grazing, but Governor Otero's message admitted "the wisdom of preserving New Mexico's forests" and sought steps "to prevent the vandalism that destroys . . . its unique, prehistoric cliff dwelling and ruins. . . ."[68] In 1908 Governor Curry was seeking Pinchot's aid to build a road through the forest reserve to the east of Santa Fe which, he maintained, "would give a scenic highway that would be used very largely by tourists, and would be a great advertisement to our Territory. . . ."[69] The governor sought the support of the Commercial Club of Santa Fe County through Abraham Staab and Levi Hughes for the route and to persuade Pinchot to locate the headquarters of the forestry service in Santa Fe.[70] When Pinchot scheduled a visit to Santa Fe in 1909, the *New Mexican* lauded him and observed that "Towns like Santa Fe and Las Vegas are firmly convinced that instead of hurting their prosperity, the creation of the Pecos Reserve . . . has made permanent the source of their existence and their promise of future growth and prosperity."[71] The new view of where Santa Fe's fortunes lay was rooting itself evermore deeply.

By 1906 diverse groups were converging to produce a broad consensus for making Santa Fe a new kind of city. The Archaeological Society of New Mexico proved to be the cohesive element. As noted earlier, it had been founded in the late nineties by John McFie and Edgar Hewett (who did not yet live in the city), aided by Paul A. F. Walter (both McFie and Walter were themselves newcomers). They formed the nucleus of this group that provided the cement for all of the interested agencies.

In the early years of the twentieth century, Hewett established contacts with important figures of archaeology in Washington, D.C. and had surveyed the condition of archaeological sites in New Mexico. His findings on the subject were incorporated by Governor Miguel A. Otero into his reports to the secretary of the interior. In them, Hewett had urged that the Pajarito Plateau be set aside as a national park.[72] In 1903 Congressman J. F. Lacey of Iowa, chair of the House Committee on Public Lands, joined Hewett to view the prehistoric sites, strengthening the latter's national connections. Under Lacey's sponsorship, in 1906 Congress passed the American Antiquities Act, which included the creation of Mesa Verde as a national park.[73]

It was at that same time that the Archaeological Society reemerged, approving the minutes of the meeting of 15 March 1901.[74] From an earlier membership of thirty-five, the list had grown to eighty-eight. The *New Mexican* felt certain that the society "will succeed in making the Cliff Dwellings known as widely as the Grand Canyon which will result in thousands of tourists coming to this city every year. . . ."[75]

The character of the membership of the society in mid-1906 pointed up the broadened range of community interest. Judges, attorneys, businessmen, bankers, doctors, and government officials filled its ranks. Significant, too, was the number of women who participated: thirty-four of the eighty-eight members were female, many married, but some also single. The society may have been the first civic organization that reflected such a widespread interest and concern with the fate of the city. On the other hand, early lists of members show few Hispano surnames among them.[76] Their absence may have been a sign that the common history of New Mexico, which deeply involved the Hispanos, may have been closer to their interests than the unearthing of the Native American past.

Moreover, a considerable overlap between the memberships of the businessmen's organizations and the Archaeological Society became evident. Such society members as Prince, R. J. Palen, E. A. Abbott, and E. H. Brodhead belonged to the board of trade as well as the Society, while Judge Napoleon Laughlin, R. H. Hanna, H. S. Kaune, Frank Owen, and Abraham Staab held membership in the commercial club and the society. The interlocking interests of the organizations rested on hopes for national parks, the promise of tourists, and, in 1907, the creation of the School of American Research. The most specific focal point which drew them together concentrated on the use of the old Palace—all could relate to that.

The growing clarity of goals for the city led eventually to institutional consolidation. As the School for American Research and the Museum of New Mexico became realities, the differences between the board of trade and the commercial club appeared increasingly unjustifiable. The *New Mexican* repeatedly cajoled both organizations to set aside their differences in the higher interest of Santa Fe. "Can't Santa Fe property owners and businessmen and citizens drop their individual prejudice and personal feelings and political and factional jealousies and get together to advertise Santa Fe . . . ?," the paper pleaded.[77] Speakers to both organizations urged unification. "Santa Fe is not a large enough city to support two civic organizations," John Wagner, a hotel builder, counseled. He added, "[S]teps should be taken to merge your organizations for the mutual and best interest of the city. . . ."[78] After protracted negotiation both groups decided to combine to form a chamber of commerce on 28 March 1911. Santa Fe had finally achieved a consensus in its business community and the future direction of the city crystallized further.

In 1917, even as work progressed on the new museum of art, the United States entered World War I. Far removed from the major centers of war-related activity, New Mexicans nevertheless responded patriotically to the emotions and needs of the moment. Santa Fe, by virtue of its political position, became the hub of the state's mobilization efforts. Many of its leading citizens became leaders in organization, with the city as the site for their activities. Its young men, like those everywhere in the country and state gave themselves to the national will and purpose. For a time, these larger issues overrode efforts devoted to city development.

Given the conditions of war, the call of the armed forces attracted primary attention and received a generous response from Santa Feans. New Mexico's National Guard, it should be noted, had just been mustered out of its duties on the Mexican border as a result of Pancho Villa's activities and its members were recalled in April 1917. All in all, some 461 men from the city alone participated in all branches of military service.[79] Ten men lost their lives and thirteen were wounded. Hispano and Anglo surnames split fairly equally.

Military enlistment aside, the issues of the war as they affected New Mexico centered mainly on increasing food production.[80] Santa Fe itself, with its limited agricultural potential, expressed its efforts with home gardens, food preservation, and the observance of wheatless and meatless days. Given the social character of the times, women played a powerful role in organizing and carrying out these activities. Such efforts diverted attention from other civic activities that had occupied them.

The war also provided the opportunity and atmosphere for linkage between moral behavior and public action in Santa Fe. The national movement for prohibition was in full swing. As early as May 1917 the city council moved to regulate retail liquor traffic, relating its use to the presence of national guardsmen. The city council unanimously passed an ordinance forbidding the sale of liquor to soldiers and closed saloons at 9 P.M. upon pain of a hundred-dollar fine and revocation of a dealer's license on subsequent violations.[81] The prohibition amendment to the national Constitution, the eighteenth, came in November 1918, the same month the war ended. In his history of Santa Fe, Twitchell noted that the event "brought about a greater change in the business life of Santa Fe than any other event in its history."[82] His conclusion that "the saloon was banished forever," however, proved quite premature, despite any immediate effects of the legislation.

The arguments against liquor linked the corruption of soldiers and the misuse of grain at a time when food production was a paramount need. The moral campaign, however, extended beyond such wartime reasoning. In October, the Santa Fe Woman's Club and Woman's Board of Trade raised the subject of immorality in moving pictures shown in the city and asked the city council to control their exhibition.[83]

Even earlier, in April, fears of invasion and sabotage based on German diplomatic activity in Mexico and the events surrounding the career of Pancho Villa led to extraordinary measures of watchfulness. The city council resolved that hotels and restaurants "take cognizance of all strangers not accounted for, or of suspicious behavior and report it to the Mayor or City Marshal without delay concerning such persons." Refusal to comply could result in "the loss and cancellation of his license to do business in this city."[84] The effects of such pronouncements clearly were chilling.

Such activities temporarily eclipsed the cultural direction city leaders had taken for a decade. The city activists, as already noted for women's groups, found themselves engaged in fund drives for bonds and private drives in the name of the Red Cross, the YMCA, YWCA, Knights of Columbus, and Salvation Army. Draft board activities involved attorneys, doctors, and dentists. Even the small artist community of Santa Fe found members leaving to paint camouflage. Any new impetus to deal with the city itself clearly had to await the end of the great war.

FIVE

The City Becomes "Different": Preservation, Style, and Tourism

AS SANTA FEANS sought to define their town's future development, they already had a valuable resource available to them—the considerable American interest in the West. Ironically, the railroad, even as it undermined the older commercial city of the Santa Fe Trail, made possible a new kind of migration fed by visitors from the East. The keys to a new Santa Fe lay in the attractiveness that New Mexico and the city held for those seeking an American antiquity based on the Indian and Spanish past, as well as the scenic beauty and climatic virtues of the region.

Long before the railroad reached New Mexico, Americans in the East had been attracted by their hinterland, which offered a landscape and climate unfamiliar to them. After the Civil War, the extension of rail lines and the creation of luxurious railway cars provided a means to transport travelers in numbers and with convenience previously unavailable. The new accessibility, however, was expensive at first, ensuring that the upper stratum of American and even English society would comprise the passengers of the private sleeping cars that came into use in the 1860s.[1]

By the early 1870s those who wished to see the West could do so with more than mere passage by rail. Thomas Cook, who had introduced the excursion train and the package tour to the British, offered these features to the tourist in America. American firms followed suit. Elegant hotels in San Francisco and Denver and resort hotels, often built by railroad capital, tended to the needs of the well-to-do voyagers.[2]

By the late nineteenth century Western travel was increasingly a large-scale phenomenon. Expensive palace cars gave way to cheaper Pullman sleeping cars for an expanding railway net and growing traveler interest. Tourist and potential settler were often one and the same. Expensive resort hotels offered termini to attract the wealthy but so did less expensive but still admirable railway station hostelries. The railroad built the greatest resort in the territory in 1882—the Montezuma Hotel—six miles from Las Vegas, New Mexico, and followed with a station hotel, the Castenada, just before the turn of the century.[3] Both facilities were ventures of a growing chain created by the AT & SF and Fred Harvey that stretched throughout the railway empire's domain. The hotels created a source of revenue for the railroad as well as altering the economies of the sites at which they were located.

Scenic attractions drew visitors, with Yellowstone and Yosemite as the earliest of such wonders. Railroads, supplemented by stagecoach, made them and other sites accessible. The mountains, deserts, and semi-arid lands of the Southwest, earlier scorned by settler and tourist alike, increasingly attracted favorable attention in the last decades of the nineteenth century. This belated interest owed its origins partly to anthropologists and artists, who depicted the area as the last contiguous American wilderness.

However favorable these conditions for a tourist trade, they did not result in immediate advantages for Santa Fe. The town had to wait almost three decades while incentives developed to marshal the resources and to build the infrastructure that tourism required. It was not that these needs were totally ignored. As early as the late seventies Santa Feans watched the human traffic through their town and mused about its significance. The *Weekly New Mexican* noted the arrival of coaches loaded with passengers every evening and the difficulty of providing accommodations for them. With anticipatory foresight, the paper predicted that when the railroad reached Santa Fe those difficulties would increase.[4]

In the months following the establishment of the rail line to the city, interest and concern regarding visitors was high. Commenting on the fact that passengers left Las Vegas on hacks bound for White Oaks, the *New Mexican* lamented this lost traffic. "What are our merchants, capitalists, and livery men thinking about?" it queried.[5] Even in 1880 the paper had found the city's hotel facilities inadequate and overcrowded; in 1881 it finally saw progress with the building of the new Palace Hotel.[6]

The reasons for the slow response lay in the time it took for the business and governmental leaders of Santa Fe to recognize that its development as a commercial center had been decisively precluded with the loss of a main line position on the railroad after 1880. For a generation after the railroad came, the attraction of permanent settlers was the city's preferred image of progress. The territory's bureau of immigration evinced a primary interest in promoting commerce and agriculture.[7] Commenting on the bookings of two thousand persons for Santa Fe in the coming winter, the *New Mexican* hoped in 1886 that a united effort could be made to induce visitors to cast their lot with Santa Fe by settling in the valley for "agriculture is the basis of all wealth."[8] Visitors and settlement were clearly linked. Fearing the loss of the town's leading position in the territory in the face of competition from other towns, the *New Mexican* spoke of the need of the town to bestir itself. Besides its other attributes, it had to maintain its standing "as a business point, as a sanitarium [and] as a pleasure resort. . . ."[9] Luring visitors to Santa Fe and hopes that they would remain had clearly become an issue of some importance.

The attractions of the town gradually became more concretely identified. By 1886 a regular newspaper column described the city's virtues, some of which concerned the actual and potential interests of visitors. They included the climate, "the finest on the continent," and points of interest in the city, among them the Adobe Palace and the collections of the historical society, the Plaza, and the Church of San Miguel. The growing awareness of a hinterland also received attention. The sightseer, it was pointed out, could go to Tesuque and other pueblos, Aztec mineral springs, or the site of ancient cliff dwellers beyond the Rio Grande.[10] In all, the inventory of attractions included forty points of interest.

Progress, however, was slow. Nearly a decade later the image of what was of interest had changed little. An *Illustrated History of New Mexico*, published in 1895 to advertise the territory, still cited only forty places in the Santa Fe area as worthy of visiting. Health had taken on increased importance, the volume proclaiming that "As a health resort Santa Fe is unrivalled."[11] But, as noted earlier, no great resort hotel existed despite frequent pleas that that was just what the city needed to draw well-to-do tourists.

By the middle of the first decade of the twentieth century, local attractions crystallized into a more comprehensive picture. By then archaeology had moved to the foreground. The movement to establish national monuments involved New Mexico and the hinterland to which Santa Fe laid claim. Pajarito Park (now Bandelier National Monument), ex-Governor Prince commented, would draw evermore visitors and "all the tourists would come and go via Santa Fe."[12] In 1906 Pajarito was touted as an attraction that the Archaeological Society would make known "as widely as the Grand Canyon."[13]

By 1907 the spatial dimensions of attractions became more specific. Newspaper articles pointed out what tourists could see in five-, ten-, and thirty-minute walks in the city. Imaginary concentric circles of ten- and twenty-mile distances depicted wonders somewhat farther away. Beyond that, trips of a day's duration were noted, some at the southern end of the Manzano mountains, a hundred miles away.[14] Albuquerque's presence, much closer to the locale of the latter sights, received no mention. Once an imperial political center, Santa Fe was translating itself into the hub of a tourist empire.

The next step was to connect the city with its hinterland. As early as 1891 the *New Mexican* looked forward to the establishment of a Pecos national park which would make the region east and north of the city "a veritable mecca for health and pleasure tourists."[15] Situated between Santa Fe and Las Vegas, however, the Pecos attracted folk to the latter town as well. In 1903, at the initiative of Las Vegas, the first steps were taken to link the cities across the mountains using the impetus of the "Good Roads" movement then popular in the West. Working together, citizens of both towns petitioned the legislature to support the project. But since the major distance ran through federal lands, the legislature could only provide for territorial roads and furnish convicts for the necessary labor force.

Santa Feans were enthusiastic about the prospects for the new road. They touted the beauties of the Pecos ("as beautiful as Yosemite and the Yellowstone Parks"), its potential as a tourist attraction, and as an example for other parts of the territory.[16] The legislature complied in 1903, passing an act that enabled the use of convict labor for the purpose of building the road.[17]

In a more general way, road building in New Mexico received a boost in 1905 when the legislature created El Camino Real. Running roughly on a north-south axis through the length of the territory, it incorporated the as yet unbuilt Scenic Road approved in 1903. The advantages of convict labor again received attention, especially the health benefits for the prisoners themselves.[18] This legislation served the interests of many towns, not Santa Fe alone.

The influence of Santa Fe and its neighboring counties in the legislature notwithstanding, actual progress on the Scenic Road was slow. In 1904 the *New Mexican* had reported on its progress warmly, citing the completion of fifteen miles of excellent wagon road.[19] Nevertheless, nearly five years later, in 1909, the same paper excoriated Santa Fe, the county, and its property owners for their disgraceful behavior in not keeping the road in good condition after the legislature had given them such a gift for the benefit of tourists.[20] A year earlier, Governor Curry, in correspondence with Gifford Pinchot of the Bureau of Forestry, implored him to build a road through the Pecos Reserve for tourism and as advertisement for the territory.[21] Concept long preceded actuality in such endeavors.

As archaeology loomed as a major path for Santa Fe's cultural development, linking Pajarito Park with the city also came under discussion. The push to create a national park at the cliff dweller ruins was already before Congress in 1903.[22] In 1906 the Santa Fe Archaeological Society planned its first excursion to Pajarito, using teams and tents for a three-day outing to the area and surrounding canyons.

Some nonmembers were permitted to accompany the expedition and future excursions were expected to follow.[23]

Roads for tourist purposes fit naturally with the growth of automobile use in the first decade of the twentieth century. By 1911 the road between Albuquerque and Santa Fe was sufficiently improved to permit such travel, albeit with difficulty. Owners of the still expensive vehicles joined in excursions between the cities. One such outing witnessed a caravan from Santa Fe joining another from Albuquerque at the top of La Bajada hill and driving together to the capital.[24] At that time the *New Mexican* estimated that Santa Feans owned a total of forty automobiles. Affluent residents owned brands such as Carter, then in vogue in the city, while Charles Catron owned a Lozier, and Bronson Cutting, a newcomer to town, a Stephens-Duryea. Motoring, enjoyable for these participants, suggested that the roads could also be used by tourists. "Good roads," the *New Mexican* told its readers, "bring good people."[25]

Santa Fe promoters of tourism had a model for their purposes. The Canyon City-Royal Gorge Highway in Colorado was held up as an example of why tourist roads should be built. The accessibility of scenic attractions in Colorado and California meant wealth to those states, the *New Mexican* argued, while the absence of such access in New Mexico resulted in the absence of wealth there. To Santa Feans it was the duty of the territory to build the roads, not the municipalities. "No one locality will build roads to open to the tourist world the scenic wonders of New Mexico," the *New Mexican* predicted. Tourist roads would bring far more into coffers than the building of "crooked highways to enable the farmer from Agua Fria to bring his chile to Santa Fe grocers."[26] In the eyes of these boosters the tourist vision was acquiring more value than the more ordinary usage of roads by the local population.

Still, progress in road development remained slow. Automobile traffic rather than tourist traffic concerned the territorial and early state legislatures. An ex-officio Territorial Highway Commission, which included the governor, was created only in 1909. This became the State Highway Commission in 1912, while an appointed commission appeared only in 1917, a year after the Federal Aid Road Act was passed by Congress. Although a tentative state highway system had been outlined in 1912, only in 1917 was a comprehensive state highway code adopted to allow participation under the federal road act.[27]

Meanwhile, the Scenic Route project went no further. Pajarito, on the other hand, continued to attract attention and, by 1916, wagon tours (six hours each way) were taking visitors there with railroad brochures advertising the fact. Overnight visitors stayed at the De Vargas Hotel.[28] Some sites closer in could be reached by auto, but Santa Fe itself and its immediate environs remained the main attraction as long as the hardships of the limited road system remained.

For the future cultural development of Santa Fe, the creation of the Museum of New Mexico and its residence in the Palace may well have been the most important decision of the twentieth century. In its enabling act the legislature informed the board of regents that

> all alterations, extensions and additions to the main Palace building shall be made so as to keep it in external appearance as nearly as possible in harmony with the Spanish architecture of the period of its construction and preserve it as a monument to the Spanish founders of the civilization of the Southwest.[29]

By this directive the legislators laid the groundwork for a major reorientation of architecture and planning in Santa Fe.

Edgar Hewett, on the eve of becoming a seminal figure in the stylistic and cultural revolution that marked Santa Fe's development, adhered to the legislature's requirements. In 1909 he recruited Jesse Nusbaum from the College in Las Vegas; Sylvanus Morley of Harvard, who joined the faculty of the School of American Archaeology; and Carl Lotave, whose murals in Denver had impressed him, as key figures in the restoration enterprise.[30] In the fall of 1913 the project was completed. It became a fitting centerpiece and marker in the city for an architectural odyssey that was just beginning, existing primarily in the minds of a few individuals.

While the Palace was a landmark of restoration, the next major step, the art museum, would be one of creation. The project grew out of an invitation to Hewett to direct exhibits at the Panama-California Exposition scheduled to open in San Diego in 1915 upon completion of the Panama Canal. Even as work on the Palace progressed, Hewett accepted the assignment, receiving the support of the state legislature in 1913 to display the products of New Mexico and to construct a building for that purpose at the Exposition.[31]

Ralph Twitchell headed the commission in charge of the project and Santa Fe architect I. H. Rapp was chosen to design it. Rapp drew heavily upon the drawings of Carlos Vierra, who found his architectural inspiration in New Mexican mission churches. Vierra and Gerald Cassidy, another artist living in Santa Fe, painted murals for its walls. In turn, the building, a great success at the Exposition, became the model for the New Mexico Art Museum that was completed in Santa Fe late in 1917.[32]

In 1909, when the restoration of the Palace received authorization, the architectural preferences of the legislature were not new in the Southwest. Architectural historians have described the path that led to the adaptation of elements of Indian and provincial Spanish colonial style of the eighteenth and nineteenth century into a distinctive regional style. The mission style of the California Building at the Chicago World's Fair of 1893 was one version of this.[33] Some of the Fred Harvey hotels and early buildings at the University of New Mexico in Albuquerque received such treatment years before the museum was created. Many Santa Feans themselves had not responded quickly to the trend.

Advocates for preservation of old structures, however, did exist in Santa Fe. The *New Mexican* noted in 1910 that "The average man from the east . . . does not come here to view Queen Anne cottages or factory chimneys. . . . But places like the Garita which Santa Fe is permitting the rains to wash away . . . and the old adobes which we despise are lodestones that help to make Santa Fe so attractive to the traveling public." And citing a prominent Bostonian's letter, the paper continued, "There is a peculiar glamour in the old Spanish style of architecture which, to us northerners is particularly pleasing and interesting." The correspondent added, "If you are to make Santa Fe attractive in the future you must preserve the old traditions. Don't be afraid to keep your old buildings." Lauding the Santa Fe railroad for its mission style stations, he charged, "preserve the architectural beauty which is the natural product of Santa Fe."[34]

In the spring of 1910 the idea of preservation and a new architectural harmony was prompting organizational activity. The *New Mexican* noted in April that "the city is threatened with a conglomerate mixture of architecture that is going to spoil it from the viewpoint of the tourist." To thwart that undesirable end, a meeting of interested citizens organized a preservation committee "with the idea of making all new buildings harmonize in idea with the general surroundings." It was declared possible to have new buildings erected in Spanish or Mission style. "Not to preserve the city's antiquities," the paper concluded, would be "contributory vandalism."[35]

By early 1912 the issue of the city's appearance had produced enough interest to warrant government action. Mayor Arthur Seligman created the Santa Fe Civic Center and City Planning Board that included H. H. Dorman, Bronson Cutting, M. A. Otero, James L. Seligman, and Marcelino Garcia.[36] Reappointed and augmented by the succeeding mayor, Celso Lopez, the board now included Hewett and S. G. Morley of the School of American Archaeology, N. L. King, a draftsman of the federal Land Office, and a stronger representation from the Santa Fe Chamber of Commerce. This planning board presented a report to the city council in December 1912 that outlined its ideas on how the city should develop.[37]

Preservation and style occupied the first paragraphs of the plan and revealed the central concerns of the board. They merit citation. Under the heading "Ancient Streets and Structure," the report stated

> It is the opinion of this Board that the preservation of the ancient streets, . . . and structures in and about the city is of the first importance and that these monuments of the first Americans should be preserved intact at almost any cost, that neither climate, healthfulness, pre-historic ruins nor scenery compare in value as an asset to Santa Fe, with these relics of a Romantic history and that it should be the duty of all city officials to guard the old streets against any change that will affect their appearance or alter their character such as widening, or straightening.

The report recommended further that

> no building permits be issued . . . to build on any of the streets listed . . . as old or ancient streets until proper assurance is given that the architecture will conform exteriorally with the Santa Fe style.
>
> The following paragraph, entitled "Architecture," argued that
>
> it can hardly be denied that the attraction of Santa Fe can best be preserved and increased by developing the town architecturally in harmony with its ancient character. We believe that everything should be done to create a public sentiment so strong that the Santa Fe style will always predominate.

To encourage that end, the report urged remitting or rebating taxes for some years on structures built in the desired style. To maintain recognition of the Spanish origins of the town the board suggested use of the old barrio names for wards.[38]

The production of a plan for the city was the work of a determined group of individuals associated with the archaeological society and the chamber of commerce. Ralph Twitchell, the lawyer and historian who was one of them, identified Edgar Hewett, John McFie, N. B. Laughlin, Sylvanus G. Morley, I. H. Rapp, Paul A. F. Walter, Carlos Vierra, James L. Seligman, A. J. Abbott, and William H. Pope as the leading lights of the group.[39] Loosely organized as the New-Old (or Old-New) Santa Fe Committee, they sought to objectify their ideas so as to bring them to fruition.

To this end and before the plan had been submitted to the city council, they installed an exhibition to portray elements of their concept at the Old Palace in November 1912. The driving force behind it was probably Sylvanus Morley, then a young archaeologist teaching at the School of American Archaeology.[40] The first annual report of the chamber of commerce noted the success of the spectacle and shared honors for supporting the project with the school, the Santa Fe Woman's Board of Trade, and the Spanish-American Alliance.[41]

Seeking implementation of the plan, the chamber sought to have its own city planning board made permanent with power to bring projects before city officials without awaiting the organization's official authorization. In addition, it urged the city to create a similar planning committee. The city, however, chose not to act immediately.[42]

Indeed, as the civic organizations pushed ahead, they encountered resistance. In July 1913 the chamber discussed the possibility of adopting the Santa Fe style of architecture for a projected new federal building, while Judge McFie, head of the New-Old Santa Fe Committee, reported a forthcoming meeting with the architects and contractors of the city to discuss the matter of "adopting the Santa Fe style of architecture for general use."[43]

Before the scheduled meeting took place, however, the *New Mexican* published a letter from Frederick Law Olmsted, a noted landscape architect, foretelling difficulties. Addressed to H. H. Dorman, then secretary of the chamber, Olmsted expressed doubt about whether the courts would hold it to be within the power of a legislature or a city council to impose upon private property owners, under police powers, an obligation such as the Santa Fe style and without provision for payment of damages. He suggested that restrictions might be imposed under the power of eminent domain to safeguard the beauty of the city, to pay claims of damages to owners, and to assess costs upon owners of land improved in value through protection of aesthetic quality.[44]

The meeting of the New-Old Santa Fe Committee and the architects and contractors was heated. Bricklayers viewed the chamber's idea as an attempt to drive them out of business. Others pointed out that of eighteen or twenty homes recently built in Santa Fe, only two used the "Santa Fe" style. Plans abounded for bungalows, but not for dwellings of the Santa Fe type.[45] A bit lamely, the *New Mexican*, which strongly supported the new direction, noted that the New-Old Santa Fe movement was misunderstood, that it never intended to interfere with building contractors or abolish brick cottages, but only "to retain, as far as possible, the old Spanish style of architecture. . . ."[46]

Despite the cautionary note introduced by opposition to the new style, some acceptance of it appeared in the middle of the teen years. Hewett noted in his reports that both new houses and remodeling reflected positive results by adopting some of its features. The Sunmount Sanatorium in 1914 and the School for the Deaf in 1916 made the case for institutional and public buildings.[47]

One result of the meeting was recognition that Santa Fe-style advocates had neither models nor technicians to implement their ideas. At the same July 15 meeting with the contractors, Sylvanus Morley announced a competition for a prize to be awarded to anyone producing the most acceptable plans for a small dwelling in the new style that could be constructed at a cost between $1,500 and $3,000.[48] In October 1913 the prize was given to Kenneth Chapman, one of Hewett's coworkers at the museum, while Carlos Vierra won the second prize. The annual report of the chamber, which appeared in 1914, noted that as a result of the competition, a number of residential designs had been created and Judge McFie, as chair of the New-Old Santa Fe Committee, recommended that these plans be published.[49]

As designs evolved for the New Mexico building at the San Diego Exposition and, subsequently, the art museum, the distinctive character of New Mexico's architecture received formal definition. Sylvanus Morley and Carlos Vierra described and advocated the local style in the middle years of the second decade of the century. Morley traced the progression from indigenous multi-storied Pueblo structures, through Spanish missions, government buildings, and residences, to the renaissance inspired and supported by the Santa Fe Railway based on the style of the California missions, and on to New Mexico's experience, without arches or pointed roofs.[50] Vierra, more forceful in his aesthetic judgments, stressed heavily the uniqueness of Pueblo architecture and the need to maintain and extend its forms to modern-day usage without compromise. He sharply distinguished the architecture of the Pueblo communities from the California missions, and like Morley, stressed the avoidance of peaked roofs and arches, while advocating the purity of adobe.[51]

Concerned about Santa Fe's heritage and future, Vierra emphasized the importance of the old architecture for the city. "Nothing," he asserted, "will push Santa Fe off the map . . . so quickly or so easily as the majestic mansion, . . . the 'cute bungalow' or the old adobe with the new razorback roof, if we persist in building them until they strangle our own architecture and individuality."[52] In his fears for the future, he wondered about what the losses of the previous generation might have cost the city in the impressions of disappointed tourists. His hopes lay in the progress of the art museum and the School for the Deaf.[53]

Although the city did not accept the plan offered in 1912, the efforts of its advocates did not cease. In the middle years of the second decade of the century, images of that architectural and city plan continued to appear. William Templeton Johnson, an architect and city planner, picked up where older city organizations had left off. "It would seem," he stated in 1916, "that Santa Fe can make the greatest progress as a tourist resort and as a pleasant place of residence for cultivated and intellectual people."[54] Johnson sought the restoration of the original Santa Fe without the brick blocks and plate glass that had crept in, "for only in this [original] aspect will it appeal most to the traveling public." He hoped the city council would decree such a restoration. The Plaza, above all, had to be restored to its ancient plan and dimensions with ecclesiastical buildings at the east side, government structures at the north and northeast corner in the Santa Fe style, a new tourist hotel on the south, along with a commemoration of the Santa Fe Trail and businesses on the west. The west and south would have *portales* as they did formerly.[55]

Edgar Hewett affirmed Johnson's views and spirit. Both worried about time. For Hewett, the next decade would tell the story "for all time." More circumspect than some of his colleagues, he expressed uneasiness with such terms as "New-Old Santa Fe Style," because the type belonged to all New Mexico and not merely the city.[56] Even so, he was pleased with the architectural progress since 1909, and like Johnson, he sought the restoration of the Plaza according to its historic arrangement.[57]

Planning itself evoked the highest aspirations of the planners—their dreams. Like those before him whose visions had imagined a Denver or a great health resort, Johnson now compared Santa Fe with Renaissance Florence. Aware of his audacity, he acknowledged, "It may seem to be a rather wide leap from Florence to Santa Fe, but why should it be?" The art colonies of Taos and Santa Fe, the Plaza returned to historic proportions, and the changing attitudes of the residents all led him to his essential query, "Why should it [Santa Fe] not become a great center for art and culture?"[58] Dreams and concepts outdistanced reality and practicality, but the spirit of the dreamers would prove a major force in the future development of the city.

After the decision to create an art museum replicating the building at the San Diego Exposition received acceptance, the issue of location arose and also met spirited resistance. Colonel Jose D. Sena, the president of the board of education, challenged the notion and legality of locating the proposed structure at the northwest corner of the Plaza on property set aside for the public schools.[59] Placing the general education of Santa Fe's children above the goals of the museum, he questioned how many of them would become artists or achieve material benefit from the gallery.[60] The art museum finally received its desired location, but the conflict revealed that the archaeological-artistic trend had not yet become the highest priority for the entire city.

Santa Fe, with advantages of proximity to archaeological sites, legislative support for an institutional base, and excellent connections with the Washington archaeological establishment, was well placed to make its mark both as a center for research and as a tourist attraction. Nevertheless, issues arose around the archaeological enterprise in the city. One of these problems concerned the relationship of Edgar Hewett's vision for archaeology in Santa Fe and New Mexico and the simultaneous development of standards being set for archaeology in prestigious academic institutions in the Northeast.

According to his biographer, Hewett had become disenchanted with the classroom early in his teaching career and fixed his gaze instead on unearthing readily accessible archaeological sites. He described himself as a "dirt archaeologist" for whom the field rather than the classroom held primary significance.[61] That perspective coincided well with Santa Fe's proximity to numerous sites available for hands-on study.

Even as Hewett moved away from the classroom to the field, developments in American anthropology were moving to some extent in a different direction—toward academic institutions and training and a new professionalism rooted in graduate education as well as fieldwork.[62] The leader in this direction was Franz Boas at Columbia University in New York City, who, through his own research and the training of his students, was emerging as a dominant figure in American anthropology.[63]

Given the differing thrust of the two positions and the contact of both men within the Archaeological Institute of America, conflict between the two was inevitable. By 1909 Boas had resigned from the Institute in protest against Hewett's administrative methods of control and because he considered Hewett's enterprise "public entertainment more than science."[64] In the following four years Boas supporters and Hewett clashed repeatedly.

Hewett was attacked on the grounds advanced by Boas. The very method by which the School of American Archaeology had been established raised doubts among the advocates of professionalism. Writing to Governor Prince, W. R. Martin, a prominent librarian in New York, described the process whereby established classical schools at Jerusalem had been founded under the aegis of specialized societies and were subject to their standards. The American School had not undergone this procedure. As a result, Martin reported, "the classical and oriental archaeologists of the Institute, ignorant of the special field, are sustaining a mere Chautauqua."[65]

Beyond the issue of the school's apparently flawed genesis lay issues of Hewett's qualifications and methods. In 1912, Alfred Tozzer of Harvard questioned Hewett's professional judgment and qualifications in a *New York Times* article. Reacting to an interview given by Hewett on matters relating to Central America, Tozzer found Hewett's errors "hardly excusable in one occupying the position of Director of the American School of Archeology" and challenged his qualifications to discuss such matters as the deciphering of Mayan glyphs as well as the "unscientific character" of his analogies.[66]

For a time the conflict was serious enough to raise fears about the continued presence of the school in Santa Fe. Those qualms, however, were probably exaggerated. Early in 1913 Tozzer responded to an inquiry by Prince "that there has been no attempt made whatever to withdraw the school from Santa Fe." Rather it was Hewett who was the problem. Harvard would send students for the summer, he insisted, "provided the School had another Director."[67] W. R. Martin also informed Prince of the difficulties of altering the situation. "I trust," he wrote with resigned irony, "that any efforts you may make to reform the School and to educate its Director may not disturb the happiness and impair the health of yourself and Mrs. Prince."[68]

Hewett's differences with the Eastern academic archaeologists could not remain hidden from the scene in Santa Fe. Governor Prince, embattled as he was with Hewett over the disposition of the historical society and considering his long interest in the city's cultural welfare, expressed his view of the conditions for success to H. H. Dorman, who in 1912 was president of the chamber of commerce. "That success," Prince noted, "requires the confidence and cooperation of the leading institutions of the land, and harmonious relations with local scientific bodies." Prince's information led him to conclude that satisfactory results "cannot exist on their part while Dr. Hewett controls the management of the so-called 'School'. . . ."[69] The inner circles at Santa Fe were clearly aware of the conflict between Hewett and the Easterners.

Differences between Hewett and his local opponents intensified after 1910 with the arrival of Bronson Cutting in Santa Fe. Probably afflicted with tuberculosis, Cutting was a Harvard-educated New Yorker whose wealth and sophistication could not but attract attention on the local scene. He soon encountered the cultural stars of the city, Hewett among them, and concluded, according to Cutting's biographer, "that he [Hewett] was a pretentious fool."[70] Hewett's comments about relations between Cutting's sister and Carl Lotave, the artist involved in the restoration of the Palace, may have added a personal dimension to the animus.[71] Cutting's qualities and resources assured him of a powerful voice in Santa Fe—especially after he purchased the *New Mexican* in 1912.

By that time the conflict between Hewett and the growing Eastern academic anthropological establishment was public knowledge even though quite muted in Santa Fe. In 1913, both the recently consolidated chamber of commerce and the new ownership of the *New Mexican* posed challenges for Hewett that were open and heated. The facts of the disputes are well known.[72] One difference rested on a chamber of commerce claim that Santa Fe was the oldest city in the United States and its use of a slogan to that effect on envelopes to be sold to merchants and others interested in attracting tourists. The preponderance of informed interpretation disputed the claim, but the chamber persisted nevertheless. Hewett, checking quietly with persons whose expert authority he trusted, opposed its use. At the public meeting where the issue was discussed, an interesting motivation for going ahead that received applause was presented by Attorney General Frank W. Clancy. "I understand," he proclaimed, "Santa Fe wants publicity. Let's provoke a controversy on the subject of the city's antiquity. There is no better way to get publicity."[73] To some, at least, the attractions that would promote Santa Fe through notoriety were more important than issues of historical accuracy.

Early in October 1913 the *New Mexican* published a report by H. H. Dorman, the chamber's president. Included was a box on work being done to advertise Santa Fe and what the city still needed. The latter portion included the following criticism: "A School of Archaeology . . . with a director who is not merely a promoter but who is recognized in scientific circles and who is able to obtain the endorsement of the leading eastern universities." That school, moreover, should "draw students from the more important institutions . . . and not a few dabblers during the summer session." A final point scored Hewett's absences (though not by name) from the Santa Fe institution.[74] Despite its disputed and dubious merit, however, the chamber upheld its use of Santa Fe's antiquity for the sake of publicity even as it claimed to seek high academic quality for the school and its director.

Other events exacerbated the tension. The chamber of commerce, housed at the Palace by Hewett's permission since 1911, fell into arrears in its rental fees in 1913. Within a week of Dorman's statement about the director, the chamber received a notice from the museum board to vacate the premises. The conflict then emerged full blown.

An open attack on Hewett by the chamber, supported by Cutting's *New Mexican*, ensued. Throughout October, front-page stories and editorials revealed publicly what had been said mostly in private. Letters from Alfred Tozzer and R. B. Dixon of Harvard, Franz Boas of Columbia, and George A. Dorsey of Chicago were printed questioning Hewett's qualifications as archaeologist and his methods at the school both as teacher and administrator. The excoriation of Hewett was neither subtle nor restrained. The above-noted scholars described him as a "laughing stock," and as having "no standing among scientists," and that they placed "no confidence in him."[75]

Hewett did not publicly defend himself. Instead, Charles Lummis stepped forward on his behalf. He lauded Hewett's efforts as a promoter for "the most important thing that ever happened in Santa Fe."[76] In addition, he cited support for Hewett from the heads of the National Museum in Washington and the Bureau of American Ethnology, who believed Hewett was the best man for the directorship of the school.

The *New Mexican* then broadened its attack. It took to task the managing committee of the school and found only three persons competent in American archaeology.[77] But that was the *New Mexican*'s last shot. A meeting of the chamber of commerce itself disclaimed responsibility for attacks on Hewett several days later.[78]

Not unexpectedly, the archaeological society defended Hewett. On November 11 it resolved to retain the director and to assure the continuity of his tenure and commended his work.[79] The *New Mexican*'s report of the meeting noted that both presiding Judge McFie and Secretary Paul Walter sought to avoid heated expressions against Hewett's attackers.[80] Essentially, both sides had aired their feelings and had reached the limits of animus. Any further conflict would lead to an abyss within the city.

In effect, the affair affirmed the direction already in place in Santa Fe. Led by Hewett, the museum would continue on its chosen path despite the disapproval of some leading academic archaeologists. The reluctance of the chamber of commerce to push the controversy further reflected a common priority shared by it and the archaeological society—to consider the welfare of Santa Fe above all else. The issue of the future of archaeology in Santa Fe and of academic archaeology carried no weight in the discussion. Lummis summarized the matter in a letter to Hewett: "[T]he School needs you—and Santa Fe needs the School."[81] Only in private correspondence did Hewett remark to Twitchell that "We must admit that in our work we have opposed to us, in the very nature of things, the intolerance of the Academician, who sees in the man outside of University cloisters, merely an interloper. That spirit has to go. . . ."[82] Similarly, Lummis's view that "the people of Santa Fe know nothing about archaeology or any other kind of science" remained a private opinion.[83]

Santa Fe embarked on a path distinct from major trends in American academic archaeology but secure in a semi-independent niche permitted by its position as the state's capital, its remnants of longevity, and, perhaps, the absence of a university. It did not have to match emerging academic standards and could, at least to some extent, stand alone. This choice was, wittingly or not, part of its becoming a city different.

The twenties witnessed a great expansion of activity in Santa Fe associated with the study of the Native American. Not until the second half of that decade, however, did its institutional development reach a high point. Indeed, the very success of the museum's activity led it to reach the limits of its sphere of influence. Artists would count on the museum for space and exhibitions, but they also developed their own independent activity. Native crafts, too, would come into their own in the Fiesta, the town's chief festival commemorating its history, and in separate organizations, such as the Indian Arts Fund.

However, it was in anthropology and archaeology, the School of American Research's most central concerns, that it faced its greatest challenge. It was inevitable that the University of New Mexico in Albuquerque would develop those disciplines as they assumed a greater visibility on the state's educational scene. The university created a department of anthropology in about 1928. Given Hewett's stature in the state and his closeness to the university's president, James F. Zimmerman, it was almost a given that he would be the first faculty member in the discipline. The school and the university department also cooperated closely in matters of publication, archaeological sites, and the use of personnel in teaching.[84]

In the mid-thirties, however, Hewett stepped aside as chairman. By that time, the anthropology department had defined its direction. Problems had arisen. Issues of jurisdiction between the museum and the university emerged over sites and conflicting views of the function of the School of American Research. Moreover, unfavorable evaluations of Hewett led one prominent young scholar, Clyde Kluckhohn, to decline appointment.[85] Hewett's departure from the university left the Department of Anthropology with its own separate mission and the capacity to fulfill it.

The late twenties also witnessed the creation of an independent Laboratory of Anthropology in Santa Fe. Funded by John D. Rockefeller in its early stages and built on land donated largely by Amelia and Martha White—two wealthy, culturally active sisters who had settled in the city—the aim of the Laboratory was to oversee Native American research and to house the craft collections of the Indian Arts Fund. Some of Hewett's longtime associates, Kenneth Chapman and Jesse Nusbaum, even joined the new center. With them stood the nationally oriented anthropologists, museum leaders, and major figures of leading Northeastern universities, including Boas, Hewett's old enemy. In 1927 they executed an organizational "end run" around Hewett, creating a Committee on the Organization of the Anthropological Laboratory.[86] The result was that Hewett's local monopoly over archaeology and anthropology was broken, but the scope of such activity in the city broadened.

Although Hewett's position in the second half of the 1920s and into the 1930s could be viewed as a "demotion" in his status, it also could be viewed in another light. The creation and growth of new and developing institutions related to the Native American must be considered a success story in which he played an important role. He and his museum simply could neither encompass all the facets of activity nor control the varied sources emerging to implement what he and his loyal supporters had initiated. Whatever the judgment of his skills as a scholar, his awareness of the role of archaeology, the broader place of anthropology and the arts, and his efforts to support and allow them to develop afford him a leading place in the creation of a new direction for Santa Fe.

By the 1920s there was ample reason to regard Santa Fe as a unique and distinctive place. In 1881, W. G. Ritch had already identified the city as a "specimen" of the Southwest's past. The artists and anthropologists later conceived a "Santa Fe style" of architecture and Edgar Hewett created an archaeological research center. The scenic attractions of the Southwest, so different from the American East, and the new access permitted by railroad travel allowed an audience to view what was to Easterners a new environment. This would give rise to a "myth" of Santa Fe in the minds of some and a conception of "the city different" as a sobriquet ubiquitously applied. Once established and supported by organized groups, this commitment to preserve the city's distinctive character became a major criterion for evaluating proposals for future development of the built environment. In the face of threat or challenge, the commitment guaranteed that change would be controversial.

SIX

Artists and Writers in the 1920s and 1930s

THERE WAS A marked broadening of cultural activity in Santa Fe in the years after World War I. The arrival of a few artists before the war, a much larger influx after its conclusion in 1918, as well as the coming of writers, altered the cultural tone of the city. In the long run, the artists and writers would be a powerful factor in shaping the views of residents about their town and New Mexico, as well as how outsiders viewed the town, a process that had begun with the interest in archaeology.

Why artists came to New Mexico and Santa Fe involves a complex answer that encompasses the state of art in America, the moods and personal conditions of its practitioners, and the development of an image of the Southwest. In Taos, the fresh aesthetic qualities of the landscape and the Pueblo community, whose inhabitants still lived close to their ancestral traditions, made it the first place in New Mexico to attract artists in some numbers in the late nineteenth century.[1] In Santa Fe, the artists' presence found connection in aesthetic trends developing around architecture in the city during the second decade of the century, in the positive working conditions for artists there, and in some aspects of weather, terrain, and that same proximity of native peoples that influenced the artists at Taos to stay. The uniqueness of the area in the United States spoke for itself and gripped those seeking something new and, in their eyes, worthwhile.

Like so many others in Santa Fe, health proved a consideration early on in drawing consumptive artists to the city. Carlos Vierra, the first of them to settle permanently in 1904, Gerald Cassidy in 1912 after a stay in Albuquerque, and in 1913, Sheldon Parsons, who would become the first director of the new fine arts museum, all came for the locale's presumed curative qualities. Before the United States entered the war in 1917, Theodore Van Soelen and William P. Henderson also joined the small cohort of health-seeking artists.[2]

Some of these early artists benefited from the fortunate circumstances surrounding the archaeological and restorative impulses already at play in the city. The work on the Palace after 1909 and the preparations for the New Mexico exhibit at the Panama-California Exposition of 1915 in San Diego created opportunities for them to employ their talents. The Exposition itself and the subsequent erection of the art museum in Santa Fe became vehicles for attracting more artists. In San Diego, Hewett convinced Robert Henri, an important figure in modern American art, to visit Santa Fe in 1916, after seeing his early Indian paintings. The new museum itself offered powerful incentives. Referring to the growing attraction of the Southwest for artists, Hewett wrote to Henri that "The building of the new Art Museum, together with the facilities which we can offer in the way of studio and exhibition galleries will be a great additional stimulus."[3] And it worked out so. Influenced by Henri, Hewett's policy toward art shows provided for open, nonjuried exhibitions and drew modernist artists to Santa Fe who faced difficulties elsewhere in gaining recognition.[4]

Attractions such as health and access to work facilities aside, the artistic milieu and atmosphere of collegiality also provided powerful attractions in producing a community of resident artists. Particularly in the early years, when Americans knew little of the area, few artists came without invitation by or recommendation from those already there. Joseph H. Sharp had sung the glories of New Mexico and Taos to Ernest Blumenschein and Irving Couse in the late nineteenth century. Blumenschein and Couse, in turn, told W. Herbert Dunton and Warren Rollins. After Henri visited Santa Fe in 1916, he informed George Bellows, Leon Kroll, Randall Davey, and John Sloan of the area's virtues and either before the end of the war or shortly afterward they too came.[5] This mode of growth reflected both the personal connections of the artists through their vocation and the relatively unknown conditions of Santa Fe and New Mexico.

News of the expanding artist community spread by word of mouth and the appearance of its work in Eastern exhibitions and galleries. The growing reputation of the area as one hospitable to artists induced others, students and friends less well connected to the earlier arrivals, to come. In 1919 and 1920, younger men, such as Fremont Ellis, Willard Nash, Wladyslaw Mruk, Jozef Bakos, and Will Shuster appeared.[6] The latter cohort would shortly combine to form their own organization, Los Cinco Pintores (The Five Painters), to better their fortunes.

Limited by isolation, the artists of Taos, the first of whom arrived nearly a generation before their Santa Fe counterparts, had sought to improve their livelihood and enhance recognition of their work. Without commercial galleries and with few tourists on the scene, six Taos artists in 1915 formed the Taos Society of Artists for the primary purpose of selling their work through traveling exhibitions.[7] The venture proved highly successful.

Meanwhile, Santa Feans, eager to expand the new cultural foundation for New Mexico, were working to make their own town its art center, as they had made it the archaeological center. The annual report of the Museum of New Mexico in 1914 spoke of the progressive nature of an art museum, the efforts of the museum to develop Southwestern art, and its importance for the tourist.[8] Writing in 1916, Paul Walter linked art activities in Taos and Santa Fe, proclaiming the practitioners "prophets of an American renaissance—founders of a Santa Fe-Taos school of art." He continued, "Who can say that the Santa Fe-Taos school of art may not in the near future mean to American art what the Barbizon school has meant to France?"[9] As in archaeology, the visions and hopes of the city's cultural leaders were quite ambitious.

The Santa Fe cultural elite, impressed with what was happening in Taos and quick to recognize the benefits of association, soon sought a tie with their more experienced northern neighbor. In 1918 they formally approached the Taos Society of Artists with the goal of uniting the two centers under the title of "The Santa Fe-Taos Society of Artists."[10] By that time the Santa Feans had, as already noted, long been linking the artists of the two communities in print. In mid-1916, *El Palacio*, the journal of the local archaeological society, had begun publishing biographical sketches of artists under the title "The Santa Fe-Taos Art Colony."

However, the annual meeting of the Taos society, held in July 1918, rebuffed Santa Fe's overtures. Blumenschein, interviewed in Albuquerque in 1919, noted playfully that "Santa Fe is so proud of the Taos art that she refers to this branch of painters as the Santa Fe-Taos school, but up in Taos, Santa Fe occupies the tail end of the hyphen."[11] The well-known artist was clearly aware of Santa Fe's desire to gain stature wherever it could by attaching itself to what it considered attractive through use of an adhesive hyphen.

By the time the Taos society turned down the Santa Feans' offer, their Palace and new art museum had become the site of frequent exhibitions by resident artists or those associated with both communities. The biennial report of the Museum of New Mexico of late 1916 had cited twenty-nine such events in the Palace between late 1914 and 1916.[12] Despite the Taos society's refusal of unification, it showed an appreciation of Santa Fe's progress in 1918. It elected Edgar Hewett, at whose Palace and museum they exhibited their work, and Frank Springer, whose fund raising and generosity helped make the art museum possible and whose financial help aided artists, to honorary membership in their own group. That same year, the society also elected Jules Rolshoven to active membership (from associate) and Robert Henri to associate membership.[13] Thus, while holding Santa Fe at arm's length, the Taos society apparently had no qualms about permitting entry to persons considered valuable to their own organization and fortunes.

The Museum of New Mexico stood at the forefront of the effort to promote art in Santa Fe. Through its official journal, *El Palacio*, it sought to make its readers aware of the importance of art to the city and New Mexico and of the activities of the artists who painted there. By 1916 no small number of its pages were devoted to such subject matter. It faithfully reported exhibitions that included locally associated painters and sales of their work, while keeping its readers informed of what other publications wrote of them—by citation or reprint of reports and articles.

From the last years of the 1900–1910 period through the 1920s, *El Palacio* developed a style of reporting, the purpose of which was to enhance knowledge of Santa Fe, and to a lesser extent, Taos, in the American art world. In its hopes and endeavors to advance the area as a culture source and disseminator, the editors readily printed the most optimistic utterances and projections. In its enthusiasm, it cited artist Walter Ufer's views of the Southwest, that "Here, some day will be written the great American opera, the great American novel, the great American epic."[14] It even compared the activities of the American Academy in Rome with its counterpart in Santa Fe and referred to the "Imperial City of Rome and in *ancient* [authors' emphasis] Santa Fe."[15]

El Palacio's editors persistently pointed out artists' ties to both New Mexican towns, which remained linked in print despite the early reticence of the Taos contingent. It employed a form of identification in which clauses such as O. E. Berninghaus, "who spent his summers at Taos," or works by Henri, "which he painted at Santa Fe last summer," or a portrait by Dunton, "first exhibited at the Museum at Santa Fe," became standard fare. When Taos and Santa Fe artists did not win a prize at a particular exhibition, the journal felt compelled to note that "they have been so much represented among the winners the past few years that . . . [they] are ineligible for most of the honors."[16]

In a similar vein, *El Palacio* sought to give any artists who had ever worked in Santa Fe or in New Mexico a stamp of permanent association for the greater glory of the city. In an offhand comment it compared a George Bellows painting (he did not particularly favor Santa Fe) on exhibit at the Pennsylvania Academy to a Rembrandt painting and drew notice that "whether one visits the staid Pennsylvania Academy . . . the men who paint at Santa Fe are to the fore. . . ."[17] The gratuitous nature of such observations, which abounded, indicated the purposes of the editors. As they had done with archaeology, they sought to portray Santa Fe and New Mexico on a par with great centers of art. Hewett's vague evaluation, that Santa Fe "is sometimes spoken of as the intellectual capital of the Southwest—to its region what Alexandria was at its age" exemplifies that attitude and objective.[18]

Exaggeration notwithstanding, the picture presented by *El Palacio* through the early twenties did depict the growth of the artists' community and activity in the city. Hewett, in his annual report for 1920, counted some eighty artists who had worked in New Mexico since the art museum opened in 1918—an impressive number for a small city.[19] The effect of its distilled and concentrated reporting gave readers the sense of a hive of activity. Indeed, for towns the size of Santa Fe and Taos that impression was accurate enough.

However, while *El Palacio*'s reporting informed its limited readership (they appeared to be largely members of the local archaeological society), it did not critically evaluate the work of its adopted cohort of artists. It praised the New Mexican content of their work and reported their successes in terms of prizes and exhibits. Its standards appeared to be set mainly by how favorably the artists' works represented Santa Fe and New Mexico.

By contrast, journals and newspapers surveyed by *El Palacio* often provided a somewhat different picture. Through their art critics, these publications discussed art by standards of criticism rather than by an artist's relationship to a particular region of the country. Although such artists as Henri were highly respected in the East, a New York critic could remark, for example, that he depended too much on formulae and that he did that "to save time, a thing valued above art."[20] The sharp-eyed editors of *El Palacio* felt obliged to defend the erstwhile Santa Fe resident, retorting, "In his best work Henri strives for truth and not to save time."[21]

Moreover, looking at the world of art broadly and historically, the Eastern commentators did not necessarily regard those who painted in Santa Fe as either the products or cultural property of that city. They separated painters from locale and sometimes from content, concentrating on style to make their judgments. But once *El Palacio* applied the glue of association it became permanent. The fact of residence became material to aid in the enhancement of Santa Fe as an art center. It advertised, but did not criticize.

Despite the differing emphases and standards of *El Palacio* and major art publications elsewhere, the effect of the art exhibitions and their reviews was to spread knowledge of New Mexico and awareness of its growing status as a place where art was produced. The content of the images spread visual impressions of the region, supplementing the well-established efforts of the Santa Fe railroad and the Fred Harvey chain of hotels in doing so. The honors some of the artists accrued did attest to their quality and added prestige to and interest in the area.

Popular journals brought both art and the region to life for readers. Writing in *Scribner's Magazine* in 1916, Ernest Peixotto described the Taos Society of Artists and asked why "moderns" in their search for the primitive had not studied Acoma and Zuni villages instead of looking to Polynesia. In the next issue, the same author also described Santa Fe in romantic imagery, dwelling on its historic and ethnic qualities, as well as its scenic beauty, in terms that would have satisfied any tourist promotion agency.[22]

In 1923, Santa Fe's art activity and museum once again received favorable attention from *Scribner's.* The friendly reception of artists, the emphasis on American art as expressed in the heritage of the Spanish conquest, and a continuing presence of relatively undisturbed Native Americans, the work of Springer and Hewett, as well as the climate and scenery all received plaudits.[23] Hewett himself could not have asked for more.

It may be impossible to measure how much the artists and the museum contributed to knowledge about Santa Fe and eventually to tourism. The work of the artists long remained more of an export matter than a product for local consumption. At the very least, however, such articles attracted the attention of travelers interested in the arts and broadened the reputation of the city from its narrower base as an archaeological center. Still regarded as exotic, Santa Fe was gaining recognition as a place where art was welcomed and created. That reputation became a part of its new heritage.

Santa Fe's growth as an art center derived from the creative urges of the artists inspired by the cultural and physical atmosphere of northern New Mexico and the city. That part of the story reflected the effect of New Mexico on the artists themselves. In turn, their presence in Santa Fe had a variety of consequences for the city. Not only did their work contribute a new cultural dimension locally, but their perceptions and activities fostered a sense of awareness among Santa Feans of their own environment, artistic and social.

The sense of community among some of the artists, particularly those who stayed for a long time, resulted in neighborhoods of common residence in the early twenties. The most compact and best known "artist quarter" grew up along Telephone Road (renamed Camino del Monte Sol), some distance southeast of the Plaza. The street name change reflected continuing efforts and the growing success of the forces seeking to retain the city's Spanish flavor.[24] There, a number of young artists, many of whom arrived in the late teens and early twenties and were bound by limited means, designed and built their own adobe houses. Ina Sizer Cassidy, wife of painter Gerald Cassidy, described the process as a necessity if Santa Fe was truly to have an art colony.[25]

Longtime artist-resident Will Shuster, more inclined to consider the perspective of struggling artists than the destiny of Santa Fe, attributed the growth of the new area to the need to survive economically and artistically.[26] It was here, in 1921, that five of the house builders organized themselves into an aforementioned group named Los Cinco Pintores.[27] Although their organizational identity lasted only about five years, their activities remain permanently embedded in the art history of Santa Fe.

The presence of working artists contributed to the artistic riches of the city. Their often shaky economic condition led them to barter their works for medical services and life's necessities.[28] The role of the museum in this process of enrichment, however, was especially noteworthy. Because the Taos society and the Santa Fe painters frequently exhibited in the museum first, those residents interested in acquiring art had an early opportunity to view and purchase these works. By 1918 exhibitions of locally owned art were taking place at the museum. Wealthier Santa Feans, often members of the archaeological society or leading civic organizations, purchased Taos society members' works and, to a lesser extent, apparently, those of artists close to the museum. At the Third New Mexico Loan Exhibition in 1921, James and Arthur Seligman, T. B. Catron, Levi A. Hughes, and I. H. Rapp were among those who showed such paintings in their possession.[29]

Many artists, and particularly those who remained permanently in Santa Fe, involved themselves in the life of the community, leaving their mark upon it by virtue of their assorted talents. The annual celebration of events surrounding the Spanish reconquest in 1693, the Fiesta, gained special attention after World War I as a community-wide affair. Will Shuster, first in 1926 and for nearly four decades thereafter, designed Zozobra, Old Man Gloom, whose immolation represented the destruction of woes for the past year and served as an important event in the celebration. In 1964 he assigned his rights in Zozobra to the Santa Fe Downtown Kiwanis Club.[30]

Some of the artists, Shuster among them, were an active element in the social life of the town through their sense of fun. In the twenties, the era of Prohibition, he and others created their own supply of illegal spirits to enliven their gatherings. The artists not only amused themselves but frequently joined tourists and their Santa Fe friends in revelry at the La Fonda Hotel or at Bishop's Lodge, where, Shuster's biographer tells us, "artists were the official court jesters."[31] The artists' behavior may also have been motivated by the prospect of sales to the visitors as well as by their own enjoyment. Whatever their purpose, such activities contributed to a permanent body of lore about the city.

Artists also contributed to the broader cultural life of the town. Mary Austin, a writer who visited Santa Fe in 1918 and was a strong advocate of community theater, may have been the driving force that induced Gustave Baumann, Carlos

Vierra, Sheldon Parsons, and others to contribute stage settings to the first performance of the new company in February 1919.[32]

In their efforts to supplement marginal incomes as well as to promote art, some of the artists engaged in enterprises that helped create Santa Fe's reputation as a place to find and buy art. In 1919 the Santa Fe Print Shop opened its doors, an early outlet for the exhibition and sale of locally produced art. Co-owned by Alice Corbin Henderson, the wife of artist William P. Henderson, the gallery solicited works by such erstwhile Santa Feans as Marsden Hartley, who gave his stamp of approval to the gallery.[33] Artists Andrew Dasburg, Wladyslaw Mruk, B. J. O. Nordfeldt, with poet Witter Bynner and Mabel Dodge's son, John Evans, founded the Spanish and Indian Trading Post in 1926—the same year that saw the Harvey Southwestern Indian Detours inaugurated.[34]

The artists also fostered the local art scene through their interest in the symbols, crafts, and artifacts of Native Americans and Hispanos. They were not the first to notice the attractions of Native American pictorial and craft work. The Santa Fe railroad, as agent for tourism, had long promoted interest in indigenous material culture, just as it had engaged painters to depict the Western landscape. Indian traders at reservations had sold Navajo blankets to tourists in some volume after the railroad arrived; by the end of the nineteenth century, they were being used as rugs.[35] By 1902 Harvey's Alvarado Hotel in Albuquerque had amassed a considerable collection of such articles. Even Santa Fe curio shops had long sold and displayed such native items and merchant Abe Spiegelberg had published an article for tourists about Navajo blankets as early as 1904.[36]

In the second decade of the century, the archaeological activity of the museum, as well as the acumen of the artists who realized the artistic importance of the native arts and crafts, fostered production as well as preservation. The discovery of prehistoric mural fragments in Frijoles Canyon inspired Native American laborers to emulate their ancestors. Under the urging of Kenneth Chapman early in the century, Hewett invited Native American craftsmen to the museum where interaction with their fellows from other Pueblo communities as well as contact with American painters advanced the work of the Pueblo artists.[37]

Santa Fe artists were active both in making these Native Americans' works visible and upholding their quality. John Sloan even arranged an exhibit of their watercolors in New York in 1920. Recognizing the artistic merit of their work, he placed it in an artistic rather than an historical or anthropological setting.[38] Then, in the mid-twenties, the artists in Santa Fe and Taos, along with writers and patrons, created the Indian Arts Fund to protect the Pueblo heritage against a major onslaught of tourists threatening to empty the area of vintage objects and to encourage inferior work because of its very popularity.[39]

The aesthetic vision of the artists and writers, and their interaction with

8. J. S. Candelario, Santa Fe curio dealer.
Courtesy Museum of New Mexico, neg. #145763.

other creative persons, also enabled them to bring the crafts of Hispano culture to the attention of the Anglo public. For the Hispanos, religion served as the enduring spark that inspired and maintained their craft in sculpture, while their need for home furnishings supported such activities as furniture making.[40] Although curio shops in Santa Fe had long collected and sold such items and Hispanos had engaged in preserving their historic monuments as early as 1913, it was Frank Applegate, Mary Austin, and John Gaw Meem, the architect, who legitimized the Hispano crafts for Anglo use in Santa Fe from the mid-twenties on. They were instrumental in creating organizations to foster preservation of every aspect of Hispano arts in Santa Fe. Austin, working closely with Applegate, organized the Spanish Colonial Arts Society and a competition "for modern examples of Spanish Colonial arts and crafts, open to any native New Mexican of Spanish descent."[41] They sponsored a Spanish Market in conjunction with the yearly Fiesta to promote and sell such native crafts. Meem and Austin added their skills and energies to the Society for the Preservation and Restoration of New Mexico Missions after 1924.[42] And Meem learned, as he began to build "Santa Fe-style" residences in the mid-twenties, that Hispano stylistic details and furnishings complemented well the interior of his structures. He utilized the skills of the Hispano craftsmen to good effect.[43]

The production of literature on the West, including the Southwest, accompanied the entire history of the American westward movement. The Santa Fe Trail, along with its terminus, had elicited a heavy volume of description. Archaeology and Indian lore in New Mexico had received literary treatment from such figures as Adolph Bandelier and Charles Lummis in the 1880s and 1890s, but at that time their efforts involved no special recognition of Santa Fe. As archaeology assumed a concrete institutional form in the museum and School of American Archaeology and as resident artists turned their attentions to the Native American, it was inevitable that Santa Fe itself would also become grist for the writers' mills.

The earlier writers devoted to Native Americans and the city itself arrived in a manner reminiscent of the artists. Alice Corbin Henderson's tuberculosis kept her in Santa Fe, along with her artist husband, William Penhollow Henderson. Her former position as an editor of the journal *Poetry* provided access to a wide circle of acquaintances and made its pages available to writing on the area, the Native Americans, and the city. In 1912, Ina Sizer Cassidy, wife of painter Gerald Cassidy, accompanied him in moving to Santa Fe from Albuquerque, where he had gone earlier for his health. She performed functions similar to those of Alice Henderson with great dedication.

The writers, like the artists, found a ready-made home for their talents and

9. L. to R.: James Forrest, Ina Sizer Cassidy, and John Pogzeba, conservator, with Gerald Cassidy's Coronado mural. Courtesy Museum of New Mexico, neg. #49479.

interests through the success of the local archaeological enterprise. By 1917 Hewett could well consider that he had laid a strong foundation for his work. The creation of the museum reflected the climax of his accomplishments. What loomed ahead was the opening of a broader field of cultural activity than archaeology alone offered. To support that new emphasis, the School of American Archaeology was renamed the School of American Research. Hewett, in his annual report for the year 1918, made it clear that he included within its purview "anthropology, ethnology, psychology, sociology, art, history, religion—in fact the entire group of subjects that proceed from the study of man."[44] Writers of every variety who loved the Native Americans of the pueblos and the Southwest and found Santa Fe admirable readily lent support to enhance the area.

The incoming writers found an open door for their skills in *El Palacio.* Its pages opened quite modestly to poetry in 1916:

"In old Santa Fe,
Throw your care far away,
There is healing for the race,
Look into my smiling face,
In my face,
In my face," says the Sun
In Santa Fe.[45]

Thus ran one of the first verses published, ushering in the "writers" era. Reviews of works on poetry, especially those in which Alice Corbin Henderson had a hand, received space, with comment that she was "now a resident of Santa Fe."[46] A year later, in July 1917, a segment of the journal entitled "Art and Literary Colony" appeared, providing writers, as had been done for artists, with recognition of an "official" place in the abundant cultural sunshine of the city.

Perhaps by the nature of their enterprise, writers were less bound to the institutional structure of Santa Fe than artists. The strictures of museum or gallery space did not apply to them. The number of publications in which they could publish were legion. They could enlighten an audience many times larger than that available to artists or scholarly archaeological publications and thus bring fame to Native Americans, to Santa Fe, or the Southwest on a scale heretofore not possible.

Writers, however, arrived more slowly than painters. Nevertheless, during the twenties poet Witter Bynner and novelist-essayist Mary Austin became permanent fixtures. They invited acquaintances to lecture or visit and added luster to the circle of residents. Carl Sandburg, who was close to Alice Henderson, came twice. Robert Frost came too, invited by Bynner, but he and his host became embroiled in a squabble that led to Bynner pouring a mug of beer on Frost's head![47]

Willa Cather also came, many times, starting long before the writer-settlers arrived. Unlike the other visitors, she used Santa Fe as material for her work, publishing *Death Comes for the Archbishop* in 1927, with the life of Archbishop Lamy serving as the centerpiece of the subject matter. This novel, however, displeased Indian and Hispano advocate Mary Austin, at whose home Cather occasionally worked. Austin disliked the French prelate and his French cathedral and one departed from her beloved cultural standards at some risk.[48] But Cather, like Sandburg and Frost, was not bound to Santa Fe by residence, scenery, or subject matter as were the local writers.

By virtue of their talents and medium, the writers became powerful advocates for Santa Fe and those ethnic traits that defined the city and its surrounding area. They reached one early peak of outreach in 1922 when they joined hands with artists, archaeologists, and Native American benefactors on the national stage to fight a congressional bill sponsored by Senator Holm Bursum of New Mexico, which, in their eyes, threatened the Pueblos with both loss of land and their communal existence. The *New Republic*, then an influential national journal, published their appeals and joined their cause with telling effect.[49] Many other prominent journals and newspapers in New York joined the campaign in sympathy.[50] Their actions inevitably drew attention to Santa Fe, New Mexico, and the Native Americans' cause.

Within Santa Fe, the creative community also showed that it could carry considerable weight on occasion. One such event occurred in the mid-twenties over the so-called "Chautauqua" affair. By that time the "culture bearers" had been joined permanently by Mary Austin, who became a force to ensure that the creative community in the city maintained the standards that she and they held dear. There was probably no one who matched her as such a voice in the decade 1924 to 1934, the last of her life, during which time she acquired the sobriquet of "God's mother-in-law."[51]

Austin went far beyond her fellows in her vision of what the area should be. Regarding herself as something of a prophet, she envisioned an American acculturation that she termed "Amerindian," in which an evolving American culture combined with Native American and Hispano rootedness to produce a new cultural synthesis. No less a literary figure than Carl Van Doren accepted her vision of herself.[52] Although her local colleagues did not always agree with her, she was a most determined advocate for Native American and Hispano arts and crafts in various forms as well as for keeping Santa Fe the kind of town it was becoming by the time of her residence.

In 1926 Austin fought successfully to keep the Chautauqua colony out of the city. Writing in *New Republic*, she claimed precedence for Santa Fe over New York as "the capital of creative effort in the Americas." She defined two types of community culture: an activist community that worked through individuals to produce cultural achievement, and a passive community that existed chiefly to hear about what had been produced by others. Seeing an example of the latter type in Chautauqua, a popular adult education movement that contained nothing "out of which golden centuries are made," she proudly labeled Santa Fe "the town that wouldn't have a Chautauqua."[53] *The Nation* backed her stance with an editorial.[54] Perhaps only a writer could have stated the case for the city's artistic purity of purpose as well as she, although her point of view about banning Chautauqua occasioned a considerable conflict within the city itself.

Austin's position and victory spelled a high point for the writers and artists. To the outside world, at least, she and her fellows created the image that Santa Fe was their jewel, a place, as an impressed *New York Times* editorial put it,

10. Mary Austin, Santa Fe, 1932.
Courtesy Museum of New Mexico, neg. #16754. Photo by Will Connell.

"where there is timeless leisure and where Americans are not ashamed to enjoy natural beauty for its own sake."[55]

Writers other than those living in Santa Fe, picked up on and contributed to the growing awareness of the city and the state. A sizable fictional literature began to appear using both locales as backdrop. Some involved Santa Fe as part of the Anglo West, a major subject matter for the American reading public. In the twenties and thirties, Santa Fe drew the writers' attentions in its own right. In addition to Willa Cather, such literary personages as Paul Horgan (*No Quarter Given*, 1935), Aldous Huxley (*Brave New World*, 1932), and D. H. Lawrence (*St. Mawr*; together with *The Princess*, 1925) used the city in their works. By World War II over thirty novels had appeared in which Santa Fe provided at least an important part of the landscape.[56] Untold thousands read of it and formed impressions that contributed to knowledge of and interest in the town.

Histories of the Santa Fe art colony often assign its "golden age" to the period occurring roughly between the two world wars.[57] If one considers the constant presence of some of the resident artists and writers as a thread of continuity, that periodization may hold. However, the economic problems that split that era in half into a time of prosperity and one of major depression belie that unity. The Depression did not strike Santa Fe with greater force than many other places. Nevertheless, its effects forced accommodations upon the artistic community that differentiated their activities in the twenties from those in the thirties.

Scholars of art history during the Depression point out some of the general problems. Between 1929 and 1933 the market index price of paintings fell by two-thirds, severely reducing the income of artists. The decline in art purchases even led to a steep drop in the production of artists' materials—by almost half. Such conditions reflected the powerful effects of the economic crisis and seemed to numb many art producers.[58]

Artists and society were thrown into a new relationship to each other. The link between wealthy purchasers and artists weakened. Artists' organizations began to view the government as the agency to improve their straitened conditions and to produce a new impetus in art. Influential artists, such as George Biddle, approached the newly elected president, Franklin Roosevelt, with ideas of supporting artists by having them produce murals for public buildings—a concept Biddle borrowed from the experience of the great Mexican muralists, Diego Rivera and José Clemente Orozco, in the 1920s.[59]

Thus, social conscience and government receptivity and support, as well as hard times for the artists, combined to create a unique relationship between government and artists, and to a lesser extent, with writers. Starting with the Public

Works of Art Project in 1933 and proceeding to the Treasury Section of Painting and Sculpture in 1934, the Treasury Relief Art Project in 1935, the Works Progress Administration's Federal Art Project in 1935, and the Work Project Administration's Art Program in 1939, the federal government designed programs to utilize artists for a variety of purposes and to provide relief for them.[60] These programs encouraged them to exercise their talents in media comfortable to them and included a broad spectrum of expression. They painted murals in public buildings, worked on easels, did lithographs and sculptures, and performed stylistic classifications and historical arrangements. Only with the coming of the Second World War did the programs cease.

New Mexico, too, experienced the pain of the Depression and Santa Fe's artists suffered the same hardships as their fellows elsewhere. Because of the town's relative geographic isolation, many depended on outside galleries and traveling exhibitions for the sale of their work and felt keenly the effects of the economic downturn. The slowing of tourist traffic, a second source of livelihood, also adversely affected their economic condition. The considerable literature on Santa Fe artists makes plain their painful plight.[61]

Santa Fe's growth as a cultural center and its political position as capital of New Mexico combined to assure it a leading role in the new relationship between government and artist. When the Public Works of Art Project (PWAP) was established in December 1933, regional committees were set up to implement its goals. New Mexico and Arizona together formed a single region, with its first committee including Jesse L. Nusbaum as director, Kenneth Chapman as secretary, and Gustave Baumann as area coordinator—all old-line figures of the Santa Fe art and museum scene. Among its members were John Gaw Meem, Mary Austin, and Bronson Cutting—a Santa Fe sweep.[62] Santa Feans continued to play an important, if not so dominant a role, in government programs throughout the Depression years.

Similarly, the artists chosen to execute the projects illustrate Santa Fe's strong position among the state's artists in the PWAP. Of fifty-one participating artists in New Mexico, twenty-five bore the Santa Fe label. Among the best known were Gerald Cassidy, Randall Davey, Fremont Ellis, William P. Henderson, Raymond Jonson, Paul Lantz, Willard Nash, Olive Rush, Will Shuster, and Theodore Van Soelen.[63] The town's artistic preeminence in the state was clear.

The government programs produced new emphases among the Santa Fe artists. To a greater extent than before, individual interest and wealthy patrons gave way to projects created for public interest. The town's artists decorated government buildings not only in Santa Fe but all over the state. While William P. Henderson painted panels for Santa Fe's federal building, Paul Lantz decorated a post office in Clovis, Theodore Van Soelen a post office mural in

Portales, and Raymond Jonson painted murals for the University of New Mexico in Albuquerque.[64] Such examples can be expanded manyfold.

The cultural legislation of the New Deal forced a measure of stylistic change on some artists. The Depression generally pushed artists' concerns toward realist representations based on life in American cities or regional culture, while drawing away from the abstract style of modernist painting.[65] Santa Fe in particular, because of the modernists there, experienced more change in style than in content. In fact, the subject matter of the New Mexican artists changed little, perhaps because it was already heavily centered on the "folk" of the area and less abstract than some of the more venturesome artists of the capital city. However, Raymond Jonson, a Santa Fe modernist, spoke of the hardships of the time for the abstractionists who reverted to objective painting, pressured by economic conditions and inability to exhibit their works.[66] Author Sharyn Udall ended her volume on modernist painting in New Mexico in 1935 because the government, as patron, she concluded, "shortchanged abstract painting" and encouraged innovators "to abandon such unpopular endeavors."[67] Although modernism at that time was not a powerful trend in New Mexico and did not assume the extreme forms exhibited in some large urban centers, the Depression appeared to suppress what there was of it.

The resident writers' mark on Santa Fe during the Depression, as during the twenties, did not prove as strong as that of the artists. Art, architecture, and the physical scenery all depended on a visual dimension that the printed word could only supplement. Yet the writers conveyed their thought in a medium that reached far and wide and received governmental recognition and support in the Depression years. The Federal Writers' Project created in 1935 was a major expression of the perceived need to record and to understand New Mexico. For a time, Ina Sizer Cassidy directed this program.

Many of those who wrote found no sharp boundary between the twenties and thirties. Yet, the effects of the Depression and the increased importance of economic issues focused attention on those matters, which had not concerned writers in Santa Fe as much in the earlier decade. New literary personages and writers came, although relatively few long-term residents were among them. Harvard professor F. O. Matthiessen spent some time in 1934 and 1935 in Santa Fe.[68] He reported on what became a famous strike in Gallup in the latter year.

Other writers may well have contributed to a small left-wing presence that developed in Santa Fe during their stay. Among them were Philip and Janet Stevenson, who lived in Santa Fe and Taos intermittently between 1930 and 1936. For a time, the city even had a John Reed Club, to which they may have belonged, since Philip Stevenson was identified as a national officer in 1938.[69] Fascinated by the Gallup strike, Stevenson wrote *The Seed*, a multi-volume work about the event and New Mexico that appeared many years later. Even after the Stevensons' departure, a modicum of left-wing activity continued in the city. In 1937, the *New Mexican* reported that a workers' lending library was opening on San Francisco Street under the auspices of the state's Communist Party. It was the second time for such an event, the paper noted.[70]

Architecture, as a part of the creative and restorative vision that emerged before World War I in Santa Fe, reached a measure of fulfillment before World War II. The earlier architects and artists, the Rapp brothers, Carlos Vierra, and Jesse Nusbaum, had already created or rebuilt the signature landmarks of the Spanish-Pueblo style in the teens. The building of the La Fonda Hotel in 1920 signified the growing vitality of those who sought to make concrete their visual image of the city. In the twenties, they were joined by John Gaw Meem, who became its best-known and most prolific executor.

Meem arrived in Santa Fe in 1920 in need of a sanatorium. An engineer by training, he soon became fascinated with the phenomenon of southwestern restoration and creation. At Sunmount Sanatorium he met other interested parties, persons of means or those known to them, and Carlos Vierra, who taught him much about the old style.[71] By 1924 he had embarked on his new career in architecture and left a remarkable legacy in Santa Fe as well as other New Mexico and even Colorado locations over several decades, including major buildings at the University of New Mexico in Albuquerque.

Meem's homes and public buildings in the twenties and thirties ensured a lasting powerful statement for those who treasured the Spanish-Pueblo (or Santa Fe) style. Starting in the mid-twenties such affluent or well-known residents as Mrs. Ashley Pond, Dr. J. R. Rolls, Mary Austin, Raymond Jonson, and Ferdinand Koch commissioned him to build residences for them. Public structures such as the Church of the Holy Faith, the Manderfield School, the Laboratory of Anthropology, and the remodeling of the La Fonda Hotel added to his mark on the city in that decade.[72] Despite hard times, a continuing stream of new Meem architectural landmarks appeared in the thirties. By World War II, his works had earned him a high place among those who sought to fashion the city as a monument to its past (with appropriate adaptations to the present).

Even as Santa Fe reached a high point in its reformation as an archaeological and art center, rather than as a trade center, those who had labored to recreate it in that image passed from the scene. In 1925, Ralph Twitchell, whose histories of the state and city were landmarks that still demand attention, died.[73] Two years later, Benjamin M. Read, a similarly minded student of New Mexico's Hispano history, passed away.[74] And among those who had labored to create an archaeological center in Santa Fe, Frank Springer in 1927 and John McFie in 1930, also died.[75] It is difficult to imagine that the course of history they sought for Santa Fe would have succeeded without their devoted efforts.

The work of the archaeologists, artists, writers, architects, and their supporters in the teens and twenties produced a permanent legacy in masonry, imagery, and print that could not be erased. It was their love of the town and its physical and human environment that lent it an aura of relaxed freedom and ethnic toleration and appreciation that would attract increasing numbers of persons in the postwar period. By their interests and concern they also roused persons already resident to express themselves as a part of the growing awareness of the arts and crafts. Moreover, there were a fair number of persons among them committed to the policy of keeping the historic elements of Santa Fe intact and building on that image who outlived both the Depression and World War II and remained steadfast in the virtue of their beliefs. The Depression would place its own stamp on how the people of the city could live, but that would not erase the labor and dreams of the generation that laid the basis for the existence of a "City Different."

SEVEN

Social and Economic Trends, 1880–1929

After the railroad main line escaped them, Santa Feans had to adapt to a changed world. Those who had anticipated increased commerce had to adjust to new conditions with few precedents to guide them. Sizable segments of an older Hispano Santa Fe, still close to their agricultural roots, remained bound to homestead, family, and church. Other segments of the Hispano community, already tied to a changing technology and new material goods, shared a readaptation process together with those Anglos who faced similar problems of adjustment. Except for the city's continuing importance in New Mexican politics, much would stand in question for nearly thirty years.

Deprived of the commerce of the Santa Fe Trail and confronted with unanswerable economic competition from Las Vegas and Albuquerque, the city slid into an unfamiliar business climate. That condition was marked not only by the disappearance of its major wholesale enterprises in the eighties and nineties but also by changes in the character of the business community itself. By the turn of the century the city had become one that hosted relatively small firms catering primarily to the local population. In 1897, the financial ratings of Bradstreet revealed that the city had only two enterprises with a capitalization of over $400,000. One was the Continental Oil Co., based in Denver, and the other, the old Staab company, which, having outlived its former locally based competitors, was not far from its own demise. Of thirty-six remaining firms rated in the city all were listed with capital of less than $35,000. A rough calculation of value in terms of today's dollar is a multiple of sixteen.

Changes in credit practices spurred changes in business itself. The rapidity with which goods became available by rail and the resultant shorter period of time necessary to settle accounts, as well as a changed consumer base altered by the loss of the old wholesale trade, encouraged specialization. General merchandise establishments fragmented into smaller components such as grocery stores, clothing stores, and dry goods firms. This process of small business growth occurred simultaneously with a population decline during the period 1880–1910. Between 1880 and 1900 there was a drop of about 27 percent in the number of wholesale and retail dealers in Santa Fe, a rate greater than the fall in population. Between 1900 and 1910, still the period of slowly declining population, the number of dealers rose again to the prior level of 1880. In essence, this represented a considerable increase in the number of smaller enterprises for the entire period relative to the size of the population.

After 1910 population growth resumed. From 5,072 persons in that year, it grew to 7,236 by 1920 and experienced a robust expansion to 11,176 by 1930.[1] In effect the city's population doubled between 1910 and 1930. The credit rating agencies confirm a commensurate picture of business growth. Bradstreet listed ninety-four firms in 1897, Dun noted 106 in 1915, and Bradstreet's list for 1925 tallied 162. By that time the town's regrowth and prosperity were fully evident.

11. Hay haulers at the Plaza, ca. 1913.
Courtesy Museum of New Mexico, neg. #61545. Photo by Jesse Nusbaum.

As general stores had slowly declined, the trend toward small food distributors increased. The great majority of groceries, meat markets, and fruit and produce sellers, insofar as they achieved credit ratings at all, were at the lowest levels of credit, arbitrarily at $5,000 or less. Grocer H. B. Cartwright, an Anglo, had the largest rated food distribution firm in 1897 with a capitalization of between $10,000 and $20,000. No one else in that field approached his wealth.

Men's and women's clothing stores (the latter appeared later), shoe stores, and especially dry goods establishments, all increased throughout the period. This indicated not only specialization of business, but also the increasing availability and use of manufactured goods. In 1897, the use of the term "dry goods" appeared in Bradstreet's rating of Santa Fe enterprises only once, while in Dun's 1915 report it appeared three times and in the New Mexico State Business Directory of 1916, six times. In the Bradstreet volume for 1925, the term appeared eight times. The formerly great wholesale house and general store of the Seligmans was listed as a dealer in dry goods in 1916. Still a large house in 1915, with a rating in Dun's of over $20,000, it had fallen to that level from the highest ratings available a quarter-century earlier.

The appearance of smaller, more numerous enterprises may have had a decentralizing effect on the town. With larger stores disappearing, the greater convenience of local shops meant that neighborhoods became less dependent on the city's center. Instead, where traditional homestead, extended family, and church already existed, the new shopping facilities enabled accustomed ways to continue without undue inconvenience. Increasingly, grocery stores belonged to Hispano proprietors on Canyon Road and Agua Fria Street, and others, at some distance from the Plaza.[2] By 1910 almost half of all Hispano dealers in the city engaged in the sale of food.

In 1912 New Mexico graduated formally from territorial status to that of a full-fledged state. As the capital, Santa Fe could not but feel the effects of its altered circumstances. When the U.S. Senate passed the statehood resolution on 18 August 1911, the whistles of the *New Mexican*, the Santa Fe Water and Light Co. and the fire company greeted the event with sheer delight. The paper's editorial equated the event with the coming of "self-reliance, independence, manhood" for the state and forecast an influx of new capital and development of material resources.[3] For the city, it envisioned the future with great potential as well as a warning:

> If Santa Fe during the next ten years does not become the largest and wealthiest city of the Southwest it will be because the people do not

deserve it because they have not made the proper united intelligent effort.[4]

Statehood, it would appear, was expected to give a new and badly needed impetus to the city such as it had not experienced in decades.

One facet of Santa Fe's changed condition derived from the new duties and powers of state government. The teen years witnessed the transfer of existing government agencies from territorial to state form. Increased independence transformed them from limited extensions of federal power into full-fledged administrative units. In addition, many new cabinet posts, boards, and commissions emerged as the state assumed responsibility for its expanded duties.

One effect of these changes was a marked increase in the number of resident government employees. In 1910 there were only 79 persons working in all three branches of government—federal, territorial, and local. Ten years later that number had more than tripled to 259.[5] In the still small town of the second decade of the century these increases amounted to a noticeable shift in how Santa Feans made their living. While only four percent of the labor force worked for all levels of government in 1910, that portion had risen to ten percent by 1920.

Between 1920 and 1928, the last full year before the Depression, the total number of government employees in the city continued to grow, although more slowly, from 259 to 354.[6] During this period most of that growth occurred among employees of state government living in Santa Fe, while federal and local government employment remained constant. By 1928, just under two-thirds of all government employees living in the city worked for the state. Clearly, state employment was assuming a powerful place in the town's economy.

After 1910, when population growth recommenced, Santa Fe showed signs of change shared by the country at large. There was sufficient wealth in Santa Fe to take advantage of the appearance of the automobile. By 1915 there were repair garages for the new vehicles; by 1925, auto sales, vulcanizing shops, and motorized delivery services became sufficiently numerous to make the entire technology an accepted fact of life. In 1926, *New Mexican* editorials sought regulation of parking around the Plaza—perhaps the surest sign of the technology's growth through use.[7] In addition, although curio shops had already been present in 1880, by the mid-twenties they had grown in number, advertised manufactured Native American goods, and were part of the great new direction of tourism that Santa Fe had begun to pursue actively.

The history of the First National Bank of Santa Fe reflected a gradual trend toward interest in the city itself. Founded in 1870 by Lucien B. Maxwell, the fabled holder of the Maxwell land grant that covered a large portion of northeastern New Mexico, the bank quickly became a territorial instrument of finance. In 1871 José L. Perea, Stanley Elkins, M. A. Otero, T. B. Catron, and W. W. Griffin comprised the largest stockholders, reflecting ranching, mercantile, and landholding interests. By the turn of the century the ownership of the Bank was changing, shifting to persons with primary interests in the city.[8] In 1905 the board of directors included locally prominent merchants Solomon Spitz, a jeweler, and John Schumann, a shoe store owner. By 1910 Levi Hughes, a wool and hides entrepreneur and Arthur Seligman, a general merchandise dealer had joined them as board members. At that time Seligman, Schumann, and Spitz were also among the bank's major stockholders.[9]

Although the bank had made loans to a variety of enterprises from its early days, sheep and cattle ranchers had been the mainstay of its lending operations. As local businessmen became the heart of the bank, city business enterprises became increasingly prominent in loan procurement, even though ranchers still remained within the purview of the bank's financial interest. In 1905, the bank made its larger loans to such well-known locals as C. W. Dudrow, Adolph Seligman, H. S Kaune, H. B. Cartwright, and Dr. W. S. Harroun.[10] To some extent, the city was replacing the territory as the focal point of the bank's attentions.

The entwining of bank and city interests continued into the second decade of the century. By 1915 the board of directors was composed primarily of Santa Fe businessmen. Moreover, the bank took actions that drew it close to those people who envisioned the city as a center of archaeological study and architectural preservation. In 1911 the board chose I. H. Rapp (who would design the art museum several years later), as architect for its own new building.[11] And when Rufus Palen died in 1916, the board promptly chose Paul A. F. Walter, a stalwart supporter and coworker of Edgar Hewett, as his replacement.[12] The bank was poised to participate in the changing image of the city even in the early stages of its formation.

The decade of the teens also marked a turning point in the physical growth of the city. The relatively small area described by the incorporation of 1891 and the much larger patent granted by Congress in 1900 to the boundary of the Santa Fe Grant had left an unreconciled difference in the city's definition of its boundary. That distinction was not erased for a generation. In 1912 the city planning committee report to the city council recommended extending the city limits to the extent of the Grant.[13] However, no action took place until 1917. At that time the city council enacted an ordinance to provide for a clear definition of city property within the Santa Fe Grant that was not claimed for deeds and was available for sale, even by public auction.[14] A clause requiring action in ninety days, suggested some sense of urgency. The opportunities presented both for private development and for a city with an increasing growth rate probably induced the changed attitude.

The final step in uniting the Grant and incorporation limits came in 1919. Perhaps the outbreak of World War I had contributed to the earlier delay. The council's formal action to extend the city limits stemmed from a desire to facilitate the leasing and managing of city lands, thereby increasing revenue and stimulating growth through improvement of such lands.[15] The council passed an ordinance to that effect and called an election to decide the issue under the rules governing the extension of county seats, of which Santa Fe was one. Residents of the area to be annexed as well as those inside the existing city boundaries were authorized to vote.[16]

The election took place on 26 December 1919. Attracting only a light turnout, the electorate voted for the grant line as the city's boundary by a sizable majority. All four wards accepted the definition of the larger city.[17] Santa Fe now had a boundary that extended nearly three miles in each direction from the plaza. That description would hold for forty years—until the late 1950s.

As noted above, after 1910 the city's population began to increase. However, a significant portion—at least half—of this growth appears to have resulted from the inclusion of the additional land resulting from the extension of the city boundary. According to the U.S. Census of 1920, these accretions occurred after 1910 in each of the four county precincts where city wards were located.[18] From another perspective, it is interesting to note that while the city population grew by 2,164, the county population dropped by 1,904 between 1910 and 1920.[19]

A more telling clarification of these accretions reveals the modesty of the growth. A considerable portion of the persons added to the city by 1920 resided in institutions lying outside the city limits in 1910 but inside its boundaries in 1920. These included the state penitentiary with 322 inmates and the U.S. Indian Industrial School with 426 students, both located in the Second Ward—the southwest quadrant of the city, and St. Catherine Indian Industrial School with 265 students, located in the Third Ward—the northwest quadrant of the town. More than half of the total increase occurred in the Second Ward. These 1,013 institutional residents comprised almost half of the total city growth from 1910 to 1920!

Population on new streets included in the 1920 census also accounted for a sizable portion of the increase. Some 890 persons can be accounted for in these new areas. Thus, the older sections of town scarcely grew, while the new areas, including the above-noted institutions, now were counted in the city proper.

Certainly the volume and nature of the increase, however welcome, did not amount to a boom.

Even during World War I, when consciousness of the conflict underlay every sort of civic activity, the condition of the city did not completely disappear as a topic of concern. By the spring election of 1918, local issues had arisen that drew the attention of the populace. In addition, a body of thought that had arisen in America generally brought new perspectives into play on how to solve urban problems.

Called the Progressive movement, this child of the early twentieth century served as a powerful generator of ideas and action in civic and social affairs. It reflected a desire for solutions to issues that arose out of the great changes the country had undergone since the Civil War. Rapid urbanization and the success of great corporations were two developments that drew the Progressives' attention. To deal with the new issues, they sought to engage the citizenry in public affairs and to motivate it to put principles above personal needs.[20]

Even though echoes of the movement reverberated throughout the city, they did not arouse overwhelming support. The *New Mexican*, which had advocated "nonpartisan" city government since 1891 took up the cry for better local governance in 1910 in the spirit of Progressivism. It called for a commission form of rule and a direct primary—efficiency and democracy—rather than the old party-run apparatuses.[21]

Between 1912 and 1928 Republicans dominated the Santa Fe political scene, despite splits within the party on both national and local levels. Politically, Progressivism affected Republican party organization more than that of the Democrats. In 1912 the Progressive Republicans made their local political appearance and joined hands with the Democrats to put forth a Democratic and Citizens ticket. Two of the candidates were of the new political persuasion. Their platform reflected Progressive principles, calling for municipal ownership of public utilities when practicable and a new city charter.[22]

The subsequent elections of the decade, from 1914 to 1918, all carried the earmarks of the Democrat-Progressive alliance. Resolutions in 1914 reiterated the virtues of publicly owned franchises and sympathy for a commission form of government.[23] In 1916 these same themes, as well as a call for voters to choose on the issue of private or public utility ownership, a budget system with published quarterly reports, and a call for city lands within the Santa Fe Grant to produce revenue for the city, headed the platform.[24]

In 1918, with the water utility franchise coming up for renewal, the issue of ownership became important. The Democrat-Independent platform of that year allowed for an extension of the franchise but sought greater control over utility policies. This time there was a call for a city manager. Still in the midst of World War I, the ticket bravely sought prosecution of the war to a successful conclusion.[25] Only that demand, the least meaningful one in terms of local reality, met with great success in the shortest time. By 1920 demands for the far-reaching urban reforms were fading in the city. Other towns in New Mexico had adopted some or all of them, but the electorate in Santa Fe passed them by. The old Republican organization swept the day.

That the traditional Republicans held on to power reflected the basic conservatism of the city electorate. For a time, in 1914, even the Republicans had taken up the cause of municipal ownership of utilities.[26] By 1916, however, they had backed off partially from this position.[27] And, in early 1918, even the joint Democrat-Citizen forces asked themselves if Santa Fe was ready for such a step. If nothing else, as Judge Hanna had pointed out to a meeting of Democrats, floating a bond issue during the war would be quite a difficult matter.[28]

After the war, Republican domination of city offices continued. No Democrat would serve as mayor between 1912 and 1928. The other citywide offices reflected similar tendencies, with no Democrat winning either the city clerk or treasurer's office. Only in city council races did a Democrat occasionally break through and then only in 1912 and 1924. In the latter year, the Democrats swept the council positions, but by 1926 the Republicans were back in full force.

In the 1912–1928 period, Anglo dominance prevailed in the citywide races. Only in 1912 did a Hispano Republican become mayor. No Hispano served as city treasurer. Before 1920 the city clerk's office favored Hispanos, but from 1920 on Anglos exclusively served in this position.

As in earlier times, ward races for city council reflected a different picture. Wards One and Two strongly favored Hispano candidates for both parties, while Ward Three favored Anglo candidates just as sharply. Ward Four came closest to a split with victorious Anglo candidates just edging out a number of Hispanos. Overall, Hispano candidates who ran and councilmen who were elected outnumbered Anglos.

■ In 1918 the twenty-five–year franchise of the Santa Fe Water and Light Company with the city expired. Some Santa Feans, in line with Progressive thought and concerned over questions of supply and service, as well as the cost of water, raised the issue of municipal ownership of the facility. Although the Company declared itself willing to sell, ultimately, the bonding capacity of the city to finance the transaction proved to be too low to meet the price. That was in 1921.[29] The desire of some Santa Feans to own the waterworks and the counter problems of cost and ability to manage it, would recur with franchise renewals throughout the century.

In 1925 the company began construction of another dam at Granite Point, which was completed a year later. The drought of 1925 led to metering and somewhat reduced water usage. In 1926, the New Mexico Power Company incorporated itself, merging with Santa Fe Power and Light as the New Mexico Power and Light Company.[30] In 1929 the city and the power company, working with the Forest Service, closed Santa Fe Canyon in order to protect the water supply. For a time, at least, the quantity and quality of the city's water were assured.[31]

In the decade after World War I Santa Fe's population increased to a point where real estate development began to hold promise. Still cautious, Paul Walter recommended in 1921 to a friend in Albuquerque against investing in building operations in Santa Fe on the grounds that "if one half of the apartments and houses are built for which plans have been drawn, there will be a glut in the market." He added, "If the Chamber of Commerce and populace knew I was writing to you like this they would tar and feather me."[32]

Nevertheless, by 1926 the real estate market appeared to explode. The pages of the *New Mexican* fairly sang with descriptions of the construction program in the city, which included hotel improvements, schools, and residences. "It is not exaggeration to say," the paper gloated, "that expenditure in the next year or two will run into millions."[33] Full-page advertisements listed available residential and commercial properties. New land opened in the Hickox addition

12. Santa Fe-style house design by Wilfred Stedman, 1936. Courtesy Museum of New Mexico, neg. #179066.

A Corner of Our Shop on Palace Avenue, Opposite Art Museum

Here the beautiful things of yesterday are adapted to today's living conditions—and your comfort—by the Southwest's finest craftsmen. The glamorous tradition of the Hacienda lives on the highly skilled crafts of the Spanish-American . . . his creations will lend your home its most distinctive touch.

Hand-Made in Old Santa Fe

Furniture, Rugs, Draperies, Wrought Iron Work, Gifts, Accessories for the Southwestern Ranch and Home.

Wrought Iron and Tin Lighting Fixtures, Goat Skin Lamp Shades, Fireplace Screens, Andirons, Upholstered Livingroom Furniture.

Interior Decoration and Complete Furnishings for the Entire Home

Southwestern Master Craftsmen

R. H. Welton

114 W. Palace Ave. *Santa Fé, N. M.*

13. Southwestern style furniture advertised in New Mexico Magazine, *May 1939. Courtesy Museum of New Mexico, neg. #179068.*

west of the railroad. More spectacularly, the newly incorporated Santa Fe Holding Company, headed by Nathan B. Stern, Dr. Robert Brown, and Burton Thompson, all well known in the city, offered over a thousand acres of property of all types. Many areas of development were in the west and south, as well as in Santa Fe Canyon.[34]

Yet, developers spoke cautiously. While admitting rapid growth and probable demand for properties, they nevertheless noted that property values were more than a third below those of cities of similar size. Significantly, they showed themselves sensitive to the issue of appearance, choosing the local firm of Meem and McCormick, the leading advocates of "the old Santa Fe style," as supervising architects.[35] In a sense, their acquiescence represented the victory of that style in the city on a mass basis a decade and a half after its advocates first proclaimed its desirability.

But if new building had its vocal and strong supporters, a push for greater infrastructure for the city met a spotty resistance. In the mid-twenties the city council spent considerable time on the issue of sewer installation. While improvements were accepted more often than not, objections and protests were numerous. With assessments on property at issue, there were those who considered the cost too high, others who felt that the isolated position of their property did not warrant the expense, and still others who resented the changes as an unwelcome form of modernization. Thus, the residents of Buena Vista Street

14. Guadalupe Church, early twentieth century. Courtesy Museum of New Mexico, neg. #15147.

15. Guadalupe Church, ca. 1957.
Courtesy Museum of New Mexico, neg. #131190.

between Don Gaspar and College Streets wanted no part of the changes. In fact, Witter Bynner, who was in New York at the time, sent a telegram to ensure that his name would be among the protesters.[36] Canyon Road residents generally expressed themselves so strongly in the negative that the Council decided "that the project be abandoned due to the opposition."[37]

While some economic changes in Santa Fe after 1910 could be linked to new technological development, such as the automobile, and to government activity as a result of its enhanced position as a state capital, another factor slowly added a new vitality—the growing attention to the city as a tourist attraction. Long a desideratum, little had actually occurred to make it so. While measurement of what later became known as "tourism" is difficult to assess, this much is clear: As Santa Fe became home to an archaeological enterprise, as interest in and knowledge of the Pueblos grew, and as artists and writers found it a suitable place to live, so did its reputation grow, along with the curiosity of travelers to see it firsthand.

It was the Anglo newcomer who pushed hard for the visitor. For example, the tubercular population wrote home and received guests. In addition, the publicity work of the AT & SF railroad continued uninterruptedly, while the institutionalization of archaeology in the form of the Old Palace as a museum lent concreteness to their boosterism. Even in 1908, as earlier noted, 10,000 visitors had passed through its portals.

Yet, however noticeable the visitor was to Santa Feans, actual growth of tourist numbers came slowly in the second decade of the century. Visitors to the Palace museum in the middle years of that decade remained at the same level as 1908—about 10,000 a year.[38] No great new hotels appeared before World War I and visitors quickly filled available space in existing hostelries and rooming houses for special events. When three political conventions involving a thousand persons overlapped in 1916, the appeals for rooms in private homes to accommodate them became urgent.[39] Such occasions, however, reflect the unprepared state of the town to handle unusually large numbers at a given moment instead of the constant, or even seasonal, shortage of accommodations.

In the middle teens it was still largely the railroad that brought the tourist to Santa Fe. Stopovers at Lamy took in the city as a day's excursion. Those who sought to stay longer could put up at the DeVargas Hotel. One-hour drives were available to various points but it was still a six-hour trip each way in wagons if one sought to go to the Bandelier National Monument. By 1916 shortages of automobile equipment due to the war in Europe were hampering improvements in transportation.[40] The American entry into the conflict in 1917 inevitably relegated the tourist trade to a lower priority.

16. Parking at the Palace, 1924.
Courtesy Museum of New Mexico, neg. #10598. Photo by T. Harmon Parkhurst.

Before World War I, shops selling crafts and curios also showed no greatly increased numbers. Candelario's, an old established firm, led the field in the early years of the century. Combined with the talents of Jake Gold, who was described as "the forerunner of all curio dealers," the shop operated on Burro Alley—the edge of the downtown area. Only the opening of Julius Gans's Southwest Arts and Crafts Shop in 1915 on the south side of the Plaza suggested increased tourist interest. His atelier, however, manufactured weavings and silver work, leaving in question how much of the product went to tourists and how much was shipped elsewhere.

In the post–World War I period tourist related activity picked up. The twenties began auspiciously with the building of the La Fonda Hotel at the southeast corner of the Plaza. It became not only the major hostelry in the city but also an architectural landmark, presenting, as one scholar put it, "a fully developed statement of the Spanish-Indian style of New Mexico."[41] Designed by the firm of T. H. Rapp, W. M. Rapp, and A. C. Hendrickson, the new hotel furthered the stylistic statement begun by the art museum. At the same time, a resort named Bishop's Lodge opened several miles north of the city at the site of

Archbishop Lamy's earlier retreat. Both institutions would prove important in Santa Fe's growing reputation as a tourist destination.

Other promising signs for the tourist trade appeared at the same time. In 1921 Erna Fergusson, of old Anglo–New Mexican lineage, in partnership with Ethel Hickey, created an instrument to tour areas outside the city. Under the name Koshare Tours, Fergusson, using large sedans and female guides, introduced visitors to landmarks and Pueblos with knowledge and elegance. In so doing, she extended the range of the tourist beyond the railroad station and city limits to the homes of the Native Americans themselves.[42]

These developments caught the eye of the Fred Harvey organization, already well established in railroad towns since the 1880s. With the outreach made possible by the automobile, a slowly improving road system, and new hotels, the Harvey organization combined these elements to form perhaps the best known of tourist enterprises in the area—Southwestern Indian Detours. It did this by purchasing the La Fonda and raising it to standards that met with Harvey's own excellent reputation and by incorporating the Koshare Tours as part of its own organization. As never before, Santa Fe was becoming a tourist destination of unique quality and style.

Nevertheless, the city's growing fame in the twenties did not always proceed smoothly. While its citizens broadly accepted their town's growth as a tourist destination, efforts to promote it on an even larger scale were deemed by some to be of a "wrong" sort and drew spirited opposition. The already noted Chautauqua affair of 1926, in which the General Federation of Women's Clubs sought to establish a permanent colony revealed the beginnings of tension between those who sought growth and those seeking to foster their own cultural values. Negotiations carried on by the chamber of commerce with representatives of the women's clubs and consideration by the city council to make city land available for erecting a sizable community mainly for summer residence created an open rift between the two sides.

Support for it came from the chamber of commerce, which lashed out at those who had continually fought against growth and change. The chamber stood for more people coming and the growth of business.[43] Hewett's forces at the museum, which would have provided intellectual fare for the proposed colony, also backed it.

Opposition came from those who viewed the city's growth as acceptable only on terms compatible with their conception of its traditions. As noted, a considerable segment of the new cultural elite in Santa Fe, with Mary Austin at its head, judged the potential newcomers as uncreative consumers of culture. In her eyes they would be destructive of Santa Fe's traditions.[44] She received support from the *New Mexican* and from wealthy residents, such as Ashley Pond, who differentiated the new Harvey Indian Detours from the "'tin-can'" type of resident coming in large numbers.[45] Members of the opposition grouped themselves into the Old Santa Fe Association, an organization dedicated to upholding their image of traditional Santa Fe—a self-conscious variant of the old lineage of distinction and superiority that had its political and religious roots in the city's Spanish origins.

Hispano cultural figures, such as Camilo Padilla, also arose in opposition. As editor of *Revista Ilustrada*, which had made Santa Fe its home in 1925, and a founder of El Centro de Cultura in 1926, which he hoped would serve as a focal point for Hispano cultural, literary, and social events, he was concerned about the discord that the issue had brought to the city.[46] La Unión Protectiva, a leading Hispano fraternal organization with several hundred members, also opposed the club women. It objected "on account of the claims of certain natives to title in that vicinity," that is, near the Sunmount Sanatorium, where the colonizers hoped to settle.[47] Thus, cultural attitudes, a desire to avoid conflict, land title issues, wealth, and the magnitude of the intrusion all contributed to the negative views. In the end, the opponents of Chautauqua won out and the project was abandoned.

Other elements of organization designed to give Santa Feans a greater sense of visible pride in their city's past and to offer the outside world evidence of its historical importance also appeared in the postwar period. The decade-long effort to revive and uphold the city as a center of tradition installed a powerful instrument in 1919 to convey those images through the adoption of a full-fledged Fiesta. The central theme around which it was built was a 1712 proclamation by city authority to honor annually the Spanish reconquest of Santa Fe in 1693 as marked by the entry of Don Diego de Vargas. This quickly turned into a commemoration of all the major periods of the city's history and a celebration of the arts and crafts of New Mexico as well.

Summer festivals had taken place before the war. The Santa Fe Woman's Board of Trade had held them to raise funds for the public library. On 4 July 1911 such an effort had been combined with a pageant depicting the de Vargas entry, a sign of the broadened ethnic awareness that had been growing for some years. Sporadic attempts followed, but the approach of war dampened further efforts.[48]

The 1919 event, although created under hurried circumstances, involved a broad range of organizations. The School of American Research handled the Native American segment of the pageant with the logistical support of St. Catherine's Indian School. The Hispanic De Vargas Association arranged the "procession" of its namesake and the Knights of Columbus honored the role of the Franciscans. The Santa Fe Lodge of Elks and cowboy volunteers organized an "Old Santa Fe Days" segment, while the Woman's Board of Trade did the same for the Plaza Market. The "Kearny Tableau," named after the American general who conquered New Mexico, was the work of the Daughters of the American Revolution and the Santa Fe Woman's Club. The parochial and public schools organized "The Children's Parade." The celebration of the Great War that had just ended fell to the American Legion, while closing summaries of Southwestern history became the responsibility of the Community Theatre and the Liberty Chorus.[49]

Not since the contrived Tertio-Millennial Celebration of 1883, which supposedly marked a third of a millennium since the city's founding—but did not in reality—had Santa Fe seen its like.[50] In retrospect, the Fiesta served as a summary statement of Santa Fe's past and, perhaps even more importantly, as an indicator of civic energy. Ethnic differences among Anglo, Hispano, and Native American were put aside in the name of a joint contribution to the existence and greater glory of Santa Fe itself. Whatever faults of interpretation existed, the celebration boded well for providing some sense of shared destiny.

From 1919 on the Fiesta became the centerpiece of Santa Fe celebrations. New elements were added to it—an Indian Fair in 1922, the art exhibitions that had been held each fall, and a fair of the colonial arts society with its presentation of crafts and cuisine. Until 1927 the School of American Research remained the primary organizer. In that year, the chamber of commerce assumed responsibility and the entire event was incorporated.

For a few years the finances of the Fiesta were a hand-to-mouth affair. But from the first, business elements in town under the umbrella of the chamber of commerce supported it as guarantors. By 1925 the event had become self-supporting and there can be little doubt that it contributed to a growing interest in the city as a tourist destination. Even though new hotels opened in the early twenties, the late-summer Fiesta produced such crowds that the chamber of commerce had to canvass the town for available rooms and arrange for the use of dormitory space at St. Michael's College, the Indian School, and the State School for the Deaf to accommodate the overflow of visitors.[51] All signs indicated the success of the event.

Throughout the 1880–1930 period the economic changes in the city helped mold relations between Anglos and Hispanos. Still a minority of the city's population in 1930, Anglos had from the beginning engaged in specialized urban occupations that Hispanos were not able to fill, given their traditional dependence on subsistence farming and manual labor. The economic strength of the Anglos, combined with the larger Hispano population promoted stable relations between the ethnic groups during the expansion of Anglo settlement. In part, the marked differences between their occupations that prevailed throughout those years tended to minimize any sense of economic competition between the two groups.[52] The numerical preponderance of Hispanos had from the beginning prompted Anglo entrepreneurs to cultivate them as customers.

Hispano numbers guaranteed the sharing of political power as well at local, territorial, and state levels of government. In territorial days Anglos held most of the appointive offices from governor on down, while Hispanos controlled the election of territorial legislators and county officers. After the incorporation of Santa Fe in 1891, Hispanos and Anglos worked together in party activities for municipal elections. With statehood in place after 1912, political leaders, regardless of affiliation, confirmed the principle that party loyalty should take precedence over ethnic difference as the basis for political rivalry. Thus Anglos came to depend on political support from Hispanos within their respective parties while Hispanos came to depend on occupational opportunities that Anglos created.

The Anglo presence encouraged Hispanos to shift from an agricultural to an urban economy. The sale of food grown on Hispano farms, at first on street corners and later in the old market house, led Hispanos into the grocery business.

17. Shipping piñon nuts, 1916, Gormley's General Store. Courtesy Museum of New Mexico, neg. #14196.

By 1880 farming and grocering had become alternative occupations. In that year almost twice as many Hispanos as Anglos were listed as grocers in the census. Twenty years later, as the city's population and urban employment declined, along with the return of some Hispanos to farming (See chapter 2), the number of Hispano grocers fell by approximately a third while Anglo grocers increased by almost half. But after 1910, when urban employment revived and the number of Hispano farmers again fell off, the number of Hispano grocers had risen to a corresponding degree. From then on to 1928, Hispano engagement in retail grocering continued to grow.[53]

From 1910 on, and almost assuredly somewhat earlier, when population growth slowly resumed, the accompanying recovery of local business provided substantial employment opportunities for both ethnic groups. Forty percent of the total increase of working Anglos between 1910 and 1928 included dealers, proprietors, and clerks of various kinds in private enterprise. For Hispanos, too, reviving business accounted for 34 percent of the increase in their work force.

Within the business sector, the two ethnic groups differed in the types of occupations that grew the most. Among Anglos, almost half of the increase consisted of proprietors, managers, or officials, while these categories made up less than a third of the increase among Hispanos. By contrast, clerical workers made up more than two-thirds of the increase among Hispanos but little more than half of the increase among Anglos. At the same time, the increase of Anglo proprietors opened employment opportunities for Hispano clerks.

Compared to those of the Anglos, Hispano business enterprises were fewer in number, less diverse in services and commodities, and on a smaller scale of organization, with a heavy concentration in food marketing. Of 118 Hispano proprietors and managers operating in 1928, 50 (43 percent) dealt in groceries, meats, dairy products, baked goods, or confections; of 299 Anglos in similar occupational status, only 30 (10 percent) dealt in these commodities, including the proprietor of a large wholesale grocery firm.

With the arrival of statehood in 1912, government jobs at all levels offered opportunities for the slowly growing population. Anglos and Hispanos found such employment in virtually equal proportions of their expanding workforces. Numbers of privately employed skilled and semi-skilled workers grew similarly.

Employment growth in other occupational areas reflected differences of education and training. Services requiring professional certification (doctors, lawyers, engineers, teachers, nurses) constituted a larger proportion of the Anglo (15 percent) than of the Hispano increase (5 percent). By contrast, other service occupations (i.e., domestic servants, waiters, cooks, bartenders, janitors) accounted for a higher percentage of employment growth among Hispanos (29 percent) than among Anglos (8 percent).

A retrospective look at the fifty years between 1880 and 1930 encourages speculation that if the railroad had run its main line through Santa Fe, many of the above-noted changes in the city's economy still might have occurred, but much more quickly. The replacement of large general merchandise firms with smaller and more diverse specialty shops, the influx of new products from elsewhere in the country, the increased investment of capital in local enterprise, the development of tourist accommodations—all this might have provided an initial level of progress that obviated a more unique development of the city's resources.

But even if the railroad had included Santa Fe on the main line, this would not have overcome the relatively low economic potential of the city's geographic setting. A limited capacity in the hinterland for agricultural production or livestock grazing, and lack of a water supply adequate for rapid population growth and industry would eventually have differentiated Santa Fe from the other growing cities in the area.

Well before 1920 local business and civic leaders had largely reconciled themselves to the loss of hoped for economic expansion. Yet, even as late as that year, newcomers could indulge extravagant fantasies about the future of Santa Fe as a hub of economic development in the Southwest. In a long article by C. S. Kennedy in the *New Mexican*, the author urged the development of Santa Fe as an industrial and agricultural center to serve the entire area west of the Mississippi. A week later in a letter to the editor, Paul A. F. Walter, secretary at the School of American Research, replied, "Mr. Kennedy is a newcomer to Santa Fe, who is not aware of the struggle that those with his vision have had in order to obtain the consent of the community to consistent city planning and building."[54]

What was perhaps most unique about Santa Fe's experience in the half-century after 1880 was the reluctance of so many local citizens to modernize the infrastructure of their urban community in ways requisite for an expanding economic posture. Not until the threat of losing its position as state capital to Albuquerque did local leaders acknowledge the need to make the city a fit habitat for the government of the state. What was unique from the political and economic point of view was not that the city began to recover and prosper, but that it almost lost its most powerful claim to existence. Without its position as capital it is doubtful that even a viable tourist trade would have received the support that emerged in the 1920s.

For the most part, the future of the business community in Santa Fe was a concern of Anglo residents. It was they who voiced their interest most conspicuously and who ran the more highly capitalized enterprises. The Hispanos, from a purely economic standpoint, as employers or consumers, were more dependent on the smaller businesses and services that met their day-to-day needs and provided employment generally less remunerative than what Anglos obtained. Between 1880 and the late 1920s the most consistent change in the Hispano labor force was the increase of those classified in the census as "clerical and kindred workers." The proportion of these workers increased from one percent in 1880 to 14 percent in 1928; and from 1910 to 1928, their increase in clerical workers accounted for most of the gain of Hispanos employed in business occupations.[55]

This gain in clerical workers by 1928 was a harbinger of upward occupational mobility for the Hispano workforce as a whole because of another change that occurred. The proportion of unskilled laborers, at 59 percent in 1880, had declined to 31 percent by 1928, indicating that many more persons were likely to be in jobs above that level. Both of these trends, paradoxically, would accelerate during the Great Depression.

EIGHT

The Great Depression, 1929–1940

AMERICAN HISTORIANS CONSIDER the Great Depression of 1929–1940 a major turning point in the history of the country. That is equally true for the West and New Mexico. In the West straitened economic conditions weakened the old empire builders—the railroads, lumber industry, and mining corporations—and reintroduced the hand of the federal government as a powerful sustaining and regulating agent.[1] New Mexico felt the full effects of the crisis and Santa Fe, as its capital, experienced its own economic discomfort as well as the sharp changes wrought by government policy.

The basic condition of the Depression, as people lived it, was economic hardship. New Mexico, as a state without a heavy manufacturing base, did not, perhaps, suffer as great a slump in its economic fortunes after 1929 as did those areas that contained such enterprises in large numbers. Reporting in late 1929 on the state's response to President Herbert Hoover's call to speed up construction projects, Governor Richard Dillon noted the absence of unemployment locally and reported some difficulty in finding labor for such works.[2] On the other hand, commercial farming in the state was already depressed in the twenties. By 1933, one-third of all New Mexicans needed government support to reach subsistence levels and in 1935 nearly 30 percent were on relief.[3] Their pain was real and widespread.

The cities were somewhat better off. Nevertheless, in 1930, before the full effects of the economic downturn took place, unemployment in Santa Fe stood at over 8.5 percent.[4] Henry Dendahl, president of the Santa Fe Chamber of Commerce, reporting for the year 1932, announced bravely, but quite prematurely, "that the depression is over; it's out, we will hear nothing more of it."[5] In fact, in 1940, of the five largest cities of New Mexico, Santa Fe had the highest proportion of its labor force employed on public emergency work (12.1 percent) or seeking work (14.2 percent), while in Santa Fe County, outside the city, these rates were even higher, at 17 percent and 16 percent, respectively.[6] Clearly, while government efforts reduced the suffering, they did not solve the basic problems of the economy—only World War II accomplished that.

Painful as economic conditions were, the state did relatively well compared to other parts of the country. It slowly improved its low per capita income from 57.9 percent of the national average in 1929 to 63.0 percent in 1940.[7] New Mexico's population also grew in the troubled thirties by over 25 percent—a larger increase than it had experienced since the first decade of the century.[8] Some out-of-staters farther east saw New Mexico, if less than paradise, as a place where they might still improve their straitened conditions.

Despite its economic problems, or because of them, Santa Fe itself underwent remarkable population growth during the thirties. Its growth rate exceeded all other urban places in the state except Hobbs, where the discovery of oil produced a phenomenal 1,600 percent upturn. While Albuquerque grew by 33 percent, Santa Fe's population rose 81 percent—from 11,176 in 1930 to 20,325 in 1940.[9] By a wide margin, the city's growth was the largest in any decade of the twentieth century up to 1990.

Although it is difficult to account for such a high growth rate, some reconstruction is possible. The factor of natural increase, of births over deaths, accounts for a small share, perhaps two to three percent.[10] The Native American population also increased by a small amount. A much larger portion came from new arrivals to the city. The social and economic programs instituted by President Franklin Roosevelt after 1933 led to expanded governmental activity on an unprecedented scale. As the state capital, Santa Fe became the home base for numerous new and enlarged agencies, state and federal, created to deal with the economic crisis. Here were jobs to be filled. In addition, certain areas of economic activity rose markedly in the thirties, providing opportunities for newcomers to join the community.

Counts made in city directories demonstrate some aspects of the increase. The directory of 1928–1929, the year prior to the Depression, reveals 99 federal employees in town. By contrast, the directory for 1940, the last full year before World War II, reveals 284 federally employed persons, nearly a tripling. For the same years, there were 223 state employees living in the city in 1928–1929 and 459 in 1940, more than a doubling. For all levels of government, 1928–1929 employment stood at 354, while the 1940 figure was 838, an increase of about 250 percent. Put another way, government employment rose from about 10 percent of the working population in the period 1928–1930 to 16.5 percent in 1940. Clerical workers of all kinds, many of whom were government employees, comprised 19.7 percent of the working population in 1928 and 27.5 percent in 1940—the largest single category of workers in the city.

Several examples illustrate this growth. The Works Progress Administration (WPA), which did not exist in 1932, employed 111 persons in 1940. Of 69 Anglo surnamed employees, 65 received no mention in the 1932 city directory. Of 42 Hispano surnamed persons, 27 had no 1932 listing. The state highway department, a very active agency during the thirties, increased its Santa Fe workforce by 58 percent between 1932 and 1940 (from 73 to 124), but there were no city listings for over 61 percent of these persons in 1932. Although circumstances other than an influx into the city can account for some of this growth, such as the achievement of working age among persons already present, in all probability, absence from the 1932 directory indicates a sizable accretion of newcomers.

The heavily depressed condition of rural areas in the state also contributed to urban growth. Santa Fe was no exception to this trend. Scholars who lived through or close to the events of the time agree generally that villagers moved to cities to improve their lot. Paul Walter, Jr., a leading New Mexican sociologist of the era, commented in 1939 that the Depression-based threat to old village life "brought thousands of refugees to the suburban villages surrounding the growing urban centers of the state, especially Albuquerque, Santa Fe, and Las Vegas."[11] Walter found that the need for cash to hold on to land forced farmers to cities in hopes of finding wage labor.[12] Besides the search for work, the need for government aid, as agencies created for that purpose grew up, encouraged relocation. Writing of Santa Fe shortly after the Depression, another scholar noted that "it was most feasible to obtain government aid at the source of its distribution, in the capital."[13]

While the pain of the Depression never disappeared during the thirties, the course of economic life in the city did not remain static. In general, the pattern of retail trade moved downward in the early years and then improved in the later years of the decade. Santa Fe sales ran about $6.5 million in 1929, declined to $6 million by 1935, and then rose to $8 million in 1939.[14] Those sales took place in a growing number of retail outlets—99 in 1933 and 231 in 1939.[15] In the former year, these 99 stores employed 283 persons full-time, while in the latter, the 231 stores employed 985 persons.[16] Growing numbers and jobs, as well as emergency help, provided resources that, in turn, led to the creation of new businesses and increased employment.

Some branches of the economy grew despite all difficulties. The expansion of automobile use was inexorable. Service stations increased from 12 in 1932 to 39 by 1940. Closson and Closson, an auto dealer already present in 1932, listed a payroll of 16 persons in that year and of 48 in 1940. Of the latter, 16 were not listed in the 1932 directory. Similarly, Santa Fe Motor Co., another firm present in 1932, grew from 25 employees in that year to 40 in 1940, with 28 of the latter not listed in 1932. Thus, as an industry, the automobile sector expanded well, hired employees—both newcomers and persons already present—and took its place as an important element in the economy, the pain of the Depression notwithstanding.

Santa Fe was scarcely alone in experiencing the growing presence of automobiles. Filling stations in the state nearly tripled in number, as they did in the city, reflecting a general increase in their use. Inevitably, this growing mode of transportation depended on an improved road system. New Mexico had committed itself to road building early. In 1919 it was the first state to institute a gasoline tax, the purpose of which was to foster the construction and maintenance of public roads.[17] Increasing automobile usage in the twenties by the local population and tourists appeared to justify this policy.

In the thirties the state adopted measures to encourage road traffic. The state highway department began to formalize the flow of information to encourage tourists to come through the creation of a state tourist bureau.[18] By 1936, the department claimed that "the tourist business is the greatest single industry in New Mexico," bringing in more than livestock, agriculture, and mining combined.[19] Although documenting actual tourist numbers is technically troublesome, the growth in the number of visitors was unquestionable. That Santa Fe gained from the upturn is equally certain.

By the late twenties, those who motored were changing the conditions of travel. Instead of the earlier hardy voyagers who "gypsied," sleeping in their vehicles or in roadside tents, those seeking more comfort were staying in "cottage camps" or "auto courts," the forerunners of the modern motel.[20]

In Santa Fe, such facilities grew considerably in number in the thirties. Seven existed in 1932 and thirteen in 1939. Four of the seven in existence in 1932 were on Cerrillos Road as were nine of the thirteen at the later date. In 1932 the last address on Cerrillos Road looking to the southwest was the United States Indian School. By 1940 a number of streets had been added composed mainly of new service stations, visitor housing facilities, a few residences, and shops of varied character. Cerrillos Road was taking on the character of a tourist terminal point of quite a different type than presented by the Plaza and its environs.

Even Santa Fe's hotels recovered after the early thirties. Several new ones opened, among them La Posada, the center building of which was the former home of Abraham Staab, one of the great merchants of the Santa Fe Trail era. Their revenue increased from $287,000 in 1933 to $592,000 in 1939.[21] By that standard, the results were a substantial comeback.

The supportive atmosphere for crafts in the late twenties also brought some desirable and needed results in the thirties in the form of woven products. Sheep and Spanish looms had been introduced by the Spaniards to Pueblo Native Americans who were already adept weavers. In turn, they adapted their existing skills to the various technological innovations, including the dyes of the newcomers. Eventually, the Navajos also learned these techniques.[22] Hispano villagers and Native Americans had never lost the art although the Santa Fe traders and their machine-made textiles cut deeply into traditional forms of production.

The positive environment for crafts, as well as tourists, promoted a renaissance in the weaving industry. In 1930 Preston and Helen McCrossen settled in town. They were experienced weavers who had visited Santa Fe several years earlier and had been impressed by the efforts of Austin and Applegate's Spanish Colonial Arts Society to foster the craft.[23] While in California, the McCrossens had created a handwoven tie, which became the featured item of their production repertoire in Santa Fe as well. Operating at first on lower San Francisco Street, the business did so well that by 1936 the McCrossens erected a building on Cerrillos Road. By that time the firm had seventy-eight employees. In the years between 1934 and 1940 the net sales of the firm totaled about $391,000, with revenue increasing virtually every year.[24] George McCrossen estimated that between 1930 and 1950 the firm brought some $6 million into the state.[25] The McCrossens marketed their product to well-known stores throughout the United States.

18. McCrossen Weavers, ca. 1938.
Courtesy Museum of New Mexico, neg. #179067.

Other firms joined the weaving trade in the same period. Santa Fe Weavers, run by Celina Padilla but financially backed by Nat Stern of real estate fame, was one. Southwest Arts and Crafts, an established shop owned by Julius Gans, also began weaving ties, which he supplied to local businesses. E. Knox followed suit in the mid-thirties, inviting young craftsmen from Truchas and Chimayó into his employ.[26] In 1936, the *WPA Bulletin* reported that some 218 persons in the city were making their living by weaving ties, scarves, and blankets.[27] Thus, the arts and crafts, even in this generally dismal period of business, became a source of profit, employment, and a means of drawing people to the city.

Artist and writer support of Hispano crafts in the late twenties resulted in retail outlets in the thirties. Members of the Spanish Colonial Arts Society opened a shop in Sena Plaza in 1930. Managed at first by Mrs. Preston McCrossen, it dealt exclusively with New Mexican crafts. It was not a success, however, possibly because of the depressed tourist trade in the early thirties and the death of Frank Applegate, an energetic supporter. It closed in 1933.[28]

Nevertheless, the seeds were sown. In mid-1934 the Native Market opened on Palace Avenue under the sponsorship and subsidy of Leonora Curtin, who had been associated with the earlier Spanish Colonial Arts Society. Despite the hard times, the enterprise fared well enough and became self-sustaining around 1936. At that time, some 200 craftsmen from New Mexico were supplying a shop of twelve employees.[29]

The impetus that the artistic community had provided for both Hispano and Native American crafts in the twenties thus served as an initiating point for the economic upturn of the thirties. The new enterprises that arose to present those crafts to the public still retained the authenticity associated with their ethnic origins, but they were businesses as well. They became part of Santa Fe's changing economic scene and proved their efficacy in this worst of times.

Economic recovery in Santa Fe had different effects on Anglos and Hispanos. These stemmed partly from the varying skills and wealth each group could draw upon and the capacity of the city's economy to provide a wide enough range of employment opportunities. At the broadest level, between 1928 and 1940, as the population of each group grew in substantial proportions, the discrepancy between them in economic advantage became markedly wider.

In 1928 the Santa Fe city directory listed the names of 1,797 Anglos whose stated occupations offer a presumption of their being employed; the same directory listed occupational information for 1,665 Hispanos. In 1940, 3,030 Anglos were so listed as compared with 2,028 Hispanos presumed to be employed. On this basis the Anglo labor force had grown at three times the rate of the Hispano labor force (69 percent and 21 percent, respectively).

19. New Mexico Exhibit at Chicago "Century of Progress" World's Fair, 1934. Courtesy Museum of New Mexico, neg. #179065.

Another measure indicates a similar discrepancy. In ten neighborhood areas of the city where the population grew between 1932 and 1940, the number of homeowners for whom no occupation was listed decreased from 35 percent to 20 percent for the Anglos but increased from 39 to 55 percent for the Hispanos. These longer-term trends provide a background for the specific means of economic recovery that each group came to rely on.

For both groups the Depression interrupted the growth of business activity but at sharply different rates. From 1928 to 1940 the number of Anglo proprietors, managers, and clerks almost doubled. By contrast the number of Hispanos in comparable positions increased by only one-fourth over their number in 1928.

One example of this difference is the share of Anglos and Hispanos in the new occupations spawned by increasing automobile usage. These ranged from car dealerships and supply stores to transport services, service stations, repair shops, and auto camps for tourists. Both groups remained virtually equal in the proportion of their total labor forces working at all automobile-related occupations, growing from 4 percent in 1920 to 9 percent in 1928. But the two groups differed in the types of occupations they pursued.

From the beginning Anglos held more highly paid executive or ownership positions within business firms. In 1928, 31 percent of Anglos in automobile-related occupations were proprietors or managers, compared to 11 percent of the Hispanos; 15 percent of the Anglos were couriers, salesmen, or in clerical jobs compared to 5 percent of the Hispanos. By contrast, 76 percent of Hispanos in the industry were drivers, delivery men, or service station attendants, compared to 45 percent of the Anglos. In each group skilled mechanics accounted for no more than 10 percent of all persons employed in automobile-related jobs.

During the Depression the fortunes of the two groups diverged even more sharply. By 1940 the total of Anglos employed in automobile-related occupations had increased by 68 percent while the increase of Hispanos so employed was only 25 percent. Hispano gains were limited to skilled workers (mostly mechanics) and semiskilled workers (mostly drivers and service station attendants). Even in this latter category Anglo workers increased threefold over Hispanos.

Clearly, the financial privation of the Depression sharpened the difference between the fortunes of Anglos and Hispanos in business occupations. The substantial increase of Anglos as proprietors and managers in automobile-related business indicates their greater access to the investment capital and financial resources necessary for business operations. The reduced access to capital overall that characterized the Depression could only aggravate the relative disadvantage of Hispanos in this regard. It became obvious that improving their lot economically would require new work opportunities as employees rather than as entrepreneurs.

Those opportunities followed quickly with the expansion of government employment in the 1930s. Between 1928 and 1940 that sector of the economy accounted for 57 percent of the increase in the entire Hispano labor force. In addition, it became the principal source of upward occupational mobility for Hispanos and Anglos alike. From 1928 to 1940, the percentage of Anglos in private white-collar jobs dropped from 56 to 53 percent of the total Anglo labor force, while those in white-collar government work rose from 10 to 15 percent. Similarly, the proportion of all Hispanos in private white-collar jobs between 1928 and 1940 increased slightly from 22 to 23 percent of the Hispano labor force while those in white-collar government jobs increased from 5 to 11 percent.[30]

Hispano gains reflected a continuing tradition of active participation in New Mexico politics from the very beginning of the territorial period and a significant broadening of such activity after the achievement of statehood in 1912.[31] In the 1930s the New Deal programs of the national administration under President Roosevelt sharply expanded the role of government in economic aid to the unemployed and the working classes. That drew support from elements of the electorate previously uninvolved in local and state politics. At the same time, the Democrat Party's working class support and its control over the new agencies of social assistance and work relief enhanced its independence as a party in ways that contrasted with the position of the Republicans prior to 1930. Unlike the Republicans, the Democrats were not beholden to local economic interest groups for electoral or financial support. Not only could the party offer jobs to its supporters but it could also assess contributions from government employees and from contractors doing highway construction.[32] This meant that opportunities for government employment became more dependent on the approval of party functionaries, chiefly the county chairmen. By 1940, a substantial overlap had developed between administration, policymaking officialdom, and the party functionaries in state government. Political scientist Jack Holmes described it as follows:

> During the period 1935–40, one could normally find on the roster of state officers and employees from a third to half of the county chairmen and other party operatives whose activities or connections assured them of state employment.[33]

The new opportunities in government employment between 1928 and 1940 strongly affected the social picture of Santa Fe's working population. Among Hispano men, it accounted for 64 percent of the increase in their workforce; and for Hispano women, 35 percent of their increase. Among Anglo women, government employment accounted for 29 percent of the growth of their workforce, while for Anglo men, it accounted for 24 percent of their gain.[34] Considering that government employment contributed 30 percent of the total increase of all workers for this period, the Hispano population acquired a major share of the newly created jobs.

New government employment also affected the type of occupations in which workers engaged. White-collar jobs increased markedly in number with Hispano women achieving the greatest gains. Without these government-based opportunities such gains would not have been realized. With them, white-collar employment rose from 31 percent in 1928 to 39 percent in 1940. Hispano males also gained greatly as a result of white-collar government employment, though not as much as Hispano women.

Anglo males also profited as a result of government work, but somewhat less than Hispano males. Anglo women, however, who already had the highest percentage of their labor force (78 percent) in white-collar work in 1928, suffered a small decline by 1940 to 75 percent. Although their share of non-white-collar work increased, they still made gains in the white-collar government category.

By contrast, Hispano women dropped steadily in their proportion of non-white-collar work from 78 percent in 1920 to 69 percent in 1928, and to 60 percent in 1940.[35] This was part of a longer historical development. In 1880, Hispano women had begun to earn wages for such tasks as laundering clothes and dressmaking, which had been customary household chores for them. Many of them had also become engaged in personal services in the homes of other families as cooks, housemaids, or domestic servants. In 1910 only about 7 percent of Hispano women in such service positions worked in commercial establishments—hotels or restaurants as waitresses or chambermaids. By 1928 independent laundresses were being replaced by women working in commercial laundries, which had begun to appear. And by 1940, 30 percent in service positions were no longer the hirelings of individual families but were employees of business firms instead. There, they were on a par with men and other Hispano women whose education increasingly qualified them for white-collar positions in commerce and government. With the onset of the Depression and the loss of employment by many men, it is tempting to speculate that access to employment by Hispano women did much to validate the new status they were beginning to acquire.

By working in similar occupations Hispanos and Anglos could become more equal in economic terms even while differences remained in language, religion, and cultural traditions. Government employment expanded the opportunities for Hispanos to do the kinds of work that formerly had been more limited to Anglos and that became even more limited in private employment during the Depression. Here one might speculate on the importance of increased educational opportunity in the city since 1920 that made such employment possible.

In the thirties, the combination of new economic opportunities with the most rapid population increase in Santa Fe's history was accompanied by the creation of new residential neighborhoods as Anglos and Hispanos alike made homes for themselves in keeping with their new employment. By 1940 signs were emerging that economic status could become as important in determining where people chose to live as ethnicity or family ties had been in the past.

In Las Vegas and Albuquerque the coming of the railroad in 1880 had resulted in the creation of "new towns" in each place that provided a geographic base separating Anglo residential areas from Hispano neighborhoods. In Santa Fe no such "new town" had developed and Anglos had domiciled themselves at the same central points of economic and political activity utilized by native Hispanos—near the Plaza for business and near the territorial capitol and later the county courthouse for governmental activity. Anglos took up residence alongside Hispanos in the streets connecting and adjacent to these sites. Even the attempt to develop real estate in the vicinity of the new railroad depot serving the spur line to Santa Fe had drawn little support from either Anglos or Hispanos.

By 1886 the residential properties of Anglos were scattered fairly evenly around the "downtown" area centered on the Plaza, where they intermingled with the residential properties of Hispanos.[36] But by 1912 Anglo residents had greatly increased in this central area of town.[37] At the same time Hispano resident homeowners had increased to the southwest of the Plaza and with continued growth this area maintained itself as a virtual Hispano "homeland."[38] Hispano residents also increased in the area to the southeast of the Plaza.[39]

By 1932 it was clear that Anglos and Hispanos had been diverging in the directions of their residential expansion. Consistent with the remnants of their agricultural tradition, Hispanos followed the east-west course of the Santa Fe River where acequias allowed irrigation for the growing of subsistence crops. Anglos, on the other hand, tended to expand into new spaces toward the north and south of the older populated areas.

Between 1932 and 1940 these divergent trends continued as each ethnic group increased more rapidly in areas where it was already dominant. Indeed, the newcomers from the villages and farms who moved into the western section of the city may have contributed heavily to that development.[40] However, with the accelerated population growth in this decade, new patterns emerged as well. In some parts of the city where rapid growth was occurring, Anglo and Hispano newcomers were approaching parity in numbers. They were becoming more similar in occupational status.

One early example of this occurred in a residential area lying southwest of the city center, where the population increased substantially in an almost equal number of new Anglo and Hispano homeowners. In 1932, of all employed Anglo homeowners in that area, 43 percent held jobs as professionals or as proprietors, managers, or officials while only 16 percent of Hispano homeowners were so employed. By 1940, 41 percent of Anglos held such jobs while the Hispano portion so employed had risen to 24 percent. This represented a reduction by more than a third of the earlier difference between the two groups. A similar change occurred in part of the Hispano "homeland" where the increase in Hispano homeowners coincided with a higher percentage of such high status jobs among them. (See figure 20.)

Obviously, this example contradicts the overall trend of a widening gap between the economic status of Anglos and Hispanos during the Depression years. But it also indicates how the occupational similarities and differences between the ethnic groups could vary from one neighborhood to another and change over time. With the higher rate of population growth in the 1930s and, later, with the economic expansion that would follow World War II, a process began in Santa Fe whereby entire neighborhoods would become more distinct from each other economically. At the same time, within each one, the

Anglo and Hispano residents would become more like each other in their economic status.

The Depression decade also proved to be a time when efforts among Hispanos to organize themselves on a broad spectrum of social issues began to bear fruit. Hispano Texans had taken the lead in one such effort in the twenties when they formed the League of United Latin American Citizens (LULAC) in 1929. Students of its history view it as a middle-class development with concern for issues of antiradicalism, race, education, and civil rights. LULAC's constitution reflected the rise of ethnic consciousness and recognition of the bicultural circumstances in which Hispanos lived.[41]

Following the lead of Texas, New Mexican chapters of LULAC emerged in the thirties, with Santa Fe Hispanos forming their own chapter. In the later years of the decade such well-known figures as J. A. Armijo, Manuel Lujan, and Carlos Gilbert were leading figures in the organization, which was providing a range of cultural and educational activities in the city. In its early years it endured some of the internal political conflict that carried over from party differences between Senators Dennis Chavez and Bronson Cutting, but these were resolved by 1937.[42] Cutting himself died in 1935, the victim of an airplane crash. By 1940 Santa Fe had become the site for LULAC's national convention.

The powerful response of Democrats to the economic pain caused by the Depression brought about equally momentous political changes. In Santa Fe, population increases related to the expansion of government services created a different political environment. The Republican hegemony of the teens and, more strongly, in the twenties, dissolved in the new climate of government action. Even with the full effects of the economic downturn not yet fully evident in 1930, the clouds of change were already forming. In the election of that year the Republicans again swept the city offices, but their vote, as the *New Mexican* noted, was "by greatly reduced majorities in comparison with the smashing victory . . . scored two years ago."[43]

In April 1932, still before the national victory of the Democrats in November, the Santa Fe Democrats were victorious for the first time in twenty years in the city. Even prior to the great increase in government programs ushered in with President Franklin Roosevelt's election, the *New Mexican* explained some of the change by pointing to a "capitol vote" of employees who had only become residents of the city in the last year.[44] The paper attributed the major cause of the Republican defeat, however, to the defection of old-guard Republicans who turned to the Democrats out of dissatisfaction with Progressive Republicans

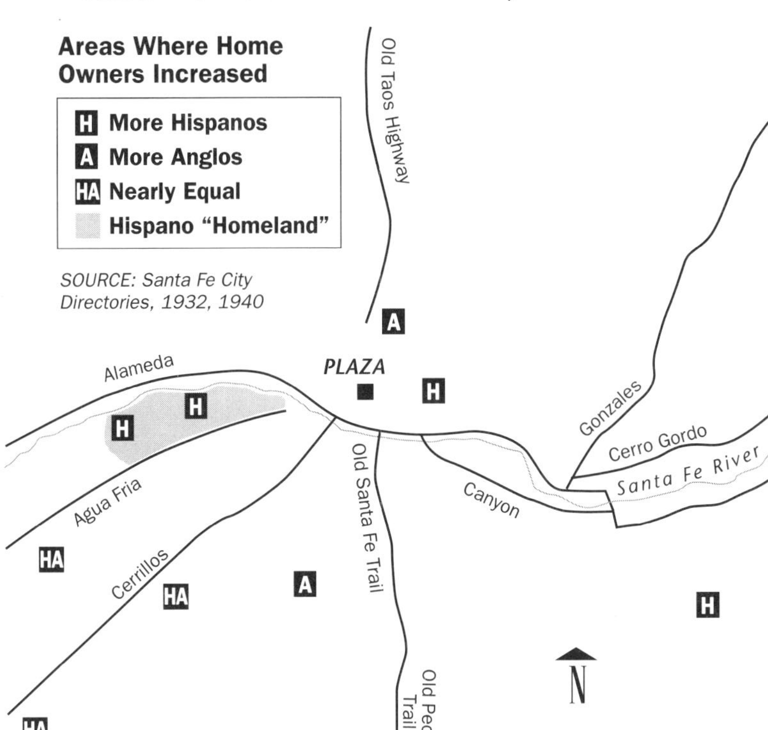

20. Map of Santa Fe residential growth, 1932-1940.

whom they regarded as "double-crossers" in earlier campaigns.[45] In any case, the Republican hold on local government was broken.

By 1934 the burgeoning programs of the federal government were clearly evident. The *New Mexican* accused the Democrats of seeking votes from the members of the Civilian Conservation Corps (CCC), an organization created by President Roosevelt to put unemployed young men to work in the nation's parks and forests. It also charged that state house employees were being solicited for campaign funds and the use of automobiles on election day to bring voters to the polls.[46] Progressives and old-guard Republicans joined hands and won the mayoral race, although the Democrats retained control of the city council. Nevertheless, the split outcome illustrated the strength of the changes that Democratic policies were bringing about in the city.

For the remainder of the decade—1936 through 1940—Democrats virtually swept the elections. The full weight of the newly created government employment in Santa Fe came to bear on the electoral process in 1936. Governor Clyde Tingley, a staunch Democrat, the *New Mexican* informed its readers, called upon state workers, some 1,500 to 1,600 strong in the city, to vote. The existence of their jobs, he suggested, depended on Democratic victories.[47] Likening Governor Tingley to Governor Huey Long of Louisiana, the paper saw Tingley's intrusion into local politics as an issue of "home rule."[48] Despite the paper's efforts, the Democrats won handily.

In 1938 the Democratic ticket openly advertised its efforts to obtain federal projects to effect civic improvements and reduce unemployment.[49] The election gave the Democrats a complete sweep of city offices. The results reflected the rapidly growing population and heavy government employment. As in 1936, a record number of votes were cast in the 1938 contest.

Republicans did not run under their own name in 1940. Instead the party offered a Better Santa Fe Ticket composed of Republicans and Independent Democrats—much as the Progressive Republicans and Democrats had united in the time of Republican dominance. The Democrats, however, again swept the election, although their majorities were smaller than in previous campaigns. This was the last election before the outbreak of World War II.

For Santa Fe the decade of the Depression proved to be a critical turning point. The economic crisis refocused the basis of the city's economy and altered the fortunes, above all, of its Hispano residents. A city that suffered more than others in New Mexico from unemployment and the need for relief, it nevertheless ended the decade with the largest increase of population in its modern history, the reexpansion of its business community, the promise of a somewhat restored tourist trade, and an unprecedented growth of new government agencies, federal and state, with programs largely engendered by the Depression itself. While Anglo residents benefited more from the new business growth, the Hispano residents found a significant new source of income and social status in government employment. If the twenties spelled the ripening of local culture through the efforts of Anglo cultural activists to define a new direction for the city, then the thirties marked the reassertion of government to a place of prominence—not only in fulfilling its obligations, but as employer and economic resource.

Altogether, Santa Fe had become more closely akin to urban areas in the rest of the country by experiencing common tribulations and responses. The general conditions of the Depression saw to that. But before the long-term effects of the change to government employment could be fully realized, the city was to become linked to the rest of the country in another way. World War II would see to that.

NINE

Santa Fe and World War II

The Second World War impacted heavily upon New Mexico. The state's vast open spaces and excellent year-round weather offered superb conditions for the creation of military bases to train a large air force. Remote areas, isolated from heavily populated centers and not even that well known locally, offered natural security for secret research facilities. The numbers of Americans drawn into all these enterprises, backed by the war investment of the national government, altered the direction of the state's economy quickly and decisively.

The war burst upon a nation still in the economic mode created by the Great Depression and geared to the government's response to it. The demands of the new conflict sharply changed both conditions. Millions of men in the prime of life entered military service. Projects related to the war effort mushroomed, offering employment for more millions of men and women. Under these conditions, programs designed to deal with the hardships of the Depression faded away before the new demands on manpower, although the transitions from stagnation to wartime urgency were not uniformly quick or easy.

Santa Fe, too, reflected the consequences of these changes. Most importantly, military service removed a host of young men from their accustomed civilian lives for the duration of the war or, for many, forever. The creation of military-related installations in the city or within a few miles of it produced some immediate short-term effects, while others, unforeseen initially, produced long-term consequences that modified the course of the town's development.

■ The greatest immediate impact of the war years upon Santa Fe was the disappearance of thousands of young men and some women as a result of the nation's buildup of its armed forces. The mobilization of the National Guard, voluntary enlistment, and the draft (the Selective Service System) changed lives to an extent unmatched by World War I. The local draft boards, which included Santa Fe County, listed 3,786 persons on their rolls through September 1945.[1] Since the city of Santa Fe held about two-thirds of the county's population in 1940, one can estimate the city's total draft rolls at about 2,524 men.

The mustering-out process at the end of the war, from September 1945 to July 1946, provides a corroborative alternative calculation of how many actually served in the armed forces. In those months about 2,400 persons who gave Santa Fe addresses received military discharges.[2] Unfortunately, some confusion resulted in duplication of names, perhaps as much as 20 percent. A reasonable estimate is that about 2,000 actually served. That figure represents 10 percent of the total population of Santa Fe in the early forties. It also agrees substantially with local press statements made during the war.[3] Government sources for numbers of veterans fall equally close to the 10 percent figure.[4] By any estimate, given both the limited age group eligible to serve and the overwhelmingly male gender of the soldiery, the extent of military service sharply altered the social makeup of the town for the years 1941–1945.

These social changes imposed by the war could not match the cost of lives lost. Santa Fe's price in manpower was part of the exceptional one paid by New Mexicans. War Department calculations showed that the state, with 0.40 percent of the national population, contributed 0.43 percent of the servicemen. Of these, some 4.77 percent failed to return, representing 0.66 percent of the country's dead and missing, a disproportionate share.[5] Put more dramatically, the *New Mexican* calculated that the rate of loss in Santa Fe County was two and one-half times that of the average U.S. community of the same size.[6]

Statistics, however, fail to convey the force of the emotional pain inflicted. New Mexicans, more than most, had to absorb the losses of the early war years caused by defeat in the Philippines. Their national guard had become federalized in January 1941 as the 200th Coast Artillery and, later, its "child," the 515th Coast Artillery. Standing virtually alone, it was overwhelmed by the Japanese and suffered the "death march," followed by more than three years of incarceration in Japanese prisoner-of-war camps. Of the original 1,800 men only about 50 percent returned. Many of these were broken in health, died early deaths, or later became invalids.[7] The legacy of that pain was part of New Mexico's and Santa Fe's daily history during the conflict and long after.

Focusing the lens of war onto the streets of the town reveals the personal cost even more poignantly. The 700 block of Agua Fria Street alone counted six deaths. The effects were not merely individual, but applied to families and the entire neighborhood. The Almanza, Anaya, Catanach, Gorman, Mares, and

Britton families all felt the agony of the loss of loved ones. In all, the county listed 117 deaths.[8]

The war also altered the economic conditions of the city. The effects of the Depression were still heavily in evidence in 1940, the last full year of peace. The census of that year indicated that over a thousand persons in Santa Fe were seeking work (14 percent of the total labor force over age 14), while another 900 (12 percent of the total labor force) were employed in government-sponsored programs created to deal with the economic crisis of the thirties.[9]

Compared to other New Mexican towns of significant size, Santa Fe was not faring well. While 26 percent of its labor force was either unemployed or employed in public emergency programs, Albuquerque's total stood at 14 percent, Clovis's at 13 percent, Roswell's at 16 percent, and Hobbs's at 9 percent.[10] Santa Fe's relative lack of employment opportunities was readily apparent.

Circumstances began to change in the year from mid-1941 to mid-1942. The WPA rolls showed a considerable drop in the state of New Mexico in numbers

21. *Inducting young men into the navy at the Palace, 1942. New Mexico State Records Center. Department of Tourism Photograph Collection, #1394.*

of applications and approvals. Applications fell by two-thirds and approvals by half. The Civilian Conservation Corps, with its population of young men, showed an even sharper drop. New applications and approvals for the entire state virtually disappeared.[11] Santa Fe County had about 130 men in the CCC for the fiscal year 1940–1941.[12] The city itself must have experienced a relatively equivalent drop in numbers during this period, which included the first half-year of American participation in the war.

The drop in unemployment had actually begun before 1942 with the selective service draft and voluntary enlistments in the armed services undoubtedly leading the way. In addition, in 1942, a small number of persons were hired at the new internment camp for Japanese Americans established in the city early in that year. In late 1942 and early 1943 the creation of the Bruns hospital and the secret base at Los Alamos withdrew many more from unemployment rolls. Indeed, the WPA itself was abolished in February 1943. Shortly before that date, the *New Mexican* had noted that the Depression-created agency had shrunk to one-tenth the size of its heyday in 1938.[13]

While national military needs played a major role in eradicating unemployment between 1940 and 1945, other factors reflected a still-troubled economy in the city. The demands of the war adversely affected the entire tourist industry in New Mexico. Out-of-state motor vehicle traffic, a major measurement of tourism, held up well through the end of 1941. The following year, however, the count of such vehicles fell by one-third and in 1943 had fallen to less than half of the 1941 figures. It did not approach the latter numbers again until 1946, the year after the war's end.[14]

The war's effects on Santa Fe business became evident during this time of restricted movement. In the first two months of 1942 the state's sales tax director reported that over one thousand businesses in New Mexico ceased to operate while only half that number of new enterprises appeared. Seventy firms closed their doors in Santa Fe and only twenty-three opened. The heaviest losses were in filling stations, cafes, tourist camps, dude ranches, and grocery stores, enterprises involved in the tourist trade.[15] In August 1942 a new report showed a continuing downward trend.[16]

The demands of the military effort impacted the tourist trade directly. Gas rationing and tire conservation loomed in the spring of 1942. Governor John Miles cautioned New Mexico's congressional delegates that the state faced the loss of $80 million a year in tourist business alone.[17] In June 1942 the Indian Detours were banned.[18] The *New Mexican*, in its editorials, finally accepted the inevitable in the fall of 1942 even while suggesting that rationing "would strike New Mexico harder than anything since Bataan."[19] Protest was to no avail; relief would come only with the end of hostilities.

In all likelihood, the most unusual development that would affect the city was the creation of the atomic research center at Los Alamos, some thirty miles away. Often heralded as the best-kept secret of the war, Santa Feans could not escape awareness that unusual activity was taking place not far from their town. Writing immediately after President Harry Truman revealed the secret to the world, a story in the *New Mexican* recalled the mysterious lights from "the Hill," as Los Alamos was called locally, the fires and smoke visible upon occasion, and ominous explosions.[20]

The mystery intrigued the local population. The arrival of newcomers who reported to an office at 109 Palace Avenue, where they received instructions from Dorothy McKibben for the completion of their journey, could be seen by all. The original estimate of project leaders that about one hundred men and their families would be needed to handle the project proved quickly erroneous. By the end of the war some six thousand persons lived in Los Alamos and Santa Feans could hardly miss both their influx and its effects upon their community.

The unavailability of many household items at Los Alamos produced a new group of shoppers in Santa Fe. Once a month wives came to town to purchase what they could not get on the Hill—everything from liquor to baby oil to children's shoes.[21] Yet, the visitors had to maintain silence about what they were doing there—security was a prime consideration.

Not surprisingly, Santa Fe buzzed with speculation. Jocular and half-jocular rumors circulated—that a home for pregnant WACs was being constructed (the birth rate on the Hill was heavy), that a new type of submarine was being constructed (naval officers had appeared), that windshield wipers for submarines were being designed, and in 1944 during the presidential campaign, that an internment camp for Republicans was under construction.[22] Almost in despair, some Santa Feans joked that the project involved building the rear end of horses.[23] The proliferation of stories led Dr. J. Robert Oppenheimer, the head of the installation, to suggest his own diversionary lead, the building of an electric rocket, news of which was to be deliberately disseminated to the curious in Santa Fe.[24] The secret of the bomb, at least as far as the general public was concerned, remained secure.

Without doubt, heavy basic construction occurred during the war years at Los Alamos. M. M. Sundt Construction Co., the earliest of the contractors, set up offices in Santa Fe in 1943. So rapidly did the bomb facility grow that in a year the original contract for $1.25 million had grown through expansion and modification to over $7 million.[25]

Such construction necessitated the creation of a large workforce. M. Eugene Sundt estimated that at the peak of employment in 1943 some 3,500 men worked on the Hill erecting the secret facilities. Figures from other sources vary between 1,800 and 3,800.[26] It is impossible to say how much of the labor force came from the city but Sundt recalled that a fair number were local. It is likely that the workers recruited in Santa Fe stayed at Los Alamos since gasoline and tire rationing made commuting difficult.[27] For recruitment of skilled workers, the company turned to local union agents for help. They, in turn, scoured the entire country for qualified workers.

In town, common laborers were a scarce commodity by 1943 when Los Alamos had to compete with such military facilities as the Bruns Hospital in town for services.[28] Eventually, Native Americans and Hispano farmers from nearby villages formed another mainstay of the atomic facility's common labor force. The special needs of that population at times created problems for the builders. The Native Americans, many of them Navajo, would return to their reservation in northwestern New Mexico for ceremonies, creating problems for Sundt. He had to rig up semi-van trailers with benches to get them home and bring them back.[29] Local Hispano farmers, too, occasionally placed the welfare of their crops above the immediate needs of Los Alamos.

The growth of the project produced ripples of economic activity in the town. The large quantities of materials needed on the Hill came from everywhere via the railroad and then had to be trucked to their final destination. Whatever could be procured locally meant increased purchases from such existing firms as Santa Fe Builders Supply Company and James Breese's Oil Devices Company.[30] These actions must have stretched the labor supply of the city quite thin in 1943.

The secrecy surrounding Los Alamos also veiled major operations within the Santa Fe banking community. The First National Bank became the repository of funds for various financial operations there. The January 1946 president's report to stockholders noted that

> Your bank not only made up the payrolls for Los Alamos, but also provided banking facilities to a large portion of Los Alamos personnel and at times covered substantial overdraughts. . . . It covered the payrolls and provided banking facilities to the contractors who built Los Alamos . . .[31]

In 1945 the bank's earnings rose 30 percent over the previous year, while its total assets tripled between 1940 and the war's end. Yet, this occurred quietly and was revealed only after the end of hostilities.[32]

Postwar investigations revealed that some exceptional efforts had indeed been made to learn of what was going on at the Hill. Klaus Fuchs and David Greenglass, both of whom worked at the atomic facility, became involved in spying for the Russians. Both had contact with one Harry Gold, who, in turn, delivered information to the Soviets, America's postwar enemy. Fuchs met Gold in Santa Fe several times in 1945 to hand over information to him there.[33] Of course, neither Santa Feans nor the American government had any specific awareness of such goings-on. However, people in the city and at Los Alamos apparently were aware of the presence of American security agents in town, both civilian and military.[34]

Santa Fe itself never became the site of any major military installations during the war. Nevertheless, the national government did locate several war-related institutions within the city that had an immediate impact on it. Moreover, although they proved to be temporary and were dismantled shortly after the end of hostilities, one of them, at least, carried longer-term consequences for the town.

The best known of these installations was the Bruns General Hospital. Occupying several hundred acres in the vicinity of today's St. Michael's Drive and The College of Santa Fe, some distance southwest of the plaza, the hospital served for a time as a specialized center for chest and pulmonary injury and ailment, but mostly as a general hospital. It was named after deceased Colonel Earl Harvey Bruns of the army medical corps and received formal dedication on 21 September 1943.

Bruns actually began accepting patients five months before its official opening. By the time of that formality, it had already treated 1,500 military personnel and had discharged 600.[35] In September 1946, three months before it closed, it still held 644 patients.

The facility had considerable value for the city. The *New Mexican* recalled how Santa Fe, which had lost ten percent of its population to the armed forces and war industries, was still ailing economically in early 1942, before construction of the hospital had begun.[36] Once that activity started late that year, it created civilian jobs. By April 1945, 227 civilian employees, many, without doubt, from the city, were working there.[37] When the announcement of its closing came in September 1946, some 400 civilians were still earning their livelihood at the hospital.[38]

The hospital's growth also aided employment elsewhere in the city. In 1944, Bruns temporarily annexed and modified the Santa Fe Inn on Old Santa Fe Trail for use as a convalescent center. And the Bruns facility itself experienced a sizable expansion that also involved the hiring of manpower. The contracting firm of Robert E. McKee undertook the work.

The hospital's presence also contributed to the growth of the city's water supply. The large requirements of the installation, estimated at some 120 million gallons, persuaded the water company to construct a new reservoir, which was completed in 1943.[39]

At the war's end, Bruns occupied some 235 acres and 200 buildings.[40] For

Santa Fe that was a large institution and as early as the summer of 1944 the *New Mexican* was asking editorially what would happen if Bruns reverted to the city. Its disappearance, the author feared, could result in a severe economic jolt. He sought unified community support to have Bruns become a permanent installation.[41] In October 1946, with the closing of the institution assured, it was estimated that the loss to Santa Fe would come to $4.5 million a year.[42]

The movement toward establishing the hospital as a permanent institution was ultimately unsuccessful. To no avail, the chamber of commerce sought support from the governor and New Mexico's congressional delegation. Veterans hospitals, military logic ran, had to be located near large cities to deal with numbers, while doctors could not be persuaded to come to small towns.[43] As a result, suggestions poured in about alternative uses of the facility. City councilman Ray P. Sharp offered the possibility that it become a playground or a gymnasium. St. Michael's put in a bid for some of the land and buildings to expand its college facilities, a proposal some city councilmen favored. Governor John J. Dempsey suggested that it be used for a health and welfare center, eliminating the need for a new office building project and making possible the treatment of tuberculosis patients.[44] Los Alamos itself sought to obtain the gymnasium, chapel, laundry, and storage facilities.[45] In the end, Los Alamos and St. Michael's, which moved its campus to the site, carried the day, and the Bruns Hospital passed into history.

Despite the hospital's demise, it nevertheless carried some important consequences for Santa Fe's medical future. Dr. Harry D. Ellis, who came to practice in the city in 1954, noted that "probably half the guys [i.e., doctors] in Santa Fe when I came were stationed at Bruns during the war and came back afterwards. Some . . . went east for their training and then returned to Santa Fe."[46] Others bear out his statement. At that time, the arrival of even a half-dozen new doctors in the period of a few years made a great difference in the quantity and quality of available care in the still small city.[47] Thus, Santa Fe gained from the hospital's presence, despite its temporary character.

A year before Bruns appeared, early in 1942, the war came home to Santa Fe through the creation of a detention center for Japanese Americans. The centers were created immediately after Pearl Harbor as a security measure presumed necessary against enemy aliens and citizens who might prove dangerous to the war effort. West-coast Japanese were so classified, and in February 1942 government officials arrived in Santa Fe to survey the possibility of using an abandoned Civilian Conservation Corps camp in the northwest quadrant of the city as such a center.

The site proved satisfactory for the national government's purposes and the Santa Fe Detention Center became a reality. Several reasons prompted approval of the specific site and Santa Fe itself. The condition of the camp, which held numerous semipermanent buildings and intact utility lines on eighty acres of land held by the New Mexico State Penitentiary all were in its favor. As for Santa Fe itself, its relative isolation in an area of low population density satisfied the security standards required by the government. U.S. Highway 66, the major east-west highway, was seventy miles away and linked to Santa Fe by narrow, two-lane roads. The main line of the railroad was about sixteen miles away.[48] Ironically, some thirty miles away and a year later, work on Los Alamos, the most secret of installations, would begin.

Feelings in Santa Fe against the Japanese ran high after the outbreak of war. Even as the camp was being readied for occupancy, a scheme to colonize 60,000 Japanese Americans permanently in New Mexico came to light, arousing a great outcry of anger from many parts of the state and from Santa Fe itself. Since it was assumed that the vast majority of the proposed colonists would be farmers and farm laborers, one objection raised in a *New Mexican* editorial pointed out that there was insufficient tillable land and not enough water for New Mexicans.[49] The same editorial admitted, however, that they would be unwelcome because they would destroy the only "golden egg" the area had, "the color and atmosphere" of the city. "No longer," the editors reiterated, "would we be able to boast of local color, of Spanish and Indian romance and influence which has proven such a valuable drawing card for this section of the southwest."[50] While national anger and the pain of war, as well as economic competition, might have satisfied most, fear of the dilution of Santa Fe's ethnic ambiance received the *New Mexican*'s additional attention. The colonization scheme never materialized.

Although Santa Feans were aware of the camp's presence, the government kept as tight a secrecy lid as it could over its existence. Contacts between town and camp were kept at a minimum until the war's end. There are indications that the motivation for this high level of discretion arose out of the awareness that problems between the two communities could produce harmful reciprocal effects on American prisoners held by the Japanese.[51] Such considerations may have sobered Santa Feans, angry over the events on Bataan, who at one point contemplated attacking the newly arrived internees.[52] Newspaper accounts of such events appear to be largely absent, possibly the result of government pressure on the press.

Nevertheless, the arrival of the internees was publicly noted. In March 1942 some 600 detrained with over 200 more arriving the following month. The rations of the Japanese Americans became an issue. The rice, fish, and soybeans sought for them put pressure on local food wholesalers from whom such items were purchased and raised some resentment.[53] The *Albuquerque Journal* merely noted that the government was asking for expensive foods for the detainees.[54]

Aside from these early events, little else of moment occurred between the camp and Santa Fe. The brighter side of the picture, as the *New Mexican* viewed it, was the creation of new jobs. Not all of them went to Santa Feans, but at least new persons who received employment moved into town.[55]

The camp's status went through several phases, closing temporarily in September 1942 after the initial hearing of the internees' cases and reopening in the following year as a permanent wartime facility. It finally closed in April 1946 after reaching a peak of 2,100 occupants in mid-1945. Writing in March 1946, columnist Will Harrison of the *New Mexican* noted its imminent closure with a sense of relief, even if it meant the loss of ninety jobs and some large purchases in town. He noted that no one had escaped from the facility and only one person had even tried.[56]

For Santa Fe, the wounds of battle, loss of life, and memories of prisoner-of-war camps left a permanent residue of sadness. The temporary installations, the hospital and internment camp, became mostly memories, although the hospital, as noted, had the lasting consequence of enticing numbers of medical professionals to join the city. The creation of Los Alamos and its conversion from a temporary into a permanent community, however, would offer far greater possibilities for sustained interaction and change.

Thus, World War II, which ended the Depression, had interrupted one exceptional series of events and replaced it with another. When it was over, Santa Fe seemed ready to revert to ways of life that preceded it. The war's effects on the town were in many ways unlike the effects on Albuquerque, where new institutions created by the war became the driving forces of its future development and sharply changed the direction of its history. Santa Fe could return more readily to patterns that were a continuation of the past.

Nevertheless, in some respects the Depression and World War II left a legacy that made any easy return to the Santa Fe of the twenties impossible. By the end of the war, Santa Fe was much larger than it had been in 1930. Moreover, the war continued to increase the governmental presence that had commenced so strongly with the Depression. A significant veteran population with new opportunities for education and claims to government support opened vistas unknown before, both for employment and for the delivery of services. Peace would provide an opportunity for the Santa Fe that was emerging in the 1920s to reassert itself, but it would do so under conditions that reflected the new realities produced by the Depression and the war and against the backdrop of an America that was also changing rapidly in many ways.

TEN

The Postwar Era: Planning and Politics, 1945–1990

FOR ROUGHLY FIFTEEN years the attentions of Santa Feans had focused on the Depression and on World War II. During the Depression the town had experienced unprecedented population growth as well as economic hardship. The war, in turn, had sharply interrupted and placed on hold every pattern of accustomed life. When it ended in 1945, New Mexico and Santa Fe were far less isolated than they had been in the late twenties. If the changes the town experienced were not as earthshaking as either the coming of the Americans in 1846 or of the railroad in 1880, they were nevertheless sufficiently great to make many of its residents realize that a new era had arrived.

The half-century that followed the end of the war, unmarked by any spectacular event to define periods sharply, was one of evolutionary change. Under these circumstances, our history, as it unfolds in the following chapters, addresses the postwar era from differing perspectives and subject matter, rather than as a single chronological sequence. The desire to retain the visual character of the city and the politics that grew out of that effort form one distinct theme. The growth and cultural broadening of the town form another, carrying it beyond the earlier Southwestern tricultural focus that had dominated its prewar dimensions. In addition, growth after the war brought to the fore urban problems that flowed from new social and economic relationships touching on everything from the formation of new neighborhoods to problems of educating children—issues of a living, growing community. And lastly, wittingly or not, attitudes and practices of both major ethnic groups merged and produced an evolving society even as old recognizable elements remained.

Forces in the city, while looking for a return to the past as the war ended, realized that growth had changed the old parameters. An editorial in the New Mexican on 13 September 1945 breathed a sigh of relief that there was no permanent army installation to disrupt the old place. However, the estimated population of 24,000 appeared too large to accommodate comfortably to the lifestyle of the twenties. Still devoted to images of development created before the Depression, the editorial regretted the absence of rules respecting new buildings and expressed the hope that appropriate regulation would come. It also found regrettable the lack of encouragement for "Santa Fe architecture" in new construction. Above all, Santa Fe had to keep up her appearance for her largest industry—tourism.[1]

Long deferred after the initial efforts of 1912, planning became an immediate issue after the war. The revelation that state and federal authorities would build a new road through the city served to raise the issue. Meanwhile, the *New Mexican* and the chamber of commerce puzzled over how to regulate expected growth in housing and business.[2]

The state of New Mexico itself had gradually created the means for cities to regulate their own fates in matters related to zoning and planning. In 1927 the legislature had passed an act empowering them to deal with the size, location, and purpose of buildings in accord with plans deemed to be for the general welfare.[3] After strengthening such regulations in 1941, the state carried the process a step further in 1947, enacting legislation that authorized city planning commissions and the creation of master plans.[4] Urban areas had now acquired sufficient power to arrange their internal affairs in accord with the wishes of their citizens and elected authorities.

To aid Santa Fe with its problems, the city council, chamber of commerce, state highway department, school board, and the Old Santa Fe Association each devoted a sum of money to employ the services of Harland Bartholomew and Associates, a St. Louis planning firm, to undertake a survey of the city.[5] It completed a preliminary study in October 1947. In turn, the city created its own planning commission in April 1948 and a zoning ordinance in the same month. The new board included many spokesmen who had long fought to preserve the old character of the town and who recognized the importance of tourism. Such persons as Amelia White, John Gaw Meem, Dan Kelly, and Witter Bynner had been on the old informal commission of 1946; and the first three were retained on the new legally endowed board that would consider the broadest aspects of the city's welfare.

Conceived as a research and fact-finding instrument, the commission was empowered to make advisory recommendations to the city council regarding long-term planning and to create a master plan for the physical development of the city. The city council was to authorize no public improvement nor contract for services of any private architect or engineer until it had requested the recommendation of the commission. The regulation did not, however, limit the power of the city council to act without such opinions.[6] Inevitably, the power of elected officials to act and of the planning commission to recommend at times became a focal point of difference.

The Harland Bartholomew plan, which appeared in preliminary form in 1947 and in published form in 1950, became the framework for discussion and decision from that time forth although the city council did not officially adopt it at that time. When it became public in April 1947, the *New Mexican* printed sections of it. It chose to highlight at the outset a rather shocking report of the effects of inadequate sewerage on infant mortality in the city and the unusually high incidence of typhoid, dysentery, and infant diarrhea. Santa Fe's rate was nearly double that for all of New Mexico.[7] For those accustomed to viewing and proclaiming the favorable conditions of clear air and high altitude—looking up—this downward look, not usually indulged in by tourists or those who touted the city's virtues, was sobering. Many other parts of the Bartholomew plan forced a similar hard look at the city's infrastructure that went far beyond preservation and beautification.

Nevertheless, planning was too complex, costly, and affected too many persons and interests in conflicting ways to make any speedy action possible. At first, the plan was a state of mind rather than a formalized political agenda and received only occasional mention by city office candidates in postwar election campaigns until the mid-fifties. Office seekers occasionally proclaimed themselves for "modern progress" while "retaining the culture and attractive atmosphere" of the city.[8] The *New Mexican* also editorialized on the same theme.[9] By the mid-fifties, however, candidates and parties were expressing their support publicly for planning and for the commission with regularity and the force of principle.[10]

The perspectives for change provided in the Harland Bartholomew plan produced an arena for considerable and continuous debate in the city. Issues concerning the use of space and appearance forced individuals and neighborhoods to consider the concrete effects of changes on their properties, while issues of zoning became an important focus for the city council's time and energy. The state, as noted, had authorized such regulations in 1927 and the city had enacted a relatively simple code distinguishing business and residential districts that served well enough until the postwar thrust toward planning began to occupy the residents.[11] The city ordinance adopted in 1948 was far more comprehensive, defining lot size within zones, reclassifying commercial and industrial areas, and eliminating commercial islands in residential districts.[12]

Perhaps the boldest and most definitive step of the entire planning movement came in 1957. That year marked a turning point when the city council adopted an ordinance to preserve and maintain historic architecture and style within certain areas of the town—the H (Historic) Zone—designated as crucial for the preservation of its character. Arguments raged passionately over the issue for the best part of the year. The Old Santa Fe Association, some of whose members could recall the original planning impulse of the 1910–1919 decade, stood as stalwarts of preservation. John Gaw Meem, who did not automatically accept a narrow interpretation of how to continue the work of the past, was nevertheless the leading spokesman for the adoption of the ordinance. Santa Feans generally accepted the concept of harmonious preservation, but some architects, in particular, considered the restrictiveness inherent in the ordinance as a limitation on their work. The adoption of the ordinance in November was significant enough to be reported in the *New York Times*.[13]

In 1960 the city finally adopted the concept of a master plan. The council, along with the capital building improvements commission, which helped to fund the work, turned to the Denver firm of Harman, O'Donnell, and Henninger to create the actual instrument that would guide the city's future development.[14] It was officially accepted in March 1962.[15] Along with its Harland Bartholomew predecessor, probably no documents in the city received more attention or occasioned more discussion in the postwar era. The plans objectified thoughts and images about the city and served as a standard for discussion about goals. Santa Feans became self-conscious through planning to a degree that few towns could match.

City elections from the postwar forties until the mid-fifties reflected little that was new. The less-than-satisfactory street conditions appeared as a perennial election issue, while the lack of funds to undertake large-scale improvements remained a hindrance to action. Juvenile delinquency and the performance of a police department hampered by political allegiances also drew repeated attention. In 1950 the issue of whether to purchase the waterworks reappeared, but the electorate rejected it. Only the above-noted formal introduction of planning was new. However, the early planners' analyses were still far removed from the field of practical action in the first years after the war and, much as some Santa Feans thought about the future of their city, the issues raised did not create immediate political heat.

In the mid-fifties, the content of Santa Fe's political life broadened beyond traditional housekeeping to include issues of professional performance by city government. Such concerns reflected the continuing growth of the town and the consequent need for both systematic procedures and skilled personnel to implement them. The adoption of a council-city manager form of government was one way to attain that objective. Similarly, the creation of a merit system for departments, which had already been adopted for the police department, caught the attention of the political parties during this period, without any immediate action being taken. It seems likely that the postwar concern with planning, too, may well have abetted the process of administrative reform. Years spent with professional planners and reliance on their expertise, as well as growth itself, may have accustomed the city and its elected officials to consider the value of professionals and full-time workers for government service.

The acceptance of planning ensured that related issues would gain prominence as electoral matters. In the late fifties and throughout the sixties candidates for office faced questions repeatedly about their stand on the master plan and how they felt about the H Zone. The Old Santa Fe Association took on the role as an agent for the public and put questions to candidates around the preservation of landmarks and traditions, assuring prominence for issues in planning that affected its interests. The League of Women Voters, through its nonpartisan forums, strengthened the focus on public issues by reducing personal mudslinging and backbiting, party-oriented campaigns, although that form of campaigning did not disappear until the mid-sixties—at least for a time.[16] This new tone in the city's politics aided those interested in keeping preservation as an element of planning in the public eye.

In the years immediately following the war, the city could not escape the pent-up pressures of the war years. Housing was in great shortage. No building had taken place during the conflict and returning veterans, eager to resume their lives or to begin families, sought living quarters at precisely the time when construction materials were difficult to obtain and shortages pushed prices up at a rapid rate.

The forces wedded to preserving the city's old character faced a frightening prospect. One could not deny returning servicemen the opportunity of an abode, but would it be adobe? While between 1935 and 1940 some 335 units had been built, the chamber of commerce now spoke of needing 500 additional units—and style could not be the commanding issue. In its discussion of the problem the chamber could only suggest that the hoped-for houses would not occur as a colony, but in a scattered fashion around the town.[17]

The shortage of building materials probably aided the protectors of the Santa Fe style. Only a few houses could be built at a time and the relatively slow process allowed a gradual resumption of a more normal pace of demand to soften some of the emergency measures contemplated. For a time in 1946 the chamber of commerce had even suggested bivouacking veterans in the abandoned Japanese prison camp. The federal government, however, would not agree.[18] Later that year the arrival of housing units from Ft. Sumner improved conditions for veterans living with families or in tourist courts.[19] The style protectors must have shuddered at their appearance.

But Santa Fe largely escaped becoming a town, even temporarily, of sizable tracts of used barrack buildings. Allen Stamm, just out of the navy, moved quickly into housing development and in December 1945 proposed to deliver Santa Fe-style homes in some number for under $5,000 on the west side of town. In doing so, he launched a career that made him the premier contractor in the city.[20] By 1957 he had built a thousand homes in which about 15 percent of the city's population lived.[21] As a result of this housing boom, by 1963 the Stamm firm had some 168 employees, mostly Hispano carpenters, in its employ.[22] In those years Santa Fe's construction industry, according to a chamber of commerce spokesman, ranked third in the city in payroll, behind the government and the tourist trade.[23] Nearly an entire generation of Santa Feans had grown up and prided itself for having been raised in a "Stamm house."

The work of the builders created new population centers in the city. From the late forties through the mid-fifties, new neighborhoods such as Casa Linda and Casa Alegre totaling almost eight hundred houses arose close to Cerrillos Road. New schools and shopping facilities followed. The balance of city population began to shift, swelling the narrow ribbon of what had been the major route to and from the city into expanded population centers of some density.

The building boom created by war stoppages and population growth continued into the sixties. Stamm was joined by other large-scale developers such as Dale Bellamah of Albuquerque, one of the largest builders in the United States. They continued to create new neighborhoods of modest homes to the southwest of the Plaza, the town's old center, beyond St. Michael's Drive in the flatland below Cerrillos Road. For these residents, the Plaza became more remote than it had been and the entire center of population gravity moved southwest—toward the outer limits of the city.

At the end of the sixties the pace of building led to the judgment of the city building inspector, Mel Hagman, that the decade had witnessed "more new building than ever built in any other preceding decade" of the city's history.[24] He included within that definition structures of all kinds and did not quite restrict himself to the city limits, but the extent of activity was undeniable. Some of the projects Hagman noted were the Santa Fe Downs, a racing facility south of the city scheduled to open in 1971 and the state police academy, just south of town, that was nearing completion. Within the city itself, a 125-unit housing subdivision being constructed by the Dale J. Bellamah Corporation was well underway. Numerous other projects were under study, including large stores, schools, and office buildings.[25] The pace and tone of activity contrasted markedly with the images entertained by the cautious old city protectors, but most of the activity was not in the H Zone.

Housing costs rose as land became an ever more valuable commodity within the city, as the population and fame of the city grew, and as inflation drove up the price of materials. Between the early sixties and the late seventies dwellings of roughly the same size and quality that Allen Stamm built in the Barrio La Cañada subdivision tripled in cost. According to Stamm's calculations the increase in land value rose one fourth more than that of building cost increases.[26] Other sources confirmed the trend in sharply rising land values in the city.[27]

From 1980 to 1990, by every measure, housing moved into a very high cost category of life in Santa Fe County. The number of owner-occupied dwellings valued at under $50,000 dropped precipitously; the largest number, valued between $50,000 and $150,000, nearly doubled. However, the greatest change came at the upper end—those valued at over $200,000. The number of such houses rose from 335 in 1980 to 3,112 in 1990—by far the largest category of growth and surpassing in number houses in the $150,000 to $200,000 category.[28]

Rental costs rose even more sharply. The number of units charging $200 to $300 fell from over 2,600 in 1980 to 1,400 in 1990. Units costing $500 or more rose from 129 in 1980 to over 3,600 in 1990—a 2,700 percent increase! Such units became the most numerous category of dwelling during the decade.[29]

The increases in housing costs reflected new problems in the city's development. While planning demonstrated a strongly and widely held desire to maintain traditional elements and to accommodate growth, the geography of the city and the pace of growth produced contradictions and increasing friction. What distinguished Santa Fe from other towns experiencing even more rapid growth was its determination to retain many aspects of past development and character even at the expense of growth. The problem arose when the sustained growth of the postwar period created new pressures that arose out of the unanticipated rate of growth.

Insofar as housing represented an inevitable response to growth, the vision of the planners affected how growth could take place. Density of housing units and the size and dispersion of new housing developments affected the space available within the city limits. As the city grew and new concentrations of population arose at some distance from older areas, every human need and convenience spoke out for accommodation. For example, the newcomers required accessible shopping and neighborhood schools for their children. Utility lines had to be extended. Moreover, as distances from the older "downtown" lengthened, automobile usage became increasingly necessary and parking in the business area an ever greater problem. The city's plan did anticipate such issues, but the pace of growth and the pressure to deal with the population were at times beyond what any plan could envision or regulate. Each element of the problems encountered developed its own constituencies—for and against particular responses. Together, they formed no small part of the content of the community's political life.

The unprecedented growth in numbers and increased motor traffic on the old streets produced broader problems in the city that could not be ignored as the war ended. Federal and state concerns led government agencies in 1946 to the conclusion that a limited access cross-city route to connect Albuquerque, Las Vegas, and Taos was a necessity.[30] No small project, a serious discussion of interested parties ensued as the matter became public.

From the outset, the new route proposed by the state highway department found opposition. Initially designed to go along Jefferson Street, at the railroad right-of-way, it was quite close to the west side of the downtown area. The Old Santa Fe Association roused and revived itself in protest, Ina S. Cassidy leading the way. Property owners in the area, led by Mrs. Charles Kiesov, also joined in.[31] Mrs. Cassidy feared that the proposed route, so close to the downtown area, would create two cities—one new and one old—and would pass through one of the few areas where inexpensive homes could be built.[32] The Association also feared the destruction of historical buildings, while Nina Otero-Warren spoke of the route as one that would segregate the Spanish-speaking population.[33] As some put it, it would create "a little Chihuahua."

The planners then recommended a route somewhat farther west of the Guadalupe Church, to which the chamber of commerce, Old Santa Fe Association, and John Gaw Meem agreed.[34] In short order, however, property owners along the newly proposed route, heavily Hispano, objected strenuously. Interested real estate developers in the area, anticipating a decline in their land values, also joined in. Led by Frank Rivera and Thomas V. Conway, the opponents of the route argued that if they were dispossessed, they could not replace their lots. Moreover, they refused to be party to moving the proposed route still farther west on the grounds that they would not do to others what they did not want done to them.[35] They would only accept a route so far to the west that it would disturb no one. The Catholic War Veterans organization backed them, resolving that the city should rescind its approval. The route planners, however, saw in a distant western route no solution to city traffic problems.

The battle raged for months on end, each side refining its arguments and organizing support. In mid-1947 the city council accepted the second plan for the trans-city highway.[36] The conflict then assumed an air of melodrama. Hardly had the city accepted the new route, when the state highway department, which had authorized it and state aid to purchase the right-of-way,

22. *Nina Otero-Warren, long-term activist and officeholder. Courtesy Museum of New Mexico, neg. #89756.*

announced that no funds were available for that purpose. The city, in turn, had insufficient credit to finance such a purchase on its own.[37]

Whatever adjustments property owners and real estate developers were able to agree to, the disputes did not end there. Business owners along Cerrillos Road had a vested interest in maintaining the preeminence of their street as a major route through the town and they used their influence to support their cause. In 1960 the Cerrillos Road Association sought to outflank city supporters of the incomplete arterial route by working with the state highway department, which was partially responsible for funding the new route, to amend the plan and to point out its shortcomings.[38]

Like the task of planning itself, the building of the road became a drawn-out affair that appeared to have no end. While the project was being completed in piecemeal fashion, the *New Mexican* could write in 1964 that the work to finish the route was ahead of schedule. Asking Santa Feans to be patient, the paper noted that "The city has been waiting nine years for St. Francis Drive."[39] By the latter weeks of that year one could traverse the entire course of St. Francis Drive, but eighteen years had elapsed since the project had first been introduced.

Even as living conditions and traffic occupied the daily lives of Santa Feans, the decade of the sixties marked another kind of divide in American history that reached deeply into the lives of many Americans, altering perspectives and challenging traditions to a degree not often experienced. The war in Vietnam, a white-hot vent in the midst of the less openly violent Cold War, the civil rights movement of the African Americans, the women's movement for social equality, and the rise of Hispano activism were all part of it. Each of the issues had its own discrete background and expression, but often several of the issues became linked, gaining both in strength and confusion as a result.

New Mexico could not escape the national turmoil and even became home to one aspect of it. Long-standing grievances of Hispanos in the north central counties of the state, feeling cheated of their land grants and beset by difficult economic conditions, found a voice in the mid-sixties to express their discontent in the person of Reies Lopez Tijerina. The lands primarily under concern were many miles north of Santa Fe, and the organizational home to unite all heirs to grants and secure restitution received incorporation in Albuquerque in 1963 under the name Alianza Federal de Mercedes (Federal Alliance of Land Grants).[40] Santa Fe lay outside the major focal points of both the organization and the arena of direct action.

Nevertheless, Santa Fe was still the state capital. Insofar as state authority became involved in solving heated controversy, the city was at times a locus of action. In July 1966 protesters marched from Albuquerque to Santa Fe in hopes of meeting with Governor Jack Campbell. There, they sought to initiate action to redress their land grant and civil rights grievances. One hundred marchers left Albuquerque on a Saturday morning, planning to reach the outskirts of the capital by Monday evening and to march to the capitol itself on Tuesday, July 5. Although their numbers apparently declined during the trek, the protesters' ranks again swelled as they entered the city. It is uncertain if that growth reflected local support or a rejoining by supporters via motor vehicle.[41] Marchers to the capitol displayed signs opposed to the war in Vietnam as "a white man's war" as well as those related to land-grant grievances.[42] When Governor Campbell, who had been absent from the state, returned several days later, he accepted Tijerina's petition and promised to forward it to President Lyndon Johnson.[43] The entire event proceeded quite peacefully.

Santa Feans, as New Mexicans and Americans, could scarcely remain aloof from the powerful emotions that swept the late sixties in general and issues of the area in particular. But Santa Fe differed from both Albuquerque and Tierra Amarilla, Tijerina's home base in northern New Mexico. Tijerina found his claims immediately challenged by State Archivist Myra Ellen Jenkins, who found little historical validity in them.[44] Letters to the editor of the *New Mexican* from local Hispanos, while obviously a highly selective source, attacked Tijerina resentfully as an intrusive outsider.[45]

Tijerina also alienated local opinion in October 1967, when he spoke at St. John's College. On that occasion, his racial, if not racist, views decried older European and Jewish "races" for despoiling the heritage of what he called his "new breed" of Hispanos. He even identified the chief despoiler, Thomas Catron, as a Jew—which he was not. At that point Tijerina was labeled an anti-Semite by the local B'nai B'rith chapter and local Hispanos. A letter to the editor by one of the latter described him as unrepresentative of the Hispano majority and commended the American Legion for denying him use of its hall to speak.[46] Clearly, while Tijerina and the Alianza found some sympathy in Santa Fe, they also encountered strong antagonism.

Tijerina aside, some evidence of external radicalism did appear in the city. An outsider Hispano (Chicano) evaluation of Santa Fe appeared in a radical San Francisco paper, *Movement*, in 1969. The author, La Simpática, described the city as a small town where wealthy liberals blocked industry so that "their air" wouldn't become polluted. In a haven for them away from the big city, they were depicted as controllers of museums, while rich artists painted quaint Hispano slums. It was a capital surrounded by an ancient barrio, a place for rich traders and poor Indians, two towns—one rich, the other poor.

Even this advocate of ethno-class description, however, found the town less than adequate in terms of support for Tijerina. Upon arrival in Santa Fe in 1966, the author found that "no movement of any kind" existed. The Alianza had no impact since there were no land-grant descendants there. The local ruling class, in the author's view, consisted of medium-sized businessmen, a mixture of Hispanos and Anglos. Those Hispanos were described as "sell-outs" or "brown noses." The handing out of the lowest state jobs reminded the writer of old Mexico.

Speaking of successes achieved, the author described the beginnings of a street theater and the creation of a Brown Beret group, which actually occurred in 1968. La Simpática acknowledged the small size of the latter organization, however active and respected, but saw their activity as a start in building a community organization that would deal with day care, bilingual education, welfare rights, and police brutality.[47] Its extravagant symbolism, expressed in uniforms and arms, seems to be in some contrast to the relatively moderate demands made.

La Simpática's account had elements of accuracy. Indeed, Tijerina did not appear to have had any major impact in Santa Fe, but some aftereffects in Hispano community organization did result from the upsurge of activism, particularly among some younger Hispanos. In 1970 they created an organization, La Gente, with the purpose of generating services for poor members of their community. It challenged the agenda of the city's urban renewal agency and demanded support for a health care facility, La Clínica, to improve the lives of local inhabitants. The organization succeeded in having such a facility opened in the summer of 1972, aided by local medical and religious institutions.[48]

In general, the aims of La Gente paralleled the goals of government action instituted by President Lyndon Johnson. Nationally, the Model Cities legislation drew its inspiration from public reaction to urban deterioration and the belief that America's health depended on the revival of urban areas.[49] Santa Fe's Model Cities program concentrated on legal aid, tutorial scholarships, health, the creation of a multipurpose center, street development, services to the aged, and community relations and citizen participation.[50]

The federal legislation and the city's reaction, as well as the presence of the new citizens' organizations, indicated a new sense of some moderately militant cultural and class identification. Santa Fe's growth and change were beginning to reflect that the city was not merely a Hispano town with some wealthy philanthropic and artistic Anglos, but one in which some Hispano areas were becoming defined as neighborhoods within a growing Anglo population. Economic and cultural differentiation, often played down in the twenties both by the character and small size of the Anglo community, now became more problematic. The growth of the Anglo population and the new building that accompanied it tended to emphasize economic distinctions, while increasingly differentiating where Hispanos and Anglos lived. The use of the term "barrio" became frequent where it had not been used before. To some younger Hispanos, it was an acceptable and honorable description. The defining of the Model Cities area as north of Cerrillos Road with St. Francis Drive and Agua Fria Street as a focal point affirms the view.[51]

In the election year of 1970 the Model Cities program carried some resonance. The efforts of an organization named the Federation of Barrios to gain official recognition created some friction between advocates and opponents of approval. In reviewing the Model Cities program several years later, its evaluators were only modestly sanguine about the state of information collected by the planning department and the failure to establish priorities, but concluded that "with all its imperfections, the Model Cities application was the first concerted look the community had taken at its poorest neighborhood."[52] However modest the social and economic gain of its poorest citizens that followed from both government programs and the efforts of local advocates for the poor, a strain of spirited advocacy on their behalf entered Santa Fe's political process.

La Clínica, meanwhile, lasted about twelve years. Housed in a former convent owned by the Catholic diocese, it provided medical care and health awareness for the poor of Santa Fe. Beset by financial problems for many years of its existence, and, facing an end to its one-dollar-a-year lease from the Church, it closed its doors in 1984. Thus ended one thread of the movement that had begun in the late sixties and early seventies.[53]

La Gente's agenda did not end with the clinic. It joined with other groups to form El Comite de los Barrios Unidos and went on to create a farmers market by linking up with farmers of surrounding areas to distribute fruit and vegetables.[54] It also founded an "all-Chicano" school that stressed vocational training and Hispano culture in the Agua Fria area.

The school venture ended badly when a shoot-out between police and Chicanos occurred on 3 September 1973.[55] The event sparked both open Hispano community resentment against Archbishop James P. Davis, who had allowed use of the former convent by El Comite, and fear of the militants.[56] Ultimately, the archbishop expelled the occupants and El Comite suffered adverse publicity.[57] The "Santa Fe 7" were eventually found innocent in the armed battle with the police. Their trial took place in Española.[58]

As noted, the raised consciousness of some Hispanos found its way into the city's political campaigns. The *New Mexican* found disturbing echoes of ethnic awareness in the election campaign of 1968, seeing in them a disruption of the relatively nonpartisan political atmosphere that had grown up several years earlier. Its editorials feared a return to party politics and complained of "blatant appeals over the radio to [the] 'raza' vote" working on ethnic pride.[59] In its stand for the election of Pat Hollis, who had been mayor since 1962, the *New Mexican* pointed out that his administration had labored in its planning efforts to take advantage of the state and federal programs to salvage run-down areas including an urban renewal project, application for participation in the Model Cities program, and the creation of special committees of volunteers to enable communication with the city's entire population.[60] The newspaper's efforts failed, however, and Democrat George Gonzales prevailed as mayor. The spirit of the 1968 election carried over into the 1970 campaign and Gonzales's victory brought him even greater support on the city council.

The militants, in their quest for a political voice and impact, did seek to cooperate with other organizations and individuals concerned with the Hispano poor in the election of 1972. La Gente joined with other barrio groups and Anglo community organizers responsive to the Hispano poor to form a Coalition of Citizens for Responsible Government (CCRG). Among other issues, it sought funds for the rehabilitation of substandard housing and improvement of water services. The slate made a creditable showing in that election, offering the city's voters a new political path in what was a lively campaign.[61]

The CCRG managed another strong performance in the 1974 election. Its three candidates for the city council all won a number of precincts, indicating a geographic preference for their views and, in general, improved on the total vote over the 1972 campaign. Emma Rivera, seeking a council seat from Ward Two, was employed as a project coordinator at La Clínica. Gerald Ortiz y Pino, running for a four-year term in Ward Three, came close to winning his race.[62]

By the election of 1976, however, new faces and issues appeared. Relative newcomers to the city gained places on the city council. One of the victors, Dora Battle, won her seat as an independent and was the first woman ever elected to the post.[63] The votes for Battle and Michael Runnels, another new council member, reflected citywide support rather than concentrated pockets.[64] By this time the names of the old CCRG candidates no longer appeared in the political fray.

The 1976 election might also stand for a broader change that appeared in Santa Fe politics. The new forces at work in the city—somewhat reduced dependence on parties and greater concern with issues—reflected a decade or more of changing attitudes. Younger candidates were one result. In the fifties and most of the sixties candidates for mayor and city council posts were rarely under forty years of age. By the late sixties and throughout the seventies candidates and city elected officials in their thirties were the rule—George Gonzales was elected mayor in 1968 at the age of thirty.

Moreover, in the seventies the electorate accepted candidates who were relative newcomers to the city. In 1970 George Scarborough, a self-described student who had lived in Santa Fe for two years, was elected to the city council. In 1976 city council electees Dora Battle and Michael Runnels had each lived in Santa Fe for only five years. The changing population and concerns, it seemed, required a fresh outlook. Old-line Santa Fean Sam Pick, who was narrowly reelected to the city council in that year, remarked, "I think we're getting an influx of new people. . . . People feel the need for change every now and then."[65]

Large concerns filled the political horizon. Candidates spoke of limiting the size of the city, relating their concerns directly to the availability of water and city services. Questions were raised about the advisability of further annexations that would extend the range of services, or whether lands closer in be utilized.[66] The inhabitants' view of the city as essentially small and the issue of whether it should be kept that way engaged many of the candidates. Efforts to maintain its visual character through planning were plainly of concern to them, supplanting to a degree the social issues of elections in the earlier seventies.

A comparison of the seventies' newcomers with those of the twenties shows some important differences in how the city was changing. The small contingent of wealthy and artistic newcomers of the earlier decade emphasized preservation of the old parts of the city and the fostering of its distinct cultural assets. Yet, a certain respectful distance separated them from the daily life of the town. They retained their own position and character—they were in the city but in many ways not of it.

The newcomers of the seventies, while recognizing the importance of the earlier issues and what had been accomplished to uphold those goals, reflected a much broader concern for problems affecting the entire city of which they were a part. They sought to deal with the community as a social organism rather than to serve only as cultural conservators. They considered issues that affected the entire city, despite the continuing (and even growing) cultural and economic distinctions that the political contingent of the twenties scarcely had begun to consider.

Growth, too, continued and intensified as an issue. One older candidate, A. B. Martinez, Jr., a native of the city, spoke plaintively of how the city had changed for him. "At one time most everybody knew each other. . . . What is overwhelming our culture now is the fantastic seemingly uncontrolled influx of new residents who live here but are not really part of the community."[67] While to him the growth of the city appeared large, it was scarcely so, as noted elsewhere, by the standards of many towns in the American West.

By 1978, growth raised issues that naturally accompanied it. The larger the city became, the greater the problem concerning the number and use of automobiles. Downtown parking became increasingly difficult. Suggestions for creating a public transportation system arose although its efficacy appeared daunting both for its cost and its desirability in the eyes of the townspeople. In 1978, too, candidates came forth in protest against reduced expenditures for social service programs. City council candidate Pete Jimenez argued for greater efforts to obtain federal funding, particularly to aid young people. Jimenez, however, was not among those chosen for office.[68]

The elections of the early eighties pursued the same themes. In part, the very fact that the city's growth was moderate allowed extended discussions of the issues surrounding it. Had there been the explosive growth of early postwar Albuquerque, the town may not have been able to afford them. The growth rate would have overwhelmed such prolonged debate. Underlying the growing parking difficulties in the downtown area and what to do about them lay the images and wishes of those who still visualized Santa Fe as the small town of their youth or as portrayed in the eyes of newcomers who still saw the city as the small community it had been in the prewar years and wished it could have stayed that way.

The dilemma became more pronounced each year. Distances between new housing developments and downtown increased, making shopping an ever longer and more inconvenient process. The answers to such problems existed in a host of western communities. However, Santa Feans, reluctant to accept growth and to accommodate themselves to the changes that accompanied it, left the issues to appear repeatedly in election years.

In 1984 census figures brought home to Santa Feans the state of their growth. The city attained the figure of fifty thousand inhabitants and became a Standard Metropolitan Statistical Area. If the figures held up, Santa Fe would be in the same class as Albuquerque and Las Cruces in terms of qualification for federal block grants that would help to fund community development projects.[69] Smallness, at least on the level that some Santa Feans hoped to retain, just kept on receding.

The election of 1988 witnessed the coming together of issues of growth, the rise of real estate values gradually separating the less affluent of Santa Fe from the wealthier newcomers, and the perception that changes were creating a new Santa Fe that reflected the values and life style of upper–middle-class America. Although shrinking relative to the whole population, the strong Hispano community and upholder of the older cultural values of the prewar town remained vital and sometimes supported by the Anglo community. The latter, however, had its own version of what parts of Hispano culture should be kept. Hispanos themselves, despite some strong preferences for traditional usage, no longer maintained parts of their material culture as they had when Santa Fe was a predominantly Hispano community with live roots in their Spanish-American and agricultural past.

The strongest political protest in 1988 lay in the election of Hispano councilor Debbie Jaramillo, who had earlier championed west-side efforts to scale down a major street project. Her message centered around bringing government back to the people, restraining the influence of developers, and narrowing widening gaps between Hispanos and Anglos.[70] Her presence on the city council proved to be a political highlight of the late eighties and early nineties.

Largely alone at first in her efforts to alter the direction the city was taking, Jaramillo proved a constant thorn in the side of the mayor and council. Despite her lonely role, her determination kept her positions in the public eye. In 1990 she ran against popular Mayor Sam Pick and lost, but remained a mem-

23. Debbie Jaramillo, first woman mayor. Courtesy the Santa Fe Reporter.

ber of the city council. A measure of her effectiveness, however, was the fact that several newly elected council members held positions close to her own, strengthening her stands against growth and for the possibility of city employees forming unions. During the campaign Jaramillo stated her belief that crime in Santa Fe, which was becoming an evermore obvious issue, be treated as a byproduct of economic conditions that needed to be addressed and that the path of the city's inequitable development was producing ethnic division.[71] By 1992 the *New Mexican* itself backed her for reelection to the council. Besides acclaiming her recognition of the importance of tourism and trade in the economy of the city, the newspaper favored her concept of the city as a crafts center for the products of native Santa Feans.[72] Her rerun bid was successful.

The importance of the issues she raised and the powerful attention she drew to them led her to run again for mayor in 1994. This time Jaramillo proved successful, campaigning against business-oriented candidates and stressing matters that to her represented the welfare of all. Her campaign revolved around issues in favor of small business and cottage industries, addressing poor housing, and paying attention to crime as an outcome of poverty.[73] The morning after the election the *New Mexican* characterized the results as a sweep for her philosophy and a victory for "the most liberal city council in the city's history" and "the end of an era in Santa Fe politics."[74]

Whatever the promise implied by that conclusion, the outcome moves beyond the time span allotted to our history. At that moment, however, the enthusiasm and joy of the victors carried a fervor that made the results appear powerful as an effort to reverse the trends of the generation that preceded the election. It seemed that the city, no longer a small town, possessed of a national and even an international reputation, might now emphasize a Santa Fe for Santa Feans and seek to regain possession of a soul some believed it had lost. The election results provided the best opportunity to achieve such goals and the delight it brought to the victors was unmistakable. Whether a state capital, a part of the United States, and a town sought out as a tourist and retirement destination could achieve such goals without becoming a free city-state remained to be seen.

A brief comparison of the economic development of Albuquerque and Santa Fe since World War II reveals some remarkable differences. Albuquerque, a regional railway and highway junction at the outset of the war, grew tenfold in forty-five years into a nationally significant high-tech production center. Like many parts of the Southwest, it drew tourists and retirees to its favorable climate and exceptional scenery. Santa Fe, which had long promoted a reputation for unique appearance and artistic presence as well as the favorable natural conditions that graced its location, moved from being a small town and governmental center, barely tripled in size, but built itself into a national and even international tourist center, adding many cultural attractions to its fare for both residents and tourists.

For Santa Fe, continued heavy government employment and tourist facilities and services remained the dominant foci of its employment base. The cultural and political leaders of the community who sought to retain that blend for the town remain partially responsible for the results—which were from their perspective highly successful. Yet, there were outcries throughout the period that the focus of the town's direction was too narrow, that it harmed segments of the town's population by producing an unhealthy imbalance, and that it served only its wealthier segments rather than the majority of its population, many of whom were not engaged in tourism.

The early planning documents of the postwar period (circa 1950) made clear some facets of attitudes and expectations toward industry. Looking at probable employment trends for the next twenty-five years (from 1950 to 1975), the planners projected some growth in government and a considerable increase in tourist activity. The latter, the planners suggested, might also lead to population growth if transport and preservation of the character and tradition of the area were maintained and improved. As for increased employment in areas beyond "the basic tourist industry," the possibilities were judged in modest terms. Other forms of economic activity did not fare even that well. As a result of limited transportation and distribution facilities, the planners asserted "Large industries can not be expected to locate in Santa Fe."[75]

The planners made plain in their zoning definitions that only industry should be permitted "that is not offensive because of emission of odor, dust, smoke, noise, or gas, in other words, any light industrial use." The areas of the city designated for industry included the Santa Fe Railroad Yards, the adjacent areas east of Hancock Street between Manhattan Street and the Santa Fe River and southward on both sides of Cerrillos Road. In all, this industrial zoning involved only 103 acres.[76]

In the mid-sixties, fifteen years after the first adopted plan, an update displayed some of the directions the city was taking. Manufacture as a category of economic development indicated that growth came largely as a result of the needs of the local population. Of the small numbers employed in manufacturing (4.3 percent of the workforce as compared with 24 percent nationally), food processing occupied a considerable segment of the firms and the employed. So too did lumber and other industries connected with construction, as well as clay and stone establishments. Hansen Lumber in 1957 had over one hundred employees, a large private firm for Santa Fe.[77]

Perhaps the main manufacturing change by 1957 was the appearance of the Eberline Instrument Division of Reynolds Electric Co., a firm "high tech" in nature that made, among other items, radiation detection equipment. In that year it employed somewhere between 20 and 49 employees.[78] By 1965 it had over 100 employees and in the early eighties that figure had risen to over 300.[79] Eberline may well have symbolized the ideal type of industry Santa Fe wished to accommodate in the post–World War II economy.

Political candidates mused sporadically about the need for industry in the city. But the boundaries of acceptability as defined in the planning documents held firm. Phrases about development "compatible with the nature of the community" in 1956 and use of the term "clean industry" dominated any consideration of a manufacturing presence.[80] A generation later, in the eighties, the issue appeared more stridently. The president of the *New Mexican* himself supported the effort to attract industry on the grounds that it would "offer a maximum of new job opportunities for our young people so they don't have to leave Santa Fe to secure decent jobs."[81]

The desire to acquire industry was not without opponents. In the somewhat radical atmosphere of the seventies, there were those who suggested growth from within, "not attracting outside industries" but aiding local small business.[82] In 1974 and 1976 there were candidates, frequently Hispanos, who stressed "growth from within" and a search for industries that fit the skills of the established population.[83] Jaramillo, in her 1992 campaign, moved along an analogous path, seeking to export "food, furniture, fashion, art and history, making them the foundation of a healthy indigenous economy."[84]

Whatever the opposition to and the difficulties of recruiting clean industry, the city made relatively small gains up to 1990. Its premier postwar builder, Allen Stamm, noted that from the fifties, "We (Santa Feans) were competing with 1,500 communities in America, all going after the same type of industry," with few interested in Santa Fe because of distance to markets and "'no right to work'" law.[85] Stamm agreed with Jaramillo's complaint that better jobs were needed than those offered in the service sector. Unlike those who sought to solve the problem from within, however, as late as 1996 he still saw the answer in light industry.

Thus, the economic picture of the postwar period showed no massive alteration of the sort experienced by Albuquerque. Industry grew more modestly than the population. In 1964 manufacturing stood at 4.3 percent of the county's employed, while government employment (federal, state, and local) stood at 34.3 percent. Trade and services accounted for another 36.1 percent.[86] In 1989 manufacturing stood at 4.17 percent, government at about 30 percent, and trade and services at 47 percent of the employed.[87] Growth in trade and tourism appeared to make the largest gains in the relatively stable distribution of employment.

The concern with growth became increasingly important in the postwar era. Whatever its unfavorable images—that it simply made the city too large, created too much traffic, or contributed to the loss of the town's traditional character—one issue remained a constant throughout the entire history of modern Santa Fe: the fear of a potential water shortage. Unlike most towns in New Mexico, private industry continued to provide water service to the city in the postwar period as it had since 1879. Indeed, it was only after World War II that the city's supply moved beyond the Santa Fe River surface flows to city wells. In the late sixties it extended to the Buckman well field along the Rio Grande.[88] As the town's population grew, water usage increased, and the source of supply was the Buckman field. Situated some 1,500 feet lower than the city and some fourteen miles away from it, the costs of development and operation proved considerable. Increases in rates followed in due course. In the seventies the city, county, and company moved to get water from the San Juan-Chama Diversion Project to the north to ensure supply.

The question of how to handle the issue had, as noted earlier, long sparked political debate in the city. It came down to matters of cost of purchase and management. The 1950 election campaign had centered around the $2.5-million purchase price for the water facilities and whether the city could run the utility.[89] The voters turned it down.

With price a continuing issue whenever contract renewals arose, the failure to purchase the system remained an issue. What had become apparent was the unwillingness of voters to engage in long-term contracts. Thus, in 1974 the city council agreed to a five-year water franchise with the Public Service Co. of New Mexico (PNM) rather than the older twenty-five-year contracts. The issue reemerged in 1978 with newly elected city council members and the mayor opposed to a twenty-five-year renewal as too long an obligation but purchase as too expensive. Again the voters turned it down.[90] The desirability of purchase grew stronger without accomplishment of the deed. In 1990 the *New Mexican* put the issue of purchase to mayoral candidates. They heavily supported purchase, but not without serious qualms about price and administrative control.[91] In 1995 the Sangre de Cristo Water Co. became the property of the City of Santa Fe.

The city had changed since World War II. In terms of size of population and developed area it might have astonished a prodigal who returned after nearly a half-century. On the other hand, the efforts of the preservationists and the planners would have left large areas of the Historical Zone quite recognizable with respect to the buildings themselves, the style and color of many new structures, and the shape of the streets. The familiarity of exteriors would not have extended to the use of interiors. The most overpowering change might well have been that downtown now catered to tourists rather than local citizens. Like many old Santa Feans, the prodigal may well have experienced a sense of loss that only the continuing presence and services of the La Fonda's bar could assuage.

ELEVEN

Beyond the Tricultural Town: Expansion of the Cultural Scene, 1945–1990

WHILE THE COMING of the railroad had ended an older commercial Santa Fe, the arrival of archaeology and the arts had sowed the seeds of a new direction for the city. In turn, the end of World War II opened the way for further expansion of that vision. Events growing out of the war—such as the creation of Los Alamos—provided unimagined opportunity and impetus to larger horizons for the city. Meanwhile, the powerful cultural and artistic images formed in the generation prior to the war not only remained intact but became the foundation for new growth. National conditions of well-being that permitted travel and tourism to grow coincided with the city's desire to attract travelers. It also supported efforts to lengthen the tourist season by allowing the creation of new interests in the city that would have seemed incredible before the war. Opera, skiing, new educational institutions, horse racing, and film production were among them. The city's increasing fame and expanding variety of activities inevitably drew a new population of artists, persons seeking to enjoy the varied activities while opening businesses or practicing professions, and some who sought retirement or a second home. As a result of its efforts, a half-century after the war, a changed Santa Fe emerged, one that now included a scale and variety in its cultural life that made it a national and even international center of repute.

The creation of Los Alamos during the war opened a new dimension for Santa Fe. With the atomic explosions that ended the war, Santa Feans learned openly what they had known but dimly—that they had a new neighbor to the northwest. Yet, with the fate of Los Alamos uncertain and the secrecy surrounding it still close, it took some time for the old capital to adjust to this new breed of settlement in its backyard. In his newspaper column, Will Harrison commented in September 1945 that unkind attitudes in the city were changing from the time when Santa Feans had regarded the base as a home for draft dodgers and foreigners.[1] Only in May 1946 did a New Mexican editorial welcome Los Alamos.[2] By that time it was becoming clear that the wartime community would become permanent.

In the next few years that did indeed happen. In 1947 the Atomic Energy Commission assumed responsibility for the program. A year earlier, the Zia Company had been created as a utility organization to provide for the maintenance of the facility. In April of that year it took over a payroll for no less than 1,500 former federal employees.[3] In the next few years Los Alamos slowly revealed its own public identity.

The two communities could only approach each other gradually. Security considerations still dominated Los Alamos's relationship to the outside world. But Los Alamos scientists, heavily preoccupied with the consequences of what they had wrought, sought to share their concerns with the outside world. They carried them to Santa Fe in late 1945, discussing openly the need for international control of the bomb.[4] Santa Feans, in their turn, noted the creation of the Zia Company to manage the facility and the involvement of local architect W. G. Kruger in creating a permanent settlement.[5]

Interaction between the two communities slowly became a fact of life. As Los Alamos achieved a strong civilian presence and the wartime restrictions on gasoline use eased, Santa Feans employed at the atomic city became commuters. Hudspeth's city directory of 1947 listed at least 58 employees of the Zia Company living in Santa Fe. By 1953 the number had risen to 153 and scientists were among Santa Fe residents employed there.[6] Six years later, some 259 Santa Fe residents commuted to Los Alamos and the number of scientists and engineers among them had grown, although still fairly small. The number of commuters seemed to stabilize at that point although the number of scientists increased somewhat. The large majority of the commuters remained Zia Company employees not involved in the research aspects of Los Alamos activities. In time, Los Alamos workers using Santa Fe and surrounding towns as their bedroom communities expanded considerably.

In 1957 the atomic center opened its doors to the public and became a new center of interest, adding to Santa Fe's breadth as a focal point of New Mexico tourism. Indeed, there were few places in the country where one could find two small cities of such fame so close to each other.

And Los Alamos made its presence known to the outside world. By early spring 1946 the *Los Alamos Times* began to cover regional events. In late 1952 some 130 clubs of all sorts had grown up within the community.[7] To the still hemmed-in citizens of the isolated town, Santa Fe allowed some measure of relief. The United Service Organization (USO) club in Santa Fe on San Francisco Street offered military personnel from Los Alamos a place to go.[8] Santa Fe businesses advertised their wares in the Los Alamos paper, as did Española and even Albuquerque firms. All of these activities slowly eroded the distance between the Hill and Santa Fe.

Arts and sports provided points of contact. The well-educated and worldly population of Los Alamos soon attracted its counterpart in Santa Fe. The practiced eye of Ina Sizer Cassidy found artistic sensibility and skill among Hill residents and she lauded their numbers, variety, and results.[9] In turn, Los Alamosans included art columns in their newspaper written by Santa Feans informing them of activities in the capital. Zia Company employees at Los Alamos and American Legionnaires of Santa Fe found basketball a vehicle for competition and camaraderie as interaction grew. In time, the Los Alamos art scene moved more actively into contact with Santa Fe. By the early fifties Los Alamos had its own art association and its painters exhibited frequently in the Museum of New Mexico gallery.[10] Despite the relatively small size of the community, its sophistication ensured frequent representation in Santa Fe.

Santa Feans also became aware of the exceptional character of their new neighbor. By 1955 the Archaeological Society of New Mexico had elected the director of the scientific laboratory, Dr. Norris Bradbury, to the presidency of their society. In the sixties, St. John's College would also recognize the proximity of the world-famous scientific personnel at Los Alamos when it chose Santa Fe as the site for its new campus. Clearly, the new town added a kind of distinction that benefited Santa Fe, while its proximity provided a pleasant and useful extension to the highly specialized and still partially closed world of Los Alamos.

In the eighties, the beginning of technology transfers from Los Alamos gave some hope to those in Santa Fe who sought high-tech industry for their town. For example, Amtech Technology Corporation found a presence in the city in 1984.[11] Thus, at least the beginning of an industrial relationship was formed between the two towns. Some political candidates savored the opportunity. If new firms wanted to remain close to their parent, they argued, then Santa Fe offered industrial parks and a nearby presence.[12] Nonetheless, industry and growth, as noted elsewhere, had their opponents in Santa Fe.

Another kind of institution also developed out of the proximity of the two towns. At the initiative of George Cowan, a senior fellow at Los Alamos, scientists and liberal arts people formed a "think tank" that found its home in Santa Fe. Called the Santa Fe Institute, it took shape in 1984.[13] Although participants came from everywhere, its presence in Santa Fe gave the city an opportunity to link itself to the world of scholarship and science in a new manner—as an "Athenic" conference and residential center. It confirmed the slowly growing ties between Los Alamos and Santa Fe and an expansion of the latter's horizons beyond the arts. On the other hand, the city also developed a small, but vocal, antinuclear community.

While Los Alamos was a creature of the war that redounded to the city's benefit, the development of skiing came about through the initiative of the Santa Feans themselves. Ambitious residents had long been concerned with the issue of how to extend the tourist season beyond the summer months. In the mid-thirties, a new possibility had come to light—the development of skiing facilities in the nearby Sangre de Cristo mountains. The rangers of the U.S. Forest Service, in fulfillment of their duties, were probably the first to glide over the ample snowpack that annually fell in the area. Los Alamos Ranch School students had also skied at that time.[14] And there were sufficient numbers of New Mexicans schooled in areas where skiing was an important winter activity, to awaken to its possibilities at home for their own enjoyment, as well as for tourist exploitation.

By 1936 Santa Fe Rotarians and the chamber of commerce had become sufficiently interested to engage the services of a professional ski instructor from Colorado, Graeme McGowan, to study the scene. He found favorably for developing facilities at Hyde Park, some eight miles from the city.[15] As a result, the Santa Fe Winter Sports Club was organized in 1937. The National Park Service and the U.S. Forest Service created a practice hill and improved trails at that time. By the time the war broke out one could find some fifty skiers at play in the late winter and spring.[16]

At the war's end, the enthusiasts resumed their efforts. They relocated to Horse's Head, completed a road through Native American land in 1949, and formed a corporation to create facilities and purchase equipment for skiers. Slowly, lovers of the sport from Texas began to arrive. In 1953 Joe T. Juhan of Colorado purchased the assets of the Sierras de Santa Fe Corporation and improved the skiing facilities.[17] By 1954 *Sports Illustrated* was listing the Santa Fe Basin as one of the twelve top ski spots in the United States. Several years later New Mexico even had local hopefuls for the American Olympic teams, John Dendahl and Mary Lind, and the Texans continued to come.[18]

Santa Fe's success with skiing coincided with the development of other ski areas in the state. Sandia near Albuquerque, Taos in the north, and Cloudcroft in the south, all moved in the same direction. Each area drew upon its own special qualities and New Mexico became an important destination for skiers nationally. In 1980 Taos appeared to be the most popular place for the sport.

There can be little doubt, however, that the growing fame and broadening facilities of Santa Fe contributed to the attractiveness of its skiing facility.[19]

In the early seventies the conjuncture of the sport's attractiveness and the fame of the town even gave birth to the creation of a garment factory—Alti of Santa Fe—and sales outlets dedicated to produce winter clothing suitable to the conditions of the sport.[20]

By the mid-eighties Santa Fe skiing was attracting greater numbers than any museum in the city, its attendance approached only by The Downs, the horse-racing facility.[21] Thus, the success of the venture contributed to the lengthening of the tourist season as its initiators had hoped. The development of skiing represented an extension of the physical environment to purposes little utilized before the war and now available to local residents as well as to visitors who could combine their love for the sport with time spent in town. A few years later, however, as with opponents of the atomic bomb, advocates of environmental causes fought efforts to expand the ski area.[22]

Other new forms of postwar activity expansion went far beyond skiing in their cultural outreach. The arts, architecture, and crafts fostered in the teens and twenties had rested firmly on the natural scenery and cultural environment of New Mexico. Santa Fe's reputation had grown as a center based on its geographic location in the midst of the Pueblo and Hispano environment and the way Anglos had presented them to the outside world.

The founding of the Santa Fe Opera in 1957 marked a sharp departure from that path. Under the leadership of John O. Crosby, who created and directed the new musical venture, Santa Fe donned a national and even international summer mantle by seeking to extend interest to cultural subject matter based on European traditions and practiced in large American urban centers. It might attract visitors and talent from everywhere, but intrinsically it belonged neither to Santa Fe nor to New Mexico in the old, prewar cultural mode.

Crosby's discovery of the area followed a familiar pattern. His poor health as a youngster had led his wealthy parents to send him to the high and dry climate of the boys' school at Los Alamos. Prior to the Second World War the family established a residence in Santa Fe. Interested in music from childhood, he had nevertheless found the path to performance difficult. His knowledge of Santa Fe, coupled with family financial support, the well-honed organizational skills of Santa Feans, and interested parties from other New Mexican towns, led to the creation of the opera company on a site several miles north of the city.

How some Santa Feans regarded the new enterprise in their midst can be seen in the early battles that accompanied its appearance. Arguments ensued as to whether it should be called a New Mexico or a Santa Fe association—and the former won out. Those who argued that Santa Fe would be known in the cultured East were in fact arguing for the broadest interpretation rather than the narrower one associated with the state. The opera itself, however, became the Santa Fe Opera.[23] Powerful support came from Los Alamos, Albuquerque, and other New Mexican towns which developed their own associations in support of the venture and contributed heavily to its financial survival in the early years of its existence. This recognition from outside the town reflected the changes occurring in the state. Albuquerque's phenomenal growth and the totally new Los Alamos indicated the importance of newcomers and their acceptance of Santa Fe's adoption of cultural forms not native to New Mexico.

The attractive power of Crosby's concept for placing Santa Fe on a new cultural map was evident from the outset. *Time* magazine covered the opening night, while Igor Stravinsky oversaw the first season's production of his work, "The Rake's Progress."[24] The notion of an apprentice program for young opera singers from all over the country who would then join opera companies everywhere ensured an expanding knowledge of the new musical enterprise. Furthermore, the effort was able to draw financial support from such prestigious institutions as the Rockefeller Foundation.[25]

24. The original Santa Fe Opera Theater, 1957. Courtesy the Santa Fe Opera.

25. John Crosby, general director of the Santa Fe Opera. Photo by Murrae Haynes, 1988.

Perhaps the greatest sign of the Opera's success came after fire leveled the house in 1967. The season continued at the Sweeney Gymnasium in town, while offers of facilities came from Los Alamos and the University of New Mexico in Albuquerque. Financial help poured in with benefit parties in Santa Fe and Albuquerque.[26] The following season opened in a rebuilt and larger structure. In 1990 New Mexicans, locals, and tourists were still upholding the Opera, which, to some, had become Santa Fe's premier summer attraction.

Santa Fe's success in attracting tourists showed up particularly well in a 1979 survey directed toward Santa Fe Opera out-of-state subscribers—5,000 in number. Over half of those who responded had visited Santa Fe more than nine times and designated the Opera as the most favorable aspect of the state, followed by mountains, Pueblo communities, and villages.[27] The Opera thus focused these tourists' attention upon Santa Fe itself as a destination, rather than as merely one more stopping place of a tour. Given the specific purpose for which they came, they spent heavily on local products. Over one-third of their purchases were for Native American goods. The opera goers, too, were highly educated, well-off, and middle aged. Nearly twenty percent were retired. They came mainly from Colorado, Texas, California, Arizona, and Oklahoma.

Once the Opera became a powerful attraction in Santa Fe, the expansion of other classical musical forms followed. The inception of the Santa Fe Chamber Music Festival came in the early seventies. Like the Opera, the Festival used the summer tourist season as its time of performance, inviting musicians who were almost exclusively from elsewhere to do the playing. As late as 1990, of 77 players, 72 were not from Santa Fe (two came from Albuquerque).[28] A few "guest" artists, as they were called, came from either the University of New Mexico or the Opera. Such nomenclature left the visiting musicians in the position of being the "home" performers. The quality of performance, however, redounded to the city's reputation and the widely spread home bases of the musicians ensured an increased knowledge of the city elsewhere.

The Festival presented itself to the public, offering open rehearsals, and, from its early days, gave concerts at Spanish-speaking villages and Native American reservations. If Opera was an extension beyond Santa Fe's traditional culture boundaries, chamber music may have been even more so. Lists of contributors from the mid-seventies through the early nineties reveal a virtual absence of Hispano surnames. By the late eighties major endowments (gifts of over $10,000 dollars) filled pages of the annual program. The downtown hotels were well represented among contributors, as were major national businesses, local businesses, and wealthy relative newcomers to the city. By the early eighties, *The New Yorker* was reviewing the Festival along with the Opera.[29] However much of a departure such events may have been from traditional Santa Fe fare, they revealed both the success of tourism and the growth of a new residential stratum of population within the city that appreciated aspects of New Mexico's old culture but also heavily supported the enjoyment of its own old culture in its new residence.

In the 1960s Santa Fe became the site of a second campus of the venerable St. John's College of Annapolis, Maryland. In the same vein as the Opera, it was an extension of a cultural vista beyond traditional Native Americans and Hispanos. However, it differed from the Opera in that the students attending were residents for a time in the city rather than mere tourists. When Richard Weigle, president of St. John's, visited the town in 1961 at the invitation of his former classmate Robert McKinney, publisher and editor of the *New Mexican*, John Gaw Meem offered him land for the new school—a generous 200 acres. After proper consultation, the offer was accepted. Among the reasons Weigle considered the offer favorably, he noted the cultural orientation of the town, the proximity of Los Alamos, whose officials warmly welcomed the college's representatives, the absence of an outstanding independent liberal arts college (he considered the College of Santa Fe's clientele as mostly vocationally oriented), and the general goodwill of the community.[30]

The new campus was dedicated on 10 October 1964. Despite the fact that it represented a disjunctive factor with Santa Fe's past, it nevertheless added distinction to the town and increased its fame. The *New Mexican*, commenting on the forthcoming event, described it as the only non-tax-supported, nondenominational college between Claremont in California and Houston and from Mexico to Colorado Springs.[31] The statement's tone was reminiscent of historian Twitchell's description of the city's political domain in the mid-nineteenth century, suggesting a condition of imperial loneliness and lofty purpose worthy of the "city different."

However remote its formal curriculum from traditional local cultural interests, town and college sought out means for rapprochement. Santa Feans created the Friends of the College group shortly after its presence became a reality and qualified local residents volunteered extra-curricular instruction in languages and the fine arts. Townspeople attended evening lectures and adult seminars.[32] Students contributed to their new environment by forming the Search and Rescue Team in 1971 to aid in the recovery of hikers lost in the surrounding mountains. The team proved to be a long-term joint effort involving both town and college students.

St. John's presence caused none of the furor in the city that many college towns experienced in the late sixties when the war in Vietnam produced so much heat and confrontation. Dissatisfied students expressed themselves to some extent in excessive class absences, drug use, or dropping out of school, but the organized turbulence—strikes and occupation of buildings—did not occur. In part, grievances expressed against many institutions, such as the desire for small classes and dialogue with teachers, did not exist at St. John's, making protest unnecessary.[33] Santa Fe would have little to complain about from its youthful temporary population.

St. John's considerable landholdings and Santa Fe's growth combined in the early eighties to improve the college's financial condition and accommodate the city's growth. Working with Zeckendorf-Colin Co. of New York, it leased forty of its acres for residential development.[34] Such reciprocal actions tied the city and the college closer to each other, although the use to which the land was put did not meet with universal approval.

The career of J. Burchenal Ault, who joined St. John's in Santa Fe in 1970 as its first vice president and spent fifteen years cementing relationships between college and town, demonstrates the path of accommodation. Ault persuaded John Murchison of Dallas, a former classmate from Yale whose asthmatic condition had brought him to Santa Fe for a time, to join the school's board of visitors and governors. Murchison contributed heavily to the college's endowment. Ault supported community seminars, concerts, and the college's art gallery, attractions and activities that would bring townspeople and college together. In town he served on the board of Santa Fe Preparatory School. And at his quasi-retirement in 1985, he chose to remain in Santa Fe.[35]

St. John's also drew closer to Santa Fe with its involvement in teacher preparation programs. These efforts brought St. John's students into Santa Fe classrooms as interns and, while producing some temporary misgivings among both parents of the school children and teachers, in the end brought satisfactory results.[36] Acquisition of large music collections by the college provided further opportunity for city persons and the college to broaden their contact and knowledge. Alumni summer seminars at the college allowed visitors to enjoy the Opera and the college. Culturally, the two communities benefited mutually and, to some extent, the same could be said for financial interaction. A college brochure of the nineties noted "The college . . . brings new residents to Santa Fe as students, staff . . . and tutors—many of whom become involved in local community events. And St. John's adds more than $40 million to the Santa Fe economy for goods and services each year."[37] What more could either entity ask?

■ The restrictive effects of World War II upon the American traveling public evaporated as automobile and fuel shortages faded. As far as Santa Fe was concerned, by 1947 a reviving tourism had brought 75,684 visitors to the Palace of the Governors—a number that surpassed the last prewar year of 1939 (69,236). In 1948 that figure passed the 100,000 mark for the first time. The number of visitors then continued to rise slowly and by 1966 had exceeded the 200,000 mark.[38] Santa Fe had reassumed that attractiveness as a tourist destination that the Depression had slowed and the war interrupted. The 1966 figure was nearly triple that for 1939. In 1990, annual hotel and motel occupancy, while not precisely reflecting tourism, stood at over 819,000 persons, a quadrupling of the 1966 number. Moreover, the number of hotel and motel rooms had risen from over 1,900 in 1978 to nearly 3,600 in 1989.[39] Without doubt, the growth of tourism had to be considered an unqualified success by 1990.

Increasingly, Santa Fe, as well as New Mexico, became a tourist destination in its own right. Whereas in earlier times the railroad allowed de-training and then a resumption of travel to other destinations, now visitors from out-of-state came and returned specifically to New Mexico and Santa Fe many times. A 1979 survey based on the nearly 42,000 out-of-state subscribers to *New Mexico Magazine* counted a mean number of over six visits per respondent to the state.[40] These visitors came from all fifty states with the largest representations from the neighboring state of Texas (17.7 percent), as well as the more distant

California (11.6 percent), Illinois (6.3 percent), and New York (4.9 percent). The survey described them as largely well-educated, well-off financially, and middle aged.[41]

These tourists spent their dollars to take some of New Mexico back to their homes. Their highest category of expenditures was for Native American jewelry, pottery, and rugs—forty percent of the total. Another 20 percent went for fine arts, paintings, and sculpture.[42] No other product lines approached these two sets of items.

Within this general category of visitors to New Mexico, purchases favored Santa Fe. Over 44 percent shopped there, surpassing the much larger Albuquerque and the smaller Taos.[43] The three towns together accounted for 85 percent of those who made purchases in the state.

The increase in tourists inevitably led to the growth, as noted, of tourist housing facilities. It was mainly the automobile that brought visitors to the city. Between the late forties and the end of the fifties the number of facilities to accommodate them increased sharply (from fourteen in 1947 to twenty-four in 1959). The terminology changed in that decade from tourist camps to auto courts and motels. Cerrillos Road, already the major entry route for automobiles into the city before the war, increased its predominance as the end of the tourist trail. Of the twenty-four motels and auto courts listed in the city in 1959, twenty were located there.[44] Through the late sixties, the number of motels continued to grow with Cerrillos Road remaining by far the major location for them. Although that increase on Cerrillos Road appeared to reach a saturation point momentarily in the seventies, it climbed again in the eighties and by 1992 there were some thirty motels along that route alone.[45]

Hotels closer to the Plaza, by contrast, increased in number later. It was in the sixties and more strongly in the seventies that major new hostelries appeared in a style acceptable to Santa Fe bearing names of major national chains—Hilton of Santa Fe, Sheraton de Santa Fe, Best Western Inn at Loretto. Throughout the eighties and early nineties, hotel building and rebuilding continued. One of the largest and most expensive of the new hostelries, the Eldorado, opened in 1986 after arousing the ire of some Santa Feans because of its size. Many of these newer hotels were within easy walking distance of the Plaza, on West San Francisco, Don Gaspar, Old Santa Fe Trail, Galisteo, and Washington Streets.

The appearance of these new establishments signaled clearly the patronage of well-off visitors. Indeed, Santa Fe, for a variety of reasons, had always attracted more than its share of them. Its position as territorial capital and trade center in the early days, its tuberculosis facilities, and as time passed, its cultural attractions, including the nearby presence of the Pueblos, had all contributed to its magnetic quality even before World War II. As American tourism expanded in the postwar era and as Santa Fe's scenic attractions and cultural attainments grew in the still small city, the better-off tourist continued to come. The newer hotels could scarcely have justified their existence without them. Their rates certainly ran considerably above the motels on Cerrillos Road—by a third to a half.

In the early eighties, Santa Fe's fame reached new national heights. Within the space of less than two years major articles about the city appeared in *Esquire, U.S. News and World Report, National Geographic, The New Yorker, Time,* and *Travel and Leisure.* The notoriety appeared to be the culmination of the decades of effort by the state and the city to trumpet their virtues as well as the national prosperity that allowed Americans to move about with great freedom to enjoy their country and its varied landscapes.

Santa Fe did not stand alone in the presentation of New Mexico, but it assumed a very notable place as a result of the style associated with its name and the extension of its facilities from purely regional to those that included its national and international cultural attractions. *National Geographic* alone had published some forty-three articles on the state between 1896 and 1988, twenty-four of them appearing in the post–World War II period. Santa Fe occupied a prominent place in many of them. Its culturally exotic character, its broadening facilities, and its relative smallness, all contributed to the growth of tourism as well as the desire of outsiders to move there. It became a romantic destination for New York and Los Angeles, as well as an attraction for persons in such neighboring states as Texas and Oklahoma.

A survey of one small local organization whose members had arrived in the city prior to 1990 helps to reveal some of the characteristics of the incoming population. Virtually every one of them had visited the town prior to moving there and many had done so on numerous occasions. Word-of-mouth knowledge, and ties with friends and relatives sometimes reaffirmed by the various media reports all played a powerful role in persuading them to relocate.

Nearly half of those who came did so to retire. Many of the others brought professions with them that they continued to practice in some measure. A number opened businesses or joined existing family businesses. On the whole, it was a population better off financially than most already-resident Santa Feans and one that hardly competed economically with them.[46] In that sense, they added to the wealth of the town and became consumers of and contributors to its arts, crafts, and cultural activity. Their function was in some measure like that of the Anglos who had been arriving since World War I. They came, however, in greater numbers into a town that had become increasingly well known in the United States and where space was becoming evermore a premium.

Santa Fe's growing fame eventually reached into the best-known stratum of celebrity—the world of movie stars. Filmmaking itself had come to New Mexico long before Santa Fe had gained its national reputation. The area's vistas, climate, and quality of light had attracted filmmakers even before 1900. The legendary D. W. Griffith's troupe had filmed in Albuquerque in 1912 and the Lubin Company West came to Santa Rita, near Silver City, in 1913.[47] These early efforts preceded the establishment of Hollywood as a permanent base for the movie industry. When that occurred, after World War I, it virtually ended the use of New Mexico for filming for a quarter-century.

Only in the 1940s did location shooting trickle back into the state.[48] It was the well-known actress, Greer Garson, who may have initiated the movement to New Mexico as a residence for movie stars. She purchased a large ranch near Pecos, after succumbing to New Mexico's beauties in the late forties.[49]

Another Hollywoodian, designer Charles LeMaire, who had retired to Santa Fe in the sixties, added an additional connection by forming a company to produce films in the town. With the enthusiastic support of Governor David Cargo in the latter years of that decade, a committee on filmed entertainment was created and filming established in New Mexico with Santa Fe as a strong focal point.[50] The governor himself even played bit parts in a number of films.

By the late eighties, the economic effects of filmmaking were being felt in many areas of the state and not least of all in Santa Fe. The field expanded to include not only movies but also videos and advertisements. In 1986, in a directory compiled specifically to highlight the industry's capabilities in New Mexico, Santa Fe listings included 50 out of 71 defined skills and services present in New Mexico. Three years later, in 1989, out of 112 skills and services, Santa Fe listed eighty-four.[51] The persons listed frequently claimed credits for pursuing their crafts in top-rated films, television programs, and advertisements, and many were at least fairly new to the city. Some thirty years after Cargo's energetic initiative, he estimated that the film industry had drawn well over a billion dollars into the state's economy.[52]

The city itself responded to the stimulus. The New Mexico Film Center was created in the late sixties. A generation later Greer Garson donated $3 million for the creation of a communication arts center at the College of Santa Fe. It opened in 1990 and bore her name.[53] To make the enterprise possible, the college even abandoned its sports facility.[54] In the interim, Santa Feans had created annual film festivals in the early eighties that involved inviting Hollywood luminaries to the event.

By the early nineties the presence of movie stars on the streets of the city and their residences within or around it had become commonplace. Some of them became involved in lecturing to students at the College of Santa Fe.

Rumors and sightings of their comings and goings abounded even though townsmen sought to downplay their presence.[55]

Whatever the fate of the stars' presence in the future, the existence of the movie industry has been of sufficient economic importance to warrant recognition in the city's development. The attention proffered the movie stars, a phenomenon that accompanied them wherever they went, offers a view of how the city was changing in the postwar period. Where the earlier focus of the town's advocates had been on its age and the cultural character of its indigenous peoples, it now exhibited at least a small interest in those who were visiting or moving to town and in judging itself by their presence. And the coming of the film stars represented a measure of tourist success undreamed of by earlier generations.

The success of tourism inevitably changed the economic geography of the city for its inhabitants. While tourists and facilities for them grew markedly in the first generation after the war, the character of the Plaza, the focal point of tourist activity, changed at a more modest pace. In 1940 the north side of the square, the site of the Palace of the Governors was, as it had long been, a premier attraction for visitors. The south side, San Francisco Street, was at that time the main shopping area of the town. From Don Gaspar Street, a little to the west of the Plaza, to the southeast edge of the square, clothing stores, large chain department emporia (Penney's, Woolworth's), pharmacies, and grocery stores formed the heart of business activity. Tourist-centered shops, however, had made their presence known. Several jewelry and arts and crafts shops had become established, while the La Fonda hotel at the southeast corner had long since established its reputation as the town's major tourist housing facility.

The east-west sides of the Plaza, now Old Santa Fe Trail and Lincoln Avenue, reflected a similar mix. Clothing, drug, and beauty and barber shops, several cafes and service stores (Western Union, Plaza Cigar) comprised Lincoln Avenue's establishments of local interest. The Old Indian Shop and Myrick's Red Saddle Shop offered tourist and Western wares. Old Santa Fe Trail, with clothing stores, the First National Bank, and a photo shop repeated the menu with the Thunderbird Shop offering tourist goods.[56] Overall, the Plaza still displayed its primary concern with shopping for Santa Feans. But the mix also indicated the presence of tourists, even if such stores did not dominate business activity.

A long generation after the war, in 1968, the changes in the Plaza remained modest. San Francisco Street, the south side of the Plaza, still had its chain department stores, clothing, and drugstores as its center of attraction. Lincoln Avenue showed some change, increasing the number of tourist-oriented shops, but the greatest change was probably that the First National Bank moved there. Old Santa Fe Trail itself gained Packard's Chaparral Trading Post as it lost the

First National Bank. Otherwise, local department stores graced the street's doorways.[57]

While changes on the Plaza came at a moderate pace until the seventies, the tempo quickened thereafter. By the early eighties many of the old established stores that drew local shoppers had disappeared from the scene. Zook's and the Capital Pharmacies were gone from San Francisco Street as was C. R. Anthony's department store, while other Plaza border streets gave up such old stores as the Guarantee in favor of division into art and jewelry shops.

By the early nineties the process of change to tourist-oriented shops was complete. The last of the old shoe stores, Kahn's, and Dunlap's department store, which had replaced Penney's, were gone, leaving only Woolworth's. In their place stood numerous art, jewelry, and clothing boutiques that did not usually cater to the local population. The Plaza had been transformed into a tourist mecca.

Santa Feans noticed the change. While some delighted in the growth of tourist numbers and the cultural image and financial benefits derived from their coming, others saw themselves as losing their town. Letters to editors and political campaigns in the eighties gave voice to dissatisfaction. "A genuine drug store or a bogus art gallery?," queried one newspaper column in 1983.[58] Candidate Arthur Sanchez noted in 1984 that "Land speculation and . . . replacement of locally oriented stores with tourist related shops is turning our city into a transient resort for the rich."[59] And candidate Debbie Jaramillo, in her 1988 campaign for city council, decried the transformation of the downtown and demanded facetiously that a Burger King replace a gallery.[60] The deed had been done, however, and even the redoubtable Jaramillo admitted that she did not know how to change the trend.

Along with the Plaza, Canyon Road, some distance southeast of the square, made a name for itself as a new artistic focal point in the city. The first Anglo artists had moved there before World War I, Gerald and Ina Sizer Cassidy being the first to do so in 1915. Randall Davey and Olive Rush followed in 1920.[61] Their choice of location appeared to be dictated by affordability and by the artistically appreciated adobe character of homes in the Hispano neighborhood. Here they could rent, buy, or build.

Early on, resident Hispanos and Anglo artists generally maintained the existing adobe structures. In the twenties and thirties, wealthy Anglos, such as Mrs. Charles Dietrich, purchased and restored buildings on the street, sometimes changing their function but not their appearance. El Zaguan, the old Borrego family house, was among her purchases. She had the interior remodeled into apartments.[62] Old Hispano resident, Anglo artist, and preservationist moved along a similar and nonconflicting path.[63]

The ethnic mix of the area began to change somewhat even before World

War II. In 1928 it was still overwhelmingly Hispano, but by 1940 Hispano and Anglo residents were approaching parity.[64] Although not a business district, the few shops on Canyon Road still reflected more Hispano than Anglo ownership. Groceries were mostly Hispano-owned, but new sorts of enterprises moved in, including Webb Young, Santa Fe Weavers, and the Rydal Press among them. The development of crafts in the city during the Depression years was also well reflected here.

The rapid population growth of the Depression years also affected Canyon Road. From 96 residences in 1928, the number grew to 188 in 1940. It was in this period that El Zaguan became an apartment compound with ten residences. While in 1928 the last listed address along the road was the New Mexico Power Co., in 1940, new addresses extended beyond that point for a considerable distance. The high rate of population increase here matched that of the city in this period.

Growth continued in the postwar years. By 1951 there were 246 residences. Anglos formed a majority of the resident population while Anglo businesses now held an edge over Hispano enterprises. The character of occupations among Hispano residents still reflected a heavy emphasis toward artisans and laborers, with some increase in government employees. The Anglo population of the street showed an increase in arts-centered employment, government work, and professionals. While the visual cultural style still maintained its Hispano character, the economic nature of the Anglo population reflected both higher income and more arts-oriented activity.

Between 1951 and 1964 the number of residences leveled off at 250, and it remained at that figure in 1983. The modest edge of the Anglo population held steady between 1951 and 1964. What changed markedly, however, was the increased business use of the street in the fifties and sixties. The listings of 1940 showed a total of twelve businesses, but by 1951 there were twenty-five, and by 1964 there were fifty-seven. That seemed to approach a saturation point for a while. Nevertheless, a generation later, in 1983, there were seventy businesses. By that time, however, the number of Hispano residents had declined fairly rapidly while the Anglo population continued to grow slowly.

The changes of the postwar period may be attributed to the new planning and preservationist regulations that the city put in place from 1957 on. In that year Canyon Road became part of the newly created historical ("H") district of Santa Fe. Five years later, Lower Canyon Road was designated a residential arts and crafts zone. These legal changes altered the character of a neighborhood that old Hispano residents and sensitive Anglos had continued in architecture and function for decades. The economic effects of these actions, however, moved beyond what the residents could have imagined.

Given the limited geographic extent of Lower Canyon Road and its commitment to the existent architectural style, the area became saturated with buildings and people. The go-ahead for business conflicted with the demands for housing. The exodus of Hispanos appears related to the increased business activity. While the early Anglo influx of artists produced no economic or cultural competition between Hispano and Anglo, the altered status of the street after 1957 brought in large numbers of arts and craft shops and increasing numbers of artists and craftsmen. A survey of the arts in the city in 1966 actually separated Canyon Road from the rest of the town because of its extraordinary number of galleries (estimated at 24).[65] Hispano resident owners experienced pressure to sell or rent rather than continue as residents. As prices rose, it was to their economic advantage to do so.

The social character of the street also changed. For a time in the late fifties Claude's restaurant and drink establishment became a focal point for bohemian behavior, departing from the more staid demeanor of earlier times. The businesses, moreover, attracted outsiders and tourists, altering the residential character of the area.[66] Renters themselves presented a less stable population base than had formerly existed. The change of designation for Canyon Road into a residential arts and crafts zone in 1962 completed the change. The street no longer carried the empathetic residential and benign character of the prewar and early postwar years. It had become a new residential and business mix geared to art production and the servicing of tourists.

During the seventies some of the Hispanos living in the Canyon Road area declared themselves Chicanos and formed organizations to serve the Hispano community. Some of their activities involved the painting of outdoor murals, which some Anglos resented in the belief that they violated Historical District regulations. For them, the victory of the Chicanos in this matter remained an irritant. More seriously, in the later seventies some Anglos felt threatened by youthful Hispano gangs as Anglos suffered some vandalism and personal injury.[67] Both Hispano and Anglo residents blamed such attitudes on economic differences between the two groups as well as on ethnic distinctions.[68] The deeper meaning, it has been suggested, lies in the conclusion that the changes made Lower Canyon Road a symbol of Anglo commercialization of Hispano culture.[69] In some respects, it was a consequence that could have meaning for other areas of the city.

The development of the Plaza and of Canyon Road allows a comparison of postwar changes in the city. Those on the Plaza indicated a sharp departure from the past. Ownership patterns and sale of the arts to large galleries reflected a shift from local interests to those of outsiders. Such enterprises not only played to tourist rather than local concerns but gradually removed Santa Feans from shopping in the Plaza. The latter, however, was not a residential area.

By contrast, even though Canyon Road changed markedly, the new business growth reflected a different pattern of displacement. Here, the smaller Anglo businesses moved against old Hispano residents. The changes, at least architecturally, seemed to maintain a Santa Fe flavor, but the remaining residential population and the new commercial interests underwent some degree of competition for turf on the basis of wealth and ethnic distinctions.

The war had interrupted the art scene of Santa Fe as it did everything else. The postwar period saw the introduction of new factors in the life of both the state and the community. Both were clearly less isolated than before. The military bases that had grown up during the conflict had introduced untold thousands of young men to the area. The development of high-technology enterprises, especially in Los Alamos, brought a different breed of inhabitant close to Santa Fe, highly trained in large and prestigious universities and with cultural proclivities of their own. Government educational programs for veterans and support for the arts allowed both to be fostered in New Mexico as never before and homegrown artists appeared.[70] The newcomers, by their number, ethnic variety, and practice of varied media diluted the close personal character and relatively narrow breadth of the prewar art community.

The postwar changes were not at first so abrupt as to destroy all recognition of the prewar era. The *Art Directory of New Mexico*, published in 1947, listed 62 artists still present and active in Santa Fe who had lived there before the war. Jozef Bakos, Gustave Baumann, Randall Davey, Fremont Ellis, Olive Rush, and Eugenie Shonnard, to name a few, were among the best known of the carryovers.[71] In all, the directory listed 115 artists working in various media in town. Albuquerque and Taos, by comparison, each accounted for 41 artists while all of New Mexico had a total of 276 practitioners. Of those who moved into the city after the war, about half were women.

By 1951 the art-producing community had grown so rapidly that the annual Fiesta Show of that year had to change the rules of participation in place since the opening of the art museum. Instead of the accustomed open-door policy of hanging paintings, the directors switched to a juried selection system since the quantity of art produced in the state and offered for the show far exceeded available exhibition space. Reginald Fisher, who had compiled the art directory of 1947, commented that there were over six hundred artists in the state and now only they could exhibit their work in the show.[72]

Santa Fe exhibitors led the way in numbers. Of 225 artists whose works were shown in 1951, seventy-five lived in the city (Albuquerque was second with forty-two).[73] Thirty of Santa Fe's contingent had not been listed in the 1947 art directory. Clearly, talented newcomers continued to move in at a rapid pace.

How many did so defies easy description. Persons concerned with keeping track of the size of the arts community struggled with the effort. The publisher of an erstwhile attempt to count some of them in 1974 looked back at Fisher's 1947 effort as the last to do so in a comprehensive manner. That more recent pamphlet estimated that a figure of two thousand resident artists in Santa Fe would be conservative![74] The number appears incredible, especially in light of a 1993 art directory that listed 140 painters and a total of just over twelve hundred artists and craftsmen of all descriptions in the city.[75] A survey made in 1966 counted 221 artists and craftspersons in the city.[76] At any rate, the more than tenfold increase between 1947 and 1993 upholds the view of an extraordinary growth of art practitioners, far exceeding the growth rate of the city itself. Along with the economic effects of their activity, it is evident that what had been a coterie in the prewar period had become an industry since that time.

The processes that led to the increase involve a complex history. Reactivation of institutions created before the war account for one part of the growth. The Spanish Colonial Arts Society, quiescent since the deaths of Mary Austin and Frank Applegate in the early thirties, received new affirmation when the Museum of New Mexico established a department of Spanish colonial art in 1951.[77] Interested originally in collection and preservation, by the mid-sixties the society's agenda included education and research. In 1965 the society sponsored a Native Spanish Market, a revival of markets held prior to the mid-thirties. After a bumpy start, it became an annual summer event, while the society's curators sought to work with craftsmen to continue and develop their talents and production.[78]

Somewhat akin to the path of Hispano crafts, the Wheelwright Museum of the American Indian founded in 1927 by Mary Cabot Wheelwright, sought to preserve Navajo ceremonial objects with the concurrence of Navajo Hosteen Klah. By 1975 those sacred medicine bundles had been given to the Navajo Community College. The museum's commitment, however, had expanded to being "more than a museum of history, but one of today."[79]

Such examples of the acceptance and broadening of public knowledge of Hispano and Indian crafts can be supplemented by other events. These include the Indian Markets that had been established in the late thirties and created the precedent for the Native Americans to set their own prices and to represent themselves directly to the buying public. The markets have been interpreted as strong links to the postwar success of their craft as well as a factor in their economic welfare.[80]

The continued linkage of Anglo-created institutions and artists with Hispano and Native American craftsmen and artists proved in all likelihood a powerful element in a broadening definition and interest in the arts of New

Mexico. Not only did their work expand the parameters of the visual arts in a process that was only beginning to include the world of native ethnic artists and craftsmen before the war, but of necessity, also included Anglo craftspersons who sought to work in their own versions of related media.

The composition of growth in the arts community of Santa Fe clearly reveals a heavy increase in the role of crafts since World War II. Of the 115 listed artists in 1947, thirty-seven were identified as craft workers, no small number of them applying themselves in more than one medium. Hispanos were virtually absent from the list, although that may say more about the compiler's capacity to find them than it does as a representation of the facts.[81] Eliminating the performing arts, sound and video media, and literary arts listed in the 1993 directory from consideration, the approximately one thousand artist listings included about three hundred craftsmen—almost a tenfold increase over the 1947 figure and roughly equal to the number of painters.[82] The number of the latter, if one holds to a definition of painting as an exclusive activity, merely doubled.

If one adds art forms either not present in the city in 1947 and the nonvisual art forms either excluded or not present in that year, then the number again swells. As examples, many new activities and activists, such as those associated with the Opera and the rise of the movie industry were included in the 1993 directory. These did not exist in the town in 1947. Thus, the enormous growth in the arts industry came about in part as the result of a change in the definition of what the arts included.

The growth of the arts community produced strong parallel effects in the city's economy. The number of galleries increased along with the number of artists and the broadening definition of the arts. While in 1947 only two galleries received mention and four in 1955, by 1964 there were twelve (nine of them on Canyon Road). After that time the number of listings seemed to explode. The 1976 telephone directory listed fifty-nine galleries and dealers (sixteen on Canyon Road) but the 1990/1991 telephone directory listed over two hundred! Canyon Road alone accounted for forty-nine such outlets.

In the midst of gallery growth, crafts plainly showed their expansion. In 1976 more than one-third of Santa Fe's art enterprises featured them as their sales product. That portion was nearly retained in 1990. The number of ethnically oriented stores remained high, especially those selling Native American and Hispano wares. The heavy increase in gallery numbers did not swamp crafts that were indigenous to New Mexico, the latter keeping pace with the growth of the art business. By 1990 this was particularly evident on Canyon Road.

The broadening of the range of arts made itself felt also in the area of style. The power of Southwest images, while still important, gave way to the acceptance of a more inclusive subject matter and attitude. The exhibitions at the

Museum of Fine Arts, which underwent a five-year hiatus for renovation in the early eighties, resumed in 1985. The still-juried shows now invited entries from an eight state area. Jurors commented that the works submitted had "no unifying characteristics," "no common aesthetic dictated by region."[83] The museum's standard, at least for this important event, demonstrated an openness and receptivity that spelled at least some measure of departure from the earlier cultural regionalism.

Proliferation in the number and variety of galleries also led to a wide range of gallery types, with fine arts at one end and trinket shops at the other. Prewar artists often arrived in New Mexico with reputations already established and outlets for their work equally set in the East. The healthy increases in both the number of art producers and tourists after the war allowed local artists to sell their work in the expanding gallery choices of the city. A survey made in 1966 noted that 98 percent of the sales along Canyon Road came from goods produced in New Mexico, while the figure for Santa Fe County dropped only to 83 percent.[84]

The Museum of Fine Arts shows had long been the major outlet for fine arts in the city. By 1966, fine art sales in Santa Fe County had passed the $800,000 mark excluding the museum sales.[85] By the early seventies Santa Fe could boast of galleries that were becoming full-fledged social and sales enterprises. The Fenn Gallery on Paseo de Peralta received considerable attention in the publications that lauded Santa Fe in the early eighties. Forrest Fenn's guesthouse, at which he catered to the famous, attracted more comment than the contents of the gallery in 1981.[86] Fenn's flamboyance irritated some Santa Feans, but his success marked how far the city had expanded in terms of the arts as business by the eighties. It became a mantra to describe Santa Fe art sales as ranking third in the nation—behind only California and New York.

Another cultural extension of interest in local crafts, the International Folk Art Museum, opened in 1953. It was the brainchild of Florence D. Bartlett, a wealthy Chicagoan who had summered for many years in Alcalde, north of Santa Fe. She gave both the funds and her extensive crafts collection to create the museum as an instrument to "contribute toward greater mutual understanding among the various peoples of the world." It became a center for the study of crafts worldwide as well as an exhibition gallery.[87] Although not as distant from earlier cultural institutions, say, as those of the purveyors of classical music, the new museum still expanded the horizons of the community's residents as well as for visitors.

Another, rather different, recreational dimension that came to Santa Fe, expanding its range of activities in the postwar era, was the horse-racing track—

The Santa Fe Downs. The track opened in 1971 several miles south of the city.[88] Four other such facilities were operating in the state at that time.

From the early seventies to the early nineties the summer season of approximately two months lured thoroughbred and quarter-horse racing devotees to the track and to betting. Daily attendance fluctuated roughly between twenty-five hundred and four thousand.[89] However, by the late eighties growth in the number of gambling establishments in New Mexico and resultant competition affected the conditions of this spectator sport. The proliferation of Native American casinos and state-sponsored lotteries in neighboring states as well as the introduction of simultaneous broadcasts of the races to Albuquerque cut into betting and attendance.[90]

The contribution of horse racing to in-state tourism is difficult to measure. Albuquerqueans formed the largest pool of racing fans in the state.[91] Living only an hour's drive from The Downs, however, they did not necessarily go to Santa Fe when the racing day had ended. Thus Santa Fe tourism might well have gained little from such visitors to the track. Furthermore, the introduction of simulcasts in the mid-nineties, a technological innovation, gave them the option of following their interests at their home track.

Nevertheless, the presence of the participants in the racing industry itself still contributed to some extent to the growth of Santa Fe's tourist income. Since considerable numbers of owners, trainers, and others who required occupational licenses to practice their skills needed lodging and sustenance during the racing season, the town could accommodate them. Throughout the history of The Downs, Texas and Oklahoma contributed by far the largest percentage of such out-of-staters. New Mexicans from distant in-state destinations added more.

The relatively modest success of The Downs may indicate the introduction of limits to what Santa Fe's tourist empire could encompass at this point of its history. The activity was not as unique to the town as were the ethnic arts, the scenery, and the appearance created by the Santa Fe–style architecture. Nor were arts, opera, and Pueblo-loving devotees necessarily drawn to sporting events.[92] As noted, when New Mexicans themselves found substitutes for attending, such as the simulcasts, attendance at Santa Fe's track dropped.

Perhaps the very success of New Mexico's and Santa Fe's traditional treasures and the tourist-accepted extensions ensured that the attention of the visitors would be skewed mainly to those who sought and enjoyed them, while local interest in the track from the small city itself could not alone support racing sufficiently to make it a great success. If so, horse racing may define one kind of boundary, at least in the present, to the growth of tourism in Santa Fe.

While horse racing may be one example of what has tested the parameters of Santa Fe's recreational interests, others also began to appear. In 1989 the town's fame and success as a recreation-oriented community led entrepreneurs seeking to create a new professional basketball league to inquire whether Santa Fe had an interest in joining it. Mayor Sam Pick rejected the offer. His reasons indicated his town's awareness of directions already defined and the limits of resources. He argued that Santa Fe had no facility sufficiently large to accommodate a professional team and would not build one. Moreover, the town was not large enough to support the activity. He concluded that "our priorities are probably going to preclude us from getting involved in this activity."[93] Santa Feans were becoming aware of what they could and could not do successfully.

The expansion of cultural horizons and institutions that Santa Fe embarked upon after the war produced one of the greatest areas of change in the city since World War II. Perhaps only the numerical growth of the city itself can match it. The variety of persons and talents involved in the new institutions and the number of visitors they attracted produced a population of wealth and sophistication that built on the prewar artistic and upper-class base and surpassed it in numbers and variety. Santa Fe's long-term capacity to gain such a population had transformed it from a center of mere political power and favor into one of even greater cultural repute. It is from these developments that Santa Fe gained its exceptional fame.

TWELVE

Social Change, 1945–1990: Residence, Class, and Education

MUCH OF SANTA FE'S modern social history has involved the entry of an Anglo population into an Hispano community and the way these ethnic groups have lived and worked together. The ethnic distinctions between Anglo and Hispano admit of many degrees of mixture but the cultural traditions and social connections of each group have remained different enough to merit recognition while becoming more like each other with the growth of Santa Fe as an urban community.

The features of that growth that made for closer connections and similarities between Anglos and Hispanos are grounded in the transformation of an economy resting heavily on subsistence agriculture into one based on commerce and in the political integration of the city with the rest of the nation through statehood. These processes, far from being interrupted by the Great Depression and World War II, actually accelerated as the city became involved in national efforts to deal with them. Following these powerful events, the developments of the next forty years, from 1950 to 1990, would further transform relationships among the city's social strata and ethnic groups.

Several changes altered the city's social structure. From 1950 to 1990, the population doubled in size, from 27,898 to 55,993. By then the accelerating influx of Anglo residents gave them a slight majority over Hispano residents for the first time. The shift toward a service-oriented economy continued to a point where almost three-quarters of those gainfully employed were in professional, executive and managerial, and clerical and sales occupations. As residential neighborhoods grew, they became distinctly different in the educational attainment, occupations, and income of their residents—marks of social class distinction that affected both ethnic groups. When limits on occupational opportunities for young people became apparent and school dropout rates prompted educators to bolster the incentive of youngsters to stay in school, the community took steps to equalize access to college education for local residents. Each of these developments affected Anglo-Hispano relations.

Between 1950 and 1990 a basic shift took place in the ways that Santa Fe residents earned their living. Among the "industry" groups tallied by the national census, the portion of the city's labor force employed in wealth-producing activities, such as agriculture, manufacturing, construction, and trade, declined from 44 percent in 1950 to 36 percent in 1990. These activities gave way to an increase in professional services (i.e., in health care, education, recreation, social welfare, and religion), and in finance, real estate, transport, and public administration. Together they rose from 52 percent in 1950 to 63 percent of the labor force in 1990.[1] Women were the chief beneficiaries. Their proportion in the labor force rose from 32 percent in 1950 to 49 percent in 1990. In this change they accounted for 59 percent of the total growth in such white-collar jobs.

Hispano workers clearly benefited from the expansion of white-collar occupations. In 1947 their estimated participation in such jobs stood at 38 percent and in 1990 it had increased to 59 percent. The women's share of the Hispano workforce grew from 29 percent in 1950 to 49 percent in 1990, matching the rate of the Anglos; and the portion of Hispano workers in administrative, clerical, and sales work matched that of the Anglos from 1950 on. The foothold Hispanos had gained by opportunities in government work in the 1930s continued to strengthen. In 1947 they held an estimated 44 percent of all the government jobs in the city and in 1980 the U.S. Census reported that in Santa Fe, 57 percent of federal workers, 57 percent of state workers, and 62 percent of local government workers were Hispanos. By a more refined measure, the Hispano proportion of workers in "public administration" was 61 percent of all persons so employed.[2]

While the white-collar share of the city's labor force grew, the part involved in precision production (as in manufacturing and skilled crafts) shrank from 34 percent to 15 percent. Although Hispanos held more of these jobs than did Anglos, both groups experienced equivalent rates of decline—Hispanos from 48 percent of their labor force to 20 percent; Anglos from 22 percent to 10 percent. Part of the city decline was due to the increase of such workers living in the county while working inside the city. Between 1980 and 1990 a large number of city residents, Anglo and Hispano, moved out to the county, possibly due to the rising cost of housing in the city. But even in the entire county, as the number of such workers increased, their proportion in the total labor force continued to decline. Altogether these changes in the entire spectrum of occupations had implications for the opportunities of younger residents looking toward their future in the city.[3]

Since 1950 another feature of Santa Fe's social structure has became more decisive in shaping economic opportunities for its residents. From early in the period of American rule, the non-Hispano population has been divided between those who were born and grew up in the city and those born elsewhere who took up residence after being hired for jobs there. Of the total population increase since 1950, Anglos have accounted for 79 percent. Since 1965 they have constituted increasing portions of newcomers—in 1970, 63 percent; in 1980, 73 percent; and in 1990, 82 percent. At each of these times, a small percentage consisted of retired persons. Moreover, since 1950 the proportion of Anglo residents in the 35- to 64-year-old age group has been consistently higher than in the Hispano population. This is the age by which one's qualifications for an occupational career would very likely have been acquired and, among Anglos, more likely to have been so before arriving in Santa Fe. This implies a relative advantage over Hispanos who sought occupational careers in their hometown.[4]

Thus far, all of our measures of growth and change have focused on the entire Anglo or Hispano population. But during forty years of postwar development, the socioeconomic differences within each ethnic group became significant and distinct from one neighborhood to another. Within each neighborhood Anglo and Hispano residents who had attained the same level of education, who worked at similar occupations and earned the same relative income, shared the characteristics of the same social class, regardless of their cultural differences. On this basis, if common interests developed among Anglos and Hispanos, then it might no longer matter quite so much how one identified oneself ethnically.

The history of the change lies in two developments during the period. There was increasing choice in the type and location of residential home sites; and the movements of each ethnic group into new parts of town brought different proportions of the two groups into the city's neighborhoods. We can trace the conditions of change by comparing neighborhoods, using census tract data for 1980 and 1990 and the Santa Fe city directories from 1928 through 1988.

Without a "new town" such as in Las Vegas, New Mexico, or Albuquerque, early modern Santa Fe did not develop even a temporary ethnic separation of its residential neighborhoods. From the start, one's place of residence had to be close to one's workplace. For some time even after the turn of the century it was not uncommon for proprietors of small stores and shops to live in the back or on floors above the businesses, or for officers or functionaries of institutions to have living quarters on the premises. Families growing crops on their household plots had to live where irrigation water was available. And many business firms were run by families whose employed members lived in homes close by. By and large the freedom to live at any distance from one's work was limited to the proprietors of large business firms, successful professionals with offices downtown, and the few highly placed government officials who could better afford to buy lots and build their own homes. In short, before the arrival of the automobile, local transportation set practical limits on where one could live.

After New Mexico acquired statehood in 1912 and the population of Santa Fe resumed growth, the establishment of state government and the expansion of local business provided more people with the means to purchase or rent living quarters and stimulated a building industry. Still, many people owned or rented small additions at the rear of homes along the main streets, originally constructed in many cases by Hispanos as their families grew larger. The use of these quarters became even more prominent after World War II when a housing shortage was most acute. Meanwhile, by 1932 apartment houses had begun to appear—in that year there were twelve with a total of 49 apartments (44 Anglos and 5 Hispanos). By 1947 there were 395 apartments, nearly a third of which were occupied by Hispanos.[5]

By the end of the Depression decade in 1940, the most rapid population growth in modern Santa Fe's history created an unprecedented housing shortage. With the end of World War II, the demand for more housing led to the Veterans Housing project at the end of West San Francisco Street with fifty-one apartments in 1947. Even larger-scale works by private contractors soon attracted new homeowners into western areas of the city where land was opened for development. By the fifties and sixties, other housing developments created residential neighborhoods that reflected socioeconomic differences among the people of the city. As with apartment houses, the occupancy of new housing developments by Hispanos was limited at first, gradually expanding with time. Between 1949 and 1958 they constituted little more than a quarter (28 percent) of the new owners; by 1988 their proportion had increased to 40 percent overall.

As already noted, by 1940 Anglo settlement beyond established areas was spreading on a north-south axis while Hispanos spread on an east-west line. After 1950 this pattern continued as the overall growth of Anglos increased proportionately in neighborhoods where Hispanos had once been the majority. At the same time the diminishing growth of the Hispano population meant that those moving to different neighborhoods were not replaced by members of their own ethnic group; movement was often to an adjacent neighborhood. Many

Hispanos moved into the same southern and western areas as did Anglos, and into the west side of the city north of the Santa Fe River.

By 1990 the overlapping of the ethnic groups had produced some neighborhoods where Anglos and Hispanos were near parity, neither group having more than 60 percent of the total. With one exception in the far northeastern part of the city, these neighborhoods were all west of St. Francis Drive but in separated enclaves extending from Rodeo Road in the south into the area north of Alameda Street in the northwest.

In one respect the ethnic composition of these tracts was the result of the flow of newcomers to the city and of residents moving from one part of town to another. Yet these choices of home sites depended more on socioeconomic status than on ethnicity. This is evident from the fact that the average of median household income was higher for the Hispano residents of these evenly divided tracts than for Hispano residents in other tracts. In those where more than 60 percent of residents were Anglos, the average Hispano median income was $30,000; where more than 60 percent were Hispano, their median income averaged $23,000. In evenly divided tracts the Hispano median income averaged $33,000.[6] In other words, Hispanos living in the latter tracts were those who could better afford to live where they chose; for Anglos in those tracts, the experience was similar.

Income difference is key to a broader range of differences among Santa Fe neighborhoods since 1950. On the basis of ethnic distinctions alone there were tracts where the Anglo majority ranged from 60 to 78 percent and the Hispano majority from 60 to 69 percent. In between were the more evenly mixed areas, where neither group had more than 60 percent. By 1990 all tracts had become more distinct along socioeconomic lines. In the city as a whole, Anglos and Hispanos could resemble each other or differ markedly in educational attainment and occupational status, as well as income. By 1990 ethnic groups had come to resemble each other in different ways in different neighborhoods.

In the city as a whole, a smaller percentage of Hispanos than Anglos had four years of college or more, and a smaller percentage were employed in professional or managerial occupations. Hispanos also had lower median incomes. However, in those tracts where Hispano residents exceeded 60 percent, Anglos had a lower percentage with college degrees as well as professional and managerial occupations than did Anglos in tracts where they exceeded 60 percent of residents.

Similarly, where Hispanos formed over 60 percent of the residents, a lower average percentage of their number had college degrees, professional or managerial occupations, and lower incomes than Hispanos in tracts where Anglos comprised more than 60 percent of the residents. Where the ethnic groups were evenly divided, their averages on these measures fell between the highest and lowest socioeconomic levels registered in other tracts.

The pattern emerging here is the stratification of neighborhoods that differ one from another according to social characteristics, regardless of ethnic composition. In a relative comparison, Anglos and Hispanos in one neighborhood can both be better off—in education, occupation, and income—than Anglos and Hispanos in another neighborhood. And, their similarity within any neighborhood resulted from a choice of location based on their economic means and preference for certain types of residential accommodation. As their means and preferences changed, so might they move to another neighborhood.

Much of the growth and movement that led to this pattern of similarities and differences occurred between 1970 and 1990. Two census tracts in particular exhibit the changes most dramatically. Both lie at the extreme western side of the city and represent areas of most rapid growth between 1980 and 1990. Tract 12 lies roughly west of Maez Road and extends to the city grant line and north of Airport and Cerrillos Roads. It grew from 786 residents in 1980 to 3,757 in 1990. In the process, its Hispano residents grew from 54 percent in 1980 to 69 percent in 1990—twice as rapidly as the Anglo population. Tract 103.02, south of Rodeo Road and east of Cerrillos Road, grew from 1,427 residents in 1980 to 2,760 in 1990. (See figure 26.) In that decade the Anglo population expanded from 65 percent to 71 percent, doubling its numbers.

In 1990 the Anglos in one tract contrasted sharply in their socioeconomic characteristics with Anglos in the other tract, as did the Hispanos. The differences are shown in the following table.

Median household income	Homeowners (%)	Bachelor's degree or higher (%)	Professional, administrative, managerial (%)
TRACT 12 *(Hispano majority)*			
Hispanos			
$25,349	49	4	9
Anglos			
$26,222	60	25	30
TRACT 103.02 *(Anglo majority)*			
Hispanos			
$53,857	86	39	54
Anglos			
$50,086	82	61	62

Thus, although these tracts differed in ethnic composition, the sharper and more decisive differences fell along lines of social class where Anglos and Hispanos shared similar positions on a scale of socioeconomic characteristics. The two tracts cited differed according to the characteristics of people who chose to move into them and the conditions that they found attractive.

By 1990 Tract 12, with its Hispano majority, had attracted a wider variety of occupational talent. Newcomers in both ethnic groups added large numbers of professionals and managers, persons employed in technical, sales and clerical

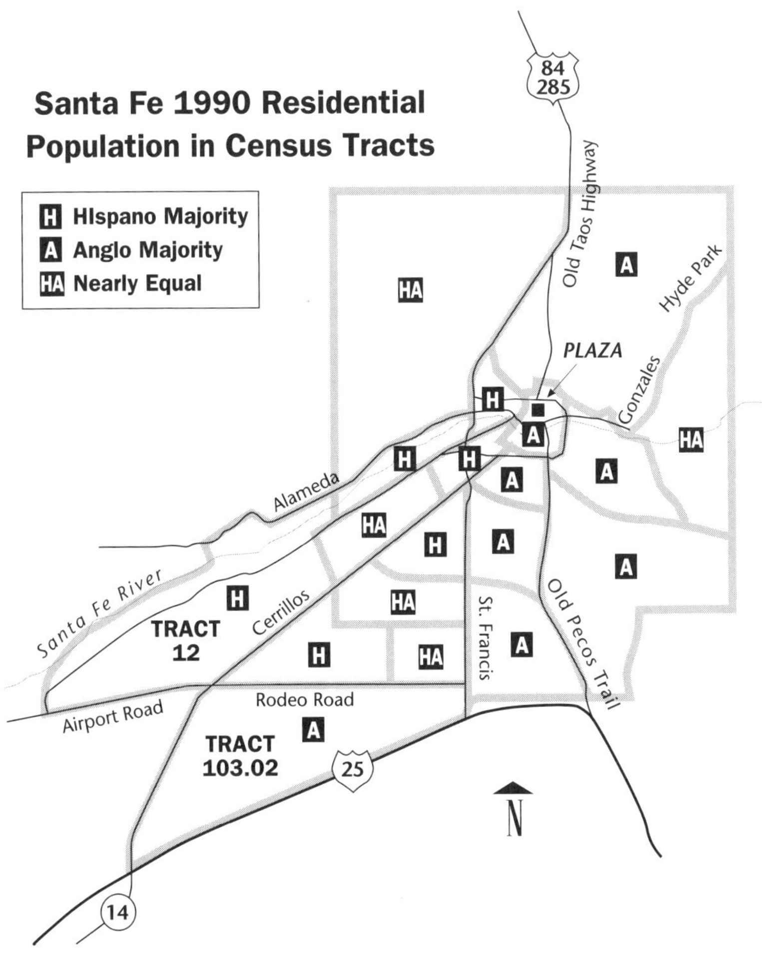

26. *Map of Anglo and Hispano residence by tract, 1990. 1990 Census. Census Tracts Santa Fe MSA.*

jobs, and service occupations. Hispanos more than tripled in precision craft and repair workers as well as the number of operators and laborers since 1980, while Anglos added no one to these categories. By contrast, in Tract 103.02, the tract of the Anglo majority, neither ethnic group added workers except in professional and managerial occupations.

Since no one else entered this affluent tract it is likely that it was too expensive for anyone not employed at these occupational levels. Indeed, the median value of owner-occupied homes in this tract in 1980 was $83,900 as compared with $51,300 for Tract 12. By 1990 the median value for homes in this Anglo-majority tract had risen to $124,000, and for Tract 12 to $76,000. Monthly rentals followed a similar path.

The choice of housing accommodations was much narrower in Anglo-majority tract 103.02. There, 96 percent of all housing units in 1990 were single family dwellings. In Hispano-majority Tract 12, only 20 percent of all units were single-unit structures, while 32 percent were multi-unit structures, and 48 percent were mobile homes or trailers, all providing a wider range of costs. This tract included the largest concentration of mobile homes in the city.

By 1990 Tract 103.02 had attracted a significantly older cohort of residents. The additional number aged 35 through 64 represented 73 percent of all residents added since 1980. Working members of this group were more likely to be established in their careers. By contrast, in Tract 12, the additional residents were much younger with 73 percent no older than 34, and for all residents, old and new, the median age was 26.9, making it the youngest tract in the city. Another notable difference was that 20 percent of additional residents in tract 103.02 were 65 and older and had evidently chosen that location for their retirement.

By 1990 the forces creating these stratification patterns were widely noticeable. The residential tracts in Santa Fe County outside the city had been outstripping the city's rate of growth since 1980. While the city's population grew by 14 percent in the decade, the county outside the city had increased by 63 percent and was approaching the size of the city's population. Persons of Hispano origin rose 50 percent and others by 79 percent. Among the newcomers not present in 1985, fully two-thirds came from outside the county but the other third came from inside Santa Fe. Between 1985 and 1990, twice as many persons (4,891) moved out of the city into the county as those who moved into the city from the county (numbering 2,174). In these movements, Anglos and Hispanos were almost evenly matched in number. With the growing proportion of lower-paid workers living in the county area, the stratification of the city's population was having an equal effect on both ethnic groups.

Economically, the Santa Fe community was spreading well beyond its municipal boundaries. By 1990, 28 percent of the city's entire labor force lived outside it and each county tract had its share of city workers, ranging from 17 to 82 percent at the extremes. In numbers, the occupational character of the workforce expanded strikingly like its growth in the city during the eighties, adding managers and professional specialists and technicians and sales or clerical personnel.

The one significant difference was the 59 percent increase of skilled workers while the city actually lost a number of them as residents. The county also outgained the city in transport and machine operators as well. And the homes of these workers were more evenly distributed in all county tracts than in the city.

From all this it appears that residents within the Santa Fe city limits had become more dependent on the labor of persons living in the county outside, among whom a growing proportion with lower-paying jobs could not afford city housing. The excess of migrants to the county over those moving to the city suggests the growing attractiveness or necessity of living outside the city as it grew.

In 1994 the planning department of the city of Santa Fe conducted two mail surveys and a series of public meetings, one for city residents and the other for county residents to a distance of five miles from the city's boundary. The purpose was to solicit comments for updating the general plan. The responses distinctly reflected the circumstances that distinguished city life from that in the "Extraterritorial Zone (EZ)" outside the city limits. For residents of the latter the top priority was to protect their control of land and resources and to preserve a rural lifestyle. Their responses reflected uncertainty about governmental agencies—county, city, and the extraterritorial zoning authority formed in 1981 to regulate land use in the area. Could they keep the city from draining off the water supply, could they regulate traffic congestion on local roads, preserve open space, and protect landowners' rights? These concerns expressed the interests of a community threatened from without. It was a collective fear of the city next door, aroused by the realization of how much they could lose because of the city's continuing growth.

The consultants for the general plan update summarized their findings. They noted that

> Many in the EZ [extraterritorial zone]—especially those who have lived there for several decades—are deeply attached to their communities. They fear the creeping urbanization of the City, and want to be able to protect themselves from what they see as a congested, materialistic, hectic way of life. They believe that EZ communities should be able to determine their own future, and that they are more in balance in terms

> of resources, than those dwelling in the city. They feel exploited by the City in some senses; water is being sucked out from under them; roads are being carved through them; neighboring chunks are being annexed.[7]

The top priorities for city residents were very different. Rather than seeking to preserve their traditional community, they sought rescue from economic pressures. While the high cost of living, particularly in housing, was near the bottom of the extraterritorial residents' priorities, for the city it was the top priority (for 55 percent of respondents) and called for relief. More than a third (36.7 percent) sought economic development and a greater job diversity:

> Many Santa Feans are discouraged, or desperate, about the lack of decent-paying jobs in Santa Fe. There are complaints about low-paying and low-respect service industry jobs. . . . At the neighborhood meetings, many Santa Feans urged the city to diversify the economy so that there are job opportunities outside the tourist industry and state government.[8]

City dwellers recognized the economic differences of neighborhoods. "Many citizens," the summary explained, "pointed to housing as evidence of inequities in Santa Fe. Expensive homes behind gates and trailers off Airport Road are symbols for many Santa Feans of an unhealthy trend."[9] These conditions portended a threat to the city's future. "There was concern that Santa Fe is losing its young people because there are no jobs or career opportunities, and because the cost of living is so high."[10]

The belief that Santa Fe was losing its young people had a basis in fact. Between 1980 and 1990 a 10 percent reduction occurred in the proportion of Anglo city residents aged 20 to 34. Most remarkably, this decline coincided with the substantial rise of Anglo population that had begun in 1970. From 1980 to 1990 the 20–34 age group was the *only* one that also decreased in absolute numbers.[11]

By contrast the Hispano population, registering virtually no growth in the city since 1980, retained essentially the same proportion in 1990 of persons aged 20–34 as in 1980. While changes in the size of this age group could result either from persons leaving the city or from new arrivals, the stability of the Hispano cohort appears to have resulted from smaller movement either way than what the Anglos were experiencing. As a smaller percentage of Hispanos (25 percent) than Anglos (61 percent) had come from outside the Santa Fe metropolitan area since 1985, the number of Anglos grew out of immigration, which was determined by their age and expectations.

Because the 20–34 category includes persons normally starting careers or advancing their education, the decline of Anglo members suggests a lack of local opportunity for employment or advanced education. What opportunities Anglos may have sought requires an estimation of what was open to newcomers by 1990.

Of all Anglos aged 20–34 who joined the city since 1980, 80 percent moved into the fastest growing neighborhoods, as had virtually all of the newly added Hispanos of that age group. Although we cannot know the occupations of the newcomers, the total increase in occupations among all residents of these neighborhoods since 1980 gives a rough indication of the range of opportunities open to them by 1990. They contributed the vast majority (94 percent) of the growth in service occupations (private households, protective services, food service, cleaning and building service, etc.), a substantial 73 percent of growth in technical, sales, and clerical jobs, a 44 percent higher gain than the city as a whole in precision production, crafts, repair, and laborers, and 34 percent of the growth in executive and professional specialty jobs. Only in the latter category did Anglos exceed (60 percent to 40 percent) the high proportions of Hispanos in the rest of the categories listed.

Apparently, the range of opportunities in higher-paying work was greater for Anglos while Hispanos had a wider range in lower-paying jobs. This could explain why, by 1990, 95 percent of newly settled Hispanos aged 20–34 had moved into the tract having the youngest population and the lowest median value of owner-occupied homes, while just 45 percent of their Anglo counterparts had settled there.

Yet since it was Anglos aged 20–34 whose numbers diminished, apparently they had choices Hispanos did not share. It was only in managerial and professional positions that the proportion of newly arrived Anglos exceeded that of Hispanos. This suggests that if more Anglos in this age group either left the city or did not come, it was because openings in that category of employment were limited; and Anglos would not seek lower levels of employment in Santa Fe if their experience or education qualified them to take high-paying positions elsewhere.

The capacity for mobility in high-income occupations had long differed for Anglos and Hispanos in Santa Fe. Between 1947 and 1990 the proportion of Hispanos in professional occupations remained at 17 percent below the proportion of Anglo workers in those specialties. In the same period, moreover, the corresponding gap in proportions with college degrees had widened from 15 percent to 37 percent. These differences were mostly due to the continuing in-migration of Anglos who had received their education and had launched their careers elsewhere.[12] This underlines how much native Santa Feans depended on the education they could receive in their own community.

For those who wanted to stay in the city, post–World War II changes had heightened the need for a college education and even postgraduate study. Given the high cost of living, such qualifications assumed more importance. Thus, Santa Fe residents, responding to the city planning department survey in 1994, called for improved educational opportunities. The survey reported that "Many feel that education is a link to a better economy, that with better educated youth there would be better jobs, and that with better jobs, there would be incentives to pursue an education."[13] Citizens expected educational improvement whether the jobs were there or not. But the efforts to achieve it over the previous forty years had shown a promise of change only in the most recent times.

In the postwar period the educational systems of Santa Fe began to reflect the economic stratification of the city's residents. Private and public schools came to be serving different segments of the population. Private schools served the interests of families who wanted their children to go to college and expected the elementary and secondary schools to provide the preparatory curricula. With a college degree, graduates could qualify for high-paying jobs that provided mobility. The public schools, however, had the additional responsibility for equalizing opportunities for all students regardless of their ultimate goals and family support.

This difference required the public schools to deal with conditions that weakened students' incentive for high school graduation. As they made the transition from elementary through junior high to high school, students in Santa Fe faced some of the same problems confronting students elsewhere. As they left their neighborhood elementary schools and their circles of longtime friends and reached the ninth grade full of students from other parts of town, many also faced new choices affecting their future without the social support they once enjoyed.

By 1970 the increased proportion of high-school–age persons enrolled in school—up to 90 percent from 33 percent in 1930—had exposed more and more students to these conditions and dropping out began to appear as one response to loss of interest.[14] In 1970 the rate of attrition was 20 percent and by 1980 it had reached 30 percent.[15] In partial response to this trend the district began to offer alternative programs. In 1971 the Vocational Technical High School opened as part of Santa Fe High School and was providing training in 25 areas. In 1982 it had 522 students with a dropout rate of 24.5 percent.[16] In 1976 the district established the Alternative High School, also as a part of Santa Fe High. It was designed to offer a flexible learning environment from the seventh through twelfth grade as an alternative to regular classroom work, with a diploma for meeting graduation requirements. This program was for students who had dropped out or were about to do so. Despite the efforts at innovation, Alternative High's dropout rate ranged from 22 percent to 46 percent between 1977 and 1981.[17]

Another effort to reduce dropouts began in 1982 as an experimental in-house suspension program to curb truancy at Santa Fe High. Students frequently absent or disruptive were separated from classrooms and assigned to study under supervision elsewhere on the campus. Assistance and counseling focused primarily on the ninth-grade students—at the entry level of the high school—who most often had "adjustment problems." One news story quoted the president of the school board in regard to this concern: "The ninth graders are lost. They don't belong in the junior high and they don't belong in the high school." Another board member replied that the board should consider shifting them to junior highs or establishing a new school for them.[18]

All these efforts suggest that the school authorities realized the limits of their ability to enforce school attendance laws. Even the state statute permitting students to leave school after the tenth grade implied a certain lack of conviction as to the obligation that remained. Thus attendance and compliance with the curriculum was in fact an option for the students and their parents, one that could be critically affected by the presence or absence of social support.

The value of such support became clear at Alternative High in 1982, soon after it was relocated at the site of the former Young Junior High. When faculty and students found themselves quartered three miles from Santa Fe High, to which they formally belonged, they asserted their separate identity. One stimulus came from an athletic director who was appointed to overcome "a lot of apathy" at the school. When he built an athletic program competing with schools of similar size, such as Santa Fe Preparatory School, St. Catherine's Indian School, and Española Alternative High, Santa Fe Alternative High students supported their teams. They selected school colors, gave themselves a nickname (the "Warriors," in contrast to the "Demons" of Santa Fe High), formed cheerleader and pep squads, and created "Warrior" T-shirts. Beyond this, they planted trees and flower beds on the school grounds, created their own student senate, and initiated their own newspaper.

The effects of such activities were powerful. Rick Powder, a faculty member, commented on the change: "People used to deny that they came to school here. Now they are proud of it." Other faculty members concurred that "The students seem more involved." Administrators noted the decline in the high truancy rate and the dropout rate.

Along with their newfound solidarity the students voiced their desire to have Alternative High recognized as a separate institution. They expressed their dissatisfaction with Santa Fe High School as having too many people and sought a separate commencement ceremony. Said one student, "We don't want to graduate with a bunch of people we don't know. We're a big family and we want to graduate with our family . . . the way we were brought up."[19]

In response to these requests, school board members gave voice to a dilemma in Santa Fe's educational system, namely, how to keep young people in school while being apprehensive about the motivation that could keep them there. District Superintendent James P. Miller supported the students' request, arguing that only a complete school with extracurricular activities would reduce the dropout rate. But board members Henry Gallegos and Eluid Martinez objected. Gallegos found Alternative High too segregated ethnically and its students insufficiently motivated to learn. Martinez echoed that if Alternative High were to become a separate school, "we'll be creating a barrio school with predominantly Hispano students, and it bothers me a hell of a lot." While the students wanted to be together in a cohesive group representing their social identity, board members feared that setting up Alternative High as a separate school would mark its Hispano students as a group set apart in the community; and different standards might develop that would discredit the academic ability of Hispano students. The board voted against separation, conceding only that Alternative High could have its own representative to speak at the next commencement.[20]

Whether intended or not, one result of setting up the new learning sites was to insulate Santa Fe High from a more arduous process of sifting out students who were losing their commitment. The dropout rates in 1980 among the three school settings were Alternative High, 37.5 percent; Vocational-Technical High, 24.5 percent; and Santa Fe High, 14.3 percent.[21]

As the principal source of education before the public school system was authorized in 1891, and continuing afterward with strong institutional support from the Catholic archdiocese, the private school system in Santa Fe retained its unique prominence into the twentieth century. In 1910 almost two-thirds of the students enrolled in the city were attending private schools. After that balance was reversed in 1930 and three-quarters of all students were enrolled in public schools, the private-school share of students varied roughly between 10 and 30 percent over the decades, a proportion higher than anywhere else in New Mexico. In the state as a whole, in 1970 and 1980, the graduates of private high schools constituted only 5 percent of all high school graduates compared to 20 percent and 17 percent, respectively, in Santa Fe. In 1980, continuing an established trend, 81 percent of the graduates of private high schools in Santa Fe declared their intention of attending an institution of higher learning, while 41 percent of the graduates of Santa Fe High, the only public high school, did so.[22]

27. *"Freshman Class, 1924," St. Michael's College. Courtesy Museum of New Mexico, neg. #51349. Photo by T. Harmon Parkhurst.*

In that same year, Catholic schools served more than two-thirds of all students enrolled in private schooling at the elementary and high school levels. Anglos and Hispanos, however, differed in the rates of their participation in private schooling, regardless of who sponsored it. Of all Hispanos in elementary schools, 13 percent were in private schools as compared with 7 percent of Anglo students. Of all Hispanos in high school, 14 percent were in private schools compared to 26 percent of Anglo students.[23]

Almost half of all private high school students in 1980 were enrolled at St. Michael's High. There, Anglos and Hispanos in varying proportions shared the benefits of a college preparatory curriculum, a popular interscholastic athletic program, and traditional support from generations of local families who had graduated from it. Since 1988, just before the new public Capital High School began to graduate its own students, the number of Hispano graduates at St. Michael's declined, from 90 in 1988 to 31 in 1996, while the number of Anglo graduates held more steady.[24] But by this time, as we shall see, a marked shift to public schooling had begun among Hispano students at the beginning of their college careers.

No history of private education in Santa Fe would be adequate without recognizing the strong inclination to regard private schools as readily available alternatives to the public system. In the early 1960s this tendency took form as a response to serious problems in the public schools. They were saddled with a quadrupled increase of enrollment since 1930 and increasing difficulty in receiving adequate funding.[25] In a survey conducted at the request of the Santa Fe Board of Education, more than half of adult respondents expressed their dissatisfaction. Overcrowding, lack of modern facilities, the need to improve instruction in basic subjects, and the need for better financial support headed local citizens' complaints.[26]

Local residents having the means responded readily. Over the next two decades, new private schools, mostly nonsectarian, began to proliferate. In 1961 a small group of business and professional men founded the Santa Fe Preparatory School. It offered a college-preparatory, liberal arts curriculum for 300 or more students in grades seven through twelve. In the eighties, the school undertook to diversify its student body and about one-quarter of the students received scholarship aid.[27]

In a parallel move inspired by a national wave of criticism and calls for reform of the country's public school systems, another small group of parents founded the Santa Fe Community School in 1968. In contrast to Santa Fe Prep, the Santa Fe Community School became a "free school" with an ungraded educational program. When the state board of education refused to accredit their secondary curriculum, the school's leaders filed suit challenging the constitutionality of the state's attempt to control private schools. After the district court dismissed the complaint, an appeal to the state supreme court resulted in a 1974 ruling that the state had no constitutional authority to regulate private schools but did have limited authority to approve courses of instruction. Still dissatisfied, the Santa Fe Community School turned to the state legislature, which in 1975 made state accreditation optional for nonpublic schools.[28] In that same year the school began to serve parents who were teaching their children at home, furnishing instructional materials and direct consultation; by the mid-nineties, nearly all of its students were being served in this way.[29]

Meanwhile, the supreme court decision and the legislative action won by the Santa Fe Community School were followed by an upsurge in the number of private schools in the city. By 1981, eleven new ones had been started, only five of which had survived by 1996. Yet even in 1980, total private enrollments amounted to the same 15 percent of total city enrollment registered in 1970. As Superintendent Miller pointed out, some of the older private schools had lost enrollments since 1975 by almost the same number of students the new schools were enrolling in 1981.[30]

By 1980 Santa Fe residents with four years or more of college education had increased to 30 percent, a sharp rise above the 10 percent level held in 1950. In those thirty years a small but certain number could have pursued their degrees entirely within the private institutions in Santa Fe. They could have finished at the College of Santa Fe, the only choice, if the required financial support existed.

In the earliest years of the college, after its establishment as a four-year institution in 1947, that choice was deliberately opened to Hispano students from the northern counties of New Mexico, as well as Santa Fe. They were to be the principal beneficiaries when the college gained the use of federal land and buildings on the site of the former Bruns Hospital. The purpose was to provide education for Hispano students who would return to their home communities and serve as teachers. Between 1950 and 1968, out of 1,017 graduates, 452 were Hispanos of whom 311 had come from the city; and of those, 97 were residents of a low-income neighborhood, the site of a Model Cities planning grant in the late 1960s.[31]

From 1968 through 1995, Hispanos comprised from 20 to 40 percent of the graduating classes. In the same period, however, the college also began to attract more students from other parts of the world. In 1976 entering freshmen came from 25 other states as well as from six foreign countries, while 30 percent still came from Santa Fe high schools. Yet, twenty years later, from 1993 to 1998, only 14 entering freshmen were Santa Fe high school graduates. Apparently the sizable increase of enrollment at the college after the mid-eighties did not widen college opportunities for the youth of Santa Fe.[32]

The opening of St. John's College in 1964, another private institution, offered some additional promise by providing scholarship aid for Southwestern students. By the mid-1990s, St. John's could count on from 12 to 15 percent of its enrollment of 350 to 385 students as coming from New Mexico and 3 to 4 percent from Santa Fe. Despite the scholarship aid, tuition costs could limit the number of students who were able to attend.[33]

It was not until the late 1970s that local residents made an effort to provide publicly supported, college-level education in the city. James Miller, who was school superintendent from 1974 to 1983, provided a strong initiative toward it. Entering a school system that had gained a reputation as a "graveyard for school superintendents," he redirected the focus of the local public to an interest in the outcome of educational activity. Miller aimed to show that if high standards were set, students in the Santa Fe public system could match the academic achievement of students anywhere. In 1982, he was rewarded by the graduates of Santa Fe High, who as freshmen at the University of New Mexico achieved the highest grade point average of graduates of any large public high school in the state, winning a special award from the university.

28. James P. Miller, Santa Fe School District Superintendent, 1974-1983.

Under Miller's persistent leadership, newspaper reporters asked how well the local school system was serving the city's young people. Articles covered the activities of high school graduates, their employment needs, and issues and disputes about meeting postsecondary educational needs. After reviewing various proposals, the Santa Fe School Board recommended an independent two-year college with its own campus. Approval by the New Mexico Board of Educational Finance came in 1982 followed by a special and successful election in 1983 that was almost lost because of a February blizzard.

The new Santa Fe Community College provided a "second chance" for those who had not graduated from high school, just as the public schools' Adult

Learning Center had done by offering instruction for the general equivalency diploma (GED). Between 1984 and 1996, enrollment at the community college for its adult basic education program and in its non-credit division together doubled. In 1983, two-thirds of enrollees in all programs were above the age of 22 (ranging up to age 62); in 1996, 81 percent were above the age of 24 (ranging up to age 75).[34]

At the same time the community college provided access to four-year degree programs by offering courses with credits transferable to other state institutions. By the end of 1996, results had become visible. Of full-time students in the credit division from 1987 to 1991, 18 percent had transferred to a New Mexico public university and eight students had completed a bachelor's degree.[35]

In little more than a decade after the community college was founded, it was evident that New Mexico's public higher education system had begun to draw more Santa Fe students. Between 1986 and 1996 the most notable difference was the increased rate of enrollment among Hispanos at the two largest state universities—the University of New Mexico and New Mexico State University. In the years 1986 through 1991, of all Hispano high school graduates in Santa Fe, 17 percent enrolled as entering freshmen at the two universities, but in the years 1992–1996, 27 percent did so. On the other hand, in the first five-year period, 22 percent of all non-Hispano graduates enrolled, but in the second period only 18 percent did so.

The difference is more striking when only graduates of private high schools are considered. Among Hispano graduates, the change from the first to the second five-year period was from 34 percent to 43 percent of the graduates; and among non-Hispanos, the change was from 16 to 11 percent. It is very likely that a larger portion of non-Hispano graduates attended institutions outside the state.

The same trends appeared among public high school graduates. Seventeen percent of Hispano graduates enrolled in the two state universities during the first period and 30 percent in the second. For non-Hispanos, the percentages fell from 23 percent in the first period to 19 percent in the second. It is plausible that Hispano students from Santa Fe were increasing their use of public institutions of higher education. At another New Mexico institution consistently attended by Hispano students, New Mexico Highlands University at Las Vegas, from 1992 to 1996, 160 Hispano Santa Fe public school graduates entered as compared with 46 non-Hispanos. Founded in 1893 as New Mexico Normal, this institution had originally trained Hispano youth as teachers for rural schools.[36]

From the earliest days of Anglo settlement in Santa Fe there has existed a measure of mutual respect between the ethnic groups. It has been evident in relations between merchants and customers, politicians and their constituents, and neighbors and fellow citizens. Chastisements have followed when the etiquette was violated. Accommodation has characterized the conduct of civic affairs and a studied reluctance to emphasize cultural differences has typified personal manners.

The strongest reinforcement of this attitude derives from the interdependence forged by the daily conduct of commerce and professional services, and from political activity requiring joint efforts in a community where Hispanos had been a majority since the Anglos arrived. Following that event, Hispanos emerged from a traditional subsistence economy into an urban one increasingly linked with the rest of the country. As each successive generation of Hispanos came closer to approximating the Anglo pattern of employment, education, and political participation, the tradition of mutual respect could reinforce the sense of likeness between both groups.

But a developing sense of likeness based on common participation in the urban economy is not the same as the one based on common ancestry, culture, or social ties. These ties—including friendships and marriage with members of other ethnic groups—confer a measure of equality in social status that is not guaranteed by the urban economy. Participation in such an economy, based on competition for scarce resources, produces its own inequities through differential rewards and life chances meted out to everyone regardless of ethnic or cultural background. Once committed to the urban way of life and livelihood, Hispanos, without necessarily shedding family ties or cultural traditions, are caught in the same system of economic differences in life chances as are the urban Anglos.

In this system, economic advantage accrues to persons whose level of education equips them for high-paying jobs wherever these may be found. In Santa Fe more Anglos than Hispanos had gained this advantage. But with the exception of the professions, where Hispanos have lagged, those with advanced education have tended to reach parity with Anglos in occupational status as well as geographic mobility. Among all the alumni of the College of Santa Fe from the class of 1947 to that of 1995, at least two-thirds of Anglos and Hispanos alike have had careers in business or education. Between 1972 and 1994 the proportion of Anglo alumni living in Santa Fe remained at 15 percent, but those living in Albuquerque increased from 2 to 25 percent. Among Hispano alumni the 40 percent living in Santa Fe in 1972 had dropped to 20 percent in 1994 while those living in Albuquerque had risen from 3 to 32 percent. These data, based on residence after graduation, demonstrate a significant shift in the locale of occupational careers and comparable mobility for both ethnic groups.[37]

These career outcomes contrast starkly with both Anglo and Hispano young people who did not graduate from high school and did not leave the city. Hispanos were affected more seriously. Although the percentage of high school graduates among them rose from 52 percent in 1970 to 69 percent in 1990, their dropout rate has been markedly higher than that for Anglos.[38] With no job opportunities to attract them elsewhere, ties of kinship and neighborhood could hold them closer to home, forcing a greater dependence on lower-paying service jobs and a diminishing range of skilled craft or manual labor employment—more recently in competition with immigrants from Mexico.

For native Hispanos one significant effect of higher levels of education is the mobility they have experienced in breaking old ties, entering into new relationships, and moving to new places as economic opportunities have become attractive. At the same time, ever since the Anglos arrived their presence has heightened Hispanos' awareness of their own cultural identity, gaining a sense of status not affected by one's economic position. Beyond the Hispanos' sharpened awareness of their own history, language, and traditions, the Anglos' reception and response have added new dimensions. In one form, Anglos in Santa Fe have celebrated Hispano culture as a tourist attraction, giving their own version of it in the process. In another form, as we show in the next chapter, Anglo residents of Santa Fe have adopted manifestations of Hispano culture as part of their ordinary lives. In health practices, intermarriage, food preferences, and language usage, the mingling has become a distinctive feature of this community.

THIRTEEN

Cultural Accommodation, 1945–1990

THE INCREASING CONTACT of Anglo and Hispano could scarcely occur without impacting both populations. Continuous Anglo growth meant a heightened presence of its culture and institutions. After 1920, when growth became a noticeable and seemingly inexorable fact of life in the city, accustomed patterns of social behavior and interaction altered slowly. From the thirties on, the effects of the Depression and World War II changed the availability of schooling, housing, and work, while increased social services permitted alteration of traditional practices to take place at a pace and in ways hitherto unknown. Interaction of Anglo and Hispano, consciously and unconsciously, became more common as the Anglo population grew and government support and legislation provided opportunity for the Hispano to move out of traditional ways and into greater contact with the growing Anglo presence.

Population increase underlay every sort of activity and Santa Feans worried about it. In 1940 their numbers stood at 20,325 and Albuquerque's at 35,449. By 1970 Santa Fe had doubled its population to 41,167, while Albuquerque's reached 243,751—a sevenfold increase.1 No matter how fast Santa Fe was growing by doubling in thirty years, its growth was quite moderate compared with the population explosion of its neighbor to the south. Santa Fe was still quite a small city while Albuquerque had become mid-sized by national standards.

In subsequent decades Santa Fe's growth continued. By 1980 its numbers reached 49,299 and by 1990 further increases brought that number to 55,859. Thus, in a half-century since 1940, the date of the immediate prewar census, the town had nearly tripled in size. Viewed in the cold light of percentage growth, the decade of greatest increase after the Depression was the forties (37.7 percent).

The following decades witnessed a slowing growth rate, 27.7 percent in the fifties and nothing exceeding a 19 percent rate until the nineties.[2] Accustomed to viewing themselves as a small town and regarding that condition as a virtue, some Santa Feans considered their growth as enormous and regarded the condition with apprehension.

The data on growth also revealed another trend. While early in the postwar period the city grew more rapidly than Santa Fe County, by 1980 that pattern had reversed, and the county outside the city was adding population at nearly double the rate of the city.[3] This new trend involved social and economic changes occurring within the city itself as well as on its periphery (See chapter 12).

The expansion of social services, which was rapid during the Depression, continued under wartime conditions and on into the postwar recovery. The greatest impact occurred precisely among that population that most needed the services: the poor, the rural, and the least educated. The tempo of change, however, could not readily be dictated from the outside. In some matters only those seeking change could choose the service and they determined the rate of acceptance.

A new/old health industry appeared in Santa Fe after World War II. It was the product of a number of factors, including the oldest of the Hispano and Native American traditions and religions, and new religious and medical attitudes within the Anglo world. This complex of views and practices established itself widely in New Mexico, but Santa Fe became an important focal point of congregation for believers and practitioners of the new arts.

New Mexico's reputation as an area conducive to health and well-being, as discussed earlier, had ebbed, but not ended, despite the discovery of new cures for tuberculosis around World War II. An artist-writer–induced view of New Mexico as a place of attitudinal health or psychological well-being had been strong in the twenties, with Mary Austin a powerful advocate in Santa Fe and Mabel Dodge Luhan and D. H. Lawrence in Taos. Serenity and rootedness were at the core of their views and contact with the Native American communities, as well as climate and terrain, provided the environment for their acceptance and elaboration.

Anthropologists, as well as writers and artists, at variance with disparaging earlier American views of the Southwestern "ethnics," pictured indigenous Pueblos and Hispano villagers with more respect and upheld the legitimacy of their traditions. Other Anglos, who had retreated from urban, industrial America, saw the still "uncontaminated" social and physical environments of these peoples as answers to the physical and mental ills they had left behind in the East.[4]

Anglos had their own cultural experiences with religiously based healing in the Southwest. Best known in New Mexico was Francis Schlatter, who in the 1890s amazed Albuquerqueans and Denverites, as well as small villagers with his curative abilities. He appears to have spent little, if any, time in Santa Fe.[5] Schlatter attracted the attention of Hispanos as well as Anglos and among the former his sobriquet was "El Gran Hombre."[6]

The use of herbs for healing and health maintenance among Hispanos and Native Americans was a practice of long standing throughout New Mexico. The appearance of the modern Anglo doctor and pharmacy may have augmented means of cure, but it did not displace folk and tribal knowledge. A study published in 1975 used as one of its sources Roybal's food store on Galisteo Street. Founded in 1917 as a general store, it was still operating in 1966 and carried a large variety of medicinal and cooking herbs labeled in Spanish. Elderly Hispanos supplied it with local products from as far away as Truchas. By the mid-sixties Native Americans and young Anglos were also bringing in varieties of herbs and California and Mexico served as major sources for nonlocal species. The clientele was predominantly Hispano, but Native Americans, local Anglos, and even tourists were among the store's customers. The store closed in 1969, but a former employee continued the operation nearby.[7]

Nor did the tradition of *curanderismo*, the folk healing system, disappear among Hispanos with the entry of Anglo medicine in the Southwest. Acceptance of the new ways came more readily in urban areas, where their accessibility was greater. Even in Santa Fe, however, the old practices never ceased even as the availability of the Anglo "alternative medicine" increased. Gregorita Rodriguez, a *curandera* who learned her craft from her grandmother and aunt, was still dispensing herbs and giving massages in the late 1980s to those in distress.[8]

While curandera Rodriguez represented the Hispano tradition, Dr. Jay Scherer represented the establishment of alternative medicine in the city. Indeed, the presence of a variety of practices ranging from acupressure to yoga, with psychic healing and palm reading in between, made the city a significant center for such healing arts. The attraction of the city for persons seeking nontraditional ways and answers to health grew after the war, as well as the population of practitioners and educators.[9] The presence of these alternatives bespoke a liberality of acceptance among the Anglos that at least paralleled and at times overlapped the growth in the range of practices used by Hispanos.

Although an outspoken Gregorita Rodriguez would challenge members of the medical profession in the city, there is evidence that Hispano cultural preferences in the processes of healing changed over time to greater utilization and acceptance of modern medicine. Speaking of Hispano patients, Dr. Albert Egenhofer, who practiced ophthalmology in Santa Fe from 1938 to 1972, noted that "they don't wait until they're half dead before they get something done."[10] Hispanos and Anglos generally shared both Anglo and Hispano doctors.[11]

Some widely accepted practices among Hispanos declined or became altered over time. One *partera* (midwife) alone in the Las Vegas area had delivered over twelve thousand children in her career.[12] But the use of midwifery in New Mexico fell sharply between 1935 and the early fifties. Whereas in 1935, 23 percent of registered live births had been delivered by midwives in the state, by 1953 it had dropped to 5.7 percent.[13] Yet, even in 1953 the use of midwives was still high by national standards, greater than in any state in the country outside of the South.[14] The number of midwives in New Mexico alone in 1948 quintupled those of all the Pacific coast states.

The reasons for decline of the practice are manifold. Certainly the scarcity of doctors and hospitals in many areas and their cost had allowed and, indeed, required the widespread use of midwives. The tradition predated the existence of any modern medical profession. State regulations on midwifery, first introduced in 1922, underwent revision in 1937 and again in 1944. Increasingly rigorous state regulation reduced the number of practitioners while medical specialization and growing numbers of obstetricians made modern treatment more readily available.[15]

In Santa Fe County, more rural than the city, delivery of infants by midwives declined rapidly in the last years before the war. Midwives had delivered nearly 49 percent of all births in 1933 (exclusive of Native Americans) but only 26 percent in 1942.[16] Among Hispano women in the county outside of the city, midwives delivered over 56 percent in 1933 and that portion had fallen to 31 percent in 1942.[17] From the perspective of physician attendance and hospital care in Santa Fe County in 1933, doctors delivered about 46 percent of all live births. By 1940, however, they delivered over 64 percent of such births.[18] Santa Fe moved from being among the highest counties in use of midwives in 1933 to the middle rank of counties in 1942.

In Santa Fe itself new agencies appeared to aid women. The Santa Fe Maternal Health Center (MHC), a birth-control facility sponsored by the Margaret Sanger movement, opened in 1937. Sponsored by non-Catholic women who believed that poverty could be alleviated in part by family planning, the strategy of the Santa Fe chapter of the MHC soon changed to dealing with maternal problems as well. For a time the MHC grew, despite heavy opposition from the Catholic Church.[19]

The Catholic Maternity Institute opened its doors officially in August 1944 to aid maternal care. New Mexico's painful record of infant death, more than double the national mortality rate in the early forties, was incentive enough.[20] Community physicians and the state health department supported the effort to train midwives, to provide maternity service directed by a qualified physician, and to offer improved birthing conditions for women who preferred home care and midwifery.[21] Thus, even before the social changes that followed the war, Santa Fe women were adapting to new methods and facilities made available to them.

In the postwar era, the hospital became the overwhelming choice as the place to give birth. Social legislation as well as benefits for the families of servicemen opened doors as never before to the general population for such treatment. By 1955 over 91 percent of births in Santa Fe County occurred in hospitals and by 1970 over 99 percent did so.[22] There was a decrease in hospital births thereafter, but even in 1990 hospital-based births stood at over 98 percent. The great majority of all births in the county took place at St. Vincent's Hospital in Santa Fe.

That the acceptance of new ways occurred so rapidly fully illustrates one limit of cultural barriers. Ethnicity may not have been perceived to be as important as self-interest in health care. When what was perceived as better care became available, the Hispanos made use of it. Dr. Bergere Kenney, with roots in both the Hispano and the Anglo communities of Santa Fe, was himself surprised at first by the willingness of Hispano women to submit to examination by male doctors, largely Anglo, as long as nurses were present and politeness shown. He likened their trust in doctors to that accorded priests.[23]

Increasing utilization of modern medical practices among Hispanos, however, did not automatically exclude the continuing use of traditional practices. Dr. Kenney noted of Hispanos that "They would be up at the Santuario de Chimayó getting holy mud at the same time they would be down here getting penicillin. . . ."[24] He and other Santa Fe doctors mentioned occasional requests to deal with afflictions caused by evil eye or witchcraft. But such instances were few and Dr. José Maldonado in particular spoke of the decline in such requests.[25] While distinct cultural traditions remained, the realities of life led to an increasing common usage, a fact of voluntary rapprochement between Anglo and Hispano cultures.

The medical profession in general also changed in the postwar period. It became more open to the meaning and importance of cultural difference in the process of healing. A literature of that genre emerged in the fifties and sixties and New Mexico, as an area containing large and distinct societies raised in non-Western traditions, could not escape the import of the different attitudes and information. The recently opened medical school at Albuquerque even invited curanderos to the classroom to demonstrate their practices as part of its student training in the mid-sixties.[26]

While mutual cultural familiarity increased in the century and a half of

Anglo presence in Santa Fe, few factors could draw Anglo and Hispano together as intimately as intermarriage. Such unions began with the earliest contacts between the two groups despite the distance between them in language, religion, and culture. Before 1880 the families that resulted tended to remain Hispano. After that time, the railroad made more accessible the increased immigration of already established Anglo families, supplanting the older pattern of single Santa Fe Trail arrivals and thus introducing new operative factors with respect to intermarriage.

Our study of manuscript census data on intermarriage in Santa Fe indicates that between 1880 and 1920 the rate of intermarriage fell.[27] In 1880, 27 percent of all marriages involving Anglos were mixed, while in 1920, that share had fallen to 12 percent. For Hispanos, the percentage of mixed marriages among their total marriages in Santa Fe in 1880 was 10 percent, falling slightly to 9 percent by 1920. Each intervening census showed declines.

Although the numbers alone do not explain the decrease of mixed marriages, the changing nature of Anglo immigration may well hold the answer. The entire period was one of population decline in Santa Fe as well; and the changed character of Anglo immigration, where many more families arrived, may simply have reduced the opportunity for such alliances to occur.

Between 1920 and 1940 the trend appears to have reversed itself. The information available, however, is quite different. Starting with 1920, after which the manuscript census is unavailable, the Santa Fe County marriage records became our major source for data. In that year, one of every sixteen marriages performed in Santa Fe was between an Anglo and a Hispano. In 1930, one of every six marriages was of that character, and in 1940, one of eight was mixed. Overall, the rate of mixed marriage appeared to double between 1920 and 1940.

In the post–World War II era, the pattern that had begun after 1920 became even more pronounced. In the year 1950 one of every seven marriages performed was mixed, and in 1960 that number had increased to one in six. From 1970 to 1990, one of every four marriages involved an Anglo and a Hispano. It is quite likely that only a considerably changed social environment underlay such an obvious rise in the interethnic marriage rate.

It should be noted that studying intermarriage poses difficulties. The use of surnames as ethnic identifiers becomes increasingly less reliable over time. In the mid-sixties, Nancie González, who was researching the subject, noted that "many individuals with Spanish surnames who, because their mothers have been Anglo, do not identify with the Hispano group. Yet if these persons marry Anglos, their marriages would be categorized as mixed." Similarly, the offspring of a Spanish-speaking mother may well have an Anglo surname. Under the circumstances, intermarriage could become increasingly difficult to study and, indeed, as acculturation takes place, she remarks, "the whole question of how much 'intermarriage' takes place will become meaningless."[28]

A variety of factors may have contributed to the long-term increase in Anglo-Hispano contact in Santa Fe. The growth of the Anglo family population, paralleling the established Hispano pattern, allowed generations of children to grow up in proximity to each other. They attended schools together and developed new kinds of familiarity. Moreover, changing patterns of Hispano employment offered opportunities for powerful barriers of social distinction to become weaker and of contact to become stronger. As the city grew, old neighborhoods lost some of their historic ethnic definition while new mixed housing developments came into existence. Growing numbers of Anglos made more marital choices available. All of these changes increased opportunities for interaction between persons of the major ethnic groups and made more acceptable alliances either unimagined or deemed impossible at earlier times. Similar studies of relatively urban Bernalillo County reveal the same intermarriage trends.[29]

Although our history does not explore many changes within either ethnic group, some comment on the effects of economic change on the traditional Hispano population is unavoidable. In 1982, the director of a Santa Fe social service agency commented on the effect of such pressure on Hispano women. One of the greatest changes was their increasing role as wage earners in the marketplace. And as careers became evermore possible and perhaps necessary in postwar society, they conflicted with the traditional female role within the family. The pressure to compete differed sharply from older Hispano values. The agency directory viewed women in that role as behaving unfavorably in the eyes of Hispano males—as aggressive.[30] Not only did such changes alter internal relationships within Hispano society, but one might ask if such circumstances also made intermarriage more possible. The changing roles of women as the economy of the city expanded and the campaign for women's rights grew, allowed them greater access to the Anglo world and easier contact with Anglo males.

How the offspring of the increasing numbers of mixed marriages identify themselves has yet to be studied, and may not be possible. The complexities and the range of possibilities are great. One may even speculate that the growing number of progeny from such marriages may bring into question the popular tricultural ethnic characterization of the city's population. The interweaving of identifiable ethnic traits within the family may make the use of such distinctions moot. That could leave the growing economic differences as a more formidable distinction and perhaps one not readily glossed over.

While the modern American economy and the Santa Fe Anglos had played an important role in redefining aspects of Hispano life in Santa Fe ever since they had arrived, the reverse was also true to some extent. Anglos, as they began to define the city as a place where the older, still existent, culture should be retained in some measure, could not help but accept aspects of that culture as desirable. The powerful presence of the Spanish language, as noted, was rooted in every aspect of daily life for the Hispanos and received at least a modicum of acceptance by many Anglos. Quite consciously, Anglo cultural leaders, from their earliest attempts at planning, sought to retain and even regain the flavor of the Spanish tradition by the use of Spanish street and place names where English had made too much headway.

The place of language itself became an obvious and important factor in the social rapprochement of Anglo and Hispano. Richard L. Nostrand in his volume, *The Hispano Homeland*, offers a parable of the stages through which Hispanos have adopted the English language. In 1900 the census taker in the village of El Cerrito, New Mexico, reported "that not one of the 136 villagers . . . could speak English." When sociologists Charles Loomis and Olen Leonard studied that community in 1940 they found that some men who had worked away from the village "knew a little English" and children were learning it in grade school. By 1980, when Nostrand was living there, adults in their thirties and forties were bilingual while children under ten were speaking English better than Spanish.[31]

Such transitions had occurred much earlier in large urban centers of the state. Yet in Santa Fe a complementary trend emerged as the earliest Anglo residents learned some Spanish and otherwise accommodated to its continued usage by native Hispanos. German-Jewish merchants, with their European background and English already a second language, had found it easy and highly useful to learn another language. Other Anglos formed business partnerships with Hispano merchants and did the same. Command of both languages helped to cement merchant-customer relationships and other business undertakings as well as the functioning of government.

Linguistic accommodation extended into the world of information. As early as 1849 to 1850, the *Morning New Mexican* was published in English and Spanish, as it was again from 1863 to 1883. From 1890 to 1958, the *Daily New Mexican* issued a companion Spanish-language publication, *El Nuevo Mexicano*. Altogether, at intervals between 1880 and 1975, ten different newspapers in the city were published in both languages as were four Spanish sections of English newspapers. In that ninety-five-year period, except for about five years, at least one paper was printing news in a bilingual format.[32]

Unlike the languages of other countries whose immigrants to the United States adopted English by the second generation, Spanish was indigenous to the Hispanos in the American Southwest and the Anglos were the immigrants. The numerical superiority of the Spanish speakers in New Mexico assured that use of their language would be politically protected. This protection began when Hispano leaders, through the territorial legislature, took steps to control the conditions under which their children would learn English in the public schools. An 1891 law specified that teachers should know English, but it also stated that "where the only language spoken is Spanish, the teacher shall have a knowledge of both English and Spanish."[33] The state constitution of 1912 prohibited the segregation of Spanish-speaking students in public schools and contained a requirement that public school teachers be trained for proficiency in both languages.[34]

The federal government confirmed the continuing need and suitability of these provisions when Congress enacted the Bilingual Act of 1968. Under this action, local schools could receive financial assistance for teaching English to children from non–English-speaking environments. Soon after, the Santa Fe schools began to receive such support. For Anglo residents of the city it also became an opportunity for their English-speaking children to learn Spanish. This was partly a response to the practical necessity of dealing with the local Spanish-speaking population but also a civic virtue.

A more immediate practical incentive stemmed from the fact that in 1980 and 1990 two-thirds of the Hispano residents of Santa Fe spoke a language other than English. In 1980, among residents of Hispano origin, only 7.5 percent reported that they did not speak English very well. By 1990, this proportion rose to 18 percent. In Santa Fe the most apparent reason for this was a more than twofold increase in residents of Spanish-speaking origin who were foreign-born, reputedly coming from Mexico.[35]

For a long time it had been advantageous for Anglos to know Spanish for employment directly serving the general public—in business, government, education, health care, and law enforcement. A recent instance was the contract negotiated by the American Federation of State, County and Municipal Employees in 1995 to secure "bilingual incentive pay" for members proficient in Spanish. Under this arrangement, for example, Santa Fe police officers could qualify by taking Spanish courses at the community college, paid for by the city. Pursuant to state requirements, notices and ballots for city elections have continued to be published in Spanish and English. Interpreters have been regularly engaged to assist persons appearing in court or involved in legal transactions.

Beyond these practical necessities, the use of Spanish by some Anglos represents for residents an identification with the city's cultural past and a source of pride. One example appeared in 1940 when the federal Works Progress

Administration published a tourist book entitled *New Mexico: A Guide to the Colorful State.* It contained a chapter entitled "Contributions to the Language" with a twelve-page glossary of words then in use by English speakers, drawn partly from French and Native American languages, but mostly from Spanish.[36] In the fifties and after, in new housing developments, the assignment of Hispano names to new streets remained customary, Anglos having long supported such designations in the interest of cultural preservation.

By 1980 almost one-third of the city's elementary school students were enrolled in bilingual education classes at their parents' request. While this program was designed to help Spanish-speaking children to learn English, after ten years of operation those students were a minority of the total enrollment in the program. According to one report, most students at that time were either non-Spanish speakers with Spanish surnames whose parents wanted them to learn the Spanish language and about Hispano culture, or they were Anglo students whose parents wanted them to learn Spanish. As the observer, himself an Anglo parent, put it: "Instead of being a remedial education program, bilingual education has become in many cases an enrichment program for non-Spanish speaking students to learn Spanish."[37] By the mid-nineties, however, the unprecedented influx of non–English-speaking immigrants, along with an increase of certified bilingual teachers (one for every school), swung the program in some schools to greater emphasis on English language teaching. Nevertheless, after more than a century of publicly backed schooling, and despite many reasons for the actual dominance of English, Spanish has remained a present and valued factor in Santa Fe's culture, primarily, of course, for the Hispano population, but with great value for its Anglos as well.

The distinctiveness of the New Mexican diet, with its emphasis on chile, convinced many Anglo residents, after some practice, that the taste and terminology were best retained. No doubt, the distance from older American centers made difficult the maintenance of diets derived from different climes, but as improved transportation erased those hindrances, the taste for the local fare did not disappear. Many continued to partake of the local foods even if they added elements not native to the area.[38] If they did not necessarily become the ordinary fare of the Anglo, they remained a specialty to be enjoyed. The number of restaurants in Santa Fe offering Hispano food has not declined despite the ready availability of international cookery of wide variety and of American ingredients used nationally. Indeed, those engaged in the artistry of cooking have combined the two in some restaurants.

The clothing and jewelry of the Native Americans and Hispanos also became a prized expression of cultural identity with the region and town for many Anglos. They sported (and sport) rings, necklaces, and bracelets, sometimes with an abandon that amused others. Hispanos, more practically, sometimes adopted the jeans that the Anglos brought in as work clothes or for informal wear. Such examples of cultural mixing are legion.

The place of sports in the modern history of Santa Fe is a broad subject involving a variety of issues. Class, ethnic identity and pride, and the process of accommodation were affected by games played, watched, or ignored by the resident population. How these interests grew and how they influenced various groups in the community provide a further measurement of changing attitudes among the ethnic groups and classes in the city toward each other. Interest in major national sports served as a factor of common interest for those segments of Santa Fe society that adopted them. Furthermore, they offered new bases of solidarity and identification within the ethnic groups as well as with persons outside of their traditional culture. Among these games were baseball, football, and basketball.

Baseball had been introduced into the Southwest by the troops of the U.S. army when they occupied the territory in the nineteenth century. Familiarity with it broadened as railroad workers and miners became residents and formed teams.[39]

The Native Americans themselves had traditions of games involving kicking or carrying balls with their feet as well as running.[40] After the Indian schools opened in Albuquerque (1884) and Santa Fe (1890), the students received exposure to American sports as part of the goal of Americanization. Apparently, knowledge of the games became disseminated throughout the Pueblo communities by the students of the schools.[41] The Native Americans adopted them and performed quite credibly. Teams from the University of New Mexico played both the Albuquerque and Santa Fe Indian schools as early as 1903.[42]

Hispanos, too, may have had some acquaintance with a game employing principles similar to baseball.[43] The organization of the modern American game, however, appeared through games sponsored by business institutions and schools. A New Mexico historian of the sport notes that its early popularity left it unrivaled in public interest and that it was played "by all levels of the territorial society."[44] St. Michael's played the game as early as the 1880s against any willing independent club. An 1888 photograph of the school's squad identifies seven Hispano and three Anglo players as its team.[45] St. Michael's and the university played each other as early as 1910 and the Santa Fe school defeated its university rival in 1911.[46]

Football contests between the university and the Santa Fe Indian School began in 1903, continuing intermittently thereafter for a number of years. After 1912 the university and St. Michael's locked horns a few times. Even the state

29. St. Michael's College baseball team, ca. 1890. Courtesy Museum of New Mexico, neg. #50262.

penitentiary and the university played each other in 1919. For obvious reasons, that was a home game in Santa Fe.

Organized basketball began a generation later. St. Michael's played the game in 1926 and a city tournament took place in 1927. St. Michael's won. The Hispano names on the 1927 squad bear witness to their interest and participation. State tournaments began in 1928.[47] However, Santa Fe schools were playing each other long before the mid-twenties. The *Cacique*, the Santa Fe High School yearbook of 1920, reported on the basketball games of the season in that year.[48] Regardless of their mediocre record, the game had clearly taken hold by then and Hispano players were on the team.

However well or ill the local schools played the various sports, their social effects were important. Anglo and Hispano students were teammates, engaged on a common platform of interaction, cooperation, and loyalty. The games themselves, as they were played in the schools, were an ethnic meeting ground, drawing Hispano youngsters into the world of Anglo activity. Here they met as equals, each offering individual skills in competition. As knowledge and interest grew, so did participation. The 1930 Santa Fe High School football squad had eighteen members, the 1949 team, fifty-four.[49] Improved organization and growing numbers meant greater popularity and an increased following.

Nor did interest stop with the players themselves. As schedules developed involving other town teams, rivalry and loyalty grew. The families of the players joined in, rooting spiritedly for their kin and favorites, and making the contests an evermore important part of their social life. Sports formed a new and deeply seated social stage for young and old alike. City institutions helped. The *New Mexican* began a sports section in January 1900, a sign at least of the subject matter's interest to a segment of the public. Later, Hispano sports writers became a part of the growing interest in the games. A student of the subject claimed that in the early fifties New Mexico had the only Hispano sports writers and editors in the United States.[50]

Inevitably, as high school sports gathered their own following, they produced their own heroes. In the early post–World War II era, Toby Roybal of

30. Santa Fe High School girls' basketball team, 1917. Courtesy Museum of New Mexico, neg. #7255.

Santa Fe High went on to the University of New Mexico, an important career stepping stone for New Mexico athletes. After a brilliant career there, he became the first university basketball player to be drafted by the professional leagues. However, he turned the offer down and returned to Santa Fe to teach and coach.[51] Coaching by Hispanos provided their youth with models of authority and excellence in activities that, while emerging from Anglo culture, gave Hispanos a sense of pride in the performance of their own.

The culture of high school sports in Santa Fe developed a checkered pattern. At times intense rivalries developed between schools. St. Michael's (at one time "the Archangels") and Santa Fe High School ("the Demons") brought private versus public school issues into play. Lack of athletic success at times led to indifference. In the seventies, a concerted effort to improve athletic quality at Santa Fe High under coach David Church, with the backing of school superintendent James Miller, who linked success in athletics with academic improvement, led to higher quality in both.[52] The effort involved rooting out favoritism, instituting summer conditioning programs, and insistence on standards. Parental involvement could be intense.[53] Efforts to honor quality athletes appeared at the schools in the form of walls of fame or honor to bestow esteem on exceptional athletes. All in all, the atmosphere of sports produced as distinctive a world of its own in the city as did the arts.

Anglos who came to Santa Fe in search of health, arts, or ethnic uniqueness, remained largely aloof from local sport interests. Those who came at an age when their children no longer required the local school system had little reason for loyalty or concern with the state of athletic prowess in educational institutions. Thus, even as one segment of the Hispano population forged bonds out of the Anglo-inspired activity through their school children, another segment of the Anglo population remained far removed and indifferent. If one speaks of Anglo interest in Hispano culture from the late twenties on, then the more recent developments that brought Hispanos closer to the Anglo world might well have been of less interest to Anglos than the older, more distinct Hispano cultural patterns.

Golf, early on, inspired only a modest level of interest in Santa Fe. As an attraction, it drew more support from local enthusiasts than for tourists. In its early days in America the game was considered one for the wealthier segments of society. Taking hold in the late 1880s in the Northeast, it made its way westward to large cities and fashionable suburbs and resorts.[54] To accommodate its enjoyment, as well as other sports in which the well-to-do engaged, such as polo, the country club came into fashion. Golf courses were expensive operations requiring extensive water usage and carrying high-class status in the early days of growth. Besides the enjoyment it provided for the players, by the 1920s, participation in

31. Toby Roybal, from Santa Fe High to the University of New Mexico, ca. 1964. Courtesy Museum of New Mexico, neg. #29679.

the game and membership in a country club were considered essential steps for successful business careers.[55] By 1931 there were 5,700 golf courses in the country, of which 4,450 were private and over 500 municipal. In addition, there were some 700 privately owned, public fee courses.[56] Clearly, the popularity of the game was immense.

In New Mexico, Albuquerque led the way in establishing a country club in 1914, near the university. With it came a nine-hole golf course.[57] By the early thirties, other golf courses had been created in the city.[58] Given the growth of business and the well-suited climate, the future of the game was secure.

The country club and its golf course became so important that it became tied to place of residence in some instances. In Albuquerque, when the country club moved from its original site to a valley location in 1928, it was accompanied by a residential addition of expensive lots and homes that would assure easy access to both club and golf course.[59]

Santa Fe's interest in the middle- and upper-class sport developed more slowly and in a lower key. In all likelihood, the better-off tuberculars, artists, and writers, seeking to express and involve themselves in the arts and to absorb the diverse aspects of Southwestern culture in the post–World War I era, did not generally look to the golf links for either physical enjoyment or for the socioeconomic enhancement of their careers.

The first known course in town appeared at Bishop's Lodge in the early twenties. Around World War II, a nine-hole municipal course had been created on Airport Road. The Japanese-American internees, whose gardening skills were unsuccessfully sought to maintain it, referred to the matter in their newsletter.[60] That modest step received no follow-up for nearly a generation.

Postwar population changes finally brought a country club to Santa Fe. The terms under which the club was chartered in 1949, however, did not represent a sharp social change in the city. Nonmembers also could play as a result of arrangements by which the golf course received its water from the city.

The continuing influx of relatively well-off newcomers led to attempts to create a golf facility and housing development by the Sangre de Cristo Development Co. in the late sixties on Tesuque Pueblo, north of Santa Fe. In 1971 lots and golf course memberships began to be sold. However, legal problems with the pueblo, as well as issues of planning both with the city and the county led to the collapse of the entire project.[61] Thus, even as new public and private courses thrived in Albuquerque, Santa Fe moved slowly in this direction.

Only in the late 1980s did the desire for golf and related housing developments become more pronounced. Even then, the county rather than the city displayed a far greater development. While such relatively expensive housing projects as Quail Run in the city offered a nine-hole course to its homeowners and a limited membership for the city, a much larger one appeared in the county. There, northwest of the city line, Las Campanas offered a course designed by famed golfer Jack Nicklaus, up-scale housing, and commercial development. In effect, some of what had appeared as a mainstream development in Albuquerque from the late twenties on now made a strong appearance on the fringe of Santa Fe.[62] The rural surroundings of the city were being replaced by suburban development and the incoming population appeared more wedded to the middle- and upper-class activities of the world from which they had come than the earlier residents who had relied far more on the traditional cultural features of the city.

Early in the last decade of the twentieth century, Santa Fe was a far more complex community than it had been at the end of World War II. After the Depression and the war, health, intermarriage, education, sport, social contact at an early age, and, to some extent, leisure, became available in forms that brought the Hispano and Anglo closer together. While economic differences did not always allow parity, they nevertheless did not preclude a growing similarity of economic identity in many areas of the town, as well as in social intercourse. If the range of economic heterogeneity in Santa Fe was greater in the 1990s than at the end of World War II, then social contact and opportunity for new responses and adaptation to cultural difference were also greater.

Old and new practices coexisted. The old remained, allowing it to be found for those who sought to continue it. At the same time, the newly provided opportunities that could be utilized by those desiring to do so and the old distinctions in many areas of everyday life lost some of their cultural distance. However much each ethnic group maintained its identity, familiarity was eroding distance and allowing the culture of the other ethnic group to be understood and, sometimes, even appreciated.

Postscript

LOOKING AT THE roughly 110 years covered by our history, one asks, how did Santa Fe change over that span of time? What problems did it overcome and what new problems, given the human condition, did it create? Clearly, by 1990 Santa Fe had become one of the major tourist centers of the United States, a far cry from its modest position as a trade terminus on the Santa Fe Trail in 1880. Yet, our basic purpose has not been to measure the growth of tourism, but to consider the lives of the city's inhabitants. Likewise, it would be difficult to ignore the tenfold growth over those years during which the small isolated town of 1880 became a substantial city.

Nevertheless, despite these momentous changes, Santa Fe in 1990 remained quite recognizable. In 1880 it was a trade terminus at the end of the Santa Fe Trail, a political capital for the Territory of New Mexico, and a religious center—a bishopric—of the Catholic Church. In 1990 it was still an important political and religious center.

The town's economic character, however, displayed a more complex nature. Before it became American territory, its status as a trade terminus coincided with its privileged position as a port of entry. After it became American territory this privilege disappeared and the town's weakened commercial position carried over even more markedly when it was bypassed by the main line of the railroad. As a result the town suffered economically for nearly forty years.

Under Spanish rule it had attracted persons who needed access to governmental permissions and services and also brought influential and wealthy persons who chose to reside there after successful careers elsewhere in the region. With the advent of American rule, the town remained a lure for wealthy persons who did not require lucrative employment. From early in the twentieth century through the post–World War II period, that attraction continued for those who came either to open businesses, practice a profession, or to retire. After statehood in 1912, Santa Fe once more became a vigorous economic entity. A strong factor in its renewed prosperity and growth rested on in-migration and the growth of government. The latter expanded greatly due to local needs and, later, national policies and trends that began with the Depression and have continued since.

Another factor in its renewed prosperity was the business of tourism. This began to take on considerable proportions in the post–World War I era. The foundations on which tourism rested lay in the national acceptance of a semi-arid climate and mountainous terrain as a place of beauty and health, in the proximity of Pueblo communities as a distinctive subject of interest, and in the deliberate expansion of Santa Fe's cultural parameters by an expanding Anglo population. The success of tourism in Santa Fe lay in its isolated geographic condition that enabled the town to present itself romantically as both a living restoration and adaptation of the past. That might not have been the case had national commerce dominated the town. The relative weakness of the city's commerce, as evidenced by comparison with nearby Albuquerque's growth, encouraged the retention of more traditional modes of life in Santa Fe.

■ Any comparison between the town of 1880 and the city of 1990 must take account of its growth. While its tenfold population increase contrasts with Albuquerque's hundredfold expansion, within its own boundaries Santa Fe's growth sorely tried (and tries) the ability of its inhabitants to maintain the image of the place in which they wanted to live. The tenfold growth became possible through the advent of the automobile. The town, seeking to keep the Plaza as its center, found itself under growing pressure to relinquish that hope. After World War II, the answer to the expanding area of populated Santa Fe was the shopping mall, which in itself was a response to the creation of new neighborhoods. Thus, instead of remaining a center of commerce for Santa Feans, the Plaza became a shopping mecca for tourists. That it remained the symbol of the town's core grew out of the determined efforts of supporters of old Santa Fe to keep it so.

■ As noted, growth required the creation of new neighborhoods. Before the Depression, despite economic differences between Hispanos and Anglos, there was a good deal of cooperation along with an absence of strong antagonism. Postwar dispersion tended to distinguish these populations in terms of wealth and class to a greater extent than before. A growing knowledge of the city in the country at large attracted wealthy Anglos—some to work and others to retire. Changes in the social and economic position of local Hispanos also contributed to the creation of new neighborhoods where they resided side by side with Anglos, even though some retained loyalties to their former residential areas and to their culture.

These developments reflected the effects of urbanization on Anglo-Hispano relations. As trade expanded and barter yielded to a cash economy, occupational diversity and specialization offered Hispanos greater employment opportunities. As the locus of self-government devolved from territorial legislature to county commission and then incorporated municipality, Anglos, as a minority in the voting population, became dependent on Hispanos for political support. The resulting interdependence—political and economic—formed the basis for an accommodation between the two ethnic segments that has lasted for a century.

In the 1950s that accommodation enabled community leaders to institute planning by city government in order to maintain features of the city's traditional character for the pleasure of its residents and to ensure its continued attraction for tourists. As the plan became a standard for community development, it circumscribed the scope of new economic activities. The desire to attract industry was curbed by fear of consequences for the image of the old city, even though small, clean manufacturing establishments were sought. While one option proposed was to expand local arts and crafts as a means of livelihood and to keep the city's character intact, that proposal developed slowly. The service jobs supported by tourism and the employment provided by state and federal governments were no longer adequate for a growing population—either in number or quality.

The effect on the city's residents was limited opportunity for young Santa Feans to find employment and careers. For some this reduced the incentive to stay in school, while others opted to move away. As the city grew in the post–World War II period, an increasing proportion of well-to-do Anglo newcomers drove up the cost of living and added urgency to calls for new jobs and better educational services. Altogether, the desire to keep the old Santa Fe as intact as possible coupled with the need for expanded employment created a difficult contradiction that did not exist in 1880 when the search for the old commerce was in full swing.

The influx of newcomers led to an Anglo majority in the city's population by 1990. Implicit in this was a threat to the interethnic balance of political power. In the past, the relatively small Anglo presence had rarely been defined as a political threat. And when it had been so considered, the issue was resolved by the normal political processes, with members of both ethnic groups working together in each contending party. More consistently, the balance of power had been defined and recognized in the respect held by each ethnic group for the cultural values of the other. The shared motivation to keep the city as it was had led to conscious as well as tacit conciliations and negotiated versions of the image of Santa Fe to be maintained.

Another postwar development with potential for interethnic strain lay in the economic realm. As Hispanos became more like Anglos in educational attainment and occupational status, the possibility of economic competition between them emerged from limitations of opportunity. Unlike a threat of political power, which could typically be resolved on a collective level in parties, competition for jobs required resolution by individuals deciding how and where to find work. Thus, the proximity of Albuquerque, as one example, offered a wider range of career opportunities that partially forestalled the frustration and discontent of the generations that faced limited choices in their home community.

Still another source of strain that impinged (and still impinges) on both young Anglo and Hispano natives of Santa Fe who did not gain enough education for jobs above the service level, was a rising cost of living. For many, this meant migration to less expensive housing areas in the city and in the county beyond. A longer-range alternative appeared in the increased enrollment in Santa Fe Community College, potentially removing limits on educational attainment.

■ Finally, it is appropriate to consider the contingencies that could affect the strength and durability of Hispano culture in the city. For this purpose it is necessary to distinguish Hispano culture as it is lived and breathed in families, extended kinship groups and neighborhoods, and Hispano culture as it is portrayed and exhibited by and for resident Anglos and tourists. On the one hand, Santa Fe is represented as the distinctively historic site of a Spanish and Hispano community and its residents seek to preserve the evidence of this for themselves and tourists. On the other hand, the history of the city has been one of steadily greater involvement in the larger Anglo world, offering greater potential for assimilation. The recently established Anglo majority of the city's population, the rising cost of living, and the limits on occupational and career opportunities threaten the younger generations in ways that may weaken native Hispano culture.

It may be that communal Hispano culture will thrive longer among the less well educated and less well paid, if only because they would have less mobility and would live closer to home. The strength of that culture depends on the social cohesion of its bearers. Being outnumbered by Anglos is much less hazardous to the culture than the mobility that disperses and separates Hispanos from each other. As for how that culture is represented by and for the non-Hispano public, its vitality is guaranteed by the collaboration of Anglo and

Hispano residents in the conduct of civic affairs and the common interest of both groups in maintaining the traditional image of the city.

Having chosen to define itself as a restoration and modern continuation of an older place, the city established a standard for itself that became a new focal point for its further development. That this new dimension created new problems reminds us that a living city neither stands still nor achieves perfection. Santa Fe, after all, is not the static restored Virginia village of Williamsburg.

Bibliographical Note

ALL SOURCES CITED in our history are noted in our footnotes. Beyond that, there lies a large body of materials, much of it duplicative in nature or extending beyond the limits of our work, that we did not cite even though we may have learned from it. Our purpose is merely to describe the major outlines of the sources we used for the enlightenment of the reader.

The materials consulted for our study have been numerous and quite varied in their character. Given the theme of the city's history, the longest continuous source has been the Santa Fe *New Mexican*, whose primary objective of informing its readers of local affairs has served us well. How much we relied upon its pages can be seen from the fact that of nearly nine hundred footnotes, somewhat over one-third of them refer to the newspaper. Its news items and opinions (regardless of outcomes) cannot be matched by any other single source. It is safe to say that without it, writing a work such as ours would have been nearly impossible.

Given our interest in themes that require quantification, several other kinds of materials have been equally, if not as broadly, important. The U.S. Census, in its raw data form, which is available through 1920, and in printed form through 1990, has allowed us to examine issues of population and social change that would have been almost as impossible to study as the flow of events would have been without the newspaper. Adding to such officially compiled sources were the directories offered by Dun and Bradstreet in the nineteenth and early twentieth centuries (they were two separate organizations in that period) and the various business and city directories compiled separately by Hudspeth and McKenney. The two types of sources, directories and newspaper taken together, account for more than half of all our notes.

A smaller, but definitive, form of source material can be found in the archives of the Museum of New Mexico and the State Archives in Santa Fe as well as the Southwest Collection of The University of New Mexico. Concentrated on particular issues, one must include here such materials as the First National Bank of Santa Fe papers, the Prince papers, the Historical Society of New Mexico papers, and various others employed by us at appropriate points in the text.

Another form of materials, secondary in nature but frequently unpublished, were master's theses and doctoral dissertations located at various university libraries, although most are located at University of New Mexico libraries. Some of those consulted most prominently were Terry J. Lehmann's "Santa Fe and Albuquerque 1870–1890" (Ph.D. diss., Indiana University, 1974); J. J. Bowden, "Private Land Claims in the Southwest" (master's thesis, Southern Methodist University, 1969); David T. Bailey, "Stratification and Ethnic Differentiation in Santa Fe, 1860 and 1870" (Ph.D. diss., University of Texas, 1975); James C. Hughes, "Three Stages of Land Use in Santa Fe, New Mexico, 1610–1967" (master's thesis, University of Kansas, 1968); Carolyn Zeleny, "Relations Between the Spanish-Americans and Anglo-Americans in New Mexico: A Study of Conflict and Accommodation in a Dual-Ethnic Situation" (Ph.D. diss., Yale University, 1944); Irene Moke, "Santa Fe, New Mexico: A Study in Urban Geography" (Ph.D. diss., University of Nebraska, 1945), and Marjorie Bell Chambers, "Technically Sweet Los Alamos: The Development of a Federally Sponsored Scientific Community" (Ph.D. diss., University of New Mexico, 1974). Many others, also valuable for their concentrated information and insights, are cited in the footnotes.

There is, of course, a rich secondary literature in both periodical and book formats that covers all but the most recent period of our work. Of periodicals, the *New Mexico Historical Review*, which began publishing in 1925, offers the greatest number of articles on a wide variety of subjects that cover New Mexico broadly and many that concern Santa Fe itself. *El Palacio*, which began publication in 1913 under the auspices of the Museum of New Mexico, provides a rich panorama of both secondary as well as primary materials that have proven invaluable.

We would be considered ingrates if we did not recall some of the major secondary works that guided us, especially those that have been in print for a generation or more. The early work of Ralph E. Twitchell, *Old Santa Fe: The Story of New Mexico's Ancient Capital*, which appeared in 1925, remains a work to read for students of the city's history despite criticism that could be leveled at it from our more modern stance. One might argue, indeed, that in some ways its age and viewpoint have added to its value by making it a document of the times in which it was written, thus displaying the goals and attitudes of the author's era.

We would be remiss if we did not mention another quite recent work on Santa Fe, Chris Wilson's *The Myth of Santa Fe*, that features the theme of architecture in a broad historical sense that raises it beyond the level of political history.

A number of older volumes broader in subject area than Santa Fe itself added greatly to our knowledge and viewpoints. Wallace Stegner's *Beyond the 100th Meridian*, 1953; Howard R. Lamar's *The Far Southwest 1846–1912: A Territorial History*, 1970, Jack E. Holmes's *Politics in New Mexico*, 1967; Earl Pomeroy's *In Search of the Golden West*, 1957; and Nancie L. González's *The Spanish-Americans of New Mexico: A Heritage of Pride*, 1967, all require specification, although the list of older works and, certainly, many newer works, could justifiably be added to the list.

For more recent times, we personally interviewed some persons whose first-hand knowledge contributed to our understanding of matters in which they were intimately involved. Some of that material will be unrecoverable and, in a small degree, places those sections of our work in the category of a primary source. Among those sources we must include our talks with M. Eugene Sundt and Allen Stamm.

The works cited here, as well as the extended list alluded to in the footnotes, do, in fact, comprise a high point of our usage. At best, our footnotes comprise a bibliography for those interested in the subject and a starting point for those who would pursue the subject matter further.

Notes

Abbreviations

CSWR	Center for Southwest Research, Zimmerman Library, University of New Mexico, Albuquerque, New Mexico
FACHL	Fray Angelico Chavez Historical Library, Santa Fe, New Mexico
LAMNM	Laboratory of Anthropology, Museum of New Mexico, Santa Fe, New Mexico
MNM	Museum of New Mexico, Santa Fe, New Mexico
NMHR	*New Mexico Historical Review*
NMSRCA	New Mexico State Records Center and Archives, Santa Fe, New Mexico
TANM	Territorial Archives of New Mexico, Zimmerman Library, University of New Mexico, Albuquerque, New Mexico

Chapter 1

1. David J. Weber, *The Mexican Frontier 1821–1846: The American Southwest Under Mexico* (Albuquerque: University of New Mexico Press, 1982), 15.
2. Ralph E. Twitchell, *Old Santa Fe: The Story of New Mexico's Ancient Capital* (Santa Fe: Santa Fe New Mexican Publishing Corporation, 1925), 11–12.
3. Ibid., 13.
4. Fray Francisco Atanasio Dominguez, *The Missions of New Mexico, 1776: A Description*, trans. and ed. Eleanor B. Adams and Fray Angelico Chavez (Albuquerque: University of New Mexico Press, 1956), 39.
5. Oakah L. Jones, *Los Paisanos: Spanish Settlers on the Northern Frontier of New Spain* (Norman: University of Oklahoma Press, 1979), 128–29.
6. Bureau of the Census, *The Seventh Census of the United States, 1850* (Washington, D.C., 1853), cx, cxi, 994.
7. Jones, *Los Paisanos*, 4, 6.
8. Ibid., 146.
9. Marc Simmons, "Settlement Patterns and Village Plans in Colonial New Mexico," in *New Spain's Far Northern Frontier*, ed. David J. Weber (Albuquerque: University of New Mexico Press, 1979), 104–5, 111–12.
10. Janie L. Aragon, "The People of Santa Fe in the 1790s," *Aztlan* 7, no. 3 (1976): 394, 402.
11. Twitchell, *Old Santa Fe*, 162.
12. Simmons, "Settlement Patterns," 104.
13. Aragon, "Santa Fe in the 1790s," 402.
14. Weber, *The Mexican Frontier*, 16, 35.

15. Ibid., 122.
16. David Sandoval, "Who is Riding the Burro Now?" *The Santa Fe Trail: New Perspectives*, no. 6 (1987): 78–79.
17. Lansing B. Bloom, "New Mexico under Mexican Administration—continued," *Old Santa Fe* 2, no. 3 (1915): 254–55.
18. House, *Acts, Resolutions, and Memorials of the Legislative Assembly of the Territory of New Mexico*, 32d Cong., 1st sess., 1852, H. misc. doc., 9–10, 36.
19. Robert W. Frazer, *Forts and Supplies: The Role of the Army in the Economy of the Southwest 1846–1861* (Albuquerque: University of New Mexico Press, 1983), 2–3, 7–8, 14–16.
20. Territory of New Mexico Legislature, *Laws of the Territory of New Mexico Passed by the First Legislative Assy., 1852*, 272–73 (Santa Fe, 1853), Territorial Archives of New Mexico, Zimmerman Library, University of New Mexico (hereinafter cited as TANM), microfilm, roll no. 1, legislature record group 1851–1857.
21. *Old Santa Fe*, 325.
22. J. J. Bowden, "Private Land Claims in the Southwest" (master's thesis, Southern Methodist University, 1969), 2:331.
23. Benjamin M. Read, *Illustrated History of New Mexico*, trans. Eleuterio Baca (Santa Fe: New Mexican Printing Company, 1912), 373–74.
24. Alvin R. Sunseri, *Seeds of Discord: New Mexico in the Aftermath of the American Conquest, 1846–1861* (Chicago: Nelson-Hall, 1979), 130.
25. Darlis A. Miller, "Cross-Cultural Marriage in the Southwest: The New Mexico Experience, 1846–1900," *New Mexico Historical Review* (hereinafter cited as *NMHR*) 57, no. 4 (October 1982): 341.
26. Calculation for Santa Fe based on National Archives, "Population Schedules of the Tenth Census of the United States, 1880: New Mexico," microfilm, T764, reel 3.
27. Bureau of the Census, *Sixteenth Census of the United States, 1940, Population*, vol. I (Washington, D.C., 1942), 695–96.
28. See Floyd Fierman, *Guts and Ruts: The Jewish Pioneer on the Trail in the American Southwest* (New York: Ktav Publishing Company, 1985). See chapters on individuals named in Henry J. Tobias, *A History of the Jews in New Mexico* (Albuquerque: University of New Mexico Press, 1990).
29. See William J. Parish, "The German Jew and the Commercial Revolution in Territorial New Mexico 1850–1900," parts 1 and 2, *NMHR* 35, no. 1 (January 1960): 1–29; no. 2 (April 1960): 129–50.
30. According to David T. Bailey ("Stratification and Ethnic Differentiation in Santa Fe, 1860 and 1870" [Ph.D. diss., University of Texas-Austin, 1975]), this percentage reflects an inconsistent enumeration practice by the Census Bureau at the time. "Many persons entitled simply 'laborers' in 1860 were called 'farm laborers' in 1870" (p. 71). In 1860 Hispano farm laborers numbered 130 and unspecified laborers numbered 260; in 1870, Hispano farm laborers numbered 513 and unspecified laborers only 9 (p. 93). Data for 1880 from National Archives, "Population Schedules of the Tenth Census of the United States, 1880, New Mexico," microfilm.
31. Fierman, *Guts and Ruts*, 31–32.
32. Arthur L. Campa, "The Spanish Language in the Southwest," in *Humanidad: Essays in Honor of George I. Sanchez*, ed. Americo Paredes (Los Angeles: Chicano Studies Center Publications, University of California, 1977), 22–23.
33. "Plat of the City of Santa Fe Grant, 1877," surveyed by Griffin and McMulan, New Mexico State Records Center and Archives, Santa Fe, New Mexico (hereinafter cited as NMSRCA).
34. Territory of New Mexico Legislature, *Local and Special Laws of New Mexico, 1884* (Santa Fe, 1885), 478, TANM.
35. Ibid., 494.
36. Ibid., 498.
37. Ibid., 474.

Chapter 2

1. James Marshall, *Santa Fe: The Railroad that Built an Empire* (New York: Random House, 1945), 150.
2. L. L. Waters, *Steel Trails to Santa Fe* (Lawrence: University of Kansas Press, 1950), 23–24.
3. Ibid., 26.

4. Ibid., 31, 39; Marshall, *Santa Fe*, 11.
5. George A. Hamm, "The Atchison Associate of the Santa Fe Railroad," *Kansas Historical Quarterly*, no. 4 (Winter 1976): 353.
6. Waters, *Steel Trails*, 56–57.
7. Twitchell, *Old Santa Fe*, 399; Waters, *Steel Trails*, 56; Robert G. Athearn, *Rebel of the Rockies: A History of the Denver and Rio Grande Western Railroad* (New Haven: Yale University Press, 1962), 94.
8. Marshall, *Santa Fe*, 164.
9. Glenn D. Bradley, *The Story of the Santa Fe: A Romance of American Enterprise* (Boston: R. G. Badger, 1920), 150; Marshall, *Santa Fe*, 164.
10. *Weekly New Mexican*, 9 March 1878.
11. Bureau of the Census, *Wealth and Industry, 1870* (Washington, D.C., 1875), 208; Bureau of the Census, *Compendium of the Tenth Census, [1880]*, rev. ed., part 1 (Washington, D.C., 1885), 890–91.
12. *Weekly New Mexican*, 1 June 1878.
13. *Weekly New Mexican*, 8 June 1878.
14. *Weekly New Mexican*, 6 July 1878.
15. Ibid.
16. *Weekly New Mexican*, 15 March 1879.
17. Ibid.
18. *Weekly New Mexican*, 28 June 1879.
19. *Weekly New Mexican*, 19 July 1879.
20. Ibid.
21. *Weekly New Mexican*, 2 August 1879.
22. Ibid.
23. *Weekly New Mexican*, 27 September 1879.
24. *Weekly New Mexican*, 11 October 1879.
25. Ibid.
26. Athearn, *Rebel of the Rockies*, 96.
27. Terry Jon Lehmann, "Santa Fe and Albuquerque 1870–1900: Contrast and Conflict in the Development of Two Southwestern Towns" (Ph.D. diss., Indiana University, 1974), 213; *New Mexican*, 23 December 1880.
28. Lehmann, "Santa Fe and Albuquerque," 234–36.
29. Athearn, *Rebel of the Rockies*, 97–98.
30. *New Mexican*, 1 November 1879. Santa Fe's major newspaper changed ownership many times during the period covered in this book. The newspaper's title underwent frequent modifications, usually, but not always, along with ownership changes. For a detailed accounting of such changes, see Pearce S. Grove, Becky J. Barnett, and Sandra J. Hansen, eds., *New Mexico Newspapers: A Comprehensive Guide to Bibliographical Entries and Locations* (Albuquerque: University of New Mexico Press in association with Eastern New Mexico University, 1975).
31. *New Mexican*, 27 February 1880.
32. Corinne P. Sze and Beverley Spears, *Santa Fe Historic Neighborhood Study* (City of Santa Fe, 1988), 63.
33. *New Mexican*, 28 September 1880.
34. Sze and Spears, *Santa Fe*, 63, 71; *New Mexican*, 12 October 1881.
35. Linda Tigges, "Santa Fe Landownership in the 1880s," *NMHR*, 68, no. 2 (April 1993): 157.
36. *Daily New Mexican*, 4 December 1880.
37. *Weekly New Mexican*, 28 June 1879.
38. *New Mexican*, 21 September 1880.
39. Sangre de Cristo Co., "Water Supply—City of Santa Fe: History and Future Additions," typescript (Santa Fe, August 1971), 34c.
40. Hubert Howe Bancroft, *History of Arizona and New Mexico, 1530–1888* (Albuquerque: Horn and Wallace, 1962), 790.
41. *Daily New Mexican*, 27 February 1880, 9 November 1880, 25 November 1880, and 25 January 1881.
42. *Weekly New Mexican*, 8 November 1879.
43. *Daily New Mexican*, 21 January 1881 and 22 January 1881.
44. *Daily New Mexican*, 4 March 1881.

45. Ibid.
46. *Daily New Mexican,* 16 March 1881, 18 March 1881, and 9 April 1881.
47. Lehmann, "Santa Fe and Albuquerque," 202.
48. See *New Mexican,* 14 October 1880, 9 March 1881, and 15 March 1881.
49. Bureau of the Census, *Compendium of the Eleventh Census, 1890,* part 1, prepared by Department of the Interior in cooperation with the Bureau of the Census (Washington, D.C., 1892), 281; Bureau of the Census, *Minor Civil Divisions, 1900* (Washington, D.C., 1901), 273.
50. *Minor Civil Divisions, 1900,* 459.
51. These data are compiled from the Bureau of the Census, *Compendium of the Tenth Census, [1880],* 997, and the *Twelfth Census, 1900, Vol. 8, Manufacturers, Part II* (Washington, D.C., 1902), 577.
52. See Wayne L. Mauzy, *A Century in Santa Fe: The Story of the First National Bank of Santa Fe* (Santa Fe: The Bank, [197?]).
53. See George B. Anderson, *History of New Mexico: Its Resources and People* (Los Angeles: Pacific States Publishing Company, 1907), I:412–26.
54. First National Bank records, Santa Fe, New Mexico, Scrap Book Archive no. 177, Special Collections, Zimmerman Library, University of New Mexico, Albuquerque, New Mexico.
55. William J. Parish, *The Charles Ilfeld Company: The Rise and Decline of Mercantile Capitalism in New Mexico* (Cambridge, Mass.: Harvard University Press, 1961), 60–61.
56. See Lehmann, "Santa Fe and Albuquerque," 219–20; *New Mexican,* 10 March 1881.
57. Lehman Spiegelberg, "Commerce of Santa Fe," [1882?], American Jewish Archives, Cincinnati, Ohio.
58. Lehmann, "Santa Fe and Albuquerque," 220; *Santa Fe Weekly Democrat,* 26 January 1882.
59. *McKenney's Business Directory of the Principal Towns of Central and Southern California, Arizona, New Mexico, Southern Colorado, and Kansas, 1882–83* (Oakland and San Francisco: Pacific Press, 1883), and *McKenney's Business Directory . . . , 1888–89* (Oakland and San Francisco: Pacific Press, 1889).
60. James D. Norris, *R. G. Dun & Co., 1841–1900: The Development of Credit-Reporting in the Nineteenth Century* (Westport, Conn.: Greenwood Press, 1978), 92.
61. J. M. Bradstreet and Son, *Bradstreet's Commercial Reports,* 30, 6 January 1872.
62. J. M. Bradstreet and Son, *Bradstreet's Commercial Reports,* 66, January 1897.
63. Data on the workforce are derived from our tabulations of the 1880 and 1900 censuses.

Chapter 3

1. Terry Jon Lehmann, "Santa Fe and Albuquerque 1870–1900: Contrast and Conflict in the Development of Two Southwestern Towns" (Ph.D. diss., Indiana University, 1974), 202–4.
2. "An Incorporated City," *Santa Fe Daily New Mexican,* 5 June 1886.
3. "Won't Stand the Test," *Santa Fe Daily New Mexican,* 7 June 1886.
4. "Judge Sloan's Views," *Santa Fe Daily New Mexican,* 7 August 1886.
5. Howard R. Lamar, *The Far Southwest 1846–1912: A Territorial History* (New York: Norton, 1970), 146–48; Norman Cleaveland with George Fitzpatrick, *The Morleys: Young Upstarts on the Southwest Frontier* (Albuquerque: C. Horn, 1971), 73, 97–99, 109–14.
6. Cleaveland, *The Morleys,* 188; Ralph E. Twitchell, *Old Santa Fe: The Story of New Mexico's Ancient Capital* (Santa Fe: Santa Fe New Mexican Publishing Corporation, 1925), 400.
7. Lamar, *The Far Southwest,* 136–70; Herbert Hoover, "History of the Republican Party in New Mexico, 1867–1952" (Ph.D. diss., University of Oklahoma, 1966), 59–82.
8. Lamar, *The Far Southwest,* 163.
9. "Incorporate the Entire Grant," *Albuquerque Morning Journal,* 20 January 1884.
10. Ibid.
11. "What Albuquerque Wants," *Albuquerque Morning Journal,* 24 January 1884.
12. Ibid.
13. *New Mexican,* 25 January 1884.
14. Twitchell, *Old Santa Fe,* 410.
15. "Territorial Affairs," *Albuquerque Morning Journal,* 20 March 1884.
16. "An Outrage Upon the People," *Albuquerque Morning Journal,* 18 March 1884.
17. "The Difference," *Albuquerque Journal,* 23 March 1884.
18. *New Mexican Review,* 27 March 1884 and 25 January 1884.
19. *New Mexican Review,* 27 March 1884; "The Capital Question," *New Mexican Review,* 28 March 1884.

20. "The Territorial Pen," *New Mexican Review*, 31 May 1884.
21. "Points on the Pen," *New Mexican Review*, 19 April 1884.
22. Lee Donohue Hilley, "The New Mexico Territorial Penitentiary: A Political and Penal History to 1899" (master's thesis, University of New Mexico, 1985), 34.
23. Lehmann, "Santa Fe and Albuquerque," 250–51.
24. Governor Edmund G. Ross to John O'Grady, 26 March 1887, Ross Papers, Center for Southwest Research, Zimmerman Library, University of New Mexico, Albuquerque, New Mexico (hereinafter cited as CSWR), microfilm, roll 102, fr. 81, p. 4.
25. Ibid., fr. 83, p. 6.
26. Edmund G. Ross, governor of the Territory of New Mexico, *Governor's Messages to the Council and House of Representatives of the 28th Legislative Assembly* (Santa Fe, 1889), lxiv-lxv, TANM, microfilm, roll 102.
27. Ross Papers, 20 July 1886, TANM, microfilm, roll 101, fr. 307.
28. See Hilley, "New Mexico Territorial Penitentiary," note 42, 73–74.
29. Ibid., 84–85.
30. Ibid., 85, 88, 89, 115, 163.
31. For a detailed discussion, see Lehmann, "Santa Fe and Albuquerque," 246–49.
32. *Santa Fe Weekly New Mexican Review and Livestock Journal*, 3 April 1884, cited in Lehmann, "Santa Fe and Albuquerque," 250.
33. Cited in *New Mexican*, 2 March 1891.
34. Ibid.
35. Territory of New Mexico Legislature, Capitol Committee, *Report of the Capitol Committee of the House of Representatives of the 30th Legislative Assembly* (Santa Fe, 1893), 7, 9.
36. See Lehmann, "Santa Fe and Albuquerque," 263–69; Miguel A. Otero, *My Nine Years as Governor of the Territory of New Mexico, 1897–1906* (Albuquerque: University of New Mexico Press, 1940), 67–70.
37. Miguel O. Otero, governor of the Territory of New Mexico, *Report of the Governor of New Mexico to the Secretary of the Interior* (Washington, D.C., 1900), 171, TANM, microfilm, roll 148.
38. Ibid.
39. *Annotated Constitution and Enabling Act of the State of New Mexico* (1911), 107.
40. "The New Incorporation Act," *New Mexican*, 13 February 1891.
41. *New Mexican*, 9 February 1891.
42. "Round About Town," *New Mexican*, 24 February 1891.
43. "Looks Like Business," *New Mexican*, 10 March 1891; "Round About Town," *New Mexican*, 30 March 1891.
44. "City Incorporation," *New Mexican*, 12 March 1891.
45. "Suspended Work," *New Mexican*, 27 May 1891.
46. "The City Incorporation," *New Mexican*, 4 March 1891.
47. "Looks Like Business," *New Mexican*, 10 March 1891.
48. Ibid.
49. "City Incorporation," *New Mexican*, 12 March 1891; "The City Limits," *New Mexican*, 13 March 1891.
50. "Incorporation Limits of Santa Fe" (Santa Fe, [1891?]), NMSRCA.
51. "City Incorporation," *New Mexican*, 24 April 1891.
52. "Turned Loose," *New Mexican*, 3 June 1891.
53. "Board of County Commissioners," *New Mexican*, 17 June 1891; *Ordinances of the City of Santa Fe* (1893), 21, NMSRCA.
54. "The City of Santa Fe," *New Mexican*, 19 June 1891; "The City Government's Expenses," *New Mexican*, 30 June 1891.
55. "Tomorrow's City Election," *New Mexican*, 1 July 1891.
56. "The City Officers," *New Mexican*, 10 June 1891; "The City of Santa Fe," *New Mexican*, 19 June 1891; "A Grand Fizzle," *New Mexican*, 26 June 1891.
57. "Santa Fe's Municipal Election," *New Mexican*, 3 July 1891.
58. *New Mexican*, 30 March 1894.
59. *New Mexican*, 6 April 1896.
60. Porter A. Stratton, *The Territorial Press of New Mexico, 1834–1912* (Albuquerque: University of New Mexico Press, 1969), 47, 86.

61. Jack E. Holmes, *Politics in New Mexico* (Albuquerque: University of New Mexico Press, 1967), 20–21, 42.
62. Bureau of the Census, *Twelfth Census of the Population, 1900, I* (Washington, D.C., 1901). Based on our estimates, in Wards Two, Three, and Four, the Hispano share of population was 61 percent, 53 percent, and 57 percent, respectively.
63. See *Ordinances of the City*, 1893.
64. *Revised Ordinances of Santa Fe, New Mexico* (Easley, 1911), 84–86.
65. See chapter 5 of this volume.
66. *Revised Ordinances*, 1911, 77–78.
67. *New Mexican*, 7 August 1891; 26 August and 11 September 1891; 29 September 1891; and 5 January 1892.
68. *New Mexican*, 30 September 1891, 2 October 1891, and 28 October 1891.
69. *New Mexican*, 5 January 1892, 24 March 1893, and 27 March 1893.
70. *New Mexican*, 28 March 1893.
71. *New Mexican*, 2 April 1892.
72. *New Mexican*, 17 May 1881.
73. *New Mexican*, 19 May 1881.
74. *New Mexican*, 10 June 1881.
75. *New Mexican*, 23 June 1881.
76. Cited in David H. Snow, *The Santa Fe Acequia Systems: Summary Report on Their History and Present Status* (Santa Fe: Planning Department, City of Santa Fe, 1988), 14.
77. *New Mexican*, 20 November 1891.
78. *New Mexican*, 18 May 1893.
79. *New Mexican*, 1 February 1895.
80. *New Mexican*, 26 May 1904.
81. *New Mexican*, 1 June 1904.
82. *New Mexican*, 20 July and 30 September 1904.
83. Sangre de Cristo Co., "Water Supply–City of Santa Fe," 3.
84. John H. Vaughan, *History and Government of New Mexico* (State College, N.Mex.: C. L. Vaughan, 1927), 216–17; C. E. Hodgin, "Early School Laws of New Mexico," UNM Educational Series, 1, no. 1 (Albuquerque: The University, 1906), 2, 8.
85. J. E. Seyfried, "Illiteracy Trends in New Mexico," *UNM Bulletin*, Education Series, 8, no. 1, 15 March 1934, 9.
86. Hodgin, *Early School Laws*, 28–29.
87. Vaughan, *History and Government*, 220–21; Jane C. Atkins, "Who Will Educate: The Schooling Question in Territorial New Mexico, 1846–1911" (Ph.D. diss., University of New Mexico, 1982), 363–64.
88. Atkins, "Who Will Educate," 362–63.
89. Ibid., 364–96.
90. Ibid., 401, 404.
91. Amado Chaves, *Report of the Superintendent of Public Instruction, March 1, 1891 to December 31, 1891* (Santa Fe, 1892), 5–6, TANM, microfilm, roll 8.
92. Atkins, "Who Will Educate," 406.
93. Chaves, *Report of the Superintendent of Public Instruction, for year ending December 31, 1892* (Santa Fe, 1893), 15, TANM, microfilm, roll 8.
94. *Report of the Superintendent, 1896*, 28; and *Report of the Superintendent, 1905*, 55.
95. *Report of the Superintendent, 1911*, table opp. p. 130.
96. *Report of the Superintendent, 1896*, 49, 52.
97. *Report of the Superintendent, 1902*, 36.
98. *Report of the Superintendent, 1905*, 41.
99. J. J. Bowden, "Private Land Claims in the Southwest" (master's thesis, Southern Methodist University, 1969), 2:326–28; John R. Van Ness and Christine M. Van Ness, "Introduction," in *Spanish and Mexican Land Grants in New Mexico and Colorado*, eds. John R. Van Ness and Christine M. Van Ness (Manhattan, Kans.: Sunflower University Press, 1980), 10.
100. Bowden, "Private Land Claims," 2:331–32.
101. Ibid., 340.
102. Ibid., 340–42.
103. "Santa Fe Title Bill," *New Mexican*, 13 April 1900.

104. New Mexico Legislature, *Laws of the State of New Mexico of the First Legislature* (Santa Fe, 1913), 32–33.
105. Ibid., 33.
106. Ibid., 82–83.

Chapter 4

1. Lansing B. Bloom, ed., "Historical Society Minutes, 1859–1863," *NMHR* 28, no. 3 (July 1943): 252–53, 255–56.
2. *New Mexican*, 24 November 1880; Hon. W. G. Ritch, "Inaugural Address of Historical Society of New Mexico" (Santa Fe, 1881), 10, Fray Angelico Chavez History Library, Santa Fe, New Mexico (hereinafter cited as FACHL).
3. *New Mexican*, 16 October 1880.
4. Ritch, "Inaugural Address," 13.
5. Ibid., 14.
6. Ibid., 17.
7. See *New Mexican*, 11 January 1881.
8. See Prince Papers, NMSRCA.
9. *New Mexican*, 31 July 1888.
10. Prince Papers, 5 January 1905, NMSRCA.
11. Historical Society of New Mexico, "Biennial Report," Publication 13 (Santa Fe: New Mexican Printing Company, 1909), 10–11, FACHL.
12. Prince Papers, 1 March 1909, NMSRCA.
13. "Report of the Historical Society for 1908," TANM, microfilm, reel 177, fr. 781.
14. Wallace Stegner, *Beyond the Hundredth Meridian: John Wesley Powell and the Second Opening of the West* (Boston: Houghton Mifflin, 1954), 116–17.
15. Curtis M. Hinsley, Jr., *Savages and Scientists: The Smithsonian Institution and the Development of American Anthropology, 1846–1910* (Washington, D.C.: Smithsonian Institution Press, 1981), 19.
16. Donald Collier and Harry Tschopik, Jr., "The Role of Museums in American Anthropology," part 1, *American Anthropologist* 56, no. 5 (October 1954): 768–79.
17. Hinsley, *Savages*, 29.
18. Cited in ibid., 240.
19. Jesse Green, ed., *Cushing at Zuni: The Correspondence and Journals of Franklin Hamilton Cushing, 1879–1884* (Albuquerque: University of New Mexico Press, 1990), 2–3.
20. Charles H. Lange and Carroll L. Riley, eds., *The Southwestern Journals of A. F. Bandelier, 1880–1882* (Albuquerque: University of New Mexico Press, 1966), 16, 26.
21. Ibid., 21.
22. "Twentieth Annual Report of the Council of the AIA," *American Journal of Archaeology* 3, no. 6 (1899): 665.
23. "The Work of the Institute of the American Archaeologist," *American Journal of Archaeology*, 2d ser., 11, no. 1 (1907): 47.
24. Charles F. Lummis, "The Southwest Museum," *Out West* 26, no. 5 (May 1907), 397.
25. "In Memoriam," *El Palacio* 29, no. 1 (1 August 1930): 19; Beatrice Chauvenet, *Hewett and Friends: A Biography of Santa Fe's Vibrant Era* (Santa Fe: Museum of New Mexico Press, 1983), 40; Paul A. F. Walter, "Twenty-Five Years of Achievement," Papers of the School of American Research of the AIA, n.s., no. 24, 1932, 4–5, Laboratory of Anthropology, Museum of New Mexico, Santa Fe, New Mexico (hereinafter cited as LAMNM); Hulda R. Hobbs, "The Story of the Archaeological Society," *El Palacio* 53, no. 4 (April 1946): 82, 86–87.
26. Historical Society of New Mexico papers, FACHL, microfilm, roll 2, fr. 129.
27. See Chauvenet, *Hewett*, for details of Hewett's early life.
28. *American Journal of Archaeology*, 2d ser., 10, suppl. (1906): 41; 11, no. 1 (1907): 47; 12, no. 1 (1908): 61.
29. Territory of New Mexico Legislature, *Acts of the Legislative Assembly of the Territory of New Mexico*, 37th sess. (Santa Fe, 1907), 302–4.
30. *New Mexican*, 18 February 1909, 1; Chauvenet, *Hewett*, 72–76.
31. Territory of New Mexico Legislature, *House Journal, Proceedings of the House of Representatives of the Territory of New Mexico*, 38th sess. (Santa Fe, 1909), 38.

32. Edgar L. Hewett, "Archaeology of the Rio Grande Valley," *Out West* 31, no. 2 (August 1909): 693.
33. Prince Papers, 11 January 1909, NMSRCA.
34. *New Mexican*, 10 April 1913, 3.
35. New Mexico Historical Society, records for 1859–1959, FACHL, microfilm, roll 1, fr. 272.
36. Karen D. Shane, "New Mexico: Salubrious El Dorado," *NMHR* 56, no. 4 (1981): 387.
37. Ibid., 389.
38. See Herbert H. Lang, "The New Mexico Bureau of Immigration, 1880–1912," *NMHR* 51, no. 3 (1976): 193–96.
39. Shane, "El Dorado," *NMHR* 56, no. 4 (1981): 388–89.
40. Hon. William G. Ritch, *Illustrated New Mexico*, 4th ed. (Santa Fe: New Mexican Printing and Publishing Company, 1883), 49–53.
41. Jake W. Spidle, Jr., *Doctors of Medicine in New Mexico, 1886–1986: A History of Health and Medical Practice, 1886–1986* (Albuquerque: University of New Mexico Press, 1986), 89.
42. Ibid., 98.
43. Ibid., 99–101; 167.
44. *Rocky Mountain Sentinel*, 7 November 1878.
45. *New Mexican*, 20 May 1880.
46. *New Mexican*, 26 January 1884.
47. *New Mexican*, 2 July 1891.
48. *New Mexican*, 14 July 1891.
49. [AT & SF Railroad], Passenger Department, Santa Fe Route, "New Mexico Health Resorts" (Chicago, 1901), 7 (brochure), NMSRCA.
50. See Lewis M. Iddings, "Life in the Altitudes: The Colorado Health Plateau," *Scribner's Magazine* 19, no. 2 (February 1896): 139.
51. Spidle, *Doctors*, 151.
52. Ibid., 145–47.
53. Max Frost, arr., comp., and ed., *New Mexico: Its Resources, Climate, Geography, Geology, History, Statistics, Present Condition and Future Prospects* (Santa Fe: New Mexican Printing Company, 1894), 172.
54. Philip P. Jacobs, *The Campaign Against Tuberculosis in the United States* (New York: Charities Publication Committee, 1908), 384–85.
55. *New Mexican*, 4 July 1882.
56. Marc Simmons, *Albuquerque: A Narrative History* (Albuquerque: University of New Mexico Press, 1982), 232.
57. *New Mexican*, 12 September 1891.
58. "Board of Trade, Santa Fe," Santa Fe Chamber of Commerce, 25 September 1907, Box #145, History Library, Palace of Governors, Santa Fe, New Mexico. Similar replies also appear for 21 December 1907, 10 March 1908, and 11 March 1908.
59. Ibid.
60. Ibid., 26 September 1907.
61. Ibid., 11 March 1908.
62. Ibid., 11 May 1908.
63. Ibid.
64. Ibid., 4 February 1909.
65. *New Mexican*, 2 May 1891.
66. *New Mexican*, 9 January 1894.
67. Chauvenet, *Hewett*, 47.
68. *New Mexican*, 9 December 1904, 3.
69. Governor George Curry to Hon. Gifford Pinchot, 13 February 1908, TANM, microfilm, roll 174, fr. 200.
70. Governor George Curry to Abraham Staab, 28 February 1908, TANM, microfilm, roll 174, fr. 253; and Curry to Levi Hughes, 22 August 1908, TANM, microfilm, roll 184, fr. 1074.
71. *New Mexican*, 13 March 1909, 4.
72. Chauvenet, *Hewett*, 42, 46.
73. Ibid., 42, 56–57.
74. "Archaeological Society of New Mexico, Minutes," 23 April 1906, LAMNM. A later meeting on 4 June 1906 noted that the old records had been misplaced. See *New Mexican*, 5 June 1906, 1.

75. *New Mexican*, 18 May 1906, 1.
76. One list of thirty-nine new members inducted in 1906 showed only one Hispano. Another list of new members dating from late 1907 and early 1908 involving seventy persons disclosed only four or perhaps five Hispano names. "Archaeological Society of New Mexico, Minutes," 19, 29, 31, LAMNM.
77. *New Mexican*, 23 April 1909, 4.
78. *New Mexican*, 10 July 1909, 1.
79. Twitchell, *Old Santa Fe*, 452–54. Note 826 cites the entire list.
80. Walter N. Danburg, "New Mexico in the Great War: III, The State Council of Defense," *NMHR* 1, no. 2 (April 1926): 112.
81. "City Council Minutes," 31 May 1917, NMSRCA.
82. *Old Santa Fe*, 451–52.
83. "City Council Minutes," 2 October 1917, NMSRCA.
84. "City Council Minutes," 12 April 1917, NMSRCA.

Chapter 5

1. Earl Pomeroy, *In Search of the Golden West: The Tourist in Western America* (New York: Knopf, 1957), 8–9.
2. Ibid., 13, 16.
3. James D. Henderson, *Meals By Fred Harvey: A Phenomenon of the American West* (Fort Worth: Texas Christian University Press, 1969), 22–24.
4. *Weekly New Mexican*, 27 September 1879.
5. *New Mexican*, 2 March 1881.
6. *New Mexican*, 3 January 1880 and 9 January 1881.
7. See Herbert H. Lang, "The New Mexico Bureau of Immigration," *NMHR* 51, no. 3 (1976): 195.
8. *New Mexican*, 28 October 1886.
9. *New Mexican*, 20 May 1880.
10. *New Mexican*, 28 October 1886.
11. Lewis Publishing Company, *An Illustrated History of New Mexico* (Chicago: The Lewis Publishing Company, 1895), 212.
12. Prince Papers, "The Pajarito Park," 23 July 1904, "Cliff Dwellings and Indian Ruins," #8, NMSRCA.
13. *New Mexican*, 18 May 1906, 1.
14. *New Mexican*, 19 October 1907, 5–6.
15. *New Mexican*, 17 November 1891.
16. *New Mexican*, 12 March 1903.
17. Territory of New Mexico Legislature, *Acts of the Legislative Assembly*, 35th sess. (Santa Fe, 1903), 113–15.
18. Territory of New Mexico Legislature, *Acts of the Legislative Assembly*, 36th sess. (Santa Fe, 1905), 26–27.
19. *New Mexican*, 9 December 1904, 3.
20. *New Mexican*, 22 April 1909, 4.
21. Governor George Curry to Gifford Pinchot, 1908, TANM, microfilm, roll 174, frs. 188, 200.
22. Prince Papers, "New Mexico's Cliff Dwellings," 19 January 1903, "Cliff Dwellings and Indian Ruins," #8, NMSRCA.
23. *New Mexican*, 5 June 1906, 1.
24. *New Mexican*, 21 March 1911, 3.
25. Ibid.
26. *New Mexican*, 17 May 1911, 4.
27. G. D. Macy, State Highway Engineer, *Biennial Report of the State Highway Engineer of the State of New Mexico, for the period beginning January 1, 1933 and ending December 31, 1934* (Santa Fe, 1935), 7–8, 10.
28. D. H. Thomas, *The Southwestern Indian Detours: The Story of Fred Harvey/Santa Fe Railway Experience in Detourism* (Phoenix: Hunter Publishing Company, 1978), 30–36.
29. Territory of New Mexico Legislature, *Acts of the Legislative Assembly of the Territory of New Mexico*, 38th sess. (Santa Fe, 1909), 6–7.

30. Rosemary Nusbaum, *The City Different and the Palace—The Palace of the Governors: Its Role in Santa Fe History, Including Jesse Nusbaum's Restoration Journals* (Santa Fe: Sunstone Press, 1978), 83, 87.
31. New Mexico, *Laws of New Mexico, 2nd regular Session of the First Legislature of the State of New Mexico* (Santa Fe: Secretary of State, 1913), 72–73.
32. Beatrice Chauvenet, *Hewett and Friends: A Biography of Santa Fe's Vibrant Era* (Santa Fe: Museum of New Mexico Press, 1983), 104.
33. David Gebhard, "Architecture and the Fred Harvey House: The Alvarado and La Fonda," *New Mexico Architect* 6, nos. 1 and 2 (January–February 1964): 18–19.
34. *New Mexican*, 23 April 1910, 4.
35. Ibid.
36. "City Council Minutes," 5 March 1912, NMSRCA.
37. "City Council Minutes," 3 December 1912, NMSRCA.
38. Ibid.
39. Ralph E. Twitchell, *Old Santa Fe: The Story of New Mexico's Ancient Capital* (Santa Fe: Santa Fe New Mexican Publishing Corporation, 1925), 458.
40. Sylvanus Griswold Morley went on to become an important figure in Mesoamerican studies, and at his death in 1948, he was serving as director of the Museum of New Mexico and the School of American Research in Santa Fe.
41. *New Mexican*, 6 February 1913, 8.
42. *New Mexican*, 9 April 1913, 3.
43. *New Mexican*, 9 July 1913, 8.
44. *New Mexican*, 14 July 1913, 5.
45. *New Mexican*, 16 July 1913, 8.
46. *New Mexican*, 18 July 1913, 6.
47. Bainbridge Bunting, *John Gaw Meem: Southwest Architect* (Albuquerque: University of New Mexico Press, 1983), 8–9.
48. *New Mexican*, 16 July 1913, 8.
49. "Annual Report of the President of the Chamber of Commerce of Santa Fe, New Mexico for the Year Ending April 1, 1914," (Santa Fe, 1914), 4, Chamber of Commerce, Box 145, Ms. Coll. Minutes of Committee Meetings, Museum of New Mexico, Santa Fe, New Mexico (hereinafter cited as MNM).
50. Sylvanus G. Morley, "Santa Fe Architecture," *Old Santa Fe* 2, no. 3 (January 1915): 278–84.
51. Carlos Vierra, "New Mexico Architecture," *Art and Archaeology* 7, nos. 1–2 (January–February 1918): 43, 46–47.
52. Carlos Vierra, "Our Native Architecture in Its Relation to Santa Fe," *El Palacio* 4, no. 1 (January 1917): 9.
53. Ibid., 5, 7.
54. William T. Johnson, "The Santa Fe of the Future," *El Palacio* 3, no. 3 (April 1916): 11.
55. Ibid., 15.
56. Edgar Hewett, "Santa Fe in 1926," *El Palacio* 4, no. 1 (January 1917), 24.
57. Ibid., 26–27.
58. William T. Johnson, "Santa Fe as the Years Pass," *Art and Archaeology* 7, nos. 1–2 (January–February 1918): 35–36.
59. *New Mexican*, 21 April 1915, 4.
60. *New Mexican*, 24 April 1915, 6.
61. Chauvenet, *Hewett*, 49–50.
62. See Regna Darnell, "The Professionalization of American Anthropology: A Case Study in the Sociology of Knowledge," *Social Science Information* 10, no. 2 (April 1971): 98–99.
63. See Robert H. Lowie, *The History of Ethnological Theory* (New York: Farrar and Rinehart, 1959), 129–32, 155; George W. Stocking, Jr., ed., *The Shaping of American Anthropology 1883–1911: A Franz Boas Reader* (New York: Basic Books, 1974), 17; Marshall Hyatt, *Franz Boas, Social Activist: The Dynamics of Ethnicity* (New York: Greenwood Press, 1990), xi.
64. Hyatt, *Franz Boas*, 116.
65. Governor L. Bradford Prince to W. R. Martin, 12 January 1913, Historical Society of New Mexico papers, FACHL, microfilm, roll 2, frs. 235–36.
66. *New York Times*, 5 February 1912, 8. Tozzer was the first fellow in American archaeology under the auspices of the AIA.

67. Alfred Tozzer to Governor L. Bradford Prince, 15 January 1913, Historical Society of New Mexico papers, FACHL, microfilm, roll 2, frs. 241–42.
68. W. R. Martin to Governor Prince, 12 January 1913, Historical Society of New Mexico papers, FACHL, microfilm, roll 2, frs. 237–38.
69. Governor Prince to H. H. Dorman, 23 December 1912, Historical Society of New Mexico papers, FACHL, microfilm, roll 2, fr. 231.
70. Richard Lowitt, *Bronson M. Cutting: Progressive Politician* (Albuquerque: University of New Mexico Press, 1992), 45.
71. Ibid., 45–46. See also Chauvenet, *Hewett*, 97.
72. Lowitt, *Bronson M. Cutting*, 47–48; Chauvenet, *Hewett*, 110–18.
73. *New Mexican*, 17 September 1913, 1.
74. *New Mexican*, 3 October 1913, 1.
75. See *New Mexican*, 16 October 1913, 1; 23 October 1913, 1; and 27 October 1913, 1. See also Chauvenet, *Hewett*, 114–15.
76. *New Mexican*, 23 October 1913, 8.
77. *New Mexican*, 12 November 1913, 1, 4.
78. Chauvenet, *Hewett*, 118.
79. *New Mexican*, 13 November 1913, 3.
80. *New Mexican*, 12 November 1913, 1, 4.
81. Charles F. Lummis to Edgar Hewett, 3 November 1913, Hewett Collection, Box 39, Folder Dorman, Cutting, Tozzer (1913–1914), MNM.
82. Hewett to Ralph E. Twitchell, 26 November 1913, Hewett Collection, op. cit.
83. Lummis to Hewett, 3 November 1913, Hewett Collection, op. cit.
84. Philip K. Bock, "UNM Centennial: History of the Anthropology Department," second draft, 1988, 2–3, Philip K. Bock private manuscript collection, Albuquerque, New Mexico. Bock is former chair of the Anthropology Department at the University of New Mexico.
85. D. D. Brand to J. F. Zimmerman, University of New Mexico president, 10 May 1936, and excerpts from Clyde Kluckhohn to Zimmerman, 7 February 1935, Philip K. Bock private manuscript collection, Albuquerque.
86. George W. Stocking, Jr., "Anthropological Visions and Economic Realities in the 1930s Southwest," *El Palacio* 87, no. 3 (fall 1981): 15; George W. Stocking, Jr., "The Santa Fe Style in American Anthropology: Regional Interest, Academic Initiatives, and Philanthropic Policy in the First Two Decades of the Laboratory of Anthropology, Inc.," *Journal of the History of the Behavioral Sciences* 18 (1982): 6–7.

Chapter 6

1. Van Deren Coke, *Taos and Santa Fe: The Artist's Environment 1882–1942* (Albuquerque: University of New Mexico Press for the Amon Carter Museum of Western Art, Fort Worth, Texas, and the Art Gallery, University of New Mexico, 1963), 9–18; Ernest L. Blumenschein, "Origin of the Taos Art Colony," *El Palacio* 20, no. 10 (15 May 1926): 190–92.
2. See Coke, *Taos and Santa Fe*, 27, 29–34, and Edna Robertson and Sarah Nestor, *Artists of the Canyons and Caminos: Santa Fe, The Early Years* (Santa Fe: Peregrine Smith, 1976), 29, 39 for biographical details.
3. Cited in Robertson and Nestor, *Artists of the Canyons*, 49.
4. Sharyn R. Udall, *Modernist Painting in New Mexico 1913–1935* (Albuquerque: University of New Mexico Press, 1984), 14.
5. Coke, *Taos and Santa Fe*, 13–14, 22, 27, 42–43, 52.
6. Ibid., 58; Robertson and Nestor, *Artists of the Canyons*, 94.
7. Robert R. White, ed., *The Taos Society of Artists* (Albuquerque: University of New Mexico Press, 1983), 3–5, 14; Coke, *Taos and Santa Fe*, 23–24. The charter members were Sharp, Blumenschein, Couse, Dunton, Bert G. Phillips, and Oscar E. Berninghaus.
8. "The Museum of New Mexico," *El Palacio* 2, no. 3 (December 1914), 2.
9. Paul A. F. Walter, "The Santa Fe-Taos Art Movement," *Art and Archaeology* 4, no. 6 (December 1916): 330, 333.
10. White, *The Taos Society*, 29.
11. "Blumenschein Is Interviewed," *El Palacio* 6, no. 6 (1919): 85.

12. "Biennial Report of the Secretary of the Museum of New Mexico, December 1, 1914 to November 30, 1916," *El Palacio* 4, no. 1 (January 1917): 69.
13. White, *The Taos Society*, 14, 29–30.
14. Walter Ufer, "The Santa Fe-Taos Art Colony," *El Palacio* 3, no. 4 (August 1916): 75.
15. "Painting and Sculpture," *El Palacio* 10, no. 8 (15 March 1921): 4. Emphasis ours.
16. Ibid., 7; *El Palacio* 4, no. 2 (April 1917): 107; *El Palacio* 13, no. 10 (15 November 1922): 122; "Art and Architecture," *El Palacio* 5, no. 22 (2 December 1918): 367.
17. Exhibits and Galleries, *El Palacio* 8, no. 5–6 (May–June 1920): 135–36.
18. "Art in New Mexico," *El Palacio* 10, no. 13–14 (15 June 1921): 14.
19. Ibid., 11.
20. "Comment on the Arts," *The Arts* 1, no. 3 (February–March 1921): 46.
21. "It Is Written," *El Palacio* 11, no. 1 (1 July 1921): 7.
22. Ernest Peixotto, "The Taos Society of Artists," parts 1 and 2, *Scribner's Magazine* 60, no. 2 (August 1916): 260; no. 3 (September 1916): 321–26.
23. R. P. Crawford, "Discovering a Real American Art," *Scribner's Magazine* 73, no. 3 (March 1923): 380–84.
24. For background on name changes from Anglo to Spanish, see Chris Wilson, *The Myth of Santa Fe: Creating a Modern Regional Tradition* (Albuquerque: University of New Mexico Press, 1997), 123.
25. *New Mexican*, 29 October 1921, 2.
26. Joseph Dispenza and Louise Turner, *Will Shuster: A Santa Fe Legend* (Santa Fe: Museum of New Mexico Press, 1989), 42–43; Robertson and Nestor, *Artists of the Canyons*, 88–90.
27. The five artists were Jozef Bakos, Fremont Ellis, Walter Mruk, Willard Nash, and Will Shuster.
28. Dispenza and Turner, *Shuster*, 60; Robertson and Nestor, *Artists of the Canyons*, 29–30.
29. *El Palacio* 10, nos. 1–2 (15 January 1921): [5–9].
30. Dispenza and Turner, *Shuster*, 15–18, 123.
31. Ibid., 15, 27, 29.
32. Drama and Pageants, *El Palacio* 5, no. 20 (9 December 1918): 334–35; Drama and Pageantry, *El Palacio* 6, no. 6 (1 March 1919): 86.
33. Udall, *Modernist Painting in New Mexico*, 43–44.
34. Van Deren Coke, *Andrew Dasburg* (Albuquerque: University of New Mexico Press, 1979), 64–65.
35. J. J. Brody, *Indian Painters & White Patrons* (Albuquerque: University of New Mexico Press, 1971), 61–63.
36. A. F. Spiegelberg, "Navajo Blankets," *El Palacio* 18, nos. 10–11 (1 June 1925): 223–29; first published in *Out West* (May 1904).
37. William H. Truettner, "The Art of Pueblo Life," in *Art in New Mexico, 1900–1945: Paths to Taos and Santa Fe*, eds. Charles C. Eldredge, Julie Schimmel, and William H. Truettner (Washington, D.C.: National Museum of American Art, Smithsonian Institution; New York: Abbeville Press, 1986), 72–73.
38. Ibid., 73, 82.
39. Ibid., 72. See also Winona Garmhausen, *History of Indian Arts Education in Santa Fe: The Institute of American Indian Arts with Historical Background, 1890–1962* (Santa Fe: Sunstone Press, 1988), 32.
40. See Withers Woolford, "Revival of the Native Crafts," *New Mexico* 9, no. 9 (September 1931): 24–26.
41. *New Mexican*, 20 May 1926, 2.
42. Arthur DeVolder, "John Gaw Meem, F.A.I.A.: An Appreciation," *NMHR* 54, no. 3 (July 1979): 212–13; John C. McNary, "John Gaw Meem: His Style Development and Residential Architecture Between 1924 and 1940" (master's thesis, University of New Mexico, 1977), 10–12.
43. McNary, "John Gaw Meem," 100.
44. "Report of the Director of the School of American Research for the Year 1918," *El Palacio* 6, no. 1 (11 January 1919): 3.
45. Clara D. True, "Voices of Santa Fe," *El Palacio* 3, no. 3 (April 1916): 9.
46. "It Is Written," *El Palacio* 3, no. 3 (April 1916): 77.
47. Lawrance Thompson and R. H. Winnick, *Robert Frost: A Biography* (New York: Holt, Rinehart and Winston, 1981), 354–55.
48. Mary Austin, *Earth Horizon, Autobiography* (Boston and New York: Houghton Mifflin, 1932), 359.
49. "In Justice to the Indians" [letter signed by forty-six persons], *The New Republic*, 13 December 1922, 70. See Alice Corbin Henderson's "The Death of the Pueblos," *The New Republic*, 29 November 1922, 11–13, and the journal's supportive editorial position in the same issue.

50. Lawrence C. Kelly, *The Assault on Assimilation: John Collier and the Origins of Indian Policy Reform* (Albuquerque: University of New Mexico Press, 1983), 220–21.
51. Arrell M. Gibson, "The Author as Image Maker for the Southwest," in *Old Southwest/New Southwest: Essays on a Region and Its Literature*, ed. Judy N. Lensink (Tucson: Tucson Public Library, distributed by University of Arizona Press, 1987), 34.
52. See Dudley Wynn, "A Critical Study of the Writings of Mary Hunter Austin" (Ph.D. diss., New York University, 1939), 1.
53. "The Town That Doesn't Want a Chautauqua," *The New Republic*, 7 July 1926, 195–97. Austin's viewpoint, if not the locale, was strikingly similar to that of William James, whom she admired. See Theodore Morrison, *Chautauqua: A Center for Education, Religion, and the Arts in America* (Chicago: University of Chicago Press, 1974), 231–32; and Esther Lanigan Stineman, *Mary Austin: Song of a Maverick* (New Haven: Yale University Press, 1989), 17.
54. Editorial Paragraphs, *The Nation* 122, no. 3176 (19 May 1926), 543.
55. "On the Trail of Santa Fe," *New York Times*, 19 December 1926.
56. Count derived from Tom Lewis, *Storied New Mexico: An Annotated Bibliography of Novels with New Mexico Settings* (Albuquerque: University of New Mexico Press, 1991). Lewis's annotated bibliography of novels with a New Mexico setting includes 1,237 titles.
57. See, for example, Arrell Morgan Gibson, *The Santa Fe and Taos Colonies: Age of the Muses, 1900–1942* (Norman: University of Oklahoma Press, 1983), and Marta Weigle and Kyle Fiore, *Santa Fe and Taos: The Writer's Era, 1916–1941* (Santa Fe: Ancient City Press, 1982).
58. Richard McKinzie, *The New Deal for Artists* (Princeton: Princeton University Press, 1973), 4–5.
59. Ibid., 5.
60. William H. Spurlock, II, "Federal Support for the Visual Arts in the State of New Mexico, 1933–1943" (master's thesis, University of New Mexico, 1974), 60.
61. See, for example, Martin F. Krause, Madeline Carol Yurtseven, and David Acton, *Gustave Baumann: Nearer to Art* (Santa Fe: Museum of New Mexico Press, 1993), 60; Peter Bermingham, *The New Deal in the Southwest, Arizona and New Mexico* (Tucson: Museum of Arizona Museum of Art, [1980?]), 5; Phoenix Art Museum, *William Penhallow Henderson: Master Colorist of Santa Fe* (Phoenix: Phoenix Art Museum, 1984), 19; Robertson and Nestor, *Artists of the Canyons*, 129; and Dispenza, *Shuster*, 32–33.
62. Spurlock, "Federal Support," 6–7.
63. Ibid., 9–11; Marta Weigle, ed., *New Mexicans in Cameo and Camera: New Deal Documentation of Twentieth-Century Lives* (Albuquerque: University of New Mexico Press, 1985), 215–16.
64. Udall, *Modernist Painting*, 121.
65. Spurlock, "Federal Support," 2; Lincoln Rothschild, "Artists' Organizations of the Depression Decade," in *The New Deal Art Projects: An Anthology of Memoirs*, ed. Francis V. O'Connor (Washington, D.C.: Smithsonian Institution, 1972), 199; McKinzie, *The New Deal for Artists*, 4–5.
66. Udall, *Modernist Painting*, 121.
67. Ibid., 207.
68. James Thorsen, "Gomorrah on the Puerco," in *Labor in New Mexico: Unions, Strikes, and Social History Since 1881*, ed. Robert Kern (Albuquerque: University of New Mexico Press, 1983), 148–49.
69. Ibid., 150.
70. *New Mexican*, 5 November 1937, 14.
71. See chapter 5 of this volume, and John C. McNary, "John Gaw Meem: His Style, Development, and Residential Architecture between 1924 and 1940" (master's thesis, University of New Mexico, 1977), 13–15.
72. See Bunting, *John Gaw Meem*, 160–68, for a partial listing of Meem's work.
73. See Ralph Twitchell obituary in *NMHR* 1, no. 1 (January 1926): 78–85.
74. See Benjamin Read obituary in *NMHR* 2, no. 4 (October 1927): 394–97.
75. See Frank Springer obituary in *NMHR* 2, no. 4 (October 1927): 387–93; and John McFie obituary in *NMHR* 5, no. 4 (October 1930): 411–18.

Chapter 7

1. Bureau of the Census, *Fifteenth Census of the United States, 1930*, vol. 1 (Washington, D.C., 1931), 730.
2. Compiled from the Dun and Bradstreet reports for 1897, 1915, and 1925, and state business directories for 1903–4 and 1916.

3. *New Mexican*, 19 August 1911, 3–4.
4. Ibid.
5. Counts made from censuses of 1910 and 1920.
6. Counts made from census of 1920 and *Hudspeth's Santa Fe City Directory, 1928–1929* (El Paso, Tex.: Hudspeth Directory Co., 1929).
7. *New Mexican*, 19 April 1926, 4.
8. Wayne L. Mauzy, *A Century in Santa Fe: The Story of the First National Bank of Santa Fe* (Santa Fe: The Bank, [197?]).
9. First National Bank of Santa Fe, "Record and Minute Book," 10 January 1905 and 11 January 1910, CSWR.
10. Ibid., 3 January 1910.
11. Ibid., 31 May 1911.
12. Ibid., "Special meeting," 22 March 1916.
13. "City Council Minutes," 3 December 1912, 88, NMSRCA.
14. "City Council Minutes," 3 January 1917, 323, NMSRCA.
15. *New Mexican*, 18 November 1919, 6.
16. *New Mexican*, 20 November 1919, 6.
17. *New Mexican*, 27 December 1919, 1.
18. Bureau of the Census, *Fourteenth Census of the United States, 1920, State Compendium, New Mexico* (Washington, D.C., 1925), Table 2, n. 21, 15.
19. Bureau of the Census, *Abstract of the Fourteenth Census of the United States, 1920* (Washington, D.C., 1923), 38.
20. See Richard J. Stillman, II, *The Rise of the City Manager: A Public Professional in City Government* (Albuquerque: University of New Mexico Press, 1974), 8–9.
21. *New Mexican*, 30 March 1910, 4.
22. *New Mexican*, 26 March 1912, 6.
23. *New Mexican*, 25 March 1914, 1.
24. *New Mexican*, 20 March 1916, 5.
25. *New Mexican*, 26 March 1918, 2.
26. *New Mexican*, 30 March 1914, 1.
27. *New Mexican*, 28 March 1916, 3.
28. *New Mexican*, 26 March 1918, 2.
29. Public Service Company of New Mexico (PNM), "Water Supply–City of Santa Fe: History and Future Additions" (Albuquerque: PNM, August 1971), 4.
30. Ibid., 7.
31. Ibid., 12.
32. Paul Walter to J. M. Hawkins, 18 July 1921, Walter Collection, MNM.
33. *New Mexican*, 22 May 1926, 10.
34. *New Mexican*, 29 May 1926, 4–5.
35. Ibid., 4.
36. "City Council Minutes," 6–7 July 1927, NMSRCA.
37. Ibid., 15 June 1926 and 1 March 1927.
38. James C. Hughes, "Three Stages of Land Use in Santa Fe, New Mexico, 1610–1967" (master's thesis, University of Kansas, 1968), Table 5.
39. *New Mexican*, 17 August 1916, 3.
40. D. H. Thomas, *The Southwestern Indian Detours: The Story of Fred Harvey/Santa Fe Railway Experience in Detourism* (Phoenix: Hunter Publishing Company, 1978), 30–37.
41. David Gebhard, "Architecture and the Fred Harvey Houses," *New Mexico Architect* 6, nos. 1–2 (January–February 1964): 23.
42. Thomas, *Southwestern Indian Detours*, 75–76.
43. *New Mexican*, 27 April 1926, 6.
44. Ibid.
45. *New Mexican*, 29 April 1926, 2.
46. *New Mexican*, 1 May 1926, 6. On Padilla, see A. Gabriel Melendez, "New Mexico's Spanish-Language Journalists: Camilo Padilla, Pioneer Publicist," Working Paper Series (Albuquerque: Southwest Hispanic Research Institute, University of New Mexico, 1994), 14–15.
47. *New Mexican*, 13 May 1926, 5.

48. John DeHuff, "The Santa Fe Fiesta," *NMHR* 6, no. 3 (July 1931): 323–24; Thomas E. Chavez, "Santa Fe's Own: A History of Fiesta," in *Vivan Las Fiestas*, ed. Donna Pierce (Santa Fe: Museum of New Mexico Press, 1985), 12.
49. "The Santa Fe Fiesta," *El Palacio* 7, no. 1 (15 July 1919): 101.
50. Bruce T. Ellis, "Santa Fe's Tertio-Millenial, 1883," *El Palacio* 65: no. 4 (August 1958): 121.
51. "The 1924 Santa Fe Fiesta," *El Palacio* 17, nos. 6–7 (30 September 1924): 134–37. For an historical analysis of the Fiesta, see Ronald L. Grimes, *Symbol and Conquest—Public Ritual and Drama in Santa Fe* (Ithaca, N.Y.: Cornell University Press, 1976; reprint, Albuquerque: University of New Mexico Press, 1992).
52. Carolyn Zeleny, "Relations Between the Spanish-Americans and Anglo-Americans in New Mexico: A Study of Conflict and Accommodation in a Dual-Ethnic Situation" (Ph.D. diss., Yale University, 1944), 192–200.
53. National Archives, "Population Schedules" for the 1880, 1900, 1910, and 1920 censuses for New Mexico, microfilm. These sources are also used for the analysis of demographic and occupational trends in the remainder of this chapter. Data for 1928 are drawn from *Hudspeth's Santa Fe City Directory, 1928–29* (El Paso, Tex.: Hudspeth Directory Co., 1929).
54. *New Mexican*, 23 May 1920, 2; *New Mexican*, 1 June 1920, 4.
55. National Archives, "Population Schedules," 1880, 1910; *Santa Fe City Directory, 1928–29*.

Chapter 8

1. Michael Malone and Richard W. Etulain, *The American West: A Twentieth-Century History* (Lincoln: University of Nebraska Press, 1989), 87; Michael Welsh, "A Land of Extremes: The Economy of Modern New Mexico, 1940–1990," in *Contemporary New Mexico, 1940–1990*, ed. Richard Etulain (Albuquerque: University of New Mexico Press, 1994), 67–69; William Pickens, "The New Deal in New Mexico," in *The New Deal: The State and Local Levels*, ed. John Braeman, Robert H. Bremner, and David Brody (Columbus: Ohio State University Press, 1975), 2:311–12.
2. *New Mexican*, 30 November 1929, 4.
3. Pickens, "New Deal," 318, 323, 335.
4. Bureau of the Census, *Fifteenth Census, 1930, Unemployment*, vol. 1 (Washington, D.C., 1931), 674.
5. *New Mexican*, 11 January 1933, 2.
6. Bureau of the Census, *Sixteenth Census, 1940, Characteristics of the Population, New Mexico* (Washington, D.C., 1943), 73.
7. William R. Watson and Shirley J. Huzarski, *Income and Employment in New Mexico, Selected Years, 1929–1969*, New Mexico Studies in Business and Economics, No. 22 (Albuquerque: Bureau of Business Research, Institute for Social Research and Development, University of New Mexico, 1973), 8.
8. Bureau of the Census, *Sixteenth Census of the United States, 1940, Population*, vol. 1 (Washington, D.C., 1942), 695.
9. Ibid., 695–96.
10. Estimates for state data of births over deaths based on Bureau of the Census, *Statistical Abstract of the United States, 1940* (Washington, D.C., 1941), 92.
11. Paul Walter, Jr., "The Spanish-Speaking Community in New Mexico," *Sociology and Social Research* 24 (September–October 1939): 156.
12. Walter, "Rural-Urban Migration in New Mexico," *New Mexico Business Review* 8 (April 1939): 134–35.
13. Irene Moke, "Santa Fe, New Mexico: A Study in Urban Geography" (Ph.D. diss., University of Nebraska, 1945), 82.
14. Bureau of the Census, *Sixteenth Census, 1940, Retail Trade, 1939* (Washington, D.C., 1941), 2.
15. Bureau of the Census, *Census of American Business, 1933*, vol. 7 (Washington, D.C., n.d.), 115.
16. Bureau of the Census, *Census of American Business, 1933, Retail Distribution*, vol. 3 (Washington, D.C., May 1935), 36; *Sixteenth Census, 1940, Retail Trade, New Mexico, 1939*, 7.
17. See Mary Bartolino, "History and Progress of the State Gasoline Tax Department," *New Mexico Highway Journal* 8, no. 1 (January 1930): 26–27.
18. Mary Severns, "Tourism in New Mexico: The Promotional Activities of the New Mexico State Tourist Bureau, 1935–1950" (master's thesis, University of New Mexico, 1951), 2.
19. "Tourist Business in State Is a Fifty Million Dollar Industry," *New Mexico* 14, no. 1 (January 1936): 35, 45.

20. Warren J. Belasco, *Americans on the Road: From Auto Camps to Motels, 1910–1945* (Cambridge, Mass.: MIT Press, 1979), 3–4.
21. Bureau of the Census, *Census of American Business, Service, Amusements, and Hotels, 1939*, vol. 3 (Washington, D.C., 1942), 578.
22. See Ann Nolan Clark, "The Art of the Loom," *New Mexico* 16, no. 11 (November 1938): 9–10.
23. George McCrossen, "The Handweaving Phenomenon in the Southwest: During the Decades Between 1930–1950," 15–16, McCrossen Collection, Mss #356, Box 1, Folder 1, CSWR.
24. McCrossen, "McCrossen Hand-Woven Textiles, Inc.," McCrossen Collection, Mss #356, Box 1, Folder 2, CSWR.
25. McCrossen, "The Handweaving Phenomenon," 17.
26. Anna N. Clark, "The Art of the Loom," *New Mexico* 16, no. 11 (1938): 36.
27. "218 Santa Fe Men Live by Weaving," *WPA Bulletin* 1, no. 11 (1936): 17.
28. Sarah Nestor, *The Native Market of the Spanish New Mexican Craftsmen: Santa Fe, 1933–1940* (Santa Fe: Colonial New Mexico Historical Foundation, 1978), 8–9.
29. Ibid., 6–11, 31.
30. The comparisons are between *Hudspeth's Santa Fe City Directory, 1928–29* (El Paso, Tex.: Hudspeth Directory Co., 1929) and *Hudspeth's Santa Fe City Directory, 1940* (El Paso, Tex.: Hudspeth Directory Co., 1940).
31. Records of Hispano office-holding in state and local government are provided in E. B. Fincher, *Spanish-Americans as a Political Factor in New Mexico, 1912–1950* (New York: Arno Press, 1974), 124–27, 251–59. Hispano participation in electoral politics from 1912 to 1960 is analyzed in Jack E. Holmes, *Politics in New Mexico* (Albuquerque: University of New Mexico Press, 1967).
32. Holmes, *Politics in New Mexico*, 199–201, 210–13.
33. Ibid., 213.
34. *Hudspeth's Santa Fe City Directory, 1928–29*, and *1940*.
35. National Archives, "Population Schedules," 1920, microfilm; *Hudspeth's Santa Fe City Directory, 1928–29*, and *1940*.
36. Linda Tigges, "Santa Fe Landownership in the 1880s," *NMHR* 68 (April 1993): 153–80; "Index to the Hartmann Map," *New Mexico Genealogist* 26 (March 1987): 18–23.
37. "King Map of 1912," NMSCRA.
38. We have borrowed the use of this term from Richard L. Nostrand, *The Hispano Homeland* (Norman: University of Oklahoma Press, 1992).
39. "King Map of 1912."
40. Moke, "Santa Fe," 82.
41. Cynthia E. Orozco, "The Origins of the League of United Latin American Citizens (LULAC) and the Mexican American Civil Rights Movement in Texas" (Ph.D. diss., University of California-Los Angeles, 1992), 288–93, 302.
42. "Santa Fe Council No. 33 says, 'Don't be afraid of politics, but don't let politics ruin you,'" *LULAC News* 5, no. 3 (1938): 24–25.
43. *New Mexican*, 2 April 1930, 1.
44. *New Mexican*, 6 April 1932, 1.
45. Ibid., 4.
46. *New Mexican*, 29 March 1934, 1.
47. *New Mexican*, 19 March 1936, 1.
48. Ibid., 7. A detailed analysis of Governor Tingley's style of political leadership and his expansion of state government in the mid-1930s is provided in Lucinda Lucero Sachs, "Clyde Tingley's Little New Deal for New Mexico, 1935–1938" (master's thesis, University of New Mexico, 1989).
49. *New Mexican*, 1 April 1938, 5.

Chapter 9

1. We counted the rolls based on "Santa Fe County Local Board #1 and #2," NMSRCA.
2. "Santa Fe County Local Board Group C," NMSRCA.
3. See *New Mexican*, 22 September 1943, 1.
4. The Bureau of the Census figures for 25 November 1947 indicate the presence of 48,384 World War II veterans in New Mexico out of a population of over a half million or just below 10 percent. *Current Population Reports, Population Estimates* (Washington, D.C., 25 November 1947), 2.

5. "World War II Honor List of Dead and Missing, State of New Mexico" (Washington, D.C.: War Department, June 1946), 1.
6. *New Mexican*, 21 August 1945, 3.
7. John P. Jolly, "History of the National Guard of New Mexico, 1606–1963," mimeograph, 65, 73–74, 76–78, NMSRCA.
8. "World War II Honor List," 9–10.
9. Bureau of the Census, *Sixteenth Census of the United States, 1940, Second Series, Characteristics of the Population, New Mexico* (Washington, D.C., 1941), 73.
10. Ibid.
11. State of New Mexico, *Annual Report of the Department of Public Welfare for the Fiscal Year Ending June 30, 1942* (Santa Fe, 1942), 22.
12. New Mexico Department of Public Welfare, *Annual Report of the Department of Public Welfare, Fiscal Year Ending June 30, 1941* (Santa Fe, 1941), 27.
13. *New Mexican*, 4 December 1942, 1.
14. New Mexico State Planning Board, *New Mexico: Facts and Figures* (Santa Fe, 1948), 88.
15. *Las Vegas (N.Mex.) Daily Optic*, 3 March 1942, 2.
16. *New Mexican*, 5 August 1942, 3.
17. *New Mexican*, 20 May 1942, 1.
18. *New Mexican*, 21 May 1942, 1.
19. *New Mexican*, 12 September 1942, 4.
20. William McNulty, "Now They Can Be Told Aloud, Those Stoories of 'The Hill'," *New Mexican*, 6 August 1945, 1.
21. Charlotte Serber, "Labor Pains," in *Standing By and Making Do: Women of Wartime Los Alamos*, eds. Jane S. Wilson and Charlotte Serber (Los Alamos, N.Mex.: Los Alamos Historical Society, 1988), 67; Laura Fermi, *Atoms in the Family: My Life with Enrico Fermi* (Chicago: Chicago University Press, 1954), 234.
22. Leslie R. Groves, *Now It Can Be Told: The Story of the Manhattan Project* (New York: Harper, 1962), 151–52; *New Mexican*, 6 August 1945, 1.
23. James W. Kunetka, *City of Fire: Los Alamos and the Birth of the Atomic Age 1943–1945* (Englewood Cliffs, N.J.: Prentice-Hall, 1978), 106.
24. Serber, "Labor Pains," 62.
25. M. Eugene Sundt and W. E. Naumann, *M. M. Sundt Construction Co.: From Small Beginnings . . .* (New York: Newcomen Society in North America, 1975), 20.
26. M. Eugene Sundt, interview by Henry J. Tobias, 13–14 June 1995, Albuquerque, New Mexico. The varying figures are noted in a letter from M. Eugene Sundt to Dr. Jesse Remington dated 8 May 1969 in the possession of Sundt.
27. Marjorie Bell Chambers, "Technically Sweet Los Alamos: The Development of a Federally Sponsored Scientific Community" (Ph.D. diss., University of New Mexico, 1974), 91.
28. Ibid. See discussion of Bruns General Hospital later in this chapter.
29. M. Eugene Sundt, "Job 444: The First Year of Zia," [197?], 74, 124, mss. compiled from the Journals of Eugene Sundt by Dewey Paxton, Los Alamos Historical Society, Los Alamos, New Mexico.
30. Chambers, "Technically Sweet," 91; Sundt, "Job 444," 76.
31. Wayne L. Mauzy, *A Century in Santa Fe: The Story of the First National Bank of Santa Fe* (Santa Fe: The Bank, [197?]).
32. Ibid.
33. Kunetka, *City of Fire*, 62; Robert C. Williams, *Klaus Fuchs, Atom Spy* (Cambridge, Mass.: Harvard University Press, 1987), 79.
34. Phyllis Fisher, *Los Alamos Experience* (Tokyo and New York: Japan Publications, 1985), 71.
35. *New Mexican*, 22 September 1943, 1.
36. Ibid.
37. *New Mexican*, 19 April 1945, 1.
38. *New Mexican*, 27 September 1946, 1.
39. Public Service Company of New Mexico (PNM), "Water Supply–City of Santa Fe: History and Future Additions" (Albuquerque: PNM, August 1971), 12.
40. *New Mexican*, 29 November 1946, 1.
41. *New Mexican*, 29 August 1944, 4.
42. *New Mexican*, 8 October 1946, 1.

43. *New Mexican*, 13 October 1945, 1.
44. *New Mexican*, 11 October 1945, 1; 19 November 1946, 1; 29 November 1946, 1.
45. *New Mexican*, 14 December 1946, 1.
46. Harry D. Ellis, M.D., interview by Jake Spidle, 6 September 1991, 1–2, Oral History Project, New Mexico Medical History Program, Archives, Health Sciences Library, University of New Mexico, Albuquerque, New Mexico.
47. Albert W. Egenhofer, M.D., interview by Jake Spidle, 19 October 1983, 10, Oral History Project, New Mexico Medical History Program, op. cit.
48. John J. Culley, "The Santa Fe Internment Camp and the Justice Department Program for Enemy Aliens," in *Japanese Americans: From Relocation to Redress*, eds. Roger Daniels, Sandra C. Taylor, and Harry H. L. Kitano (Salt Lake City: University of Utah Press, 1986), 58–59.
49. *New Mexican*, 5 March 1942, 1; 6 March 1942, 1.
50. *New Mexican*, 7 March 1942, 4.
51. Jerre Mangione, *An Ethnic At Large: A Memoir of America in the Thirties and Forties* (New York: Putnam, 1978), 323. Mangione directed the public relations program of the Immigration and Naturalization Service, the custodian of the camps, during the war.
52. Ibid., 323; Koichiro Okada, "Forced Acculturation: A Study of Issei in the Santa Fe Internment Camp During World War II" (master's thesis, New Mexico Highlands University, 1995), 9.
53. Culley, "The Santa Fe Internment Camp," 60.
54. *Albuquerque Journal*, 5 March 1942, 1–2.
55. *New Mexican*, 6 March 1942, 1 and 12 March 1942, 1–2.
56. *New Mexican*, 21 March 1946, 6.

Chapter 10

1. *New Mexican*, 13 September 1945, 4.
2. *New Mexican*, 18 September 1945, 1.
3. New Mexico Legislature, *Laws of the State of New Mexico Passed by the Eighth Regular Session of the Legislature of the State of New Mexico, 1927* (Santa Fe, 7 March 1927), 31–35.
4. *New Mexico Statutes 1941*, vol. 1, 909–14; New Mexico Legislature, *Laws of the State of New Mexico Passed by the Eighteenth Regular Session of the Legislature of the State of New Mexico, 1947* (Santa Fe, 20 March 1947), 444–53.
5. Harland Bartholomew and Associates, "Comprehensive City Plan: Santa Fe, New Mexico," [1950], iii, CSWR.
6. *The Code of the City of Santa Fe, 1953: The Incorporation Proclamation and the General Ordinances of the City, Enacted as a whole March 31, 1954, effective May 1, 1954*, 253–57.
7. *New Mexican*, 1 April 1947, 10; 3 April 1947, 14.
8. *New Mexican*, 28 March 1946, 1.
9. *New Mexican*, 1 April 1946, 4.
10. See the *New Mexican*, 16 March 1956, 1, for a Republican campaign statement of this attitude, and 23 March 1956, 1, for the Democratic view.
11. City of Santa Fe, *Code of Ordinances* (Santa Fe, 1930), 115–16.
12. *New Mexican*, 15 April 1948, 1.
13. *New York Times*, 3 November 1957, viii, 1:1. Some of the most important articles on the progress of the ordinance can be found in the *New Mexican*, 10 January 1957, 1, 11; 31 March 1957, 7A; 12 April 1957, 1, 2; 9 May 1957, 1, 2; 25 October 1957, 1, 2; 27 October 1957, 1, 2; and 29 October 1957, 1.
14. *New Mexican*, 10 April 1960, 1.
15. *New Mexican*, 15 March 1962, 3.
16. See *New Mexican*, 27 March 1958, 4; and 30 March 1962, 8.
17. *New Mexican*, 3 July 1945, 1.
18. *New Mexican*, 3 May 1946, 4.
19. *New Mexican*, 23 November 1946, 1.
20. *New Mexican*, 4 December 1945, 1.
21. *New Mexican*, 28 April 1957, 10.
22. Count based on *Hudspeth's Santa Fe City Directory, 1963* (El Paso, Tex.: Hudspeth Directory Co., 1963).
23. *New Mexican*, 10 April 1960, 13.

24. *New Mexican*, 1 March 1970, A-3.
25. Ibid.
26. Ellie Becker, "Allen Stamm: A Standard of Excellence in Building and Business," *Santa Fe Real Estate Weekly*, 15 March 1996, 18.
27. *New Mexican*, 26 February 1970, 1.
28. Bureau of Business and Economic Research, University of New Mexico, *The Census in New Mexico* 1 (January 1992): 73.
29. Ibid.
30. *New Mexican*, 5 January 1946, 5. See also "Survey Intra-City Travel," *New Mexico* 24, no. 1 (January 1946): 29.
31. *New Mexican*, 5 January 1946, 5.
32. Ibid.
33. *New Mexican*, 21 January 1946, 6.
34. *New Mexican*, 19 April 1946, 1.
35. *New Mexican*, 14 September 1946, 1.
36. *New Mexican*, 12 June 1947, 1.
37. *New Mexican*, 19 June 1947, 1, 4.
38. *New Mexican*, 31 March 1960, 1.
39. *New Mexican*, 30 August 1964, A-7.
40. See Richard Gardner, *Grito! Reies Tijerina and the New Mexico Land Grant War of 1967* (Indianapolis: Bobbs-Merrill, 1970), 96.
41. *New Mexican*, 3 July 1966, 1, and 5 July 1966, 1.
42. *New Mexican*, 6 July 1966, 1, 3.
43. *New Mexican*, 11 July 1966, 1.
44. Ibid., 2.
45. *New Mexican*, 22 June 1967, A-6.
46. *New Mexican*, 5 October 1967, A-6, and 7 October 1967, 7.
47. La Simpática, "Viva La Raza," *Movement* 5, no. 6 (July 1969): 6–9, in Nabokov Papers, Mss 93 B.C., Box 6, CSWR.
48. Mauricio Vigil, "Ethnic Organizations Among the Mexican Americans" (Ph.D. diss., University of New Mexico, 1974), 376–81.
49. Charles M. Haar, *Between the Idea and the Reality: A Study in the Origin, Fate, and Legacy of the Model Cities Program* (Boston: Little, Brown, 1975), vi–vii.
50. *New Mexican*, 4 January 1971, A-2.
51. A rough map of the area is shown in Department of Housing and Urban Development, Office of Community Development Evaluation Division, *The Model Cities Program, Ten Model Cities: A Comparative Analysis* (Washington, D.C., [1973]), 144.
52. Ibid., 145.
53. See the *New Mexican*, 1–3 March 1984.
54. Vigil, "Ethnic Organizations," 383–84.
55. *New Mexican*, 4 September 1973, A-1.
56. *New Mexican*, 5 September 1973, A-1.
57. *New Mexican*, 1 October 1973, A-1; Vigil, "Ethnic Organizations," 384–86.
58. *New Mexican*, 12 March 1974, 1.
59. *New Mexican*, 8 February 1968, 1, and 28 February 1968, 8.
60. *New Mexican*, 23 February 1968, 8.
61. Vigil, "Ethnic Organizations," 382–83; *New Mexican*, 8 March 1972, A-1, A-8.
62. *New Mexican*, 6 March 1974, B-1.
63. *New Mexican*, 3 March 1976, 1.
64. *New Mexican*, 4 March 1976, A-6.
65. *New Mexican*, 3 March 1976, A-10.
66. *New Mexican*, 29 February 1976, A-11, B-10.
67. *New Mexican*, 12 February 1978, B-7.
68. *New Mexican*, 26 February 1978, B-7.
69. *New Mexican*, 22 February 1984, 1.
70. *Journal North*, 3 March 1988, 1.
71. *New Mexican*, 25 February 1990, 5.
72. *New Mexican*, 1 March 1992, D-6.

73. See *New Mexican*, 27 February 1994, D-1, D-2.
74. *New Mexican*, 2 March 1994, A-1.
75. Harland, Bartholomew and Associates, "Comprehensive City Plan Santa Fe, New Mexico," [1950], 13–14, CSWR.
76. Ibid., 49–50.
77. Arthur A. Blumenfeld, comp., *The 1957 Directory of New Mexico Manufacturers* (Albuquerque: Bureau of Business Research, University of New Mexico), 32–34; Harman, O'Donnell, and Henninger Associates, Inc., "Santa Fe Comprehensive Plan Update: City of Santa Fe, New Mexico" (Denver, Colo., January 1966), II–4, CSWR.
78. Blumenfeld, *1957 Directory of New Mexico Manufacturers*, 33.
79. Harman, et al., "Santa Fe Comprehensive Plan," II–4.
80. See *New Mexican*, 16 March 1956, 1, and 25 February 1966, 1.
81. Wayne Vann, "Behind the Scene," *New Mexican*, 15 February 1984, A-5.
82. *New Mexican*, 3 March 1974, A-6.
83. Ibid.; *New Mexican*, 29 February 1976, B-8.
84. *New Mexican*, 23 February 1992, D-2.
85. Ellie Becker, "Allen Stamm," *Santa Fe Real Estate Weekly*, 15 March 1996, 18.
86. Ralph Edgel and Peter J. LaLonde, *Income and Employment in New Mexico, 1960–64* (Albuquerque: Bureau of Business and Economic Research, University of New Mexico, 1964), 40.
87. Santa Fe Community College Business Assistance Center, *Santa Fe Stats, 1990–91* (Santa Fe, 1991), 12.
88. Brian McDonald, John Tysseling, and Lee Brown, "Evolving Urban Water Pricing Policies in Selected New Mexico Cities," *New Mexico Business* 33, no. 4 (May 1980): 8–9.
89. *New Mexican*, 29 March 1950, 4.
90. See *New Mexican*, 19 February 1978, B-9; 26 February 1978, B-7; 5 March 1978, B-10. The voters turned down the twenty-five–year franchise by a three-to-one margin. *New Mexican*, 8 March 1978, 1.
91. *New Mexican*, "Voter's Guide," 25 February 1990.

Chapter 11

1. *New Mexican*, 12 September 1945, 1.
2. *New Mexican*, 10 May 1946, 4.
3. See Robert E. McKee, *The Zia Company in Los Alamos* (El Paso, Tex.: C. Hertzog, 1950), 2, 8.
4. *New Mexican*, 1 December 1945, 1.
5. *New Mexican*, 5 April 1946, 1, and 10 May 1946, 5.
6. Counts based on *Hudspeth's Santa Fe City Directory, 1953* (El Paso, Tex.: Hudspeth Directory Co., 1953).
7. Marion B. Williams, "Life on the Hill," *New Mexico* 30, no. 12 (December 1952): 45.
8. *Los Alamos Times*, 18 October 1946, 3.
9. Ina Sizer Cassidy, "Scientist-Artists," *New Mexico* 28, no. 1 (January 1950): 24.
10. See *El Palacio* (January 1950): 29; (March 1950): 92; (July 1950): 221; (January 1951): 25.
11. New Mexico Legislature, Science and Technology Commercialization Commission, *Integrated Statewide Plan for Technology-Based Economic Development* (Santa Fe, November 1989), 15–16.
12. *New Mexican*, 27 February 1986, C-1.
13. Harold Morgan, "SFI is a Center for Science of Complexity," *New Mexico Progress* (April 1990): 1–3.
14. Virginia Nordhaus, "Ski Trails at Sky Line," *New Mexico* 24, no. 12 (December 1946): 23.
15. Graeme McGowan, "Ski Skill," *New Mexico* 14, no. 12 (December 1936): 3, 35; Thomas B. Catron II, "Snow Trails at Sky Line," *New Mexico* 16, no. 2 (February 1938): 19.
16. Perl Charles, "Snow Trails," *New Mexico* 19, no. 12 (1941): 13.
17. D. D. Van Soelen, "Snow in the Desert," in *This Is Santa Fe: A Guide to the City Different*, eds. Charles H. Comfort and Mary Apolline Comfort (Santa Fe: Comfort, 1955), 50–51.
18. James Laughlin, "Skiing in America," *Sports Illustrated* 1, no. 17 (December 1954): 62, 64; Tony Perry and Earl Howey, "Holiday on Skis," *New Mexico* 38, no. 2 (February 1960): 8, 11.
19. Abigail Adler, "Confessions of a New Mexico Ski Addict," *New Mexico* 65, no. 11 (November 1987): 54–55.
20. Bertram Gabriel, "Confessions of a Repentant Ski Bum," *New Mexico* 60, no. 10 (October 1982): 34.

21. Santa Fe Community College Business Assistance Center, *Santa Fe Stats, 1990–91* (Santa Fe, 1991), 23.
22. *Sunday New Mexican*, 1 March 1992, A-1–2.
23. Eleanor Scott, *The First Twenty Years of the Santa Fe Opera* (Santa Fe: Sunstone Press, 1976), 15.
24. Frank Magee, Jr., "Opera and the Royal City," *New Mexico* 38, no. 6 (June 1960): 11, 38.
25. Farnsworth Fowle, "Your Public is With You," *The Rockefeller Foundation Quarterly* (April–June 1967): 2, 9.
26. Ibid., 7.
27. John Temple, *Out-of-State Visitors Expenditure Survey* (Albuquerque: Bureau of Business and Economic Research, University of New Mexico, August 1979), 13.
28. Santa Fe Chamber Music Festival, "Santa Fe Chamber Music Festival: the Eighteenth Season, 8 July–20 August, 1990" (brochure).
29. Musical Events, *The New Yorker*, 9 August 1982, 74 and 16 August 1982, 68–69.
30. Richard D. Weigle, *The Colonization of a College: The Beginnings and Early History of St. John's College in Santa Fe* (Annapolis, Md.: St. John's College Print Shop, 1985), 17–18, 22–23, 34.
31. *New Mexican*, 9 October 1964, 1.
32. Weigle, *The Colonization of a College*, 121.
33. Ibid., 143–45.
34. *The St. John's Reporter*, September 1981, 1, 3.
35. *The St. John's Reporter*, February 1985, 1, 7, 15.
36. *The St. John's Reporter*, September 1985, 1, 5, and April 1986, 4.
37. St. John's College, "Reaching Out Giving Back" (Santa Fe, n.d.).
38. James C. Hughes, "Three Stages of Land Use in Santa Fe, New Mexico, 1610–1967," (master's thesis, University of Kansas, 1968), 89.
39. Santa Fe Community College, *Santa Fe Stats, 1990–91*, 23.
40. Temple, *Out-of-State Visitors*, iii, 4.
41. Ibid., 5–6.
42. Ibid., 10.
43. Ibid., 11.
44. *Hudspeth's Santa Fe City Directory, 1947* (El Paso, Tex.: Hudspeth Directory Co., 1947), and *Hudspeth's Santa Fe City Directory, 1959* (El Paso, Tex.: Hudspeth Directory Co., 1959).
45. U.S. West Marketing Resources, *1992 Catalist: Business and Household Digest of Santa Fe and Vicinity* (Loveland, Colo.: U.S. West Marketing Resources, 1992), B-43–46.
46. We surveyed the Santa Fe membership of the New Mexico Jewish Historical Society in 1998. The number of members who responded and had arrived prior to 1990 stood at fifty-nine.
47. Robert Anderson, "Early Film Making in New Mexico: Romaine Fielding and the Lubin Company West," *NMHR* 51, no. 2 (April 1976): 145–46.
48. Joseph Dispenza, "On Location in New Mexico," *New Mexico* 62, no. 11 (November 1984): 78.
49. John Bowman, "Greer Garson," *New Mexico* 68, no. 11 (June 1990): 25, 27.
50. Walter Briggs, "Hollywood on the Rio Grande," *New Mexico* 47, no. 9–10 (September–October 1969): 4.
51. New Mexico Economic Development and Tourism Department, *New Mexico Film and Video Personnel/Business Directory, 1986* (Santa Fe, 1986), and *New Mexico Film and Video Personnel/Business Directory, 1990* (Santa Fe, 1990).
52. David Cargo, telephone conversation with Henry J. Tobias, January 1999.
53. Bowman, "Greer Garson," 22, 25, 28.
54. Bowman, "College's Blockbuster Success: A Home Away from Hollywood," *New Mexico* 72, no. 6 (June 1994): 100.
55. *Albuquerque Tribune*, 2 July 1991, C-1, C-4.
56. *Hudspeth's Santa Fe City Directory, 1940* (El Paso, Tex.: Hudspeth Directory Co., 1940).
57. *Hudspeth's Santa Fe City Directory, 1968* (El Paso, Tex.: Hudspeth Directory Co., 1968).
58. *New Mexican*, 15 August 1983, A-6.
59. *New Mexican*, 29 February 1984, A-6.
60. *New Mexican*, 14 February 1988, B-10.
61. Heidi Hinton, "The Changing Composition of Lower Canyon Road—A Neighborhood in Santa Fe, New Mexico" (bachelor's thesis, Colorado College, 1977), 29.
62. Ibid., 29–30.
63. Ibid., 33.

64. *Hudspeth's Santa Fe City Directory, 1940; Hudspeth's Santa Fe City Directory, 1928–29* (El Paso, Tex.: Hudspeth Directory Co., 1929).
65. Jim Gilbert, *A Survey of the Arts in New Mexico* (Santa Fe: State Planning Office, 1966), 29.
66. Hinton, "Changing Composition," 49–50.
67. *Santa Fe Reporter*, 26 August 1976; Hinton, "Changing Composition," 43–44.
68. *Santa Fe Reporter*, 26 August 1976; Hinton, "Changing Composition," 44–45.
69. Hinton, "Changing Composition," 44–45.
70. Edna Robertson and Sarah Nestor, *Artists of the Canyons and Caminos: Santa Fe, The Early Years* (Santa Fe: Peregrine Smith, 1976), 153.
71. Reginald Fisher, comp. and ed., *An Art Directory of New Mexico* (Santa Fe: Museum of New Mexico, 1947).
72. Ina S. Cassidy, "Arts and Artists of New Mexico," *New Mexico* 29, no. 10 (October 1951): 28.
73. Ibid.
74. C. R. Wenzell, *Artists of Santa Fe: Their Works and Words* (Santa Fe: C. R. Wenzell, 1974).
75. Our counts are based on The City of Santa Fe Arts Commission, *Santa Fe Arts Directory, 1993* (Santa Fe, 1993).
76. Gilbert, *Survey of the Arts*, 49.
77. Ann Vedder, "History of the Spanish Colonial Arts Society, Inc, 1951–1981," in *Hispanic Arts and Ethnohistory in the Southwest*, ed. Marta Weigle (Santa Fe: Ancient City Press, 1983), 205.
78. Ibid., 210–11.
79. Linda Monacelli, "Mary Cabot Wheelwright's Hogan," *New Mexico Magazine*, February 1983, 17–19.
80. Bruce Bernstein, "From Indian Fair to Indian Market," *El Palacio* 98, no. 3 (summer 1993): 54.
81. Fisher, *Art Directory*, 64–68.
82. Our counts are based on the *Santa Fe Arts Directory, 1993*.
83. David Bell, "Once More With Feeling," *Art in America* 73, no. 9 (September 1985): 29.
84. Gilbert, *Survey of the Arts*, 28.
85. Ibid., 27.
86. Lee Eisenberg, "The Right Place," *Esquire*, May 1981, 33. See also William S. Ellis, "Goal at the End of the Trail Santa Fe," *National Geographic* 161, no. 3 (March 1982): 332–33.
87. Museum of International Folk Art, "Museum of International Folk Art: The First Ten Years 1953–1963" (Santa Fe, n.d.); Karen Meadows, "Sisters in Spirit: Florence Dibell Bartlett, Mary Cabot Wheelwright, and Amelia Elizabeth White," *El Palacio* 92, no. 1 (summer/fall 1986): 8.
88. New Mexico State Racing Commission, *1970–1971 Biennial Report* (Santa Fe, 1971), 8, 11.
89. New Mexico State Racing Commission biennial and annual reports.
90. Arlene Odenwald, "Are They Off or Are They Gone?" *New Mexico Business Journal* 20, no. 9 (September 1996): 17.
91. *Journal North*, 24 May 1990, 1.
92. Temple, *Out-of-State Visitors*, 27.
93. *Journal North*, 26 August 1989, 1, and 23 September 1989, 1.

Chapter 12

1. Data for comparisons of 1950 and 1990 population characteristics are drawn from Bureau of the Census, *Seventeenth Decennial Census of the United States, Census of Population, 1950*, vol. 2, *Characteristics of the Population, Part 31, New Mexico* (Washington, D.C., 1952), 33–36, and *Special Reports, 3C, White Persons of Spanish Surname* (Washington, D.C., 1952), 54; and *1990 Census, General Social and Economic Characteristics, New Mexico* (Washington, D.C., 1993), 374, 386, 401, 415, and *Census Tracts and Block Numbering Areas, Santa Fe, NM MSA* (Washington, D.C., 1993), 19, 51, 84, 89, 94, 99.
2. Our counts are based on *Hudspeth's Santa Fe City Directory, 1947* (El Paso, Tex.: Hudspeth Directory Co., 1947), and Bureau of the Census, *1980 Census of Population*, vol. 1, *General Social and Economic Characteristics, Part 33, New Mexico* (Washington, D.C., 1983), 138, 142, 153.
3. Data are drawn from Bureau of the Census, *1980 Census, General Social and Economic Characteristics, Part 33, New Mexico* (Washington, D.C., 1983), 142, and *Census Tracts, Selected Areas in New Mexico* (Washington, D.C., 1983), 97–99; and *1990 Census, General Social and Economic Characteristics, New Mexico*, 384, and *Census Tracts and Block Numbering Areas, Santa Fe, NM MSA*, (Washington, D.C., 1993), 61–64.

4. Bureau of the Census, *1970 Census, General Social and Economic Characteristics, Part 33, New Mexico* (Washington, D.C., 1973), 169, 185, 187; *1980 Census, General Social and Economic Characteristics, Part 33, New Mexico*, 134, 147; and *1990 Census, Census Tracts and Block Numbering Areas, Santa Fe, NM MSA*, 51, 84.
5. Data for occupancy of apartments and housing developments for 1932 and subsequent years are derived from *Hudspeth's Santa Fe City Directory* for the designated years.
6. Data for the population characteristics of census tracts in the discussion below are drawn from *1980 Census of Population and Housing, Census Tracts, Selected Areas of New Mexico* (Washington, D.C., 1983), H-15–17, P-15–17, P-46–47, P-80–82, P-97–99, P-163–64, P-175–76; and *1990 Census of Population and Housing, Census Tracts and Block Numbering Areas, Santa Fe, NM MSA* (Washington, D.C., 1993), 31–34, 51, 54–57, 61–64, 84–88, 89–93. Census tracts are small, numbered subdivisions of a county's area designated by the Census Bureau. Each tract is designed to include 2,500 to 8,000 persons, to be homogeneous in population characteristics, economic status, and living conditions. Boundaries can change in accordance with population density and altered physical features.
7. Blayney Dyett, Urban and Regional Planners Western Network, Public Participation Consultants, *Santa Fe General Plan Update, Summaries of Public Meeting and Survey Responses for Extraterritorial Area* (Santa Fe: City of Santa Fe Planning Department, 1994), 6–7.
8. Ibid., 4, 5, 54.
9. Ibid., 4.
10. Ibid., 54.
11. Data pertaining to the age group 20–34 are drawn from Bureau of the Census, *1980 Census of Population, General Population Characteristics*, vol. 1, *Part 33, New Mexico* (Washington, D.C., 1983), 56; *General Social and Economic Characteristics, Part 33, New Mexico*, 140; *Census Tracts, New Mexico Selected Areas* (Washington, D.C., 1983), 15–16, 46–47, 97–98, 175–76; *1990 Census of Population, Social and Economic Characteristics, New Mexico* (Washington, D.C., 1993), 374, 384, 401; and *1990 Census of Population and Housing, Population and Housing Characteristics for Census Tracts and Block Numbering Areas, Santa Fe, NM MSA* (Washington, D.C., 1993), 4–6, 16–17, 31–33, 54–56, 61–63, 86–87, 91–92.
12. Occupational data for 1947 are based on our counts from *Hudspeth's Santa Fe City Directory, 1947;* and for 1990, *1990 Census of Population and Housing, Census Tracts and Block Numbering Areas, Santa Fe, NM MSA*, 89, 99. Data on educational attainment for 1950 are drawn from Bureau of the Census, *Seventeenth Decennial Census of the United States, Special Report P-E, No. 3C, Persons of Spanish Surname* (Washington, D.C., 1952), and vol. 2, *Part 31, New Mexico* (Washington, D.C., 1952), 34; and for 1990, *1990 Census, Census Tracts and Block Numbering Areas, Santa Fe, NM MSA*, 84, 94. Data on new residents are drawn from Bureau of the Census, *1970 Census, General Social and Economic Characteristics, New Mexico* (Washington, D.C., 1973), 169, 187; and *1990 Census, Census Tracts, Santa Fe, NM MSA*, 51, 84.
13. Dyett, *Santa Fe General Plan Update* (responses of city residents), 5.
14. Bureau of the Census, *Fifteenth Census of the United States, 1930, Population*, vol. 3, part 2, *Reports by States* (Washington, D.C., 1932), 243; *Sixteenth Census of the United States, 1940, Population*, vol. 2, part 4 (Washington, D.C., 1943), 1,017; *Census of Population, 1950, Characteristics of the Population, Part 31, New Mexico*, 34; *1960 Census of Population*, vol. 1, *Part 33, New Mexico* (Washington, D.C., 1963), 104; *1970 Census of Population*, vol. 1, *Characteristics of the Population, Part 33, New Mexico* (Washington, D.C., 1973), 171.
15. Leonard J. DeLayo, Superintendent of Public Instruction, State of New Mexico, *Annual Statistical Report of the Superintendent of Public Instruction, July 1, 1969 to June 30, 1970* (Santa Fe, 1970), 185; New Mexico Department of Education, *Annual Statistical Report, July 1, 1979 to June 30, 1980* (Santa Fe, 1980), 74.
16. *New Mexican*, 24 November 1981, A-3, and 6 June 1982, A-1, A-7.
17. *New Mexican*, 14 January 1976, 2, and 24 August, 1976, A-10; *Santa Fe Reporter*, 7 April 1982, from clippings file of James P. Miller, Albuquerque, New Mexico.
18. *New Mexican*, 20 January 1982, A-1, and 8 September 1982, A-1, A-7; *Santa Fe Reporter*, 24 February 1982, from clippings file of James P. Miller.
19. *New Mexican*, 20 October 1982, A-1, A-9; *Journal North*, 21 October 1982, 1; *Santa Fe Reporter*, 8 October 1982, from clippings file of James P. Miller.
20. *New Mexican*, 20 October 1982, A-1, A-9; *Journal North*, 16 October 1982, 4; *Santa Fe Reporter*, 8 October 1982, from clippings file of James P. Miller.

21. *Santa Fe Reporter,* 8 October 1982, from clippings file of James P. Miller.
22. *Nineteenth and Twentieth Annual Reports of the Territorial Superintendent of Public Instruction to the Governor of New Mexico for the Years 1909–1910* (Santa Fe, 1911), 130–31; Bureau of the Census, *1930 Census, Population,* vol. 3, part 2, *Reports by States* (Washington, D.C., 1932), 243; Leonard J. DeLayo, *State of New Mexico Annual Statistical Report, July 1, 1969 to June 30, 1970* (Santa Fe, 1970), 178–79, and DeLayo, op. cit., *July 1, 1979 to June 30, 1980* (Santa Fe, 1980), 13–15.
23. *Superintendent of Public Instruction Report for 1979–80* (Santa Fe, 1980), 10–11; *1980 Census,* vol. 1, *General Social and Economic Characteristics, Part 33, New Mexico,* 136, 147.
24. Data on high school graduates in Santa Fe provided by Henry F. Borgrink, Division of Statistics, New Mexico State Department of Education, Santa Fe.
25. Paul V. Petty, Devoy A. Ryan, Bonner M. Crawford, Daniel C. Tredway, Frank Angel, and Harold Lavender, *Report of the Survey of the Santa Fe Public Schools, 1963–64* (Albuquerque: Bureau of Educational Service and Research, University of New Mexico, 1964), 25–32, 41–50.
26. Ibid., 27–29.
27. Information provided by Jim Podesta, director of development, Santa Fe Preparatory School.
28. Ed Nagel, *Cheez! Uncle Sam: What Price Justice? A Resourceful Struggle on Behalf of Freeing Our Children* (Santa Fe: SFCS Publications, 1978), 116–17, 125–26, 133.
29. Ed Nagel, telephone conversation with Charles Woodhouse, February 1999.
30. *New Mexican,* 5 May 1981, 8.
31. Brother Raymond Ogden, "A College Comes of Age" (College of Santa Fe, 1969), mimeograph, 1–2, Archives of the College of Santa Fe, Santa Fe, New Mexico.
32. Our count is based on College of Santa Fe, *1996 Alumni Directory* (White Plains, N.Y.: Bernard C. Harris Publishing Company, Inc., 1996).
33. Information provided by Office of Development, St. John's College.
34. Data on enrollments provided by Richard C. Rindone, Coordinator, Institutional Effectiveness, Santa Fe Community College.
35. Data provided by Dr. Bill Simpson, deputy director for educational programs, New Mexico Commission on Higher Education, Santa Fe.
36. Data on college and university enrollments were provided by Tom Field, Office of Institutional Research, University of New Mexico; Miriam Meyer and Judy Bosland, Institutional Research, Planning and Outcomes Assessment, New Mexico State University; Esther Hamerdinger, Office of the Registrar, New Mexico Highlands University; Amy Holt, Office of Planning Services, Eastern New Mexico University; and Gloria Taylor, Admissions Counselor, College of Santa Fe.
37. Our counts are based on College of Santa Fe, *1996 Alumni Directory.*
38. *1970 Census, General Social and Economic Characteristics, Part 33, New Mexico,* 187; *1990 Census, Census Tracts and Block Numbering Areas, Santa Fe, NM MSA,* 84. In the Santa Fe school district for the year 1989–90, in grades 7 through 12, the dropout rate for male Hispanos of 5.9 percent exceeded the rates for males of all other categories; for Hispano females the rate of 3.8 percent exceeded the rates for females in other ethnic categories but equaled that for African American males. See New Mexico State Department of Education, *New Mexico Dropout Study, 1989–90* (Santa Fe, March 1991), 75. For the entire state in 1993–94, dropout rates for grades 9 through 12 were 6.0 percent for Anglo students and 10.2 percent for Hispano students. See Carrol L. Hall, Peter Abeyta, Louise Cavata, Kathleen Forrer, Patricia Rael, and Jim Travelstead, *The New Mexico Accountability Report* (Santa Fe: New Mexico Department of Education, November 1995), 19.

Chapter 13

1. Bureau of the Census, *1970 Census of the Population, Characteristics of the Population,* vol. 7, *Part 33* (Washington, D.C., January 1973), 12.
2. *New Mexico Statistical Abstract, 1989* (Albuquerque: Bureau of Business and Economic Research, University of New Mexico, 1989), 106; Bureau of the Census, *1990 Census of Population, General Population Characteristics, New Mexico* (Washington, D.C., 1992), 2. We performed the percentage calculations.
3. *New Mexico Statistical Abstract, 1989,* Bureau of the Census, *1990 Census of Population, General Population Characteristics, New Mexico,* 1.
4. A summary of this background may be found in Stephan D. Fox, "Healing, Imagination, and New Mexico," *NMHR* 58, no. 3 (July 1983): 213–38.

5. See Ferenc M. Szasz, "Francis Schlatter: The Healer of the Southwest," *NMHR* 54, no. 2 (April 1979): 89–104.
6. Ibid., 89.
7. Karen Cowan Ford, *Las Yerbas de la Gente: A Study of Hispano-American Medicinal Plants* (Ann Arbor: University of Michigan, 1975), 81–83.
8. Bobette Perrone, H. Henrietta Stockel, and Victoria Krueger, *Medicine Women, Curanderas, and Women Doctors* (Norman and London: University of Oklahoma Press, 1989), 107–9.
9. "Alternative Health Care: An Overview," *Santa Fe Lifestyle*, Summer 1987, 24–25.
10. Albert Egenhofer, M.D., interview by Jake Spidle, 19 October 1983, 9, University of New Mexico Medical School Archives, Albuquerque, New Mexico.
11. Bergere Kenney, M.D., interview by Jake Spidle, 17 October 1984, 27; José Maldonado, M.D., interview by Spidle, 20 October 1983, 21; and Carol K. Smith, M.D., interview by Spidle, 11 September 1985, 11, University of New Mexico Medical School Archives.
12. Fran Leeper Buss, *La Partera: Story of a Midwife* (Ann Arbor: University of Michigan Press, 1980), 2, 87.
13. Paul H. Jacobson, "Hospital Care and the Vanishing Midwife," *The Milbank Memorial Fund Quarterly* 34, no. 3 (July 1956): 257.
14. Ibid., 256–57.
15. Myrtle Greenfield, *A History of Public Health in New Mexico* (Albuquerque: University of New Mexico, 1962), 123, 253; Mary N. Marquez and Consuelo Pacheco, "Midwifery Lore in New Mexico," *American Journal of Nursing* 64, no. 9 (September 1964): 81.
16. "Vital Statistics," Section Three, *New Mexico Health Officer* 11, no. 2 (June 1943): 33.
17. Ibid., 36.
18. Bureau of the Census, *Vital Statistics of the United States 1940, Part II* (Washington, D.C., 1943), 50.
19. See Michael Anne Sullivan, "Walking the Line" (master's thesis, University of New Mexico, 1995), xi–xii.
20. Sister Rosemary Smyth, "History of the Catholic Maternity Institute" (master's thesis, Catholic University, 1960), 1, 10.
21. Ibid., 15–16, 18, 26.
22. New Mexico Health and Human Services Department, *1975 Selected Health Statistics Annual Report* (Santa Fe, 1975), 17.
23. Kenney interview, 27.
24. Ibid.
25. Ibid.; Maldonado interview, 21.
26. Dr. Lesley Libo, then teaching at the school, informed us of this teaching practice in 1999.
27. The figures are derived from counts we made in the censuses from 1880 through 1920.
28. Nancie L. González, "The Spanish Americans of New Mexico: A Distinctive Heritage" (Mexican-American Study Project, University of California-Los Angeles, September 1967), 115. For a discussion of the surname issue, see also Nancie L. Solien González, *The Spanish-Americans of New Mexico: A Heritage of Pride*, rev. and enl. ed. (Albuquerque: University of New Mexico Press, 1967), 24–25. Mixed ancestry resulting from intermarriage is also the basis for Chris Wilson's claim that "coyotism" is increasingly characteristic of Santa Fe's population. He recognizes "Coyote" as an ethnic designation equivalent to Anglo, Hispanic, or Native American identity. See Wilson, *The Myth of Santa Fe: Creating a Modern Regional Tradition* (Albuquerque: University of New Mexico Press, 1997), chapter 5 and "Interlude: Coyote Consciousness," 169–80.
29. González, *The Spanish-Americans*, 68–69; Carolyn Zeleny, "Relations Between the Spanish-Americans and Anglo-Americans in New Mexico: A Study of Conflict and Accommodation in a Dual-Ethnic Situation" (Ph.D. diss., Yale University, 1944), 334; Irma Y. Johnson, "A Study of Certain Changes in the Spanish-American Family in Bernalillo County, 1915–1946" (master's thesis, University of New Mexico, 1948), 45–51.
30. Angela Pacheco, quoted by William Heinbach in "Image and the Hispanic Woman," *New Mexican*, 21 October 1982, Sec. C, 1.
31. Richard L. Nostrand, *The Hispano Homeland* (Norman: University of Oklahoma Press, 1992), 122–23.
32. Pearce S. Grove, Becky J. Barnett, and Sandra J. Hansen, eds., *New Mexico Newspapers: A Comprehensive Guide to Bibliographical Entries and Locations* (Albuquerque: University of New Mexico Press in association with Eastern New Mexico University, 1975), 438–94.

33. Lynne Marie Getz, *Schools of Their Own: The Education of Hispanos in New Mexico, 1850–1940* (Albuquerque: University of New Mexico Press, 1997), 17.
34. Zeleny, "Relations Between the Spanish-Americans and Anglo-Americans in New Mexico," 295–301. For more detail see Getz, *Schools of Their Own.*
35. Bureau of the Census, *1980 Census, Census Tracts, Selected Areas in New Mexico* (Washington, D.C., 1983), 163–64; *1990 Census, Census Tracts and Block Numbering Areas, Santa Fe, NM MSA* (Washington, D.C., 1993), 84.
36. Reprinted as *The WPA Guide to 1930s New Mexico,* compiled by the workers of the Writers' Program of the Work Projects Administration of the State of New Mexico (Tucson: University of Arizona Press, 1989), 107–19.
37. Robert E. Storey, "Parents Seek Better Bilingual Plan," *New Mexican,* 27 January 1980, A-5.
38. Huntley Dent, *The Feast of Santa Fe: Cooking of the American Southwest* (New York: Simon and Schuster, 1985), 20.
39. Richard Knight Barney, *Turmoil and Triumph: A Narrative History of Intercollegiate Athletics at the University of New Mexico and Its Implications in the Social History of the City of Albuquerque and the State and Territory of New Mexico 1889–1950* (Albuquerque: San Ignacio Press, 1969), 9.
40. Glenn Steimling, "A Comparison of New Mexico Tribal and Municipal Sports and Recreation Facilities for Risk Management" (Ph.D. diss., University of New Mexico, 1997), 16–17.
41. Ibid., 18.
42. Barney, *Turmoil and Triumph,* 307–8.
43. See Dioniseo Costales, "Spanish Games in New Mexico" (master's thesis, University of New Mexico, 1937), 77.
44. Barney, *Turmoil and Triumph,* 43.
45. St. Michael's High School, *A Hundred Years of Service* (Santa Fe, 1959), 194, Special Collections, Albuquerque Public Library, Albuquerque, New Mexico.
46. Barney, *Turmoil and Triumph,* 307.
47. *A Hundred Years of Service,* 192.
48. Santa Fe High School, *Cacique,* 1920, 73.
49. Santa Fe High School, *El Conquistador* (Santa Fe: n.p., 1930); Santa Fe High School, *Para Mañana* (Santa Fe: n.p., 1949). Both are high school yearbooks.
50. Ricardo Dow Anaya, "An Historical Perspective of Influence Sport Had on Sports Legends of New Mexico 1925–1975" (Ph.D. diss., University of New Mexico, 1997), 28.
51. *Albuquerque Journal,* 12 February 1995, E-6.
52. James P. Miller, interview by authors, Albuquerque, New Mexico, 16 May 1998. See also *New Mexican,* 22 February 1980, B-4.
53. See *New Mexican,* 25 March 1982, B-1.
54. Foster Rhea Dulles, *The History of Recreation: America Learns to Play,* 2d ed. (New York: Appleton-Century-Crofts, 1965), 242.
55. Ibid., 358; Frederick Lewis Allen, *Only Yesterday: An Informal History of the 1920s* (New York: Perennial Classics, 2000), 172.
56. Nevin H. Gibson, *The Encyclopedia of Golf With the Official All-Time Records* (New York: Barnes, 1958), 28.
57. "Country Club Turning 75," *Albuquerque Journal,* 11 November 1989, C-1.
58. See *Hudspeth's Albuquerque City Directory, 1932* (El Paso, Tex.: Hudspeth Directory Co., 1932), 413.
59. Marilyn Lobdell, "Chronology Of Albuquerque History, 1870–1976," typescript, 51, 65, 67, CSWR.
60. Toby Smith, "The Story of an Internment Camp," *Albuquerque Journal Magazine,* 31 March 1981, 6.
61. Chuck Hundertmark, "After Decade, Santa Fe Housing Project Still in Court," *Albuquerque Journal,* 21 February 1982, B-1, 4.
62. See Ralph Odenwald, "The Grand and Glorious Game of Golf Is Also a Business," *New Mexico Business Journal* 19, no. 5 (May 1995): 20; and *Journal North,* 13 September 1991, 1.

Index